THE JEWISH WAY IN LOVE AND MARRIAGE

The Jewish Way

in

Love and Marriage

MAURICE LAMM

HARPER & ROW, PUBLISHERS

SAN FRANCISCO

Cambridge London
Hagerstown Mexico City
Philadelphia Sao Paolo
New York 1817 Sydney

*I dedicate this book to my wife, Shirley,
for our twenty-fifth wedding anniversary.
Her love, understanding, and self-sacrifice
have made our partnership a marriage
and this work a reality.*

Acknowledgment is made to the following publishers for permission to quote from their books:
Jonathan David Publishers, New York; Keter Publishing House, Jerusalem; and Philip Feldheim
Publishers, New York.

First Harper & Row paperback edition published in 1982.

Designed by Jim Mennick

Library of Congress Cataloging in Publication Data

Lamm, Maurice
  THE JEWISH WAY IN LOVE AND MARRIAGE

  Bibliography: p. 240
  Includes index.
  1. Marriage—Jews.   2. Marriage (Jewish law).
3. Marriage customs and rites, Jewish.   I. Title.
HQ525.J4L29   1979   301.42   79-1760
ISBN 0-06-064915-1

82 83 84 85 86   10 9 8 7 6 5 4 3 2 1

Contents

Acknowledgments

I acknowledge my profound debt to the following people for assisting me in the production of this work:

My brother, Dr. Norman Lamm, my mentor and colleague, President of Yeshiva University, who sacrificed precious hours to critically review the entire manuscript;

Rabbi Zvi Schachter, Rosh Yeshiva, and Head of the Kollel at Yeshiva University, who tested all my halakhic decisions;

Rabbi David Bleich, Rosh Yeshiva, and faculty member at Cardozo School of Law, who reviewed the chapter on prohibited partners;

Shimon and Anita Wincelberg, authors and playwrights, who made important suggestions regarding style;

Adaire Klein, librarian at Yeshiva University, Los Angeles, who contributed dedicated and invaluable research assistance in the preparation of the bibliography and manuscript;

Ben Zion Jerusalmi, who diligently reviewed the sources;

John Loudon, my editor, who was persistently confident of the need for this work;

Last and most, my parents, Samuel and Pearl Lamm, who serve as models of the Jewish Way in Love and Marriage. May they continue to find their dreams fulfilled for many years to come.

NOTE ON TRANSLITERATION, NOTES, AND BIBLIOGRAPHY

The system of transliteration used here generally follows that of *Encyclopaedia Judaica* (Jerusalem: Keter Publishing House, 1972), with the following variations and clarifications:

1. The guttural *het* is written as *ch* instead of *h* with a dot under it;
2. *Tzaddi* is *tz* instead of *z* with a dot under it;
3. An apostrophe is used to separate a she'va from the major part of the word that follows;
4. A hyphen separates a full vowel from the major part of the word that follows;
5. Biblical names and place names are rendered according to the Bible translation of the Jewish Publication Society of America (1917).

This book is intended for both scholars and laymen. Because the profusion of superscript numbers can be distracting to the general reader, an unusual system of notation is employed here. Those who wish to read the notes will find them immediately following the text itself, identified by page and line number. Sources frequently cited are abbreviated in the notes; the Bibliography provides full source information and an explanation of abbreviations.

Introduction

WHO HAS THE ANSWER?

My grandfather once told me that no one ever died from asking a question. But our grandchildren may suffer from asking this one: How do you make a marriage work in this modern world?

This is a question to which few people have found a truly satisfactory answer. The proof is that we have contrived so many contemporary answers: living together arrangements, serial monogamy, open marriages, communal marriages. Or no marriage, at all: no bonds, no family—and alas—no ties, no knots; no breakup, no breakdown.

This book will set forth one answer that has succeeded in outliving every attack on the institution of marriage since the dawn of civilization. That answer, the Jewish answer, is alive and well today. It is not foolproof, nor is it appropriate for every person in every circumstance. It is not just a biblical demand; it is engraved in the scheme of creation, and it will last forever.

I

This work was conceived in the recognition of two important contemporary trends. First, society is in bedlam. A million people trapped in troubled marriages dash for the nearest exit. If *their* marriage cannot work, the whole institution must be headed for extinction. They seek new options and alternatives, heady words of new-found liberty that are not "new" at all; they were discarded centuries ago because they did not work.

Living together without benefit of marriage seems like a "new" option, but it was once called "concubinage" and was eventually replaced by a contractual arrangement, which bound equal partners with mutual obligations. Serial monogamy was replaced by a reasonably permanent marriage, because children did not benefit from short-term parents. And communal marriage was succeeded by strict monogamy, because women simply were not satisfied with a partial husband, just as husbands rarely even considered settling for a fraction of a wife.

Second, the number of fragmented families and unhappy marriages continues to increase despite these "free" alternatives and a liberated sexual atmosphere. Divorce and unhappiness are the gravestones that pockmark the open fields of the free society. That fact alone is eloquent testimony to the sophisticated barbarism of our "Brave New World." In the midst of this social turbulence, Judaism can serve as a light in the too-long tunnel that people enter as free singles and from which they are expected to emerge as responsible adults.

II

Marriage has succeeded as a vital and stable institution in spite of its frequent alternations between the extremes of Christian asceticism and the anarchy of free love. Judaism steered clear of these dangers. It cannot be simplistically categorized as a puritanical religious view that celebrates celibacy and virginity as intrinsic virtues, and settles for marriage as a concession to human frailty. It did not adopt the ascetic pattern of total self-denial, nor has it ever advocated unrestricted freedom of sexual practice.

If asceticism is unnatural to Judaism, hedonism is abhorrent to it. The Jewish faith not only approves of love and sex within marriage, it positively mandates it. Marriage is part of the fabric of creation. With no apologies, Judaism speaks of the dynamic continuity of the tradition of marriage in the midst of constant social upheaval.

III

This book will describe the traditional Jewish view on such topics as romantic love, premarital sex, homosexuality, interfaith marriage, and extramartial affairs. It will also deal in detail with the outward symbols and practices of the traditional wedding ceremony that encase enduring values, and which are practiced in bits and pieces in almost every wedding ceremony in western civilization.

The religious values that people must bring to marriage are old, tested, rich—and nearly forgotten. But they encourage both durability and excitement in marriage. The Jewish way needs to be articulated today because it is the Jewish concept of marriage which was, and can again become, the foundation of the family in Western civilization.

This book is not concerned primarily with sociological surveys, the supposed mythological roots of religious practices, or anthropological research into rites of passage. Nor does it make any pretense to being an "original" or totally comprehensive treatment of this complex subject: the themes discussed are covered, for the most part, in the Jewish Codes, although the information is scattered in many places and is not generally accessible. Rather, it is an interpretation and popular presentation of the institution of marriage in light of the traditions and laws of the Bible and its accepted interpreters through-out the millenial Jewish history as it relates to today's experience and mood.

It is also not intended as an apologetic. In this time of sexual revolution I may be criticized for espousing a perfectionist ethic inappropriate to the modern world; religious liberals and conservatives may be caught short by rigidity here or elasticity there. But I have tried to enable the tradition to speak for itself, applying its principles to our times rather than adjusting the law to new movements or philosophies. Although the ideas issue from the great tomes of Jewish law and custom, they are of necessity refracted through the prism of my personality. Thus, "if this be error and upon me proved," the fault is with me and not with the heritage.

The scope of the topic, the scarcity of single major works covering the entire field, the urgent, relevant nature of the academic research, the need to present meaningful concepts to a public largely uninitiated in the logic of the Halakhah —all these have made the effort both difficult and fascinating.

Because this book breaks some new ground it is perhaps a first word. It surely is not a last word. Readers would do well to use the bibliography to mine deeper into the living tradition. People today have too many answers and too few questions. My effort will be amply rewarded if people learn what to ask of those who are able to respond.

A word about the form of the book: I have tried to write a text that is easily readable by laypeople, supplemented by end-notes providing research sources for the scholarly community. To that end I have eliminated note numbers and italics from the body of the work; footnotes are listed by page and line in the back. Only biblical citations remain in the text.

IV

Of course, my grandfather is right. Society will not die because it can find no solution to the problem of marriage. But it will continue to suffer the anguish of broken families unless it can rediscover the traditional values of marriage and family living. Margaret Mead once said, "No matter how many communes anybody invents, the family always creeps back." Marriage has lasted too long and generated love and beauty and happiness for too many centuries to be hastily written off by contemporary society.

Can any other human institution provide so much warmth and intimacy? In what other structure can young lovers reach the lyrical heights they do in marriage? Is there another setting in which one generation can bestow so much care on the next?

Marriage is so promising, so potentially satisfying, that separation is almost always deeply traumatic. Is there any better testimony to that beauty which can never be sociologically analyzed and statistically measured? Is there any other relationship which can so surely guarantee the survival of the human species and better perpetuate the moral life? Where else but in marriage can we equally discover the full mystery, dignity, and sacredness of life?

Of course, marriage is *not* a state of perpetual bliss. Someone once remarked that "All marriages are happy; it is the living together afterward that causes all the trouble." There will always be problems in marriage, as in the rest of life. There are daily tensions, sometimes savage controversies. But it is the failures of marriage that tend to be documented. The successes are largely left to the unspoken, intuitively sensed, emotional part of life that has little academic standing and cannot be weighed and tested.

My hope is that this book will speak for those who believe in the ideal of traditional marriage, which has survived—despite formidable challenges—in the Jewish way of life.

Maurice Lamm
Beverly Hills, California

Part One

FINDING A MARRIAGE PARTNER

CHAPTER 1

The Matchmaker

The story is told that a Roman matron once asked Rabbi Yose: "How has your God been occupying his time since He finished the creation of the world?"

"He has been busy pairing couples," answered the Rabbi.

She was astonished. "Is that His trade? Even *I* can do that job. As many man-servants and maid-servants as I have, I can pair."

"Perhaps it is a simple matter in your eyes," replied the Rabbi. "For God, it is as intricate as the splitting of the sea."

She promptly placed one thousand man-servants opposite one thousand maid-servants and declared, "He will marry her, she will marry him," and so on.

The next morning, two thousand servants came to her door, beaten and bruised, complaining, "I do not want her, I do not want him!"

She sent for Rabbi Yose, and conceded: "Rabbi, your Torah is true." The Talmud explains: Matchmaking was a simple matter in her eyes because she, unlike God, could not understand the fundamental differences in the human character that militate against one stranger being successfully matched with another.

There is no doubt, the talmudic Sages conclude, that God Himself had to be the first and ultimate *shadkhan* (matchmaker). Who else could blend two disparate personalities so that they cleave together "as one flesh"? Did he not arrange the union of Adam and Eve? The conclusion was irresistible, and it was written no fewer than five times in midrashic literature: "Marriages are made in Heaven."

This is not a romantic American cliché, but a serious statement of predestination. God determines which people will unite successfully and serve as vehicles for human survival. Does not the Talmud say: "Forty days before the birth of a child, a heavenly voice proclaims: 'The daughter of so-and-so will be married to so-and-so?' " The Talmud even illustrates how this idea induced a spirit of quietism in some people, with the tale of a young woman who refused to wear pretty clothes, jewelry, or cosmetics to attract a husband, because she believed that—regardless of what she might do—her suitor would be brought to her by God.

This raises a thorny question: If the selection of a mate is preordained, why is it necessary to go through the elaborate charade of selecting a suitable mate? And why do so many marriages fail?

Rabbi Akiva responds to a similar question of predestination by saying, "Everything is known to God, yet free will is given to man." God knows what we will do and how things will work out, but it is still up to us to arrange our own life. Only after all of the arrangements have been made can we say confidently that this is what God had originally ordained.

A HISTORY OF THE *SHADKHAN*

The tradition of the matchmaker traces its human origins to the "super-*shadkhan*" of all time, Abraham's masterful servant Eliezer, who arranged no less a marriage than that of the patriarch Isaac to the matriarch Rebekah. The biblical chapter (Genesis 24:1–67) that records the story was read in synagogues when the groom was called to the Torah on the Sabbath before or after the wedding in order to announce the marriage publicly. Western European communities abrogated this custom in the 1700s, but the Sephardim (the Jewish community that originated in Spain) continue it to this day. Abraham, having realized that the native Canaanite women were morally unsuitable, decides to search abroad for a suitable wife for his son Isaac. He sends Eliezer, under oath, to find the right bride for Isaac "from among the members of his family and the house of his father," which he had left behind when at God's bidding he had set out for Canaan. Eliezer believes he has found a suitable match in Rebekah, daughter of Bethuel, the nephew of Abraham; but she must first pass a test designed to determine the quality of her kindness and hospitality. Rebekah succeeds admirably in meeting all his expectations—she is generous, extraordinarily hospitable, and selfless, kind to total strangers and even animals. Eliezer brings Rebekah to Isaac, who welcomes her into his home, and "he loved her."

The significance of the function of the *shadkhan* in ancient times can be seen from the derivation of its root word *shidukh* (match). The Aramaic translation has it as *sheket,* "silence," and the term *shidukh* signifies tranquility or peacefulness. The connotation is that the *shadkan* pacifies parents who are anxious about their child's marital prospects. It also implies a sense of tranquil arrival for two people tired of the dreams, the frustrated expectations, and the long search for a loving spouse.

The classic *shadkhan* has a long and honorable tradition in Jewish life. No huckster could become a unifier of human beings. He had to have deep personal integrity and balanced judgement to be entrusted with so vital a task as arranging a permanent union. From the days of the Talmud and for centuries thereafter, it was the headmasters of the Higher Torah Academies who were customarily asked to recommend eligible students for marriage. The reason is obvious: in addition to possessing the necessary moral qualifications, these rabbis were also intimately acquainted both with the elite young scholars who were considered the prize grooms and the leading families of the community who supported the communal institutions.

After the *shidukh* was arranged, informal negotiations took place at which the preliminary arrangements were settled. The future alliance was agreed upon and the dowry and presents were clearly specified. But the agreement was still informal, and if one of the partners decided to withdraw because of disaffection or other grounds that were not previously known, there was usually no legal penalty—although undoubtedly it must have led to some bitterness, frustration, and quarrels.

The role of the *shadkhan* reached its height in the darkest days of oppression and dispersion of the long Jewish exile in Europe. At a time when the survival of the people was in danger, and high standards of personal morality seemed threatened with extinction, this institution provided a stabilizing, fortifying and encouraging influence. This was especially true during the thirteenth and fourteenth centuries, after the Crusades had ravaged the Jewish people and scattered them over the entire continent. Communities had been splintered and isolated, and there was little communication between one group of Jews and another.

It was also at this time that the concept of romantic love was formally introduced to the world and young people considered it the highest—indeed, the only—test required for life's permanent union. In light of the new emphasis on romance, Jewish leaders reminded the community repeatedly of the words of the Talmud: "Rav says, 'He who marries without *shidukhin* (preliminary marital arrangements) deserves corporal punishment.'" Although physical punishment could not be inflicted by a Jewish court in those days, the statement served to underscore rabbinic distrust of the romantic impulse as the only basis for marriage. The *shadkhan* short-circuited the long search for a mate, encouraging earlier marriages and lessening the chances of romantic dallying with a variety of people.

Although the estimation of beauty was the *shadkhan's* stock in trade, he was encouraged not to arrange a union based exclusively on physical attributes. Instead, he based his choices on qualities of character, piety, intelligence and competence that would lend permanence to a marriage and encourage a high degree of moral stability in the community.

Toward the end of the Middle Ages, a new type of individual began to occupy the position of *shadkhan*—the paid professional. It is very likely that the *shadkhan* began to be paid as the community became anxious about the contagion of romantic love and its potentially disastrous effects on Jewish society.

By the fifteenth century, scholars as great as Maharil, earned their livelihoods as professional *shadkhanim*. Questions and answers are recorded in medieval rabbinic Responsa indicating how, how much, and when the *shadkhan* is to be paid. If a match proved to be unhappy, *he* could be banned and his fee refused. If things went unusually well, he could reasonably claim twice the fee. Jewish law, therefore, established his fees, and Jewish ethics determined his integrity.

At the same time a formal contract (*tena'im*) replaced the informal preliminary agreement between the families. This contract specified the date of the wedding, financial arrangements, the assurance that neither party would marry anyone else, and the monetary penalties that would be imposed, if any part of the contract was broken.

THE SHADKHAN AS A PRESERVER OF JEWISH VALUES

The talmudic Rabbis say about God, the first *shadkhan:* "He pairs two people, even if He must . . . bring them from one end of the world to the other." In the same way, the *shadkhan* traveled from city to city in an intricate network of cross-pollination, telling the father of a young man that a perfectly-suited young lady had been discovered two hundred miles away. Considering that highway robbers made the medieval roads notoriously dangerous to travel without armed escort, and difficult as well as time consuming to navigate even at the best of times, there was virtually no way such families would have met without the *shadkhan*'s unique combination of courage, psychological acuity and brokerage talents. In fact, Jewish law recognized this aspect of the *shadkan's* function and stipulated that he was to be paid a higher fee when the bride and groom come from widely separated communities. In this way he literally interrelated whole communities and provinces.

At the same time, he performed an important subsidiary function by carrying news of Jewish affairs to widely separated Jewish communities. Although to us marriage and news-bringing may be ordinary events, in those days they served the vital function of encouraging small pockets of Jews not to despair: they were not alone, but part of the larger world of Jews—related to the big cities, the great scholars, and to Jerusalem itself.

The *shadkhan* was familiar with the backgrounds of scores of families, and he held the key to the successful marriages of their children. As a result, the community developed a greater concern than ever for the authenticity of family descent. A mixed marriage, the conversion of one of its members to another faith, or the birth of an illegitimate child would significantly diminish the opportunities for a good *shidukh* for every child of each family. Since the selection of a spouse was not left to a chance meeting, the rate of interfaith marriage was kept so low as to be insignificant. Because the *shadkhan* would not only match inner qualities but family pedigree and scholastic and economic achievements, families knew that their futures depended on their religious and moral reputations. The Rabbis frequently decried those who contracted unworthy marriages and ignored the potentially disastrous effect upon future progeny. This spurred families to achieve a better quality of Jewish life, resulting in a religious and moral stability that was the envy of surrounding peoples.

In these times, the ideal of well-to-do parents, was to have their daughter marry a Torah scholar of great potential. This only the *shadkhan* could arrange, and he was often a genius at wedding scholarship to wealth. He thereby performed feats of genetic engineering which assured the survival of the intelligentsia. Unlike Roman Catholicism, which developed a priestly intellectual class and then did not permit priests to marry, the Jews considered marriage an obligation of the highest priority, especially for scholars. Thus, a groom's scholarship became the most sought after quality for Jewish brides.

Interestingly, this process served society in another crucial way: because the scholar was able to reach the top of the social ladder, the poor learned that the fastest way out of poverty was intellectual achievement. Similarly, the girl born to poverty had at least a reasonable hope of rising socially by bearing children whose scholarship would make them eligible to marry into wealthier families. Even the sisters, parents and children of a scholar were invested with his prestige. The Rabbis said, "Take heed of the children of the poor, for from them will issue scholars of Torah."

Although this "wedding of scholarship to wealth" worked well, it had an ironic side-effect: often the only books that survived the frequent pogroms and communal destruction, were those printed and reprinted by the wealthy fathers-in-law of Torah scholars or by the well-to-do daughters-in-law married to the scholars. Many of the rare handwritten volumes of greater, but poorer scholars were lost to posterity.

THE DECLINE OF THE *SHADKHAN* AND HIS RE-EMERGENCE

Gradually, over the centuries, the societal need for the *shadkhan* diminished. Communities were more stable, communication and travel became easier, and there was a greater concentration of Jews in the larger cities. Also, many young people who were suddenly emancipated and imbued with the ideals of the romantic tradition sought to experience this romance personally. C. S. Lewis called the thirteenth century "the era of erotic institutionalism." Young people would allow no one, not even parents, to suggest a choice of mate. The traditional clients of the *shadkhan* now felt demeaned merely by talking to him, since it was a clear sign of their own inadequacies.

Further, the profession of *shadkhan* succeeded so well that it bred its own demise. Because it offered income and status to people who had no apparent skill, worthier men or women were discouraged from this work. The *shadkhan* evolved from a heaven-sent master doing God's will to an unsavory, umbrella-toting charlatan. He took on the image of a fleshtrader, an image that hung on for centuries. By the end of the sixteenth century, his activities were closely watched, and many commentaries and ethical tracts scorned his techniques. In five hundred years, the *shadkhan* declined from an exalted position to an object of mockery and social anathema.

Of course, the *shadkhan* is, in large part, a figure from a world long passed. Yet in a 1959 article (reprinted in a text on marriage in 1977), Eleanor Stoker Bell analyzed the applicability to modern society of the arranged marriage.

There are solid arguments for reviving the function of the *shadkhan*. First, people tend to marry at an early age—one out of three, under 18; most frequently at age 21 and 22 for men, 18 and 19 for women. Their sober judgment at this age is at least questionable, and intellectual compatibility at school is frequently confused with abiding love. Dr. Judson Landis at the University of California notes that divorces in families where both mates marry under age 21 are six times the average. Second, in our highly mobile society, most children will have moved approximately five times before they complete high school. This instability is not a good base for a reasonable choice of mate, and strong parental guidance is surely called for. Third, the burden of failed marriages will frequently fall on the shoulders of parents, and they should therefore have more influence over the crucial aspect of mate selection.

On the other hand, the traditional matchmaker is not well suited to today's society. Even strong parental control is often deleterious to marital success. Parents may be status-oriented, seeking to realize their own interests through their children's alliances. In addition, many parents fared poorly in their own marriage. How will street-wise children accept such parents' judgments for their own lives? Further, marriage requires a base of affection, not only shared values. Partners must start their lives together not only as paired clones, but with warmth and tenderness. That calls for a personal acquaintance on which the future can reasonably be based.

While the *shadkhan* cannot effectively be transplanted from Europe to

America, from another century to the twentieth, the new world can seek to create a new instrument for arranging marriages that will incorporate the positive values of the *shadkhan* with the needs of contemporary people.

In recent years, with the growth of an indigenous American Orthodoxy that finds the contemporary moral environment repugnant, the *shadkhan* has re-emerged, dressed in the new garb of the university and the computer matching service. Orthodox Jewish communities now avail themselves of some fifty such modern marriage brokers who demonstrate none of the ridiculed qualities of their predecessors. These *shadkhanim* are found largely in New York. Private enterpreneurs, they rarely advertise and are best discovered by personal recommendation. Organizations such as the Union of Orthodox Jewish Congregations are considering computerization of available data, and the conservative movement already operates such a computer successfully from its base in New York.

It would not be surprising if the Jewish world, seeking desperately to preserve itself, fearful of the imminent collapse of the host culture and astonished by the growing divorce rate, would warmly welcome back, in a new guise, the old *shadkhan* who traces his lineage, after all, to God Himself.

CHAPTER 2

Romantic Love and the
Jewish Concept of Love

ROMANTIC LOVE AS AN IDEAL

With new-found freedom, a wider intergenerational gap, heightened mobility, greater individuality, and expanded opportunities for employment and travel, the fever of romantic love grew contagious and in time became the dominant criterion for choosing a mate. This transition from *shadkhan* to romance was confusing to many Jews, as illustrated by two songs in the musical "Fiddler on the Roof." Singing "Matchmaker, Matchmaker," Tevye's daughter hopes that the *shadkhan* will bring her a mate who is both suitable to her parents and attractive to herself, while her mother begins to question her own successful twenty-five year marriage when she asks, "Do You *Love* Me?" Tevye does not understand: he works for his wife, cares for her; for twenty-five years he has helped her raise the children. "If that is not love, what is?" Love, to him, is demonstrated in action. But his wife has caught the fever of romance, and nothing else matters.

Romantic love, passionately experienced by humanity throughout the ages, grew as an ideology in France during the last quarter of the twelfth century. Its theoretical basis was formulated by Andrew Capellanus (the Chaplain), in *The Art of Courtly Love,* and in the poetry of Chrestien de Troyes. Carried to the countryside by troubadors, the idea of romantic love took hold and spread rapidly throughout Europe—even into the narrow confines of the Jewish world.

Rabbi Judah the Pious comments on this in *Sefer Hasidim* with the oft-quoted phrase, "as the Christian goes, so goes the Jew."

Romantic love was originally conceived of on two levels: "pure love," which consists of "the contemplation of the mind and the affection of the heart" but finds no ultimate physical fulfillment; and "mixed love," whose desire has been fulfilled, however infrequently. It is the ideal of pure, unfulfilled love that is celebrated by the poets and acted out in so many of the great dramas—the stories of Romeo and Juliet, Tristan and Isolde, Heloise and Abelard are the classic examples.

The void left by the disappearance of the *shadkhan* has been filled today by an elaborate courtship procedure. While it is true that most people cannot and will not go back to the old days of the cantankerous *shadkhan,* we need to ask ourselves whether our complicated and frustrating dating game really leads to more marital happiness. In their book *Marriage: East and West,* David and Vera Mace describe the dating game as "a vast Noah's ark". Perhaps arranged marriages were not terrible as we moderns think—after all, we have inherited only the caricature, not the reality. Surely, they suggest, more intense parental control of mate selection, a sort of *parent* matchmaker system, would make for more stable and joyful unions than we in a free society achieve.

Other writers declare that the trouble with American marriage is our style of courtship. It is artificial, juvenile, and premature, and emphasizes romance, sex appeal, charm, and affluence to the exclusion of the deeper, more enduring aspects of character. Charles Darwin once observed that men scan with far more scrupulous care the character and pedigree of their horses when they breed them than they do their potential marriage partners.

Denis de Rougemont, a contemporary French scholar, says, "We are in the act of trying out—and failing miserably at it—one of the most pathological experiments that a civilized society has ever imagined, namely, the basing of marriage which is lasting upon romance which is a passing fancy." We must ask ourselves these questions: Are we happier? Do our marriages last longer? Are our children more satisfied with their parents? Will romance ever be able to replace the *shadkhan* in producing the stable families that characterized Jewish life from its inception?

THE HAZARDS OF ROMANCE

Romantic love is often expressed in terms of "sickness": romantic poems repeat endless variations on the theme of "Why so pale and wan, fair lover?" and even the origin of the word "passion" is "suffering." Upon reflection, the irrationality of it all is astounding. People fall "madly" in love, their love is "out of this world," the lover is "moonstruck." It is more than coincidental that the propitious time for passionate love is during the full moon—in primitive society, that was thought to be the time for madmen, *luna*tics, to be active. *Sefer Hasidim* in the thirteenth century records the question of how to handle a married man who is 'bewitched' and irrationally pursues another woman whom he does not know. (*Im adam me'khushaf ve'rodef acharei ishah?*) It is assumed that such a man is under a spell, and the object of his adultery is referred to as an "exotic fruit."

Romantic love is also associated with sadness. Like parting, it is sweet sorrow. Denis de Rougemont notes that, "Happy love has no history." The sadness arises from the fact that the lovers cannot fulfill their souls' yearning to "become as one," either because one lover is married to someone else or because they are separated by too great a distance. Romantic love is based on an idealized notion of the other person, which requires remoteness—psychological, physical, or social—to be maintained. Hence the inherent paradox: romantic love desires intimacy, but at the very moment of intimacy, love evaporates.

Pure romantic love is applied only to love outside of marriage. While it is true that romantic love did become a sort of precondition to married life at the end of the sixteenth century, its outlook could never be suitably adapted to this state. The potion of romance must contain an ingredient of secrecy and mystery—the furtive glance, the "stolen waters." The love relationship, therefore, is primarily a premarital or extra-marital association. Singers do not often sing of romantic love within marriage, the care for children, on the mutuality of love in old age. Romantic love, by its own definition, is something "beyond," "out of this world," which cannot be contained in the restricting narrow walls of married life.

Love is blind. Cupid's arrows have always been shot indiscriminately, and in the twentieth century his aim is often completely off the mark. Love is not usually altogether blind—but it is nearsighted, able to see only what is agreeable to the five senses, not necessarily to common sense. Burdened with this romantic myopia, the nearsighted lover cannot discriminate between true love and infatuation. A lover chosen in this way may be utterly unfit for marriage. Is a cute smile a qualification for responsible child raising? Are broad shoulders sure-fire indications of integrity? Benjamin Franklin was right when he said, "Keep thy eyes wide open before marriage and half-shut afterwards."

Romance foists upon the world the illusion that a mate must be capable of providing a life of continuous ecstasy. Unfortunately, passion has the tendency to spend itself quickly. Romantic love, by holding out the possibility of perpetual passion, raises unrealistic expectations. When no passion is experienced and the embers have cooled, many people think their marriage has failed and start looking for the exit sign. As Oscar Wilde noted cynically, "One should always be in love. That is the reason one should never marry."

The religious ethic holds that sex and love must be integrally related; secular ethic that the two may be totally separate phenomena—sex is physical and love is emotional. This classic conflict leads to one of the most dangerous hazards of romantic love in a society with professed religious ideals: the equation of sexual desire with love. Too often the words "I love you" are only a come-on for a physical relationship. We do not allow ourselves to call sex "sex," so we call it love. John Ciardi observes, "Love is the word used to label the sexual excitement of the young, the habituation of the middle-aged, and the mutual dependence of the old."

Most marriages are failures. Not because most marriages end in divorce, but because in most unions one or both partners are miserable. Most of marriage's ills, perhaps, can be traced to faulty selection of a spouse that was precipitated by a glorious moment, a flash of insight, or an uncontrollable passion.

Romance is not known to bring clear perception and a sense of balance in weighing future marriage possibilities. The sickness and the sadness and the "magic" distort the vision and transport the emotions. Selecting a lifelong partner under such heady intoxication is hazardous in the extreme.

"Pure" romantic love is immensely powerful. If the passion of love can hardly be controlled, making life decisions on its basis alone is absurd. It is surely thrilling—the stuff of dreams, the throbbing heart, the quickened pulse—but is it also right?

JUDAISM ON ROMANTIC LOVE

Judaism treasures the love of husband and wife and surely knows the power and attraction of romantic love. Judaism gave the world the Bible and the Psalms and the Song of Songs. It knew of love and sang of love, but not of the "pure love" that is never consummated—there is no "Romeo and Juliet" in Jewish literature. Judaism is suspicious of powerful drives that cannot be disciplined, regarding "blind" decisions as non-ethical. It considers ecstasy temporary and undependable in terms of long commitment, unless it can be transformed into everyday acts of love.

Does that mean that romantic love plays no part in marriage? (Ernest Van Den Haag has said that love is "a *goyish* invention.") Of course not. No knowledgeable Jew could agree with such a premise. Judaism considers romantic love and affection in marriage to be very desirable, *if* it is one of a cluster of values that brings man and woman into the marital partnership, and can reasonably serve to sustain the union. There is much in our historic character, echoed in the Bible and Talmud, that calls for that mysterious, undefinable binding love between man and wife. The qualification is that the romantic component of love must be transposed into complete, fulfilled love. For that to happen, romance cannot play an *exclusive* role in mate selection; other components must enter into the decision-making process.

Judaism understands that the romance of the first year of marriage seems specifically designed to overcome the initial adjustment difficulties, but it does not tolerate the demands of romance to completely control selection of a mate. From its first chapters on the beginnings of human life, the Bible speaks of the sexual relationship as *yada* (knowing), as in "Adam *knew* Eve" (Genesis 4:1), "carnal *knowledge.*" When the ideal of marital intimacy is expressed by *yada*, a root word the Torah also uses for "reason," it implies a profound knowledge of one's beloved that includes both feeling and understanding. Marriage partners must be selected with reason, as well as with the love that "informs" the heart.

The Book of Proverbs ends with a gentle but curious phrase: "Grace is deceitful and beauty is vain, but a woman who fears the Lord, she shall be praised" (31:30). This does not imply that Jews believe grace and beauty are evil. Rather, comments Rabbi Elijah, the Gaon of Vilna: Grace *alone* is deceitful. Beauty, *by itself,* is vain. But a woman who has grace and beauty that are coupled with the value system that makes for the fear of God, she shall be praised.

The whole world loves a lover, and Judaism does too. In fact, Judaism holds that romantic love, *in the proper framework,* adds a dimension to life that can come from no other source. But romantic love becomes a very foolish idol when it supplants all other values.

The most poignant illustration of the agony and ecstasy of love within a religious setting is the ancient odyssey of Jacob as he set out to marry Rachel (Genesis 28ff.). Isaac, the first man born a Jew, had his marriage to Rebekah arranged by Eliezer, the servant *shadkhan* (Genesis 24:1–67). But the romantic Jacob, Isaac's son, finds Rachel himself, thus providing us with a different model of mate selection. In contrast to Eliezer who approaches the new bride with a well-laden entourage, a meticulously planned route, detailed planning and smooth execution, Jacob makes a precipitous and lonely flight on foot from his father's home to that of his bride, arriving empty-handed and unkempt. He finds Rachel and is struck by her beauty—"he kissed Rachel and wept aloud." (Gen. 29:11) But her cunning father keeps the lovers apart for seven years.

The commentaries wondered why the Bible goes out of its way to record that he "wept aloud." Rashi, the classic biblical commentator, notes that at that moment Jacob realized the difference between *his* approach to Rachel and *Eliezer's* approach to Rebekah and he wept in consternation at being reduced to penury and at his inability to shower his beloved with gifts.

In contrast, the author of the *Biur* says that Jacob wept aloud out of the sheer uncontained joy of great love. As a true romantic, he could not repress his feelings and keep them within the bounds of propriety and gentility, but allowed the cry to burst from his throat.

Jacob was willing to spend seven years heroically doing menial work in order to marry his beloved, and he never argued with his father-in-law about the exorbitant cost of that love. Ramban notes that Jacob became a shepherd, though he had never been one in the past, so that he might be close to her.

How, then, does this story differ from the romantic ideal of "pure love"? Jacob could not have acted on his romantic desire if he had not assured himself that he was in the proper milieu, one in which he could be sure that the fundamental bases of ethics and religion were part of the family tradition. He had seen, in his own youth, how his father suffered when his brother, Esau, married women from Canaan, and he understood the necessity of seeking his bride from within his family, just as Abraham before him had sent Eliezer to find a wife for Isaac. He knew that if he would choose a girl from his own extended family, she would be heir to the value system of his grandfather Abraham, and could understand the uniqueness, mission, and obligations of the Jew. In this way, he was able to choose a spouse and allow himself to seek romance at the same time.

Jewish tradition consistently stresses that the wise person should examine the nature *not only* of the chosen mate, but also of the prospective family. Generations of solid family life lend security to a marriage. Of course, there are no guarantees—but romantic love that is combined with this sort of reasonable selection assures us as fully as possible of a successful and stable marriage.

Jewish literature uses powerful symbols of romantic love to portray humanity's love of God. In the Song of Songs, the shepherdess pursues her beloved. But when she finally is within reach, he is out of grasp. She believes she sees him, but he is not there. She thinks she hears his voice, but he is elsewhere. In its religious interpretation, the story is a metaphor for our constant search for God, Who is ultimately unattainable. At every turn we believe we have communicated with Him, and yet we can never touch His essence. As we reach out for the love of God, so do we reach out for a man or woman.

The ideal of love percolates through Jewish literature, life, history, and law. Ecclesiastes (9:9): "Enjoy life with the wife whom thou lovest." The Song of Songs (6:3): "I am for my beloved and my beloved is for me," and (8:7) "Many waters cannot quench love; neither can the floods drown it." The Prophet Hosea (2:21): "And I (God) will betroth you (Israel) to me forever."

So much is the love for a wife *assumed* in Jewish society that the Bible explicitly commands us to love God, to love our neighbor, to love the stranger, but never once does it explicitly demand of man that he love his wife. That is because to love God we must relate to the supernatural; to love our neighbor requires the sometimes impossible feat of associating with a disagreeable person, and to love a stranger we must overcome ubiquitous xenophobia. But the love of a wife, as the love of one's homeland, is taken for granted as natural and needing no explicit command. One who perverts that love—except in the normal course of a marriage in the process of dissolution—is beneath contempt. The Rabbis said, "You are called *Adam,* but an idolator is not called Adam." That is, as man without loyalty to God is not truly a man, so man without loyalty to a wife is not truly a man.

The idea that romantic love is desirable when associated with other values is reflected in the practical *Halakhah* (the body of Jewish law as written in the Talmud and codes). For instance, the law confronts the question of whether a man should marry a woman he loves despite his parents' objection. In a Responsum, Maharik says that if the girl is suitable to the boy in terms of values and piety, the father has no right to reject the girl with whom his son has fallen in love. Considering the enormous value that Judaism placed on the Fifth Commandment, this decision to overrule parental objection in favor of love is astonishing. As further confirmation, the law even permitted a poor woman to sell a Torah scroll in order for her to have sufficient funds to marry; but the law does not grant permission to do something similar in honor of a parent. According to Rabbi Phinehas Halevi Horowitz, there is a lesson to be learned from the Talmud's comment that Jacob, by absenting himself from honoring his father for twenty-two years (because he had to spend that time working in order to marry his Rachel), demonstrates that the ideal of marriage to a good person is greater than the honoring of a father.

If a man wishes to marry a woman he loves, although she is seriously ill, more power to him. The Sages affirm this in reference to the prophetess Miriam, the sister of Moses and Aaron, who was called *azuvah* (abandoned) because all of the young men abandoned her when she became sick. But Caleb, the son of Chezron, did marry her, and because he nursed her during her illness he was considered her "father" (I Chronicles 2:18); and it was accounted a marriage for the sake of heaven and much praised.

The Rabbis in the Talmud extoll the virtue of a beautiful woman, but declare that a man who marries an unsavory woman simply because of her beauty will ultimately give birth to unsavory children. The Talmud tells of the daughter of Caleb who was called *Achsa,* which means anger, because all who saw her went home and quarreled with their less beautiful wives. It is interesting that even Maimonides, who appears to have been influenced in sexual matters by Aristotle —a man who did not greatly value women—considered it perfectly permissible and within the bounds of halakhic and moral propriety, following the Talmud, to look at a woman with amorous intent in order to determine whether she was physically suitable and lovable as a wife. Such looking, he says, would not be considered to be motivated by immoral desires.

Further, in recognition of both the value and power of love, the Sages avoided applying certain rabbinic enactments if these meant disturbing ideal love. The Midrash tells the following story:

"A certain Israelite of Sidon, having been married more than ten years without being blessed with children, determined to be divorced from his wife. With this view he brought her before Rabbi Simeon, bar Yochai. The rabbi, who was unfavorably disposed to divorces, tried to dissuade him from it. However, seeing that the man was not inclined to accept his advice, he said this to the couple: 'My children, when you were first joined in the holy bond of wedlock, did you not rejoice? Did you not make a feast and entertain your friends? Now, since ye are resolved to be divorced, let your separation be like your union. Go home, make a feast, entertain your friends, and on the morrow come and I will comply with your wishes.'

"So reasonable a request, coming from such an authority, could not, with any degree of propriety, be rejected. Accordingly, they went home and prepared a sumptuous party to which they invited their friends.

"During the entertainment the husband, elated with wine, said to his wife: 'My beloved, we have lived together happily these many, many years; it is only the lack of children which makes me want a divorce. To convince you, however, that I bear you no ill-will, I give you permission to take with you out of my house anything you like best.'

" 'Be it so,' rejoined the woman.

"The cup went round and the people were merry. Having drunk rather freely, most of the guests fell asleep, among them the master of the feast. The lady no sooner perceived it, than she ordered him to be carried to her father's house, and to be put into a bed she prepared for just that purpose.

"As the fumes of the wine gradually evaporated, the man awakened. Finding himself in a strange place, he wondered and exclaimed, 'Where am I? How did I come here? What does this all mean?'

"His wife, who had waited to see the result of her stratagem, stepped from behind a curtain. Begging him not to be alarmed, she told him that he was now in her father's house.

" 'In your father's house!' exclaimed the still astonished husband. 'How did I come to be in your father's house?'

" 'Be patient, my dear husband,' replied the prudent woman, 'and I will tell you all. Recollect, did you not tell me last night, I might take out of your house whatever I valued most? Now, believe me, my beloved, among all your treasures there is not one I value so much as I do you; no, there is not a treasure in this world I esteem so much as I do you.' "

YICHUD: A JEWISH CONCEPT OF LOVE

Yichud, the word most descriptive of the Jewish idea of love, is defined as "together," "alone, with no one else present, in a room or in an enclosure." This one-word concept describes many of the aspects of the love that Judaism proposes. Before we can fully understand *yichud,* we must clarify what it is not by contrasting it with *ahavah,* the word traditionally associated with love in general.

In over two hundred references to *ahavah* in the Torah, there are only a few instances in which *ahavah* is associated with married love. Most often, it refers to nonromantic relationships—"love" of family, of God, of good or of evil, of the neighbor and the stranger, the servant's love of his master, the woman for her mother-in-law. Often it means simply "friendship," as when David laments the death of Jonathan (II Samuel 1:26): "Wonderful was thy love for me, passing the love of women." So too, the Book of Esther (6:13) describes Haman's followers as "Zeresh, his wife and all his *ohavav* [friends]."

When *ahavah* is applied to man-woman relationships, the reference is usually to pre-marital or extra-marital love. It is often a substitute word for "passion," as in Amnon's "I love Tamar" (II Samuel 13:4), which culminates in sexual assault and the transformation of his love into hate. In Hosea (3:1) and elsewhere, the word is used in a situation where love and adultery alternate thematically, with no relation to stable married love. *Ahavah* is also used in Jeremiah's chastisement (2:25), "There is no hope. No, for I have loved strangers and after them will I go"; and Ezekiel's charge (16:33), "To all harlots gifts are given; but thou hast given thy gifts to all thy lovers."

When *ahavah* is used in the context of married love, it does not express the uncomplicated Jewish ideal of marital love but only connotes a comparison—the loved one as opposed to the "hated" one, or a new love replacing an old love. For example, "and Jacob *loved* Rachel" (Genesis 29:18). Surely here was deep, abiding love. But the term *ahavah* is used in anticipation of the statement 12 verses later (29:30) "and he *loved* Rachel more than Leah." When Deuteronomy (21:15) uses *ahavah* in the phrase, "If a man has two wives, the one *beloved,* and the other hated," this does not indicate love or hatred, but preferred and less preferred. So "Ahasuerus *loved* Esther above all women" (Esther 2:17), and "Rehoboam *loved* Maacah above all of his wives" (II Chronicles 11:21). Even Elkanah's magnificent unqualified love for Hannah is not convincingly portrayed by the term *ahavah* by itself. For here, too, it is comparative: "And he had two wives, the name of one was Hannah, and the name of the other was Peninah, and Peninah had children, but Hannah had no children. . . . But unto Hannah he gave a double portion, *ki et Channah ahev,* for he *loved* Hannah" (I Samuel 2:5). The same is true, in a different sense, of Isaac's love for Rebekah after he brought her "into his tent," "and she became his wife; *va-ye-ehaveha,* and he *loved* her" (Gen. 24:67). "Love" here is also comparative. It indicates "that he was consoled" for his mother's death. The "love" for Rebekah was a replacement "love" for the vanished "love" of his mother. (For all of the understanding of *ahavah* as either non-marital or purely erotic, or only as a comparative sentiment, there remains the statement of *Kohelet*, the wise but embittered, cynical King: "Enjoy life with the wife whom thou lovest all the days of the life of thy vanity. . ."[Ecclesiastes 9:9].)

Especially as used in the "Song of Songs," *ahavah* is connected with the deepest, nonrational level of sentiment, *ahavat nefesh,* a "soul-love" (Song of Songs 1:7 and elsewhere); or with the sickness characteristic of romance, *cholat ahavah;* or with such extreme notions as, "If a man would give all his substance for love, he would be utterly contemned." (Song of Songs 8:7). As traditionally interpreted, this is a symbolic tale of the relationship of humanity with God in which the striving for union can never find satisfactory culmination.

Thus *ahavah* almost always connotes a unilateral love that deals with relationships requiring an act of faith, such as the love of God, or a supreme commitment to justice, as in the love of a stranger or the love of a neighbor as oneself. In these instances, *ahavah* must be commanded. In contrast, *yichud* bespeaks an intimacy, a balanced, mutual relationship, and a love that is simpler, more natural, and lasting—such as the love of a spouse. There is no need to formally command *yichud.*

VALUES IMPLIED IN *YICHUD*

Unlike *ahavah, yichud* connotes both complete, sustained love *and* the sex act within the framework of marriage. The Rabbis do not permit *yichud* before marriage and certainly not outside of marriage. For this reason, it is the name given to the concluding ceremony for establishing the covenant of marriage. *Yichud* is effected by the ceremony after the *chuppah* when bride and groom close themselves off in one room. Consciously and expressly, with no interruption, the couple joins together and remains briefly alone to show they have chosen each other to the exclusion of everyone else. This is not a random or casual act, but a singling out for the purpose of belonging to one another. The *yichud* ceremony symbolizes the rule that love is never to be sought outside of the marriage chamber. All future fulfillment must be contained within these walls, and all tender love directed only to one another.

The word *le'yached* means to select with the specific intention that both become as one. The Torah speaks of *basar echad* (one flesh) (Genesis 2:24) *echad* and *yichud:* one and alone. This expresses the new reality of being alone with someone in order to *know* him or her fully. The biblical carnal knowledge is possible only in an environment of *yichud,* where one person focuses only on the other—not to compare or assess relative merits, but to delve profoundly into the soul of the other. Comparisons are always invidious and signify, as the philosopher Santayana says, "A lack of understanding of each in its own uniqueness." This is especially true in marriage, where even a verbal comparison is the intrusion of an outsider into the exclusive precincts of marriage. The Bible's "And he shall cleave unto his wife" (Gen. 2:24) implies that the embrace is meant only for one's wife.

In ancient times, the bride was festively carried on a litter coach followed by a huge retinue through the streets of the town and into the groom's home. The *process* of leaving one home and entering another was celebrated as *chuppah,* effecting the *yichud* love, and she was legally considered to be married. The advocators of this halakhic understanding of *chuppah* emphasize that the essence of marriage is expressed in the tie to the home. In order to *build* a home and family, one must *come from* a home and family—*mi-beit avikha le'veit chatunah. Yichud* implies this family-centeredness. It is said that *beito zu ishto* (a man's home is his wife), and it is not by chance that the Jewish people are described as *Beit Yaakov,* (the *House* of Jacob), or *Beit Yisrael* (the *House* of Israel).

Thus unlike the poetry of romantic love that concerns itself solely with the intimacy of two individuals, *yichud* implies the designing of an environment in which both love of spouse *and* love of children can flourish. Although the Bible reports the romantic swoon of Jacob *before* he married Rachel, prior to that it records a reverse process: Isaac brought Rebekah to his *home,* and only *then* did he *love* her (Genesis 24:67). *Yichud* is symbolic of that complex of ideas and sentiments that ties love to home, to the efforts of raising a family, and to the daily work required to maintain the ideal of *shelom bayit,* peace in family living.

While *ahavah* denotes an emotional relationship, *yichud* speaks of affection within a cluster of rational values. Leone Ebreo, son of 15th-century biblical commentator Isaac Abrabanel, says, "It is obvious that the love of husband and wife is pleasant, but it must be bound up with good too; which is the reason why a reciprocal love does survive the enjoyment of its delights, and, not only persists, but grows continually, through its participation in the good. Moreover, the good and pleasurable elements in married love are supplemented by that of advantage; for each of the spouses is ever deriving benefit from the other, which greatly contributes to the fostering of their love. Thus, married love, being pleasurable essentially, is preserved by its connections with both advantage and good."

The foregoing interpretations are based on the fact that the ancient *chuppah* was the couple's new bedchamber. The reenactment of *Yichud* therefore implies total privacy. The couple is not permitted *yichud* before marriage, precisely because its very privacy may result in immorality. *Yichud* thus makes an unqualified statement: it sets the locus for love indoors, within the home. Love is privacy and secrecy and mystery, and the concern of two people only. No one else may have the key to the bedroom door.

Yichud is the culmination of the ceremony of *kiddushin,* and so sanctity must be a component of any relationship that is to succeed as a Jewish marriage. This sanctity enables the love of God to be couched in the familiar words of the love of man and woman. Since the close of the Bible, monogamy, the bond of one man and one woman, has come to reflect monotheism, the bond of one people and one God; *yichud* is based on *achdut ha-borei* (the oneness of the Creator). The theme of unity that is so prominent in Jewish mysticism and theology also underlies the structure of the Jewish family. *Sanctification* means *separation.* As God chose the Jews and thereby sanctified them, we select our spouses and thereby sanctify the relationship. *Yichud* love assures that married life can continue to be imbued with a sense of the sacred.

Lastly and most importantly, *yichud* means that marriage must provide latitude for *relationship modalities other than love.*—a variety of nonromantic relationships. These may be a non-sexual intimacy, affection, deep respect, or simply an acceptable partnership arrangement to assure that children are raised in a pleasing and wholesome atmosphere. As long as there is caring, empathy, and closeness between the partners, a community of *thought*—like a community of *feeling*—is an altogether proper setting for successful marriage.

To those committed irrevocably to romantic love as the only way, these words may seem heretical. But nonromantic relationships exist in millions of households, Jewish and non-Jewish. The *"Playboy* Report on American Men," a Louis Harris poll taken in 1979, ranks what people today consider the important qualities of the ideal lover. "Someone to be totally honest and open with" headed the list with fifty-three percent of the 1,990 men surveyed, while only twenty-four percent cited "someone who is sexually exciting."

The halakhic structure of *chuppah* that expresses this idea is unusual. It says that *yichud* may be accomplished even if bride and groom were *not alone,* so long as they were *together.* How can marriage, which is fundamentally a sexual relationship, be symbolized by a togetherness which cannot be accomplished because of the presence of others? How is that original bedchamber to be represented by a *yichud* in the company of a crowd? *Ran,* a medieval commentator, holds that the union must be *re'uyah le'bi'ah,* potentially to be consummated. But marriage must be able to accommodate more than sensual love. Even if they are not totally alone the couple must live together peacefully under one roof.

Minimally, then, marriage must assume the possibility of living together in friendship, and in that sense satisfy the basic biblical charter for any two humans sharing a life together: "Love thy neighbor as thyself." (Leviticus 19:18) Therefore, every precaution must be taken *before* marriage to make sure that the boy and the girl not be personally repelled by each other. That is the reason why, according to the *Halakhah,* even if the marriage was arranged by a matchmaker the couple must also meet face-to-face prior to the marriage. Maimonides rules that if, after the wedding, the husband or wife maintains that the other is personally repulsive, divorce may be granted on those grounds alone.

If parents cannot act decently with one another, they have no right to expect to be able to raise decent children. The Rabbis, in the talmudic discussion of the "Rebellious Son" (*ben sorer u'moreh*) rule that if parents do not at least have the facility to communicate openly, their child may not be punished as a delinquent. Hence in the law, if there is too great a disparity between parents— in height or in temperament, or if they do not speak the same language, or in a similar tone of voice, or if one is mute or deaf—the son cannot be prosecuted.

One of the frustrations of a marriage based solely on romance is that the smitten lover seeks from romantic love what it may not be able to give. When marriage produces no transcendent purpose or new significance, and the world turns out to be the same ordinary world, marriage undergoes severe strain. Friendship, as a base for love and marriage, contains the seeds for growth in a life of shared commitment.

YICHUD AND MARRIED ROMANCE

The most painful paradox of romantic love is that the very qualities that characterize "pure love" are those that most commonly evaporate on the first day of marriage. One of the basic tenets of "pure love" is mystery, but there can be little mystery when the conquest has been achieved and the lovers are not only ready, but available. The breathlessness of pursuit cannot be recaptured because there is no longer any pursuit—the unattainable has been attained. Total unavailability and untouchability may be good for romance, but they are certainly contradictory to good marriage.

Interestingly, this sustained love called *yichud* often encourages the aims of romantic love—ecstasy, desire and pursuit—within marriage. Experience has proved that the Jewish concept of *tze'niut* (modesty) in all of its varied expressions (such as the veiling of the bride and the covering of the hair and nonexposure of the body) unintentionally enhance the exotic motif more than blatant and unadorned exposure of the body. The physical body was a paradox to philosophy and religion because its very physicality somehow did not accord with theoretical modes of thought. The Greek philosophers solved the paradox through aesthetics, and glorified the body by exposing it. Judaism solved the paradox through the concept of *kiddushin* (sanctity), which calls for withdrawal, hiddenness, covering.

"Absence makes the heart grow fonder." The laws of *niddah,* which demand total physical and sexual withdrawal from one another during twelve days following menstruation, impose a rhythm of passivity and activity, scarcity and availability, passionate fervor and disciplined withdrawal. After this period, there is almost a reenactment of the honeymoon, and the revitalizing of the pursuit and discovery of romantic love.

The Jewish tradition urges that husband and wife design for each other a *romantic environment* for marital intercourse. The Talmud speaks of using affectionate words (*ritzui u'piyyus*), and of being on the same physical level during intimate conversations; Maharam of Lublin says that "not intercourse alone is a religious command, but all forms of intimacy (*kiruv*) by which a man rejoices his wife." This environment has components of the psychic rhythm and the physical rhythm, of words and thoughts that move the couple to blend harmoniously in mind and body.

With these traditions, Judaism tries to domesticate desire and to place romance well within the framework of marriage rather than to have it disappear the moment the veil is lifted.

Authentic *yichud* love must express a sensitive balance between reason and romance, discipline and spontaneity, dream and realism, aggressiveness and withdrawal, fusion and independence. It must be sustaining throughout life, able to weather the daily prosaic crises that come not only between the lovers, but also between them, the family, and the community. It is not selfish, but it is also not impersonal. It is not shut off from society, but it is also not solely communal. It is not exclusively spiritual, and it is also not exclusively social. It is not wholly an idealistic love, and it certainly is not an exclusively sensual love.

CHAPTER 3

The Sexual Component in Love and Marriage

THE POWER OF SEX

Sex is the most powerful, all-pervasive force in human experience. It may be intensely personal, meaningful, and creative at one moment, and depersonalized, meaningless, and careless the next. Much of its glory is that it can bring us as close as we may get in life to experiencing the mystery of our mortality, and because of this it is sanctified. Yet it can also be a blind, nearly irresistible force seeking wanton release on the biological level, and in this way its sanctity is perverted. Paradoxically, sex—the most chaotic, powerful, and untutored drive—can only be fully experienced when it includes an element of discipline and precision.

Theologian Helmut Thielicke postulates a theology of sex on the premise that not even an iron will can truly withstand its force. *En apotropus le'arayot,* the Talmud teaches: "No one can guarantee another's sexual innocence." Long ago the Rabbis said, "The greater the man, the greater the desire," equating personal power and libidinal power. "The sexual attraction first engages the eyes," say the moralists, "and the only effective way to eliminate immorality is to *avoid* its grasp at every turn."

But temptation, in the form of magazines, books, and movies, is a multibillion dollar industry and permeates our society. The abuse of human sexuality has reached the stomach-turning point, and there seems to be no way to avoid it—no exertion of universal will, no permanent cover for the eyes. It is ironic that this situation should exist at a time when cults are multiplying, more people are praying, and atheists are being ridiculed into extinction. It seems we are at a time of religious boom and moral bust.

You may ask, "what else is new?" Haven't religious and ethical leaders throughout history decried society's lack of morality? Yes, but it *is* different today. Not because the sanctity of sex is violated in practice, not because television brings temptation into the family's inner sanctum, and not because sexual gratification is readily available. Today sexual morality is rejected as an *ideal,* modesty is scoffed at, and chastity is rejected as anachronistic. Worse, those who articulately uphold moral standards, modesty, and chastity are disappearing; their arguments appear irrelevant.

The Bible rejects one who does only "whatsoever is right in his own eyes" (Deuteronomy 12:8). Today, the philosophy that "man is the measure of all things" is not confined to one group, it is the heritage of our whole society. If we are to be the final arbiters of all value, it follows that whatever serves our needs is declared "good." "The *good* life" is a life devoted to sensual experience —tennis, water-skiing, the theater. These activities are not intrinsically wrong; but it is noteworthy that the most basic ethical term is so easily transferred to physical pleasure.

We have adopted an ideology of narcissism informed by situational ethics: if you have pleasure and mutual consent anything goes—as long as no one gets hurt. For example, what is disturbing is not the ethical merit of a particular abortion, but the rationale for wholesale abortions: "It's my body and I can do what I want with it." Similarly, there is hardly a trace of guilt to be found in those responsible for media presentations of what is now considered "old-fashioned" sexual immorality. No attempt is made to correct the situation— that's just the way it is. But worse is the accepted justification for casual sex or an adulterous affair: "It makes me happy."

Today *contra*ception, not *con*ception, is the focus of research. The sex act has effectively been separated from its fulfillment—one is play, the other pro-creation. In a day when coitus is no longer necessarily connected with reproduc-tion or with responsibility, not many pregnancies are likely to survive both contraception and abortion.

Today there is no talk of standards, God's or society's. It seems sex is all right in every form—so long as it is not repressed, Freud forbid. We are faced with this question: What shall sex be used for now that it is no longer tied to that sacred, cosmically significant function of perpetuating the family, the faith, and the human race? Society's answer appears to be very simple: fun—and fun has no rules.

JUDAISM ON SEXUAL BOUNDARIES

There is no single term for "sex" in the Bible. The title for the list of the Bible's prohibited sexual offenses is *gilui arayot,* "uncovering the nakedness" (Leviticus 18:6ff), and Maimonides classifies these chapters of the law under the rubric of *Kedushah* (Sanctity). Although Jewish tradition does not treat sexual experience systematically, reference to it can be found in every one of the Five Books of Moses, in every book of the Prophets, and *Ketuvim,* the "Writings." Even the Talmud contains candid, sometimes explicit clinical analyses and intimate details that would make a Victorian blush. What emerges is a moral discipline that is strict, yet highly sensitive to the human condition; one that affirms the joyfulness of the sexual experience, but insists that it express itself in controlled circumstances; and one that never deprecates marriage and at every opportunity deplores monastic asceticism.

Judaism's philosophy of sexual experience, love, and marriage begins with the Bible's first recorded paragraphs describing Adam's relations with Eve. This philosophy has weathered every new fad and every radical style that boldly declared its doctrine to the world, from the celibacy of Augustine to the free love of Bertrand Russell. Judaism has focused its greatest minds on understanding God's law and nature's demands, and throughout its history has succeeded in elevating sex, sanctifying marriage, and firmly establishing the family as the primary unit of the community.

Traditional Judaism makes the following general propositions about sex and its place in human society:

1. *Sexual relations may take place only between a man and a woman.* This means that sex with an animal is considered a perversion, and intercourse with a member of one's own sex prohibited.
2. *Sexual relations and marriage are not permitted with someone outside the circle of the Jewish people (mixed marriage) or inside the circle of close relatives established by the Bible and the Sages (incest).*
3. *Sexual relations are a* mitzvah, a religious duty, *within a properly covenanted marriage in accordance with Jewish law.* Outside of that covenant, premarital sexual relations are not condoned and extramarital relations are considered crimes.
4. *Sexual relations within marriage must accord with the laws of family purity with respect to the wife's menstrual cycle.*

Rabbi Akiva deduced these fundamental ideas from a single verse (Genesis 2:24): "Therefore shall a man leave his father and his mother and shall cleave unto his wife, and they shall be one flesh." By extension, "his father" also includes his father's wife, even if she is not his mother, and his "mother" is meant literally—to *exclude incest*. "And he shall cleave," but not to another male—to *exclude homosexuality;* "to his wife," not to his neighbor's wife—to *exclude adultery;* "And they shall be as one flesh," not to animals—to *exclude buggery*.

SEVEN AXIOMS FOR SEXUAL CONDUCT

These propositions are based largely on the following axioms that form the fundamental concepts of human sexuality in Judaism.

1. The Human Being Is Not an Animal

Simple observation teaches us that we have the genitalia of animals and participate in a similar sexual process. Why, then, can we not act like animals? It does seem to be nature's way. Indeed, Freudian psychology teaches us generally that we must see ourselves as we are, pleasure-seeking animals, and that we will not succeed in negating our essential animality except at the risk of neurosis. In the physical and psychological sense, then, human beings are considered to be fundamentally no more than animals.

Convinced of the truth of this specious reductionism—that we are nothing but animals—we begin to act that way without guilt, and even with gusto. There are no rules for beasts to follow other than blind obedience to instincts, satisfaction of needs, and "doing what comes naturally." The consequences of this irresponsible behavior can be disastrous, resulting in broken homes, broken hearts, loneliness, children born out of wedlock, loveless marriages, and infidelity. Ecclesiastes (3:19) declares only in bitterness, "Man has no preeminence above a beast, for all is vanity." But if that is all we are, then the world, humanity, the soul, and all of life becomes meaningless and empty. We were created in the image of God, and Judaism does not permit us to squander our humanity. *Ha-nèshamah lakh ve'ha-guf Pa'alakh* ("the soul is Yours [God's] and the body is Yours, too") is a cornerstone phrase of the Yom Kippur liturgy. At the wedding service, a blessing is recited to remind the bride and groom that the human being is created in God's image.

Despite the similarity of sexual anatomy and parallel reproductive processes, the essential humanity of our sexuality can be discerned in the very fabric of the physical act. If it is to be successful, the sexual act must be based on a sense of concern for the partner. Helmut Thielicke notes that "there is a two-way communication in the structure of the libido, for the prerequisite for the fulfillment of pleasure is that the other person give himself to it, that he participate. . . . The other person should not be a passive object upon which one's own urge is simply 'abreacted.' " Without this communication, coitus is disguised autoeroticism. We cannot successfully follow the animal instinct and achieve release, but must be synchronized with our partner in order to satisfy ourselves.

This "synchrony" required of sexual partners reflects a unique factor that is fundamental to our understanding of the difference between animal sex and human sex: A man's curve of sexual excitement tends to rise sharply and fall precipitously, while a woman's may rise more slowly and taper off gradually. At first this may appear to be an imperfection, when compared to the easy harmony of animals. But perhaps this apparent incongruity is designed to prevent human beings from merely following the erotic impulse in blind animal fashion. To achieve genuine satisfaction, we are forced to express our humanity. Sex exposes us to failure and success, and in all this it confronts us with the theme of human communication instead of mere animal copulation. It is precisely this human need to correct the natural impulse that impels the thirteenth-century author of *Iggeret ha-Kodesh,* a document on the mystical significance of marriage, to give detailed advice to his son on preparing his wife for the sexual act and designing the proper erotic atmosphere.

This exception of the human being from the rule of instinct in the natural realm teaches us that we must exercise our essential humanity in the area of sexual relations as in all other critical areas of life. We must reasonably and intelligently choose a life partner, make proper human covenants, order our lives and our priorities, control our urges, and submit to a higher discipline: a *halakhah,* the law we were given by God. This is a law that we need in order to protect our love, both from other humans who act like animals, and from the internal animal that we sometimes allow to crouch at the door of our souls.

While some segments of society attempt to animalize our humanity, Judaism tries to humanize that which is called animal.

2. The Human Being Is Not an Angel.

If we are not animals—and thus not permitted to abuse our sexual gift—we are also not angels who may abstain from sex altogether. We must live according to a higher ethical and moral law as beings created in the image of God, but reality dictates that we are not, and will never become, angels.

Judaism therefore frowns on celibacy. As recorded in the Talmud, Ben Azzai (one scholar among the thousands recorded) chose to remain celibate in order to study Torah and was chastised severely. This is in stark contrast to the celibacy of the two founders of Christianity, Jesus and Paul, and the pronouncements against the institution of marriage (I Corinthians 6 and 7), which accept it only as a concession to human frailty. To wit, Paul: People should marry only "... if they cannot contain ... ; for it is better to marry than to burn" (I Cor. 7:9); and Matthew: "Be a eunuch for the sake of Heaven" (19:12); and John

Calvin, at the beginning of the Protestant Reformation: Marriage is "a necessary remedy to keep us from plunging into unbridled lust." Reinhold Niebuhr considers the Christian development of the family a triumph over the negative Christian attitude to sex and marriage.

Judaism posits that sex is a gift from God. How could such a gift be considered evil or sinful? Properly used in a legitimate framework, sex is to be viewed positively as joy and as *mitzvah*. The patriarchs marry, the kings marry, the *kohanim* marry, the prophets marry, the Sages marry. Nowhere is there the slightest indication that sex or family interfered with their mission. The term used for Isaac's sexual relationship with his wife is *me'tzachek*, rejoicing (Genesis 26:8). The author of *Iggeret ha-Kodesh* writes: "Let a man not consider sexual union as something ugly or repulsive, for thereby we blaspheme God. Hands which write a Sefer Torah are exalted and praiseworthy; hands which steal are ugly."

While the sexual act is considered good in the proper context, there were some ascetic pietists who viewed the sheer pleasure of even the legitimate act with some disdain. In the seventeenth century, Rabbi Hayyim Vital established the rule of Kabbalists: "He should sanctify himself at the time of intercourse so that he should derive no pleasure from it." However, the Seer of Lublin indicated that this applies *before* the act, as it is impossible to have no pleasure during the act. The Seer quotes Rabbi Elimelech of Lyzhansk, active in the eighteenth century, as saying that there is no benediction before performing the *mitzvah* of intercourse, "because it cannot be performed without an admixture of the 'evil' inclination." Nonetheless, while one should not *seek* pleasure from it, and while a full blessing may not be recited over it, the author concludes that we should thank God if we have received pleasure, so that we should not be guilty of using sacred things without proper acknowledgement.

Sex is not sin, and it does not need to be spiritualized. It must, however, be humanized, by affirming the reality of its power and attractiveness, rejoicing in its presence, using it as a blessing for the benefit and development of humankind, and abstaining from it when its Creator forbids it. A corollary of the two statements—that we are neither animals nor angels—may be that we have aspects of both. In this case, our humanity would consist of proper resolution of the tensions and contradictory demands made upon us by our dual nature.

3. Human Sexuality Is Clean and Neutral.

Judaism believes that sex is morally neutral. Libidinal energy is an ambivalent power, the effect of which depends on what the human being does with it. Sex does not even have the status of an intrinsic value, but can function as a means to express love and build family, or as random personal gratification. Sex is neither bestial nor sinful, neither sacrament nor abomination, and so may not be abused or discarded. It is not to be denigrated as a necessary concession to human weakness, nor is it to be worshipped as an idol.

Genesis (1:31) tells us that at the end of the creation, God saw everything that He made and that it was *tov me'od* (very good). Interpreting the verse, Rabbi Samuel ben Nahman said: "*Tov,* good—that is the *yetzer tov,* the good inclination; *tov me'od, very good—that is the yetzer ha-ra,* the evil inclination. But how can an admittedly evil inclination be considered *good,* let alone *very good?* Because without it, man would not care to build a home, he would neither marry nor beget children, nor would he pursue a livelihood."

Judaism does not believe that sex in itself is evil, it is the *abuse* of sex that is evil.

4. Sexuality Cannot Be Separated from Character.

If we agree that the sexual force is neutral and that its good or evil qualities depend on how we use it, we can begin to appreciate that our sexuality can never be separated from our total personality. Thus the way we handle our own sexuality is not primarily a matter of facts, but of values. Indeed, sex can be a revealing indication of character—is our partner a giver or taker, sensitive or gross, caring or selfish, religious or irreligious?

If sex were merely a matter of physiological function, it could be treated like a mechanical problem—get the best engine, use the best technique, and achieve the best result. If it doesn't work, trade it in. If this were the case, then sexual partners would be interchangeable, and society would function as a warehouse for suitable parts. This mechanical concept is analogous to prostitution, which is concerned solely with the biological function. It follows, therefore, that the more one's life is motivated by isolated instinct, the more one tends to polygamy and the less one seeks a single person with whom to share everlasting love.

The Jewish world view makes it clear that sex cannot be mechanically abstracted from the totality of human activity. Thus, the problems of premarital sex, adultery, and casual sex are really questions of values.

5. Human Sexuality Has Meaning Only in the Context of Relationship.

Perhaps our greatest fear is that our lives will be meaningless. If sex, the most powerful and sensitive area of our lives is to have meaning, it must be used as an expression of love or affection for another person. If we depersonalize the act by relating to another person only on a biological level, we dehumanize our partner and rob ourselves of our own integrity. To be successful, the act of sex requires the sensitive involvement of both partners. Noninvolvement results in a mechanical orgasm that is ultimately meaningless and demeaning.

If simply sleeping together would produce happiness, then the prostitute would be the happiest person in society. According to Helmut Thielicke, what is an ethical *deficiency* for the person who seeks the prostitute—the need for the physiological function rather than the person—is for the prostitute a *positive* element of moral self-defense. She saves her sense of self-worth by withholding her "self" during sex.

It is this distinction that determines whether the act is merely another sensation, or a true step toward relationship. It is becoming characteristic of our society that old as well as young people seek experiences rather than relationships, episodes rather than the continuous growth toward greater love. Ramban, in his commentary to the fundamental verse of love and marriage in Genesis (2:24), notes: "First one must cleave to his wife, then they will become one flesh. There can be no true oneness of the flesh without first experiencing a cleaving together of the heart."

The later Rabbis analyze the specific commandment of *onah,* the *mitzvah* that requires the husband to care for his wife's conjugal needs. They ask whether the *mitzvah* requires only the object of the act (*cheftzah*), or the subjective involvement of the *person* in the performance (*gavra*). After finely dissecting the *mitzvah* and reducing it to its several legal components, they firmly maintain that the sex act ordained by the Bible as the right of the wife must by accompanied by closeness (*kiruv*), and joy (*simchah*). Both of these qualities require *gavra,* the involvement of the total personality, not merely a physical performance.

The sexual union of two people on a primitive, impersonal, casual, biological level is a gross misfortune. If it is by mutual consent, it is simply mutual exploitation. It has met the test of liberty in that it is not coerced, but it has failed the test of meaning, sensitivity, decency, and responsibility to the future.

6. Sexuality Has Value Only in a Permanent Relationship.

In the Jewish view, it is insufficient to affirm that the act must have meaning: it must also have value. For Judaism, value in human sexuality comes only when the relationship involves two people who have committed themselves to one another and have made that commitment in a binding covenant recognized by God and by society. The act of sexual union, the deepest personal statement that any human being can make, must be reserved for the moment of total oneness.

The sexual act is the first and most significant event of married life, and its force and beauty should not be compromised by sharing coitus in the expectation that some day a decision will be made to marry or not to marry. The act of sex is not only a declaration of present love, it is a covenantal statement of permanent commitment. It is only in this frame of reference that sexual congress is legitimate, because only then is it a religious act, a *de'var mitzvah.*

Love by itself is not a sufficient motivation for sexual expression; love that is authentic will want to reserve the ultimate act for the ultimate commitment. The test of a good marriage is not compatibility in bed, but compatibility in life. Given love and respect, sexual technique can be learned. Engaging in sex to "test it out" de-sanctifies the act. It is not a rehearsal for marriage, it is a rehearsal for divorce.

The Torah speaks of the sexual act as carnal knowledge, as in (Genesis 4:1) "Adam *knew* his wife Eve" (Gen. 4:1). *Ye'diah* is the most sublime human knowledge because it *knows* the mystery, the soul of the beloved. In the sexual act, knowledge comes not only from physical intimacy and harmony and one-ness, but also from experiencing the very depths of passion and extremes of emotion emanating from the loved one. It is a knowledge *from the inside.* All such knowledge has two aspects: We learn about the other person, and we also experience ourselves at the extreme of our potential. Perhaps that is why taboos surround both love and death. A taboo is designed to protect us where we are most vulnerable and most mysterious—as we generate life in the privacy of our room, and as we take leave of life.

The increasing freedom from sexual restraint in this post-Freudian era is testimony to the demystification of sex and the irretrievable loss of precious "knowledge." We can conjecture further that perhaps the use of the term *yada* (revealing knowledge) for the sex act is contingent upon the prior existence of hiddenness, mystery. This *he-alem,* (concealment) exists both on the biological level—the internality of the female genitalia—and the societal—the idea of modesty, *tze'niut,* and its use of clothing to cover the body. As society sheds its clothing, there is progressively less to "know" by means of sexual exploita-tion. If the object of carnal knowledge is to know our *self* as well as our *mate,* then the demystification of sex adversely affects our self-knowledge as well.

7. Sexuality Needs to Be Sanctified.

If sexuality is that deepest personal statement, filled with ecstasy and in-formed by knowledge, it follows that even within marriage sex is not considered simply a legitimated biological function. The Torah motivated the Jew to sancti-fy sex within marriage, for sex as a part of daily routine threatens to become wearisome and a dread bore, and sometimes more divisive than supportive. The laws of "family purity," which require abstinence during and shortly following the menstrual period, place the sexual act in a special category.

On a basic level, sanctity means separating oneself consciously from immoral-ity and illicit thoughts. Maimonides incorporates the laws of sexual morality in a section of *Kedushah* (the Book of Holiness), and states that the deliberate separation from the illicit is an act of self-transcendence that constitutes sanctifi-cation. Ramban goes beyond Maimonides in his comment on the verse in Leviticus "Be you holy" (19:2): "Sanctify yourself even with that permitted you" is a call to those who strive to a higher level of spirituality and sensitivity to separate themselves from gross acts and uncouth behavior, even that which is technically permitted, so as not to become *naval bi-re'shut ha-Torah,* "a knave within the realm of the Torah".

Kiddushin—which signifies sanctity and betrothal—leads inevitably to *nissuin*—nuptials, elevation. Thus sanctification raises the physiological act of sex onto a higher, more spiritual level. This understanding of sanctity as leading to elevation is implied in the suggestion of the Talmud that it is preferable for a pious scholar to perform the conjugal act on the Sabbath. Rashi explains, "It is the night of joy, of rest, and of bodily pleasure." Such an affirmation is descriptive of how the Sabbath invested even bodily joys such as wearing special clothes and eating special foods with a special significance, elevating them to the realm of *sanctified physical pleasures.*

Sanctity also implies mystery. The Holy of Holies of the Temple, its inner sanctum, was visited only once every year, and then only by the High Priest. In the imagination of the people, it was a subject of awe and mystery.

Our society has lost the sense of the sacred, and there is little mystery attached to sex. Its physiology and technique have become commonplace to children, and teenagers are already tired and bored veterans.

Judaism teaches that the erotic act has wide significance, and that this *physical* act operates transcendentally. The creation of family and the consecration of marriage are events of which Jews sing at the wedding feast, *she-ha-simchah bi-me'ono,* "there is joy in His [God's] abode."

There are two terms for the sexual act. The better known is that which is used in the Bible and Talmud, *bi'ah,* which means "a coming" as in "he *came* unto her." The second is a Kabbalistic term, *chibbur,* which means "joining." It is used in *Iggeret ha-Kodesh,* which is subtitled *Sefer Chibbur Adam ve'Ishto,* "The Book of Joining of Man and His Wife." The word and concept are based on the mystical vision of the cherubim facing and embracing one another in spiritual mutuality. It also connotes the ideal of *ye'diah,* "knowledge from the inside." The Kabbalah considers knowledge and joining synonymous—true "knowledge" derives only from an interpenetrating and joining of the two bodies, the knower and the to-be-known.

Where *bi'ah* is simply descriptive of the physical position of the male, *chibbur* implies a coming together of equals. While rape or seduction must be referred to as *bi'ah, chibbur* implies a need for consent.

Chibbur also recalls the fundamental Jewish mystical drive of uniting and mending into oneness the fragmented world of "broken vessels." Genesis records the separation of the rib from ancient Adam, and *chibbur* refers to the rejoining of that rib to the side of Adam. Judaism strives for an understanding and an affirmation of the concept of *chibbur* in the context of *yichud,* the mutual love of husband and wife. The contemporary writer I. Lewald says: "In the consciousness of belonging together, in the sense of constancy, resides the sanctity, the beauty of matrimony, which helps us to endure pain more easily, to enjoy happiness doubly, and to give rise to the fullest and finest development of our nature."

Part Two

PROSPECTIVE PARTNERS:
THE PROHIBITED AND
THE PREFERRED

The conjugal act is the only *physical* act in Jewish law that may evoke dire biblical penalties or elevate the soul to a glorious partnership with God in the creation of a new human being. The deciding factor is the identity of the partners: Adultery is considered the most heinous misuse of sex, while sex within marriage is the most honorable. The prostitute is *kedeshah, set aside,* apart from the moral community; but the newly married couple enters *kedushah, set above,* elevated beyond their former status. Prohibited partners can produce the *mamzer,* the illegitimate offspring of incest or adultery; preferred partners can produce the light of future generations.

Jewish matrimonial law is divided into two categories: the prohibitions of forbidden acts and the preferred, positive laws of marriage. The prohibitions are clearly defined, proclaimed as absolutes, and read aloud to the congregation on the holiest day of the year, Yom Kippur. The positive laws, which deal with the obligations and conduct of marriage, are primarily inferred from the violations, loosely constructed in biblical sources but painstakingly formulated by the Rabbis in the Oral Law.

This apparent imbalance is instructive. The Torah wanted to provide the widest possible latitude for the boundaries of permissible marriage in order to encompass the full *legitimate* variety of human passions and combinations. But the restrictive boundaries had to be carefully observed to ensure that the integrity and purity of the Jewish family would be preserved. Thus, the law of endogamy—a Jew must marry a Jew—marks a line beyond which marriage is prohibited, encircling the furthest limit of the nation. The prohibition against incest draws a circle within which marriage is proscribed, enclosing the nearest limit of the family.

Both prohibited and preferred unions embody the idea of holiness: the very rejection of a prohibited partner is considered to be as sacred an act as embracing a permitted relationship. The incest prohibition can be found in Leviticus 18 (called the Holiness Code) and Maimonides, in codifying the law in the twelfth-century, included the laws of incest in *Kedushah.* In the same way, the positive laws of marriage are to be found in the Codes under the category called *kiddushin* (sanctity), as marriage itself is called *kiddushin.* This pattern is reflected in the betrothal blessing that is recited at the opening of the wedding ceremony.

The benediction contains two separate and distinct references to the two themes of holiness: "Who has sanctified us and commanded us regarding incestuous unions . . ." and "Who sanctifies His people Israel through the wedding canopy and the sanctification ceremony, *kiddushin.*"

The unions of prohibited partners fall under five categories, according to the severity of the prohibition: (1) death decreed by "heaven" or excision from the Jewish people, *karet;* (2) capital punishment administered by the courts, *mitat beit din;* (3) negative command, *issur lav;* (4) positive command, *issur asei;* and (5) Rabbinic enactment, *divrei soferim.*

The laws do not refer to the actual present-day meting out of punishment and, in any case, the actual implementation of capital punishment in ancient times was rare. However, in Temple days these were the kinds of cases for which—if all technical halakhic requirements were completely satisfied—the Sanhedrin could either issue a verdict of death at the hands of the court or declare the crime deserving of punishment by God only.

The categories of prohibition are also divided by the legal nature of the prohibition: some are *prohibited and void,* others are *prohibited but valid. Prohibited and void* means that if the partners are biblically prohibited to each other—even if the marriage ceremony is otherwise performed in full compliance with the law—the marriage union is null and void. Under this heading fall the laws called *gilui arayot* (uncovering of the nakedness), which are punishable both by court-ordered death or by heavenly-decreed excision. This category lists twenty-two prohibited partners, including adultery, homosexuality, buggery, and incestuous relations with any one of eighteen relatives.

Prohibited but valid means that if partners who are prohibited to each other marry despite the law, the marriage is legally valid and can only be dissolved by divorce. The courts may attempt to persuade the couple to be divorced but they cannot today compel them to do so. The category of prohibited but valid includes those biblical laws which are imposed and punishable as plain prohibitions (*issurei lav*) for which there is no death sentence and those which are rabbinically enacted.

Plain prohibitions include the union of a *mamzer* and a legitimate Jew; a Jewish woman with a castrated man, or one with certain genital injuries; a divorcee who married and then divorced (or was widowed from) a second husband and wishes to remarry her first husband; a woman whose husband died childless and was not formally separated from the obligatory Levirate marriage (a marriage in this instance would be void); the marriage of a Jew and a gentile; and the specific partners prohibited the *kohen*—the divorcée (*ge'rushah*), *zonah,* or *chalalah* (profaned woman). Rabbinic enactments include prohibition of secondary incest, and bigamy committed by a man. (A woman who is married to two men at one time is considered by the Bible to be an adulteress.)

The status of prohibited but valid is a difficult concept to comprehend. How can something be not allowed and allowed at the same time? The concept may be clarified by explaining the difference between the secular and the Jewish concept of marriage. The secular law considers marriage a contract validated and sanctioned by the state. For example, according to California law first cousins may not marry. If they marry in defiance of that law, their marriage is simply not recognized by the State. Judaism, on the other hand, holds the marriage to be a covenant between two *persons*. It has either been done or has not been done, as they agree; the courts cannot undo the fact of a private agreement. Therefore, a marriage which violates a plain, negative commandment is valid, even though the couple is committing a sin and clearly violating a prohibition. The court can compel a divorce, but the contract is a contract.

The category of prohibited and void is much easier to understand. In this case, Jewish law considers the marital bond as non-existent. A union that the Torah considers worthy of capital punishment is no union, because the participants are "as good as dead." Hence, the marriage is not a marriage.

CHAPTER 4

Prohibited and Void

INCEST

Throughout history, virtually every society has had laws prohibiting incest. These laws are almost always under the severest moral sanction, and their violation evokes terrible penalties, usually death. Most prohibitions against incest are axiomatic, and offer no rational explanation (although they are often defended on eugenic grounds), and they vary somewhat from group to group. For example, while modern society forbids marriage within the immediate family, in ancient Egypt the Pharaohs were encouraged to marry their sisters or half-sisters. According to Diodorus, sibling marriage was not only permitted but considered an obligation for Egyptians.

The Bible lists the incest laws, some of which took effect only after the Sinaitic revelation, when some marriages which had been permitted earlier became prohibited (e.g., Jacob married two sisters; Amram and Yocheved, Moses' parents, were nephew and aunt). While we do find violations of the incest laws down to the days of Ezekiel in the sixth century B.C.E., the rules have generally been very strictly observed.

Biblical law lists primary prohibitions, which were expanded by the Rabbis of the Talmud. These rabbinic extensions are called *she'niyot*, secondary incest. They were not intended merely to lengthen the list of incestuous possibilities, but to protect the biblical prohibitions from ever being violated. This is in consonance with the important talmudic principle of protection, "Make a fence around the law." The relationships forbidden by secondary incest laws are those that may approximate or sound like incest. Allowing such marriages might lead people to believe that the biblical laws have been relaxed, and even primary incest laws might ultimately come to be violated. The incest table at the end of this section is based on blood relationships such as mother, daughter, and sister, and widens to include relations of legal marriage such as daughter-in-law and step-mother. It continues to spread out in descending lines (grandchildren), ascending lines (grandparents), and lateral lines (sister-in-law).

The practical differences between the biblical primary incest and rabbinic secondary incest are important. A marriage contract that would also be a relationship of primary incest is prohibited and *void*, a marriage in violation of secondary incest is prohibited but *valid*. The offspring of primary incest is illegitimate, a *mamzer*, the offspring of secondary incest is *kasher*, legitimate.

Violators of primary incest suffer *karet*, death "at the hands of heaven," which is a combination of Divine vengeance and human punishment. It is distinguished from the death penalty in that the latter is "executed by man," while the former is "executed by heaven." *Karet* is believed to bring the wrong doer childlessness or sudden (or at least premature) death. The human court in Temple times, imposed only the penalty of flogging if the violation was knowingly perpetrated, or required a sacrificial offering for the sin if done unwittingly. Incest violations that incur capital punishment by human courts include such relations as a man with his mother, step-mother, mother-in-law, daughter, daughter-in-law, or granddaughter.

Although violation of secondary incest was objectionable the offender was only flogged, as a punishment for arrogant defiance of basic rabbinic edict. Because the censure for secondary incest was relatively light the violations were more frequent, and the Rabbis took other steps to ensure observance of their injunctions. Thus, a woman could not collect the payment promised in her *ketubah* (marriage contract) if she were married to a man forbidden her by the Sages, and her husband had to issue a divorce or suffer flogging at the hands of the court.

Jewish law did not permit even kissing or hugging any relative listed on the incest table, if it was done out of carnal desire or for the thrill of it. It is written, "None of you shall approach to any that is *near* of kin to him, to uncover the 'nakedness' " (Leviticus 18:6). Not only is the "uncovering" (a euphemism for the sexual act) prohibited, but even the "coming near." Maimonides would penalize even this by flogging; Ramban would withhold flogging for technical legal reasons, but considers the act utterly reprehensible. Innocent gestures, of course, are not considered *taavah* (sensual desire).

There are indications that certain incestuous relationships are more frequent today than in previous eras. While this may be a consequence of our uninhibited society, in our world where "everything goes" even the historically sacrosanct incest prohibitions may go. In an age when it is fashionable to say, "It's your body, do what you want with it," what is to prevent the violation of traditionally

INCEST TABLE

Biblical Prohibitions	Rabbinic Extensions
Mother	Grandmother Grandmother's mother, ad infinitum Grandfather's mother and (according to Maharshal) even grandfather's mother's mother
Stepmother	Father's stepmother, ad infinitum Mother's stepmother Maternal grandmother's stepmother Paternal grandmother's stepmother
Sister,* father's sister Mother's sister	Paternal grandfather's sister Maternal grandmother's sister
Brother's wife and father's paternal brother's wife	Father's maternal brother's wife Mother's paternal or maternal brother's wife Paternal grandfather's paternal brother's wife Maternal grandmother's paternal brother's wife (according to Rabbi Asher)
Daughter and granddaughter	Great granddaughter, ad infinitum
Son's wife	Grandson's wife Great grandson's wife, ad infinitum, (i.e., only if it be the wife of son's son's son, etc.)
Wife's mother and grandmother	Wife's great grandmother, ad infinitum
Wife's daughter and granddaughter	Wife's great granddaughter, ad infinitum
Wife's sister	No secondary prohibitions
Half-Sister on father's side or mother's side	No secondary prohibitions
Son's daughter	No secondary prohibitions
Daughter's daughter	No secondary prohibitions
Wife's son's daughter	No secondary prohibitions
Wife's daughter's daughter	No secondary prohibitions

*Unrelated boy and girl, though raised together in one family as brother and sister, *may* marry.

sanctified laws? It is necessary, in these times, to develop a greater respect for tradition and moral law. Perhaps the growing excesses will cause us to return to our roots, if only because we are disgusted by what goes on in the name of freedom and individualism. Coming to religious observance out of disgust with the profane may be the true embodiment of the rabbinic idea that the very rejection of an incestuous union is an act of *kedushah,* sanctity.

ADULTERY

Adultery is a remarkable pastime. It is the stuff of novels, the subject of political scandal, and the dream of couples who feel trapped by duty and boredom. Adultery is the topic of thousands of jokes, and is by no means considered to be a serious moral threat.

Conversely, fidelity in marriage is becoming an anachronism. In the public imagination, those who practice it are conventional bores or unadventurous dullards who have no opportunity to relish what they condemn. Their attitude is thought to be the result of poor imagination, excessive timidity, or reactionary, bourgeois moralism. When morality, in this setting, speaks of fidelity and honor and sexual purity, it comes up hard against social reality. But is this a reason to dispense with forty centuries of fidelity?

Superficially, fidelity does seem old-fashioned. It denies that the only excitement in love is that of a stranger, and that happiness is the only worthwhile goal. It denies that "I" am the most important person in the world, and that "experiencing" is the chief value in life. It denies that the great lover is the multiple lover, and that the satisfactions of a moment are more valuable than the lasting relationship of a lifetime. But if fidelity is dismissed as an irrelevant ideal, then marriage, which demands fidelity in order to survive, must also be thrown away.

At first glance, the biblical statement on adultery seems purposely obscure: "And the man that commits adultery with *another man's wife,* even he who is committing adultery with *his neighbor's wife,* both the adulterer and the adulteress must surely be put to death" (Leviticus 20:10). The phrases "neighbor's wife" and "another man's wife" seem needlessly repetitive. However, according to the author of *Ye'shuot Yaakov* the verse should be read as, "Any man who commits adultery with a married woman, whose husband is also committing adultery. . . ." In this way the author learns the nature of the prohibition, and comments insightfully, "The prohibition of adultery with a married woman is one of the *mitzvot sikhliyot* [a rationally understood duty]. But when the Torah requires death even though the woman's husband is himself violating that very prohibition, that is *chok,* [a divine law that is beyond reason]." In our society, when "everybody" appears to be violating the traditional sexual code, we are duty-bound by *chok,* even though it seems absurd—to uphold the ideal of fidelity.

The romantic notion of love has convinced the world that love happens to people whether they participate or not. Judaism teaches that if you are not in control of yourself you are not a human being.

The Seventh Commandment, prohibiting adultery (Exodus 20:13 and Deuteronomy 5:17), is buttressed by the Tenth Commandment, prohibiting the coveting of a neighbor's wife or his possessions (Exod. 20:14 and Deut. 5:18). This last commandment is considered in some ways the most important of the ten, because if you eliminate desire you do not violate the law. The person who does not covet his neighbor's possessions will not swear falsely against him, or rob or murder or commit adultery. The first rendition of this commandment in Exodus (20:14) reads *lo tachmod,* "Thou shall not *covet.*" The second, in Deuteronomy (5:18), adds *lo tit-aveh,* "Thou shalt not *desire.*" Most of those who enumerate the Torah's commandments consider "covet" and "desire" as two distinct prohibitions. Coveting is a hunger that ends in an act of violation, while desiring is a passive fantasy. The Torah warns that coveting precedes action; whether it is scheming or conscious wishing, it is not permitted. This implies that we *can* control our desires, because if we could not it would be nonsense to make such control an eternal obligation.

The author of *Sefer ha-Chinukh* says: "Do not be astonished and say, 'How can a man deny desiring the whole treasure trove of delights that his friend owns, while he has naught? And how can the Torah prohibit that which man cannot possibly endure?' This is not so. Who would say this except fools who desire in their own interiors to transgress? Because, in fact, man is able to deny himself his desires and his fantasies concerning anything he wants and likes. And his heart is in his hand to do what he wishes."

Nineteenth-century German scholar Rabbi Samson Raphael Hirsch notes that human rulers can judge only actions, but the King of Kings knows our innermost thoughts and can demand that we think properly as well as act properly. But how in the world can we accomplish this? How can we control seemingly autonomous feelings? Ibn Ezra answers that we have to train ourselves to understand that certain objects of desire are impossible to achieve— that which we can never hope to attain cannot be the object of our dreams. We must rule them out of the framework of our reality because of our fear of God. An example given by later commentators is of the beautiful queen who arrives in her gold carriage. The poor peasant who sees the queen has no romantic fantasies about her because it is beyond imagining that such wishes could be fulfilled. Hence we are able to insist to ourselves that sex outside of marriage is impossible, and then erotic fantasy will have less tyrannical control of our imagination. We can do it—the Torah says so—despite the wisdom that derives from our own experience and from the stentorian proclamations of our foremost psychologists.

"A woman cannot be the wife of two men," says the Talmud, deducing from the Bible's "Thou shalt not commit adultery." Thus a man may not marry a woman who is married to another man. That is the prime violation of fidelity, and as such it is prohibited and void. As an act of adultery, it was biblically punishable by death. *Kiddushin,* the sanctity of marriage, implies a wife's *exclusive* dedication to her husband; obviously, exclusivity cannot be applied to two simultaneous marriages. (The situation is not always this clear: For example, if the first husband is missing and assumed dead, and the wife remarries only to have her first husband reappear, the Rabbis would be called upon to make a determination that would have to consider the charge of adultery. Great compassion and much sensitivity were engendered in deciding such cases, and it is a complicated question of *Halakhah* better left to acknowledged rabbinical authority.)

Adulterous marriages were not uncommon, and the Torah decreed capital punishment for violation of the law for both men and women. In cases that are provable, since there is no capital punishment today, the Torah requires a divorce from the husband, and many authorities hold that the Sages require a divorce also from the adulterous paramour. The Rabbis decreed this because, although the second marriage is void, people ignorant of the first marriage might assume that the second marriage is authentic and that a Jewish divorce is no longer a necessity for terminating marriage.

Adultery is the only sexual offense recorded in the Ten Commanements, and is recorded again in the Holiness Code of Leviticus 20. It is called "The Great Sin" in the Bible (Genesis 20:9) and *ha-averah,* (*The* Sin) in the Talmud. The marriage bond is divinely ordained, and adultery divinely proscribed. As a metaphor for idolatry, it signifies that as woman owes exclusive loyalty to one man, so Israel owes undying loyalty to the one God. It is considered one of the three sins (along with idolatry and murder) that people should avoid even at the pain of death.

The Seventh Commandment is placed between "Thou shalt not murder" and "Thou shalt not steal," among the second set of five commandements that deal with interpersonal relations. This would appear to suggest that the crime of adultery is a crime exclusively against the husband. Indeed, there are those who assume that adultery is a remnant of the *property* concept of marriage and say that its motive force is violation of a man's *possession*—his wife. In Babylonian, Assyrian, and Hittite annals, the husband therefore had the right either to kill the adulterer or to forgive him. The wife was, after all, the husband's property. The husband, as the aggrieved party, could naturally be expected to seek revenge for the infamy brought upon his household. There was surely an element of that sentiment in Jewish history for two thousand years, even until the first century, and it is not unknown today.

In contrast, however, the Torah and the whole of Jewish law and tradition consider adultery to be a heinous affront to *God*. In the Bible, adultery is a moral crime, not primarily an injury to the husband. Whether he prosecutes or not is immaterial, and it is irrelevant to the court whether the husband is or is not willing to forgive his wife, whether or not he wishes to continue to live with her, or whether or not her actions were justified. Indeed, the Bible provides no way out for the adulterer—it made no difference if the woman freely consented, if she solicited, whether or not he knew that she was married, or even if the husband pardoned him. The woman did have one defense—she was guiltless if she was coerced. Thus a betrothed woman who committed the offense in the city generally did not claim violence, for in the small and close quarters of ancient urban areas, she could have cried out and probably would have been saved. In a rural area, however, her claim was considered valid (Deuteronomy 22:25–27). Her husband's willingness to have her back made not one whit of difference to the law.

This is ingeniously inferred from the unusual wording of the verse (Leviticus 20:10): "and the man that commits adultery with *eishet ish* [another man's wife], even he who commits adultery with *eishet rei-ehu* [his neighbor's wife], both the adulterer and the adulteress shall be put to death." The Rabbis were initially puzzled by the apparently unnecessary repetition of "another man's wife" and "a neighbor's wife," but they drew a number of conclusions. Rabbi Burukh ha-Levi Epstein elaborates on the commentary of *Ye'shuot Yaakov*. "A man who commits adultery with the wife of another man who *himself* commits adultery with *his* neighbor's wife." This is indeed the literal translation of the Hebrew words. It refers to people who believe that wives are the property of their husbands and that men may do as they please. The verse is directed to those people "who eat and drink together and exchange wives." It is to them that the Torah directs its pronouncement. No matter her agreement, no matter what her husband does, it is adultery and deserves the most severe punishment as a crime against God and a violation of His divine law as well as a sin against the members of the family.

Imrei Shefer comments that though a woman's husband is not pure, this does not give her the right to cohabit with another, and no stranger may use this as an excuse to have carnal relations with her. The Torah declares that both the adulterer and the adulteress are punished.

Finally, Rabbi Samson Raphael Hirsch states that one might think that if the husband does not mind, it is permissible for the wife to commit adultery. That is why the Torah qualifies "another man"—even though he be *r'ea*, "your friend, your neighbor," and it is with his consent that you do it, your sin is not diminished for you have offended God.

Marriage, therefore, transcends the civil contract that society uses to assure mutual compliance with its minimal standards. It is a divine institution, invested with holiness. The two partners have a third partner, God, and the moral code of the family must sanctify this third partner. Immorality by mutual consent is still a breach of *his* trust.

The divine ordinance reflects not only a concern for people fouling their own nest, but for those who destroy another's family. That is why even if the male is single, his actions are punishable. The Talmud, in teaching concern for other families, interprets *lo tin-af,* "Do not *commit* adultery," as *lo tanif,* "Do not *cause* adultery." Simeon, ben Tarphon, says "This is a warning to procurers." The Bible warns not only against the sin itself, but against trafficking in the sin. It is God's decree that every family is sacrosanct and dare not be endangered, and any relationship to adultery is abhorrent. Jewish courts today have no power to levy punishment for adultery, and only in the rarest historical circumstances have they ever declared for capital punishment. While it is true that the Bible explicitly provides for the death penalty and the Talmud delves into its manner of execution and associated technicalities, before that penalty could be administered it had to satisfy a number of stringent requirements: The existing marriage had to be valid according to *Halakhah;* the crime had to be committed with full and free volition, not by physical compulsion or threat of death; the couple had to have been warned of the punishment for the crime in very specific terms; and the violation had to have occurred before two valid witnesses. The probability of exacting the death penalty under such circumstances is truly remote.

The Rabbis were generally averse to capital punishment for any crime unless it was subject to the strict laws of evidence. Indeed, for two thousand years Jewish courts have not exercised the power of capital punishment even when Jews enjoyed limited self-rule. Even theoretically, the Rabbis made it difficult to declare the crime to be adultery of a nature requiring capital punishment. The Sages substituted corporal punishment in certain cases, in order to prevent doing public violence to the high standards of family morality and to protect the community's moral fiber. Another type of punishment was given the adulteress who was considered "defiled": If the crime could be proved according to the above rabbinic standards, she could be prevented both from continuing to live with her husband and from marrying her paramour after the divorce.

The appeal to observe the law, to live with personal dignity, and to protect marriage might have fallen on deaf ears when it had to compete with passion and romantic attraction—biology is often more persuasive than morality. For this reason, it was necessary to use the most powerful force available to the law—the effect adultery would have on children. Hence the law established that an offspring of an adulterous union is a *mamzer.*

A *mamzer* is the issue of a couple whose sexual relationship is forbidden according to the Torah and punishable by *karet*. Since such a couple is legally "as good as dead," their relationship is held not to exist, and their child is not a legitimate Jew. Thus the child of an incestuous union is a *mamzer*, but the child of an interfaith marriage (whether the Jewish mother was married or single) is not a *mamzer* because no death penalty is involved. In contrast to other systems of law, a child born out of lawful wedlock is not a *mamzer*, or illegitimate in any way.

The rights of a *mamzer* to marriage are severely limited: "A *mamzer* may not enter the congregation of the Lord" (Deuteronomy 23:3). A marriage with another Jew is not permitted for him or his offspring, though there is no question that he may marry another *mamzer* or a proselyte. Restrictions on the *mamzer* have no bearing on personal status, rights or privileges, and apply only to marriage. Thus the *mamzer* can hold public office or even become king of a Jewish state. The rabbis of every age went to unbelievable extremes to avoid labeling any offspring *mamzer*, but the title alone had sufficient force to send shudders through anyone contemplating an adulterous dalliance.

According to Ramban, the primary goal of the adultery prohibition was the protection of the child. He says that adultery "robs the child of an acknowledged and recognized father," and that "It robs parenthood of all glory, as there can be no fulfillment of honoring parents." It fills a child born of his parents' personal indulgence with lifelong shame.

ADULTERY AND RELIGIOUS DIVORCE

The Torah's zealous guardianship of the family caused the Rabbis to build a protective fortress of marriage laws. Marriage is legally, morally, and socially binding; private, sacrosanct, and untouchable from the outside. That spirit accounts for the religious divorce laws. As the marriage is a personal agreement sanctified by Jewish law, the dissolution of marriage is a personal agreement sanctioned by the law of God and Torah. The State has no authority in religious law, and it is religion that fosters and protects the institution of marriage. Of course Jewish law takes account the state law, but it does so as an *additional* requirement.

The Torah demands absolutely and unequivocally that marriage be terminated by formal religious divorce (*get*). If marriage were open-ended, without a formal termination, a second marriage could not claim any integrity. If a relationship to the first spouse existed in a marriage that was begun but not terminated, the succeeding marriage could not have sanctity. The integrity of the family must be preserved even through successive marriages. Perhaps this is the reason that the law of divorce is most prominent in the section of the Bible dealing with remarriage.

The Jewish divorce, *get,* is a no-fault divorce, and has been so for two millenia. No questions are asked other than to assure proper identification of the principals and unquestioned voluntary participation. Settlements are not usually made by the Jewish court (although ideally the alimony should be adjudicated by the Jewish court rather than by the state). A Jewish divorce requires fifteen minutes for response to the questions, and the time it takes for a scribe to calligraph the divorce document of twelve lines written specifically for the couple. This document simply declares that the marriage is terminated "according to the laws of Moses and Israel" (the identical wording used in the marriage ceremony), and the permission is given "to remarry any man."

Without this formally executed divorce, Jewish law holds that the marriage is still in effect, regardless of any oral agreement of the couple to the contrary, the edict of the state, the number of successive marriages, or that the other partner subsequently married a non-Jew. *Only a Jewish divorce ends a Jewish marriage. Only a Jewish divorce permits remarriage.* This is a *sine qua non* of all rabbis (except Reform); they will *not* marry anyone whose previous marriage was not terminated by a Jewish divorce.

The lack of divorce then, means that the previous marriage is still in force and the "remarried" partner is living in an adulterous union. Because most people are not aware of this, they may unwittingly violate the law, an act that would otherwise be unthinkable. If this has happened, the remedy is to speak at once with a rabbinic authority and then communicate with the first husband or wife and arrange at once for the Jewish divorce, preferably *before* the civil decree is issued. This may be an unpleasant chore, but it is absolutely and unequivocally required.

With this arsenal of moral and legal weapons, Jewish tradition passionately and effectively defended the institution of the family. Anyone thinking of a forbidden flirtation had to contend with being prohibited to paramour as well as to husband, and to bearing a child who will carry the disgrace through all of life. The sense of communal outrage and the sense of personal shame, coupled with these severe legal restrictions, enabled Jews to reach the heights of moral purity even during eras of externally-imposed social degradation.

The Jewish people will survive only if the Jewish family survives. The family will survive only if that old, powerful fortress of marriage is preserved in the form in which it has existed since Sinai—the sanctified, immovable, inviolate rock of civilization.

INTERFAITH MARRIAGE

Interfaith marriage—the union of a Jew and an unconverted non-Jew—serves as a warning that there is disease in the Jewish body politic. Like fever, which warns of an underlying problem, the symptom itself may kill. In order for the patient to survive, we must be able to manage the symptom as well as treat the infection.

We will not diagnose here. It will be more instructive to cite relevant statistics, which have become historical record. A survey taken in Europe in 1929 yielded these statistics: Berlin, 23.5 intermarriages out of every one hundred Jewish marriages; Hamburg, 33.9; Budapest, 16.5; Amsterdam, 14.8; Vienna, 14; Copenhagen, 31.8 (in older families over 50 percent); and Trieste, 56.1. These figures are significant for a number of reasons. First, five years later Hitler retrieved the defectors and returned them to their families so that they could die in the gas chambers as Jews. This is a stark illustration of the ultimate failure of assimilation as the purpose of interfaith marriage. Second, if those were the figures for socially conservative communities, what must they be for a fluid, untraditional society like Jewish America? Third, world Jewry survived those statistics and the Holocaust that followed, and it will survive this year's statistics. Individual communities, however, may eventually self-destruct.

The latest figures released by the American Jewish Committee in January 1979, indicate that the average rate of interfaith marriage rose from 10 percent in 1960 to 31 percent in 1978, and is even higher in smaller cities. What centuries of pogroms could not do to us, we have done for ourselves in years of plenty. If that is not disease, what is?

THE HISTORY OF AN IDEA

There have been many reasons given throughout Jewish history for the profoundly negative attitude towards interfaith marriage. This attitude appeared at various times to be based on political or military considerations, or motivated by ethnic pride or the danger of social disintegration. But whatever the given reasons, the primary motive was to keep the religion of the Jew intact.

The threat of interfaith marriage is graphically illustrated by the following story: When the Jews were still wandering in the desert, they had an enormous population, were militarily well prepared, and were virtually unconquerable. But the pagan prophet Balaam, recognizing the destructive influence of mixed relationships, simply loosed idol-worshiping Moabite women upon them, recounts the Midrash. Immorality, idolatry, and assimilation quickly weakened the Jews and wrecked their spirit, their cohesiveness, and their will.

The historical tradition of marrying within the religion at any cost is evident from Abraham's choice of a wife for Isaac (Genesis 24:3); Rebekah's sending Jacob back to her family to marry (Gen. 27:46); Esau's marriage to Hittite women, which brought grief to his parents (Gen. 26:34–5); and Jacob's sons who were horrified that their sister Dinah might be married to one not circumcised (Gen. 34:14). When Samson fell in love with a Philistine woman, his parents sought to dissuade him: "Is there no wife among the daughters of thy brothers or among all my people that thou goest to take a wife from the uncircumcised Philistines?" (Judges 14:3). Thirty-nine kings of Judah and Israel reigned for three hundred and ninety-three years and only two married out of the faith. Exogamous marriages were contracted by Judah, Simeon, Joseph, and Moses, but these came before the legal restriction was pronounced at Sinai. (It is traditionally assumed that all their wives were converted.)

Jewish literature in different centuries cites interfaith marriage as the cause of a number of communal failures and historic tragedies. The blasphemy record-ed in Leviticus 24:10 is specifically ascribed in the Torah to a child of a mixed marriage (an Egyptian man and his Jewish wife), and the inordinate difficulties of the Jews during the early period of the Judges is blamed on those who "resided in the midst of" the local nations (Judges 3:4-5). King Solomon's decline is ascribed to marriage to foreign wives "who sacrificed unto *their* gods" and caused him to "do evil in the eyes of God" (I Kings 11:1-6). The murderers of Joash (II Chronicles 24:26) are listed as children of mixed marriages of Jewish fathers with Shimat the Ammonite woman, and Shimrit the Moabite woman.

The prophet Malachi attacks interfaith marriage: "Judah has dealt treacher-ously and an abomination is committed in Israel and Jerusalem. For Judah has profaned the holiness of the Lord. For he has loved and married the daughter of a strange god. May the Lord cut off the man that does this, that calls and answers from the tents of Jacob, and offers an offering unto the Lord of Hosts" (2:11-12).

The cornerstone of the interfaith-marriage law is Deuteronomy 7:3, which says: "And thou shalt not make marriages with them; thy daughter thou shalt not give unto his son, nor his daughter shalt thou not take for thy son. For he will turn away thy son from following after me, and they will serve other gods . . ." This refers to the seven idolatrous nations that occupied the Promised Land, but the Talmud inferred that the prohibition applies to all, because the Torah's reason refers "to all who would turn their children away" (Deut. 7:4). Exodus (17:8-16) speaks of the Amalekites, the arch-enemies of the Jews, who were to be blotted out of existence by God. Naturally, marriage to them was prohibited. Ammon and Moab, who refused the Jews bread and water and hired Balaam to curse them, were prevented from marrying "into the assembly of the Lord even unto the tenth generation . . ." (Deut. 23:5). Milder, but still vigor-ously prohibited, was marriage to the Egyptian, "because thou wast a stranger in his land" (Deut. 23:8); to the Edomite, "because he is thy brother" (Deut. 23:8); to the Midianites (Numbers 31:15-17); to the Sidonites and Hittites (I Kings 11:1-2) because of their worship of Ashtoreth; and to the Ashdodites (Nehemiah 13:23) because of their cult worship.

With Ezra comes the most dramatic historic enactment of the interfaith-marriage prohibitions. When the Jews returned from the Diaspora, he mandated that they set aside their heathen wives (Ezra 10:11). Zerubbabel set about the task of separating from the Israelites their foreign wives, children of mixed marriages, and descendants of Solomon's foreign slaves. He established family records and set up a special court to investigate problem cases. The idea of purity captured the imagination of the Jew. The Jewish community was "holy seed," and the heathens belonged to "the uncleanness of the nations." Mixed marriage was thus considered "defilement." The ethnic aspect of Judaism, which encases the religion, was never to be compromised.

The absolute rejection of interfaith marriage has been charged with emotional force from that day to this. The charisma of Ezra's personality and the sheer moral power of his idealism gave the problem of interfaith marriage an awesome importance that continues into the twentieth century. Ezra taught that it is not only a terrible problem; for Jews it is nothing less than a choice between existence and nonexistence.

The next three centuries saw a very rich spiritual development. But then "progressive" Hellenists "joined themselves to the gentiles and sold themselves to do evil" (I Maccabees 1:5). The future of Judaism hung by gossamer threads. The Hasmoneans responded with great force, not only in terms of military leadership and "war on the internal enemy," but with new enactments designed to prevent socialization with the heathen, and which succeeded in saving the Jewish community by erecting a wall around it. This was fortress psychology in a war for survival.

The teachers of the Talmud who became leaders of the Jews were more successful than the prophets and the kings in destroying every vestige of idolatry: their instrument was the power of the law. They considered paganism to be repugnant, and the associated immorality, superstitions, and orgies disgusting and intolerable. Thus the carriers of paganism would not be allowed to "sell their wares" within the Jewish community. The Talmud records ordinances designed to accomplish this, which succeeded where prophetic preachments and bloodshed did not. Any service that might be helpful to the spread of paganism was absolutely prohibited: No apartment could be rented to a heathen because he might use it for a house in which to worship his idol; no land in Israel could be sold to him, for he is "defilement"; no Jew was permitted to deal in merchandise the pagan could use for his idolatrous feast; and since a heathen wedding feast was considered a religious ritual, no Jew was permitted to attend a heathen service.

The lines had been drawn, the enemy had been met, and the war had been won. Paganism was dead in the Jewish community. Two centuries later the Rabbis could relax somewhat on the more stringent details of the social ordinances, but no one ever compromised on the unqualified, unyielding prohibition of interfaith marriage. It kept the Jews intact, and enabled Judaism to live to this day.

One thousand years later Maimonides, who lived in Spain, ruled that Mohammedans were not heathens and Rashi and the Tosafists, who lived in France, ruled that Christians were not idolators. But the law against interfaith marriage preserved the integrity of the tiny Jewish people in the chaos of international events and the pressure of history to liquidate them, and no attempt was ever made by any teachers of the Law to relax the prohibitions for Christians or Mohammedans.

For the next six hundred years, the prohibition of Deuteronomy and Ezra remained unchallenged. In 1806, Napoleon presented this question to the Great Sanhedrin, the assembly of Jewish nobles: "May a Jewess marry a Christian, or a Jew a Christian woman? Or has Jewish law ordered that Jews should marry only among themselves?" The newly-liberated rabbis and lay leaders, while responding with a tact that is a classic illustration of Diaspora language and philosophy, clearly expressed its opposition and ruled that no rabbi should officiate at an interfaith marriage.

Early Reform leaders at the 1844 Braunschweig Conference in Germany took a different course. The protective wall so laboriously built in the Hasmonean and talmudic age was to them a prison wall. Since free men and liberals (as they considered themselves) are supposed to demolish walls, they permitted mixed marriage "with all monotheists," provided the children were brought up as Jews. How was such a radical notion able to gain favor? One reason was that there was no longer a national motive; the Jews were citizens of the same country as Christians. As the law was "only" religious, not civil, marriage was permitted with all monotheists. Some nineteenth-century Reform leaders, notably Abraham Geiger, David Einhorn, and Isaac M. Wise, rejected this stance, but even their response was astonishing. Louis Epstein characterized it in this way: "The position of modern Judaism, in general, regarding the question of intermarriage, is similar to that taken by Protestantism or Roman Catholicism, both of which discountenance mixed marriages, on purely religious grounds."

Eastern European Jews, however, responded to mixed marriage traditionally, expressing rage at the defectors and horror at the mere thought of relaxing the standards. They intensified their opposition, considered interfaith marriage apostasy, and built the wall of separation even higher to protect the people against an unpredictable, unrooted society. Congregations expelled those who intermarried and families sat *shiva* for their loss, even as they mourned the deceased.

Despite changed conditions, the absence of idolatry, and the parity between members of different faiths (especially in the United States), the Jewish people is in danger as never before of disappearing beneath a calm sea of pleasure and cooperation. Hence the commitment to survive *as a distinct people* must remain paramount. The community's claim to survival transcends the individual desire to make personal choices.

THE STRATEGY OF THE LAW

Interfaith marriage is no marriage; it is prohibited and it is also void. Although this principle may appear to be obvious, its explanation is somewhat complex and therefore constitutes a major statement by the Rabbis. One might think that interfaith marriage, like all other marriage that violates ordinary negative commandments (*issurei lav*), should be valid although prohibited. The reason it is not valid lies in the difference between Jewish and secular concepts of marriage, explained earlier. Secular law considers marriage a contract validated and sanctioned by the state, which can declare the marriage valid or void. If a proposed marriage is in violation of the law the state says it is prohibited, and if the couple is married in spite of the law, the marriage is considered void. Judaism, however, holds the marriage to be a covenant *between persons of the same religion.* It has either been done or not been done as they agree, and the state cannot invalidate a private agreement. Thus a marriage that violates an ordinary negative commandment is valid, although the couple is committing a religious sin and clearly violating a prohibition. The court can compel a divorce, but the contract remains a contract.

Interfaith marriage is void not because it is prohibited, but *because one party to the contract is incapable of contracting a marriage with a Jew within Jewish law.* The contract never was a contract because both parties were not Jews. The Sages derive this law from the verses in Deuteronomy (7:3–4) that state there is no such thing as an institution of interfaith marriage and the logic is impeccable.

The Child of an Interfaith Marriage

If the marriage is not valid, what is the status of the child? Obviously, it is a product of its mother. Although a child is also a natural product of its father, specific paternity is not necessarily an undisputed fact, and at times it must be legally determined. Thus, a mother is a mother regardless of marriage or legal sanction, but a father needs a legal document to establish his fatherhood—whether it is a marriage document or, if the parents are single, the testimony of one of the parents.

In interfaith marriage, therefore, the child is always classified according to the mother's origins. If the mother is gentile, the child is gentile; in order ever to be considered Jewish, conversion is required. This conversion is the same as for any other gentile: Jewish paternity does not lend any special merit, because legally there is no father. Nor is there special merit attached to a Jewish upbringing or working for the good of the Jewish community, although both are commendable.

The Rights of the Intermarried

The following questions of Jewish law concerning the rights of Jews who have married out of the faith have been answered by contemporary scholars and incorporated in the growing responsa literature on this subject. The term "intermarried" as used here technically refers to a Jewish person married to a gentile not converted by traditional halakhic procedures. Before following any course of action, a competent authority thoroughly versed in *Halakhah* should be consulted on this question.

Burial Rights.   The rights of burial are fundamental rights extended by the Jewish community to its members. The law has the power to withhold such rights when its authority has been flouted; this is based on the practice that the righteous are not to be buried alongside the wicked. Although this option is rarely exercised, it is often enforced in such cases as intentional suicides, unremitting apostates, and intermarried Jews. This is one way the community can promote adherence to its standards when it has no police power to do so. While the decision may appear to be harsh, it is required.

An intermarried Jew may be buried in a Jewish cemetery. The principle concern is the concept of "not burying the righteous alongside the wicked." Interfaith marriage is comparable to renunciation of one's Judaism, but since even a Jewish apostate legally remains Jewish according to Jewish law, such a person is buried in a Jewish cemetery, sometimes near the outer gates.

The non-Jewish mate is gentile and may not be buried in a Jewish cemetery.

The child of a Jewish mother is Jewish and is accorded full Jewish burial rights. *The unconverted child of a non-Jewish mother* is gentile and may not be buried in a Jewish cemetery.

The Right to Be Called to the Torah.   The majority of the scholars hold that a Torah honor should not be extended to one who has defied the Torah and endangered the survival power of the Jews. This is qualitatively different from one who violates other laws of the Torah, because it strikes at the roots of Jewish existence and because the community must take emergency precautions due to the nature of the crisis.

In cases where this results in embarrassment, as when the person is already standing at the Torah, the restriction is often relaxed. Such decisions must be rendered by competent, learned authority.

The Right to Be Counted Toward a Minyan.   Not every Jew may be counted. Although a Jew remains a Jew despite his sin, in the old days those who were excommunicated were not to be considered an integral part of Jewish society. While excommunication is not relevant to the American Jewish community, a judgment has to be made as to whether one would deserve such punishment were it enforceable. Interfaith marriage has always brought this response from the community because of *migdar milta,* the need to establish boundaries, to affirm and protect its standards. Therefore, *Se'ridei Esh* rules that the intermarried person is not to be counted, and is to be considered *mumar le'khol ha-Torah kulah* (as having denied arrogantly every law of the Torah).

In complicated or unusual situations, a competent authority should be consulted. These are not open-and-shut legal cases, and because they involve practical communal procedures, local learned authority should decide. If there is no *minyan* without the person in question, or if the ruling is counter-productive, the more lenient ruling of *Iggerot Moshe* that he be counted at all times should be relied upon.

The Right of Children of a Non-Jewish Mother to Attend the Jewish School.
Although technically one of the questions in this regard concerns the principle of teaching Torah to a non-Jew, the crucial issue is this: Is it wise to enroll a child who is legally not a Jew in a Jewish school?

Our first concern is for the child. Should we subject a child who is not obligated to perform as a Jew to the frustration of studying Judaism at school only to return home to a mother who has denied the value of the Jewish people? No matter how fine and ethical a person she may be, she has not converted to Judaism, the formal step that is absolutely required by law, by history, and by community. While it is unfortunately true that there are Jewish mothers and fathers who are the living antithesis of everything their children are taught by their teachers, at least the parent is Jewish and is counted as Jewish. A situation in which the mother is not even Jewish must create intense confusion for the child. (One authority does permit a child of this type to attend a Jewish school, in the case of a father and child who assure the authorities of the child's intention to convert to Judaism when he comes of age. But even this permission must await the solution to the following question.)

Our second concern is for the integrity of the community. Attendance at a Jewish religious school is a public statement of the child's Jewishness. Children simply assume their classmates at the synagogue and Jewish school are Jewish. They have every right to socialize and decide to marry without investigating family history. If we permit children who are not legally Jewish to attend a Jewish school, we run the risk of interfaith marriage.

In addition, what is to prevent such a boy from being counted in a *minyan* or becoming *bar mitzvah* on the basis of his schooling? Should the child participate in this unwitting fraud? Should the Jewish community permit this to be the reward for interfaith marriage? The community must set its limits at this point. If the child is being tutored privately in preparation for conversion, however, there does not appear to be any danger to communal policy or to the child's needs.

Undeniably, some good and well-intentioned people may suffer. A Jewish father who has intermarried, and deeply wants his children to be Jewish, but who refuses to convert the child, is an object of compassion. But more worthy of our compassion is the innocent child who wishes to study alongside his friends and who likes the synagogue and Judaism. Why is he to suffer? That question must be placed on the doorstep of his parents. Perhaps more than father or child, the person most hurt is the non-Jewish mother. Although she is gentile, she is quite willing that the child should have a Jewish education. That is a commendable position—there are Jewish women less willing to educate their children Jewishly. Historically, however, the Jewish community has demanded a commitment to Jewish survival in order to participate in its program. Education without conversion is much like love and passion without a resolve to marry. All the declarations of love are high-sounding and noble, but a denial of commitment is by itself— for whatever reason—a negation of love. As one may not enjoy the rights of marriage without accepting the responsibility of marriage, so the education and willingness to cooperate and to love Israel are commendable, but a formal commitment to Judaism is required. If that is lacking, nothing can be done.

The Dietary Laws and Interfaith Marriage

The eternity of the Jewish people is guaranteed by God, but only people can ensure its preservation. While philosophers reflected on the causes of the Jews' survival, the Sages framed the laws that made it possible. The Jew can and should cooperate fully with the non-Jew in every way except that which would encourage interfaith marriage.

The physical activity that most encourages socializing is eating. The Torah required families to come together as their first act of freedom as they ate the Paschal lamb before leaving Egypt (Exodus 12), and the *Halakhah* subsequently urged all Jews to eat the *Seder* with others. The most illustrative law of food-companionship is *zimmun,* the presence of three or more adult Jews, who have the duty to recite grace over the meals as a unit. When three or more people eat together, they become a cohesive body, not unlike the *minyan* quorum of ten for worship.

There has developed a whole social etiquette around eating—children are taught rules of social grace; parties are food-and-drink gatherings; businesses could not thrive without luncheon meetings; and the successful person does not eat alone.

But we are also taught when to withdraw from the eating fellowship. Knowing when to *forego* food is as important to our growth as *individuals,* as knowing when to *share* food is important to our development as *social beings.* The Bible's first prohibition relates to food. Although God gives the herbs and trees for food to all creatures ("To you it shall be for food; and to every beast of the earth . . ." [Genesis 1:29]), he adds a prohibition for Adam: "Do *not* eat of the fruit of the tree . . ." (Gen. 2:17). But when Adam becomes a social being in the presence of Eve, he finds the food irresistible. Unable to withdraw, he sins. The dietary laws are supreme examples of man's learning to *retreat* from food.

The Rabbis carefully used food to hedge the pattern of assimilation. Because they enacted the food laws to prevent intermarriage, these laws were not categorized under the *kosher* laws, but under the *marriage* laws. Therefore, unless there are exceptional circumstances, one should not even attend a non-Jewish wedding feast, let alone the religious service.

Wine manufactured by non-Jews was not permitted by the Rabbis. This is called *stam yeinam,* the reason for which is *mishum be'noteikhem,* the fear of interfaith marriage. Wine is even more conducive to fellowship than food—no one toasts over a steak, or becomes light-hearted over breakfast rolls. Observant Jews keep these rules to this day. For the same reason, privately-baked gentile bread was forbidden. Today, kosher bread baked in commercial bakeries is permitted; it would not be conducive to an "eating fellowship," since one does not need to partake of it with his host who baked it.

These laws appear very restrictive and required spartan observance, but they were very effective in preventing interfaith marriage.

THE STRATEGY OF THE COMMUNITY

Historically, Jews lacked the legal ability to stop an interfaith marriage, and the community had to take steps to prevent it. Josephus, the ancient Jewish historian, records an incident about Joseph, a tax farmer for Ptolemy III in 229 B.C.E. Joseph fell in love with a gentile actress and asked his brother to help him keep it secret in order to avoid a scandal. Instead, the brother dressed up his own daughter in the guise of the actress and gave her to Joseph. Joseph, thinking her to be the actress, lavished affection upon her, and finally married her—to everyone's great delight!

What steps can the Jewish community take today to prevent intermarriage?

We *must* build exclusivity—even in the midst of freedom. Exclusivity may be cumbersome, perhaps even embarrassing—but what choice is there if survival is our goal? Meeting a non-Jewish partner under Jewish auspices is an open declaration of communal approval. Most young people begin social life with the confident feeling that "it can't happen to me," but proximity and ease and social acceptability remove the distance very quickly and very subtly. The Jewish tradition built a wall because the wall was needed. Today we have all but demolished the wall. Where then do we draw the line? If we Jews do not create a wall of flowers, others may create a wall of thorns.

We must act out what we proclaim. If we pronounce against interfaith marriage, we should not honor Jews who are themselves intermarried, even if it be for fund-raising for Israel or for orphaned children, nor should we elect them president of philanthropic federations or other "secular" organizations that daily agonize over our "assimilated youth." If we do, young people, who sense the duplicity of public honors given in return for public dishonor, will develop a cynical attitude to all things Jewish and find no horror in interfaith marriage.

We should not permit the non-Jewish partners to become members in our synagogues. It is illogical to claim that the Jewish people will be decimated by interfaith marriage, and then invite them to participate fully in the life of the synagogue. The rationale that we are "trying to bring them closer in order to have the gentile partner convert" is a signal that interfaith marriage will be tolerated.

The Need for Jewish Education

Jewish education is absolutely necessary. Education is the only way to foster identification. Ignorance has always been the Jews' nemesis: If they don't know about Judaism, they won't care. Young people may earn graduate degrees in chemistry or history, but have only a kindergarten acquaintance with Judaism. Thus they may simply characterize Judaism as a cluster of primitive folkways and walk away from it. With this attitude, why should they not intermarry?

Jewish education must be free for all. If we accept that Jewish education is necessary, it will be far more accessible if it is free to every student. Family budgets are often strained, and high tuition can become a good reason, and also a good excuse, for keeping children home. Many people will neither ask for nor accept scholarships. The children must be saved in spite of their parents, and they must be viewed as independent Jews in need, rather than the wards of parents who should know better but do not.

At the present time the exorbitant costs involved in such a program would be staggering to the community, the administration overwhelming, and the whole business therefore unfeasible. But we have reached far more difficult goals—Israel is eloquent proof of this. A universally free Jewish education may not be realistic right now, but it must be on the Jewish community's agenda.

Conversion As a Cure

Conversion will not save us. There are those who consider conversion of gentiles to be a means of offsetting the loss of those who marry outside the faith. In fact, a number of rabbis, academics, and others now view interfaith marriage as a new source of gain for the Jewish population. Leonard Fein, Professor of Contemporary Jewish Studies at Brandeis University, says: "Our continued rejection of the intermarried does not seem to affect the popularity of intermarriage very much. A redirection of our efforts [is needed], a welcoming of intermarried couples into our midst . . ." Alexander Schindler, President of the Union of American Hebrew Congregations, called for an aggressive effort by Jews to convert non-Jewish marriage partners. This proposal represents a distinct departure from the Jewish historical pattern of not seeking converts. Indeed, some members of the Reform rabbinate, who do not require the gentile partner to convert, claim that providing the couple with a religious ceremony will tend to make them feel more Jewish, associate them with a rabbi, incline them toward eventual conversion, and ultimately increase the number of Jews in the world. How are we to respond to this argument?

First, there is a basic mistake in the logic: The crisis is not one of quantity, but of quality. While it is true that there are not a large number of Jews, and the loss of a million souls cannot be contemplated with equanimity, that is not the overriding problem. In our mechanized world we tend to see life in terms of "more or less" rather than "better or worse." We have absolute faith and long historical proof that the Jews will continue to survive. The question for the future is not whether we will be more Jews or fewer Jews, but what sort of Jews we will be.

The Jews in the Middle Ages numbered only about one million, yet they produced scholars, diplomats, saints, Kabbalists, philosophers, scientists, and an incredibly rich literature. No one worried about survival. Today, Jews number thirteen million and are worried sick about survival. What is happening today is that the center of the Jewish people is intensifying, becoming more committed, observant, and vigorous, while the periphery is assimilating. Historian Irving Agus claims that all Jews today are descendants of a small portion—only about two percent—of the Jewish population of the ninth century. Only the spiritually fit will survive.

The real catastrophe is that families are lost to God, to Jewish tradition, to the Jewish historical destiny. Their defection is horrendous because they break the chain of their family's loyalty, and because their children will not know the beauty and truth of Judaism. It is difficult to come to faith as a reasoning adult, although many do just that. Ideally, one should experience Judaism as a child, surrounded by the smells, the sights and the sounds of Judaism, the glory of its celebrations and the sadness of its fast days.

The *Halakhah* is repelled by conversion for ulterior motives. The proper criterion is not love of Jews, but love of Judaism. History has taught us the painful lesson that you can't have one without the other, and the *Halakhah* has insisted on maintaining this integrity. The tradition calls one who converts *le'shem shamayim* (for the sake of heaven) a *ger tzeddek* (righteous proselyte). Such converts bring glory to the Jewish people. They add to its sanctity, raise its communal standards, and inject the fire of idealism into the moribund embers of those who are born into the faith but do not appreciate its greatness.

But if conversion is performed with a desperate concern for the disappearance of the Jew, virtually any prospective convert will be accepted. Every motive will be rationalized as *le'shem shamayim:* Are you converting for the sake of your girl friend? Fine. Because of the dogged insistence of your future mother-in-law? OK. These ulterior motives appeal to the basest reasons for conversion, and the prospective convert will know that it is a conversion of convenience, performed because the Jewish community is deathly afraid of losing the life-long battle in the competition for souls.

Converts for ulterior motives are referred to as *gerei arayot,* "Lion Proselytes," after the Samaritans who converted under miraculous circumstances (II Kings 17:24) when beseiged by devouring lions which they regarded as being sent by God. The Samaritans were never considered full converts because their compelled belief in God coexisted with their former idolatry. In fact the *Halakhah* discerned two types of lion converts: those who accepted Judaism fully but for inauthentic reasons, and those who never genuinely took upon themselves the "yoke of the Commandments." Both were strenuously discouraged, but the law dealt more leniently with the first, while totally rejecting the second. What they had in common and what the Rabbis sought at all costs to avoid was sham. Neither the fear of lions nor the fear of mothers-in-law is respected as an authentic reason for converting to Judaism.

The imagination of the Jew in regard to conversion is beset by the myth that the convert becomes "more" Jewish than the Jewish mate. First, this observation, were it true, would be eloquent testimony to the failure of the Jewish community. Second, it is hardly a recommendation for conversion. The standard for the convert's acceptability is not relative to the fiance's nonobservance and noninvolvement. Third, it is unquestionably not a provable truth. Statisticians make grand claims for their profession, but they have not quantified the soul or the quality of Jewish life. I cannot believe that a person who converted not for the sake of Judaism but for the sake of marriage to a peripheral Jew, is going to make an ideal or even acceptable convert. If this popular observation is true of anyone, it is the *ger tzeddek* who is often more committed than a Jewish-born spouse.

The most important aspect of conversion—after genuine love and commitment—is the *process* of conversion, which is clearly defined by the Bible, the law, and the tradition. There must be circumcision for men, and immersion in a ritual pool (*mikvah*) for both men and women. This process must be approved by a specially convened court (*beit din*) consisting of an authoritative, competent halakhic expert and two of his associates. Only these conversions are accepted by the worldwide Jewish community. Conversions that fall short of this process or are not conducted by reliable authorities will not be universally accepted and will cause those involved much frustration.

The importance of the process of conversion is similar to the naturalization process required for an alien to become a citizen. This process is formal and precise; an alien cannot simply announce that he loves his adopted country and intends to uphold its laws, and receive citizenship in return. It would not help to argue that native citizens who know less of the law and history than the immigrant never have to make a statement of loyalty. More is required of a rational, adult immigrant than of native citizens.

There is no way to determine conversion by testing the quality of the convert's soul; this would require subjective analysis and be open to much error. The formal process assures a lifelong, binding commitment. The law must deal with an action that conveys a feeling—it cannot deal with feeling alone.

The law does look with more compassion upon situations that are *fait accompli,* such as children of mixed marriages whom the community considers Jews and who seek conversion, and those already married civilly. These are very serious and weighty questions, and a reliable halakhic authority should be consulted.

THE STRATEGY OF THE HOME

Precautionary efforts do not *begin* when children are of marriageable age; they *end* at that time. They begin with the dawn of consciousness of the growing child. We can do a number of things at home to ensure that our children are not tempted to look for a marriage partner outside Judaism.

Design a Jewish Environment

The Home. The home must be genuinely Jewish. The association of joy and Judaism is vital, and Jewish moments such as lighting Sabbath and holiday candles must be joyously and continuously celebrated. Symbols of Judaism such as books of Jewish interest and Jewish journals and newspapers must be visible and accessible. The family must belong to a synagogue, contribute to the Jewish community, and be concerned about the fate of Israel.

The College. We Jews have made of education an idol to which we pay unquestioned obeisance, with which we share a common faith, and which we regard as our chief pride. Ironically, by worshipping that idol we may be sacrificing our very Jewishness.

In order to test this apparently radical proposition, I posed a value problem to a Jewish audience. The question I asked was strictly hypothetical but simple, and I assumed it would elicit a spontaneous yes or no answer: "If you had definite advance knowledge that by sending your son or daughter to a distant college the young person would behave immorally and relinquish Jewishness, would you nonetheless send your child away to school? Or would you accept the alternative of having them remain at home without a college education, perhaps having to work at the supermarket, but with the absolute assurance that Jewishness and moral behavior would be retained?

The response to my question was stunned silence. After a few moments, paralyzed indecision gave way to defensive questions: "What do you mean by 'immoral' and 'un-Jewish?' " I said that I would consider as "typically immoral" random premarital intercourse or the taking of drugs, and as "typically un-Jewish" the total assimilation into the secular environment, or interdating. I still did not receive a yes-or-no answer to my question, but rather a response typical of today's religious and ethical minimalism: "Premarital sex? *So long as* she doesn't become pregnant. Interdating? *So long as* he's a nice boy. Dope? *So long as* it is not addictive. Assimilated? *So long as* she is happy. What else does a Jewish mother want?" I persisted "Would you choose a college education for your daughter if you knew she would opt for premarital sex without pregnancy, or interfaith marriage with a 'nice' gentile, or take nonaddictive dope, or be assimilated but happy?" I received no answer from any adult in that audience, but I did receive one response from an eighteen-year-old girl who was about to leave home for college: "I would work in the supermarket."

Of course no one has to settle for the supermarket (there are good children and schools), but unfortunately the lack of academic credentials has become a more heinous sin for Jews than immorality. You may be giving your child no alternative to interdating. No matter how strong the child or how supportive the home, a young person sent to a small out-of-town college or even to a large university in a small town will have little choice of Jewish partners and will always be surrounded by non-Jews. If a student is forced to stay at the dormitory on weekends, or cannot attend the Friday night football game, it is an invitation to disaster. If you cherish your Jewishness, you may have to compromise on the college of your dreams.

School and Camp.   Jewish education, formal or informal, is the greatest bulwark against interfaith marriage. Hence a Jewish child should attend a Jewish summer camp. Informal education is more subtle and closer to the home environment than is the formal instruction at school, and often the child can absorb more in that setting than at school.

Friends should be carefully screened, since peer influence is often greater than parental influence. You should be concerned for their ethical values, attitudes to life, to Judaism, to school, and to community.

Teach Real Values.   Parents may themselves have married exclusively on the basis of romantic love, but often they reject this motivation for their child. Unfortunately they do not often replace romance with substantial values, but with advice to marry a wealthy or professional person. Happiness is a by-product of marriage, not a goal, but in our society it has become the ultimate test of success. We must train children to look for more enduring values, such as quality of belief, Jewish loyalties, ethical conduct, and moral demeanor.

Jewish Social Welfare Participation.   Israel is a self-contained Jewish environment, and identification with it serves as a marvelous support for identification with Jewish tradition and with the Jewish people. It is also important to inform your children of the Holocaust and discuss it with them. Although an over emphasis on the tragic aspects of Jewish history may wrongly identify Judaism with pain, an intelligent introduction to the subject can be very effective. Participation in Jewish social causes, such as the problem of Soviet Jewry, is also of inestimable value in strengthening your child's Jewish identity and evoking idealism.

Parents must not forget that they are an important part of a Jewish environment. It does not consist only of symbols and celebrations, but also of souls. If you are pretending your Judaism, your child will detect it with unfailing accuracy.

Negotiate for Jewish Marriage from Day One

Permit no interdating—not once, not even in a group. Interdating may appear innocent enough, but if it is *ever, for any reason,* considered acceptable, it will eventually be naturally assumed. There should be total agreement between both parents on this matter. Make the child positively and absolutely aware of your horror at the prospect. You have more influence than you suspect.

Do not attend wedding services or receptions of intermarried friends or even relatives. It may cause temporary embarrassment, but it may also have a great impact on your child and save you lifelong grief.

At the sign of crisis, be *more firm and more loving.* Ba'al Shem Tov, the founder of Hasidism, said that you must respond to children's problems with more, not less, love. This does not mean a collapse of parental will, or the sentimentalism we sometimes mistake for love. It must approximate, in a modern framework, the talmudic adage, "Bring him near with the right hand and keep him distant with the left." Love does not always imply acquiescence; it means "no" as often as it means "yes."

You must not accept a mixed marriage at all. Do not ask if your child's intended spouse will convert; this is a last resort that may never be available to you. Pull out every stop. Parents used to sit *shiva* and tear their garments in mourning at such times, and some still do. Of course it is heartbreaking to be severe with your own child, but do not melt. Have faith, place your trust in God, and pray.

A NOTE TO THOSE WHO ARE PREPARING TO MARRY OUT OF THE FAITH

This is not addressed to those who are totally indifferent to their Jewishness. If you were one of those, you would not be reading this book. It is also not addressed to those looking to shed their Judaism. Interfaith marriage is a passport to the gentile world, and is close to *she'mad,* conversion to another faith, the most horrendous word in the lexicon of Judaism. You are probably not in that category if you are sufficiently interested in Jewish marriage to read this book. If you are positively oriented to Judaism and to your parents, and harbor no Jewish self-hatred, you should know these facts. Romance cannot vitiate them.

Interfaith-marriage is treason against the Jewish people, its Bible, its history, and its laws. It means victory for those forces, ancient or modern, which have sought to destroy us. It is a terminal malignancy for your family's Judaism. You are most likely the last generation of a people that has lived continously for thirty-five generations. The chances are that this is the end of that continuity, no matter how good your intentions or your spouse's high hopes. Jewish history will continue, but you will have caused a blow that will have weakened imperceptibly, though most definitely, the very fiber of our faith.

The family today is in critical condition. It has suffered violent disruptions, and is badly in need of cohesive components. By marrying out of the faith, you will be beginning married life as a house divided against itself.

Ironically, it is on those occasions when families most often experience cohesion that you will probably experience conflict. Will your wedding be held at a state office? When a son is born, will he be circumcised or baptized? Do you name the baby at synagogue or at church? December will be crisis month: is Christmas or Hanukkah to be the family's holiday? If you celebrate both, the cost may well be permanent confusion and loss of integrity. These moments in life that are most meaningful, which religions have invested with sanctity, may become for you milestones of anguish and predictable conflict.

How will your families feel? Marriage is not only a union of two individuals, but of two kinship groups. Is it possible that they would cause no dissension. If they do, should you cut them off and thereby cut off any chance of an extended family? One of the unconscious motives for having children is the desire to assure your life beyond your own existence, a sort of immortality. Will parents see in their grandchildren some continuation of their own lives? Do you have the right to withhold this from them?

Children have a way of becoming demanding realities, forcing parents to make decisions. There can be no more theories when your child asks, "Dad, are you coming to church today?" Children who did not ask to be born have a right to be protected from dissension. Should your child be asked to choose the preferable religion? That is very democratic and very thoughtful, but to do so involves choosing one parent over the other. You, in your interfaith marriage, are two people, but your child is only one.

Worst of all, who is your child? No less a personage than former Prime Minister of England Benjamin Disraeli, the son of a baptized Jew, was asked by the Queen of England, "What are you?" He walked to the Great Bible on the mahogany stand. He turned to the New Testament—but he was not a Christian. He turned back to the Old Testament—but neither was he a Jew. He turned to the blank page between the two, and said to the Queen, "This is what I am."

HOMOSEXUAL "MARRIAGE"*

According to Jewish law, two men may not relate sexually. Hence, homosexuals are prohibited marriage partners. At almost no time in the past two millenia would such a statement need to be made. But today, when freedom is the chief idol of the academy and being "consenting adults" who have a "loving relationship" is the criterion for love and marriage, the ancient Jewish teaching on homosexuality must be forcefully restated.

A "marriage" that sanctions a bond between two members of the same sex is not only void but unthinkable. The demand that Rabbis solemnize such relationships and that congregations admit such couples to their family membership indicates a faulty conception of the Jewish religion.

BASIC JEWISH TEACHINGS ON HOMOSEXUALITY

Reference to homosexuality in the halakhic literature is rare, indicating that it was virtually absent among Jews. This is interesting in light of the fact that the ancient Greeks accepted it as normal (Plato in the Symposium considers love between man and man to be nobler and more spiritual than love between man and woman), and that according to social researchers C.S. Ford and F.A. Beach, sixty-four percent of primitive societies accepted it as within the framework of normalcy.

Biblical References to Homosexuality

The Bible prohibits homosexual intercourse and labels it an abomination: "Thou shalt not lie with a man as one lies with a woman: it is an abomination" (Leviticus 18:22). In Leviticus 20:13, capital punishment is ordained for both transgressors. In the first passage, sodomy is linked with buggery [sex with animals], and in the second with incest and buggery. . . .

---

*Much of this section is extracted from an article by Dr. Norman Lamm in *Encyclopaedia Judaica Yearbook,* 1974. I cannot improve on his commentary.

The city of Sodom had the questionable honor of lending its name to homosexuality because of the notorious attempt at homosexual rape when the entire population ("both young and old, all the people from every quarter") surrounded the home of Lot, the nephew of Abraham, and demanded that he surrender his guests to them "that we may *know* them" (Genesis 19:5).

The decimation of the tribe of Benjamin resulted from the notorious incident, recorded in Judges 19, of a group of Benjamites in Gibeah who sought to commit homosexual rape.

Scholars have identified the *kadesh* proscribed by the Torah (Deuteronomy 23:18) as a ritual male homosexual prostitute. This form of heathen cult penetrated into Judea from the Canaanite surroundings in the period of the early monarchy. Rehoboam, probably under the influence of his Ammonite mother, tolerated this cultic sodomy during his reign (I Kings 14:24). His grandson Asa tried to cleanse the Temple in Jerusalem of the practice (I Kings 15:12), as did his great grandson Jehoshaphat. But it was not until the days of Josiah and the vigorous reforms he introduced that the *kadesh* was finally removed from the Temple and the land (II Kings 23:7).

Talmudic References to Homosexuality

Rabbinic exegesis of the Bible finds several other homosexual references hidden in the scriptural narratives.

Of Ham, the son of Noah, we are told that "he saw the nakedness of his father" and told his two brothers (Genesis 9:22). Why should this act have warranted the harsh imprecation hurled at Ham by his father? The Rabbis offer two answers: One, that the text could be taken to imply that Ham castrated Noah; second, that the biblical expression is an idiom for homosexual intercourse.

On the scriptural story of Potiphar's purchase of Joseph as a slave (Genesis 39:1), the Talmud's comment is that he acquired [Joseph] for homosexual purposes, but that a miracle occurred and God sent the angel Gabriel to castrate Potiphar (*Sot.* 13b).

Post-biblical literature records remarkably few incidents of homosexuality. Herod's son Alexander according to Josephus, had homosexual contact with a young eunuch.

The incidence of sodomy among Jews is interestingly reflected in the *Halakhah* of *mishkav zakhur*. The Mishnah teaches that Rabbi Judah forbade two bachelors from sleeping under the same blanket for fear that this would lead to homosexual temptation (*Kid.* 4:14). However, the Sages permitted it because homosexuality was so rare among Jews that such preventive legislation was considered unnecessary (*Kid.* 82a). This latter view is codified as *Halakhah* by Maimonides. Some four hundred years later, Rabbi Joseph Caro, who did not codify the law against sodomy proper nevertheless cautioned against being alone with another male because of the lewdness prevalent "in our times." About a hundred years later, Rabbi Joel Sirkes reverted to the original ruling, and suspended the prohibition because such obscene acts were unheard of amongst Polish Jewry. Indeed, a distinguished contemporary of Rabbi Caro, Rabbi Solomon Luria, went even further and declared homosexuality so very rare that, if one refrains from sharing a blanket with another male as a special act of piety, one is guilty of self-righteous pride or religious snobbism.

Lesbianism as such is not mentioned in the Bible, but it is discussed in Rabbinic literature. *Sifra* considers it implicit in the abhorrent practices of the Egyptians and Canaanites, against which the Jews were warned. The Talmud extends the prohibition of male homosexuality to the female, but not the penalty. It is not considered *arayot*, a specifically sexual sin, but *issur*, a general religious sin. Maimonides classifies it as *pe'ritzut*, promiscuity, rather than *ze'nut*, a violation of a sexual prohibition. There is in lesbianism no genital intercourse and no wasting of seed. Thus it is not considered a perversion of God's intent.

Rabbi Huna held that lesbianism is the equivalent of harlotry and disqualified such a woman from marrying a priest. The *Halakhah* is more lenient. While the act is prohibited, the *Halakhah* decrees that the lesbian is not punished with death as the male homosexual would be, and is permitted to marry a priest. However, the transgression does warrant a disciplinary punishment—flagellation. The less punitive attitude of the *Halakhah* to the female homosexual than to the male does not reflect any intrinsic judgment on one as opposed to the other, but is rather the result of a halakhic technicality: There is no explicit biblical proscription of lesbianism, and the act does not entail genital intercourse.

Three reasons are offered for the prohibition of homosexuality. First, it is a perversion of man's natural endowments. Such a perversion diminishes man's dignity, which he derives from being created in the image of God. The genitalia of male and female were obviously designed by the Creator for mutual complementation, and—following Sigmund Freud's insight that "anatomy is destiny"—their psyches are also designed to be complementary.

Second, homosexuality frustrates the primary purpose of sex procreation. The purposeful "wasting of seed" in masturbation is not tolerated in Jewish morality, and the sin is compounded when it is performed by another in a homosexual union. Judaism views procreation as a blessing transformed into a command. According to Isaiah 45:18, not only was procreation necessary to the development of humanity (*lo tohu be'raah, lashevet ye'tzarah*), it meant the survival of the Jewish people.

The third reason is one offered by the Tosafists and Rabbenu Asher. This is the destruction of the family, which strikes at the roots of Judaism. The Rabbis erected fortresses of laws to preserve clean family life so that the home might be sensitively attuned to raising the next generation, through whom will be transmitted the faith in God. Saadiah Gaon considers the rational basis of most of the Bible's moral legislation to be the preservation of the family. Homosexuality precludes the perpetuation of the human species (and hence the interaction of humanity with God), and it betrays the survival of the Jewish people.

When a man indulges in homosexual tendencies he commits *to-evah,* an abomination.

> The Talmud records the interpretation of Bar Kapparah who, in a play on words, defined *to'evah* as *to'eh attah bah,* "You are going astray because of it" (*Ned.* 51a). The exact meaning of this passage is unclear, and various explanations have been put forward.
>
> The *Pesikta (Zutarta)* explains the statement of Bar Kapparah as referring to the impossibility of such a sexual act resulting in procreation. One of the major functions (if not the major purpose) of sexuality is reproduction, and this reason for man's sexual endowment is frustrated by *mishkav zakhur.*
>
> It may be, however, that the very variety of interpretations of *to'evah* points to a far more fundamental meaning: namely, that an act characterized as an "abomination" is *prima facie* disgusting and need not be further defined or explained. Certain acts are considered *to'evah* by the Torah, and there the matter rests. It is, as it were, a visceral reaction, an intuitive disqualification of the act, and we run the risk of distorting the biblical judgment if we rationalize it.

THE HOMOSEXUAL ARGUMENT AND A JEWISH RESPONSE

I remember reading the account of a gay Jewish couple's "engagement" announcement a few years back. The couple described the joyous response of the Chavurah gathering, who danced around the couple, singing *siman tov, mazal tov.* "It is natural that we should want to celebrate our friends' happiness; why shouldn't we rejoice over the good fortune of two men who have found a loving relationship?" The homosexual argument is paraphrased as follows in an article by Hershel Matt:

> Granted that marriage in Judaism has always been heterosexual; and granted that one of the major purposes of marriage has always been procreation—in order both to populate the world and to pass on the Covenant way of life. But is that the sole purpose and meaning of Jewish marriage? What of the legitimacy of sexual pleasure and release—is that not also Jewish? Longterm abstinence is no more feasible, bearable, or desirable for homosexuals than for heterosexuals. And does not marriage have other purposes as well: the fostering of mutual affection, care, trust, sacrifice and support; the encouragement and sustenance of growth—intellectual, esthetic, moral and spiritual; the sharing of pain and anxiety; the nurturing of joy and hope; the overcoming of loneliness—all of these on the basis of an enduring commitment of faithfulness? Is not marriage the primary and preferred—and, indeed, the only fully acceptable—context for furthering these purposes? If it is Torah-teaching that the fullest possible meaning of personhood is to be found in and through marriage,

shall we, because we are homosexuals, be denied the right to seek such meaning and to develop such personhood? If God, in whose image we homosexuals, too, are created, has directly or indirectly caused or willed or allowed us to be what we cannot help being—men and women unable to function heterosexually—can we believe, and can you heterosexuals believe, that He wants us to be denied the only possible arrangement whereby we can live as deeply a human life as we are capable of?

Here precisely is the focus of the homosexual argument—The union will bring into being a caring and loving relationship. Is the purpose of marriage not also companionship? Unlike celibacy and masturbation, this strikes the note of a meaningful partnership with another human being.

Norman Lamm offers a Jewish response:

"Loving, selfless concern" and "meaningful, personal relationships," the great slogans of the now dated "new morality" and the exponents of situation ethics, have become the litany of sodomy in our times. Simple logic should permit us to use the same criteria for excusing adultery or any other act heretofore held to be immoral; and indeed, that is just what has been done, and it has received the sanction not only of liberals and humanists, but of certain religionists as well. "Love," "fulfillment," "exploitive," "meaningful"—the list itself sounds like a lexicon of emotionally charged terms drawn at random from the disparate sources of both Christian and psychologically-oriented agnostic circles. Logically, we must ask the next question: What moral depravities cannot be excused by the sole criterion of "warm, meaningful human relations" or "fulfillment," the newest semantic heirs to "love"?

Love, fulfillment, and happiness can also be attained in incestuous contacts and certainly in polygamous relationships. Is there nothing at all left that is "sinful," "unnatural," or "immoral" if it is practiced "between two consenting adults"?

According to midrashic teaching, the generation of Noah was eradicated by the Flood because it had descended to such forms of immorality as the writing of formal marriage contracts for sodomy (homosexuality) and buggery (a man-beast relationship), a practice prevalent in the Athens of Plato and the Rome of Nero but unheard of in the long history of the Jewish people.

HOW SHALL WE VIEW THE HOMOSEXUAL TODAY?

The act of homosexuality is prohibited, but all practicing homosexuals cannot be arbitrarily lumped together. The response must be to each individual and appropriate to his motives.

Dr. Judd Marmor delineates four types of homosexual activity:

"Genuine homosexuality" is based on strong preferential erotic feelings for members of the same sex. "Transitory homosexual behavior" occurs among adolescents who would prefer heterosexual experiences but are denied such opportunities because of social, cultural, or psychological reasons. "Situational homosexual exchanges" are characteristic of prisoners, soldiers, and others who are heterosexual but are denied access to women for long periods of time. "Transitory and opportunistic homosexuality" is that of delinquent young men who permit themselves to be used by pederasts in order to make money or win other favors, although their primary erotic interests are exclusively heterosexual. To these may be added, for purposes of our analysis, two other types. The first category, that of genuine homosexuals, may be said to comprehend two subcategories: those who experience their condition as one of duress or uncontrollable passion which they would rid themselves of if they could, and those who transform their idiosyncracy into an ideology, i.e., the gay militants who assert the legitimacy and validity of homosexuality as an alternative to heterosexuality. The sixth category is based on what Dr. Rollo May has called "the new Puritanism," the peculiarly modern notion that one must experience all sexual pleasures, whether or not one feels inclined to them, as if the failure to taste every cup passed at the sumptuous banquet of carnal life means that one has not truly lived. Thus we have transitory homosexual behavior not of adolescents, but of adults who feel that they must "try everything" at least once in their lives.

Clearly, genuine homosexuality experienced under duress (Hebrew: *ones*) most obviously lends itself to being termed pathological, especially where dysfunction appears in other aspects of the personality. Opportunistic homosexuality, ideological homosexuality, and transitory adult homosexuality are at the other end of the spectrum and appear more reprehensible. As for the intermediate categories, while they cannot be called illnesses, they do have a greater claim on our sympathy. . . .

Hence there are types of homosexuality that do not warrant any special consideration, because the notion of *ones* or duress (i.e., disease) in no way applies. Where the category of mental illness does apply, the act itself remains *to'evah* (an abomination), but the fact of illness lays upon us the obligation of pastoral compassion, psychological understanding, and social concern. In this sense, homosexuality is no different from any other anti-halakhic act, where it is legitimate to distinguish between the objective act itself, including its ethical and moral consequences, and the mentality and inner development of the person who perpetrates the act. For instance, if a man murders in a cold and calculating fashion for reasons of profit, the act is criminal and the transgressor is criminal. If, however, a psychotic murders, the transgressor is diseased rather than criminal, but the objective act itself remains a criminal act. The courts may therefore treat the perpetrator of the crime as they would a patient, with all the concomitant compassion and concern for therapy, without condoning the act as being morally neutral. To use halakhic terminology, the objective crime remains a *maaseh averah* [a violative action], whereas the person who transgresses is considered innocent on the grounds of *ones*. In such cases, the transgressor is spared the full legal consequences of his culpable act, although the degree to which he may be held responsible varies from case to case.

The response to the homosexual must contain a number of ingredients: intelligence, compassion, personal strength, and an abiding loyalty and commitment to Jewish belief and Jewish history.

THE LEVIRATE MARRIAGE

A Levirate marriage occurs in the following circumstances: A man, Reuben, is married to a woman, Sarah. Reuben dies before he can father a child. The widow is now obligated to be married to Reuben's eldest brother, Simon, so that she may bear and raise a child in the "name" of the deceased Reuben (The brother in this position is termed a *yavam* or *levir,* hence "Levirate" marriage). If there are no succeeding children, Reuben's name will not be continued in the family tree. If Simon and any other brothers in succession refuse to do *Yibbum,* they must perform the ceremony of release, called *chalitzah,* in which they formally state their refusal to marry Sarah. Of course, Sarah may also refuse to marry them. In ancient times, however, widowhood without children and family was so difficult a burden to bear that most women were glad to accept the offer of marriage by one of the brothers-in-law.

The law of *yibbum* (Levirate marriage) which is not well known and therefore not widely observed in contemporary times, is important for the spiritual protection of the integrity of the traditional Jewish family. The Bible (Genesis 38:7–10) recounts a fascinating narrative of a Levirate marriage that was frustrated. Judah had two sons, Er and Onan. Er was married to Tamar, but had no children. When Er was put to death by God for committing a sin, Judah instructed Onan to marry Tamar, as it is the obligation of the *levir* to "raise up seed to thy brother." Onan, realizing that the first child would be accounted his brother's seed, not his own, "spilled his seed upon the ground" and refused his Levirate responsibility. For this act he was punished by death at the hand of God. Eventually, Judah himself formally married Tamar, fulfilling the *levir* requirement (after Revelation, Levirate marriage was restricted to brothers only).

The law is codified in Deuteronomy (25:5–10): If a man died without any child from his present marriage or from any previous marriage, then his eldest surviving brother (of the same father) is obligated to marry the widow. The law stipulates that the Levirate marriage had to be potentially productive of children; that (in the polygamous society of that time) it did not matter whether he was himself married or not; and that if he did not perform Levirate marriage, the duty fell upon the brother next in age. The widow was not permitted to marry anyone else until she was formally separated from the brother by the *chalitzah* ceremony.

The patriarchal family is like a branched tree. If a son dies without offspring, his branch must be continued by his surviving brother *lo yimacheh she'mo me-yisrael,* "that his name be not erased from amongst the Jews." The Bible, in order to assure the continuation of the brother's immortality, suspended a fundamental prohibition of incest, the marrying of a sister-in-law: "Thou shalt not uncover the nakedness of thy brother's wife: it is thy brother's nakedness" (Leviticus 18:16). Thus marrying a sister-in-law is accounted a great sin if she had a child by the brother, and a great *mitzvah* if she had none. Because by the slightest turn of a technicality this act could be either incest or *mitzvah,* a mortal sin or an immortalizing act, an entire tractate of the Talmud (*Yevamot*) is dedicated to its myriad details.

THE PURPOSES OF THE LEVIRATE MARRIAGE

"The Raising of Seed"

Everyone is entitled to be blessed with immortality and one way of ensuring that our ways live on is through our children. "When your days are fulfilled, and when you sleep with your forefathers, I will set up your seed after you, that shall proceed out of your body ..." (II Samuel 7:12). Because the natural extinction of a family is equivalent to its annihilation, virtually every consideration had to give way to parenthood. This feeling was vividly expressed by the daughters of Lot, who, thinking the world had collapsed after the destruction of Sodom, committed incest with their father in the cave, "that we may preserve the seed of our father" (Genesis 19:30–38). In the case of Levirate marriage, the Bible suspends another form of primary incest—between a man and his sister-in-law—but only under strict conditions and in order to preserve seed.

Ruth seeks to continue her dead husband's lineage and is willing to "sacrifice" herself for that goal. In an interesting and telling phrase, her name is linked with Tamar's: "and let your house be like the house of Perez, whom Tamar bore unto Judah, of the seed which the Lord shall give you of this young woman" (Ruth 4:12). Tamar and Ruth are considered righteous and shining examples of courage.

Rabbi Samson Raphael Hirsch embellishes on the idea of "raising the seed." If no child survives in whom the deceased continues to live, his wife allies herself with his brother, the man who is nearest to him in nature. In this way the household most closely related to him "will be built up under the aegis of his own outlook."

Protection of the Widow

The second reason for Levirate marriage is the protection of the wife. Thus, the codification of the Levirate laws in Deuteronomy (25:5–10) is not found among "marriage laws," which would account for the "raising of seed" motive only. They are included in the laws of kindness which are designed to protect the disenfranchised. These laws include laws of equity; the rejection of injustice to strangers, widows, and orphans; the sensitive treatment of laborers; generosity to the landless; and kindness to animals. Josephus notes, "This procedure will be for the benefit of the public, because thereby families will not fail, and the estate will continue among the kindred; and this will be for the solace of wives under their affliction, that they are to be married to the next relatives of their former husbands."

In ancient times, an unattached woman was considered to have little right even to exist. Ryder Smith, surveying ancient Eastern civilizations, says that when a single woman was encountered she was assumed to be a harlot. The status of female singlehood was probably the most unenviable in all of society. This is why the Prophets speak passionately of the protection of the widow and often concern themselves more with her treatment than with war and peace, religion and morality. The situation was even worse for a widow who had no children to care for her and to provide the continued means for her livelihood. The Levirate laws guaranteed the young widow a family, continued status, and funds. This motive of protection argued for the full marriage of the widow with the *Levir* rather than one single productive cohabitation, which may have sufficed to accomplish the minimum requirement for "raising up the seed."

CHALITZAH, THE CEREMONY OF RELEASE

By now *yibbum* (the Levirate marriage) is academic, having been superseded by *chalitzah,* which is now *compulsory for all childless widows who have surviving brothers-in-law.*

There is a provision already in the Torah for an alternative to the obligation of *yibbum* (Deutetonomy 25:7–10). Levirate marriage is preferred, but *chalitzah* is a clear alternative, although it does reflect shame on the *yavam* for having shunned a duty to his family. The scholars of the Mishnah in the first century began with the tradition that *chalitzah* is legitimate only if the Levirate marriage was impossible. In the second century, Abba Saul held that since marrying a sister-in-law is incestuous without the command of *yibbum,* any Levirate marriage entered into without the pure intention of "raising the seed" is incest.

The Talmud later codified this view: "Now that the *yavam's* intention is not for the fulfillment of God's command, it is decided that *chalitzah* is preferable to Levirate marriage." In the Geonic period of the eighth and ninth centuries, the two great academies were still divided on the subject. The Sura Academy taught that marriage was preferable, while the Pumbedita Academy taught *chalitzah* was to be preferred. In the twelfth century, Maimonides favored *yibbum,* while Rashi decided for *chalitzah.* Since the ban on polygamy by Rabbenu Gershom at the beginning of the second millennium C.E., and the concern that the widow and the *levir* must enter a marriage free of personal interest (coupled with the constantly threatening possibility that such a misjudgment qualifies the act as incest), the Jewish tradition has opted for *chalitzah* over Levirate marriage. As early as the nineteenth century Rabbi Zevi Hirsch Chajes noted that morals had become so loose that one could never be sure that the deceased brother had not in fact sired a child unbeknownst to others. This would disqualify him for the Levirate act to "raise seed" in his name and the act of *yibbum* would become an act of incest.

Today the *chalitzah* ceremony is performed not to cast shame on the *levir* for refusing to continue his brother's name, but to free his sister-in-law so that she may remarry. It is "no-fault" *chalitzah*. The official decision is this: The formal ceremony of *chalitzah* must be performed, the Levirate ceremony marriage may not, and only by the process of *chalitzah* is the widow free to marry.

Chalitzah is an official public ceremony requiring a rabbinic court of three, plus two others present, who are known by the Yiddish term *shtume dayanim,* silent Judges. Like all court actions, it must be performed during daytime.

The widow must first wait a period of three months after her husband's death. This wait, called *havchanah,* is the same as that for a divorcee. Its purpose is to determine whether she was pregnant from her former husband. The law was very firm regarding the purity of paternity. This is especially important in *chalitzah,* because if the widow was pregnant and a living child subsequently issues, there is no need for a Levirate marriage.

The ceremony is ancient and starkly simple. It recalls such forbears as Tamar, daughter-in-law of Judah and granddaughter of Abraham, Isaac, and Jacob; and in its unusual symbolism it spans all of the history of the Jewish people.

The judges sit and the *levir* and widow stand before them. The court ascertains that they are of age and that three months have passed since the husband's death, and they call witnesses to testify to the identity of the *levir* and the widow. The *levir* is asked whether he consents to the *chalitzah* rite. Upon his affirmative answer he is placed in position for the removal of his shoe, leaning against the wall or an indoor post. The *levir's* right foot is washed before the ceremonial boot is put on. The boot, a special ceremonial kind made completely of leather, is donned, laced up, and tied below the knee. He then presses his foot on the floor. Facing the *levir,* the woman, audibly recites in Hebrew the biblical phrase, "My husband's brother refuseth to raise up unto his brother a name in Israel; he will not perform the Levirate duty unto me." The *levir* also replies audibly in Hebrew the biblical phrase: "I do not wish to take her." Bending down, the woman loosens the strings of the shoe with her right hand and, holding up his foot with her left hand, she pulls off the shoe with her right and throws it on the ground. She straightens up and expectorates on the ground before the *levir's* face in sight of the court, and exclaims in Hebrew, "So shall it be done to the man that doth not build up his brother's house, and his name shall be called in Israel, the house of him that had his shoe loosed." Those present at the ceremony all exclaim together in Hebrew, *chaluz ha-naal* (he that hath his shoe loosed) three times.

The ceremony is concluded with a few prayers that have no talmudic origin. One, recited by the judges when the *levir* returns the shoe to them, is as follows: "May it by Thy will (O, God) that the daughters of Israel be not in need of *chalitzah* or Levirate marriage." When the court is dismissed its head offers the benediction, "Blessed art Thou, O Lord, our God, who hast sanctified us by Thy commandments and statutes, even by the commandments and statutes of Abraham our father."

Through the centuries, many conjectures were offered as to why the shoe was the central feature of *chalitzah*. Rabbi Samson Raphael Hirsch says that shoelessness symbolizes the "forfeiture of position and progress on earth." Sociologist David R. Mace assumes the shoe is the symbol of possession, "the right to walk over the estate." Anthropologist Robertson Smith records that removal of the shoe is the Bedouin form of divorce, the husband reciting, "She was my slipper and I cast her off."

But in Jewish tradition the shoe has a closer connection to the *chalitzah* ceremony and dramatizes the symbolic rejection of raising up the seed of a dead brother. Removing the shoe is a practice of the mourning observance. If the brother would have performed the Levirate ceremony, he would have kept his brother "alive." Now that he refuses to keep him "alive," and the deceased has no children to mourn him, the brother has his shoe removed as though in a renewed bereavement for a "second death."

Expectorating is also an ancient rite, and its origins are shrouded in the mystery of centuries. Today our sensibilities are ruffled by this act, but not long ago spittoons were a requirement in public places. Two theories as to the inclusion of spitting in the *chalitzah* ceremony present themselves.

Expectorating is a reference to a biblical incident of disgrace. After Miriam spoke ill of her brother Moses, God punished her and Moses prayed for her recuperation (Numbers 12:14). "And the Lord said unto Moses: 'If her father had but spit before her face, should she not hide in shame. . . .'" Miriam demeaned her brother by diminishing his honor; spitting is a reaction to the demeaning act. Thus it was originally an act of disgust by the wife who was willing to sacrifice for her husband's memory, in the face of his flesh and blood brother who would not.

It is also a graphic portrayal of the first recorded frustration of the Levirate marriage. Saliva, says the Ba'al Shem Tov, founder of Hasidism, looks like "seed." Spitting on the ground is a symbolic replay of Onan, spilling his seed on the ground to avoid "raising up the seed" for his brother, Er. The saliva symbol implies that the *levir* is *wasting* his seed rather than "*raising up* the seed."

THE MARITAL STATUS OF THE CHILDLESS WIDOW

If there is no surviving brother-in-law, the widow is free to remarry after the three months of *havchanah*. The status of the widow from the death of her husband until receiving *chalitzah* from her brother-in-law, which terminates for all time her relationship to her husband's family and enables her to remarry, is called *zikah* (tied). This indicates that although her husband died she is still tied to his family. It also signified in ancient times that the widow was destined to marry her *levir* and until that time she was tied to him.

If *zikah* is similar to betrothal (*erusin*)—because the widow is not free either to live with the *levir* or to marry anyone else—is she guilty of adultery if she has sexual relations with someone else during this time? The Talmud ponders this critical question and determines that *zikah* is legally inferior to betrothal, and she has not violated biblical adultery laws. If the *levir* has relations with the widow's sister, is that incest? Again, Rav holds that *zikah* is legally inferior to betrothal, and there is no sin of incest. On the other hand, Samuel holds that it is considered betrothal, and incest has been committed. This question in its varied details and ramifications should be referred to rabbinic authority.

What happens if the widow marries without *chalitzah?* The major concern of the Rabbis with regard to Levirate marriage *today* is the prohibition of the childless widow to remarry before going through the formal religious ceremony of *chalitzah*. Without *chalitzah* she remains in the state of *zikah,* which is almost synonymous with marriage itself. Legally there is still doubt whether her subsequent marriage is void or valid. Because of this technical doubt, all stringencies are observed. A Jewish divorce is required of the second husband, *chalitzah* is still required of the *levir,* and she may not subsequently marry the *levir.* One who is in this situation should consult a halakhically authoritative rabbi.

CHAPTER 5

Prohibited but Valid

The unique legal phenomenon of a prohibited marriage, which if contracted is still recognized as valid by the law, has been analyzed in the previous chapter. Following are cases included in this category.

DEFECTIVE LINEAGE: *THE MAMZER*

It is true that marriage is a private agreement between the partners to the covenant. But Jewish law is concerned with more than the individual character and goals; it is also concerned with family background. Traditionally, a moral stain in the family made one unacceptable for Jewish marriage. The child of a defective union, such as adultery or incest, was prohibited from marrying into a family of pure and proven lineage.

At first blush, our egalitarian sensibilities may be offended. Is the child of an adulterous union to blame for the moral infractions of his parents? Clearly our Jewish sense of justice and fairness makes us uncomfortable with the idea of punishing children for the sins of their parents. But the law was designed to serve the Jewish community by defending the integrity of the family unit. To a people who had no weapon of enforcement other than moral suasion, the threat of branding a child *mamzer* was of such force that it prevented immorality from destroying the whole institution of marriage. People might sacrifice their marriage, themselves, even their standing in the community, for the sake of love and sexual fulfillment; but the law correctly saw that they would rarely risk endangering their children. To have caused children to bear the stain of their own immorality was an intolerable burden. That is why the law assumed, according to Maimonides, that an abandoned child (*asufi*) was of doubtful legitimacy, *safek mamzer*. The father would never own up to siring the child, as it would be a living reminder of his waywardness.

Ramban (Deuteronomy 23:3) traces the word *mamzer* to *muzar me-echav*— estranged even from his own family, in his own town, with no one to identify him, because his natural parents will be ashamed to admit the relationship. That is why the commentary, *Baal ha-Turim* (Deut. 23:3) notes that the law of *mamzer* follows the law of the eunuch—as the eunuch cannot father a child so the *mamzer* does not father a child (because, presumably, to do so would be to continue the stain of *mamzer* "even unto the tenth generation"). Because of the fear of the socially horrendous consequences of the state of *mamzerut,* the law was largely successful in keeping Jewish marriages pure.

Rabbi Abbahu, in the Jerusalem Talmud, derives *mamzer* from *mum zar,* which can mean either a blemish, *mum,* derived from two people who should be separate, *zar,* or a blemish that is strange among the Jewish people. Cases of *mamzer* were rare in the Jewish tradition. The Jewish family historically was an institution of great integrity, but the emphasis was not on racial purity— converts could marry into distinguished Israelite families. Indeed, the Rabbis said it is better to marry a convert with good personal qualities than a person of good Jewish family stock who is moody, perpetually angry, and excitable. Their insistence was on the development of *moral* purity and a sense of mission, and that required careful breeding. One of the tests by which one could determine the Jewishness of a spouse was whether he or she was compassionate, humble, and shy, qualities which are touchstones of the Abrahamic heritage.

The Bible says starkly: "A *mamzer* shall not enter into the assembly of the Lord; even unto the tenth generation shall none of his [progeny] enter into the assembly of the Lord" (Deuteronomy 23:3). "Enter into the assembly" is the biblical idiom for marrying into the Jewish community; the "tenth generation" is a round and large number indicating an infinite time.

The *Halakhah* defines a *mamzer* as the issue of a union that is forbidden by the Torah and is punishable by death or *karet*. The Rabbis therefore said, "If she cannot contract a legally valid marriage to others, her offspring is a *mamzer*."

The first category of such prohibition is incest, as outlined in the Bible. The second category of union productive of *mamzerut* is adultery, the sexual union of a man with a woman who is already married to another man. In other words, marriages which are void, such as incest and adultery, produce *mamzerim*. Interfaith marriage is not a marriage voided by the law because, technically, it is not a violation of a prohibition—it never took place. Therefore, its progeny are not *mamzerim*. The third category is the child of parents, one of whom is a *mamzer*. The offspring of the *mamzer* retains that blemish.

No other union, no matter the prohibition, produces a *mamzer*. Thus, the fruit of the union between two unmarried people (who are not incestuously related) is a child without legal stain, and the parents may susbequently marry one another. They need not marry each other, but in the eyes of the law it would be preferable so that the paternity and integrity of the family lineage may be maintained.

Because the *mamzer* suffered a fundamental injustice, the Rabbis of the Talmud limited the application only to progeny of incest and adultery, and absolved the children of other indiscretions. It is remarkable that in this case, the view of Rabbi Akiva—that the offspring of practically *all* biblical violations are *mamzerim*—was not upheld by the *Halakhah*. Instead, the law opted for the view of an obscure sage, Rabbi Simon the Yemenite, who restricted the number of *mamzerim* only to incest and adultery.

It was also for this reason that the Rabbis made every effort to solve all cases of *mamzerut*. The Talmud implies that the biblical verse (Deuteronomy 23:3) that states the *mamzer* may never marry into the Jewish community refers to "tenth generation" rather than "forever," because "in the future world (*le'atid la-vo*) *mamzerim* will be purified." Jewish sensitivity modified the use of "forever" to offer a fragment of hope that the stain might yet be washed out. They went so far as to suggest ways in which to terminate the *mamzer* status for future generations by selective mating, a suggestion that is viable even today.

Indeed, there was no unduly detailed investigation into family lineage when there was no suspicion of *mamzerut;* the tradition wanted no part of crusades or vigilantism to discover ancient, long-buried sins in order to punish innocent progeny. Necessary as the Torah's law is for the protection of the people, its harsh consequences on individual Jews must be limited to those cases that come clearly into focus.

Mamzerim are Jews and are considered so by the law. They are bound by its statutes and, like other Jews, they are expected to conform to them. Their relationship to God is no different from that of any other individual; indeed, a *mamzer* who is a *talmid chakham* (a Torah scholar) takes precedence in terms of honor over a High Priest who is ignorant. Further, biblically, the *mamzer* can become a king of the Jewish people, conforming to the Torah's requirement that he be "thy brother" (Deuteronomy 17:15). His defective ancestry also does not prejudice his rights of inheritance.

The *mamzer's* descendants, however, always remain *mamzerim*. The Talmud's principle is that, in the case of a prohibited marriage, the children follow the "defective" parent.

Thus a *mamzer's* marriage to a legitimate Jew is productive of a *mamzer*. If, however, a *mamzer* married a non-Jewish woman, the paternity is considered legally nonexistent and the child is non-Jewish. If the child subsequently converts to Judaism, there is no stain of *mamzerut*.

The only legal disability imposed upon the *mamzer* is that of marriage. The

Bible is clear on this: (Deuteronomy 23:3) The *mamzer* may not marry into the community. If a *mamzer* violates the prohibition and marries a legitimate Jewish person, the marriage is valid but the community is under instruction to encourage divorce. The *mamzer* may marry another *mamzer* provided they are both definitely *mamzerim,* not questionably or doubtfully so. There was a debate in the literature as to whether a *mamzer* may marry a convert to Judaism, and it was finally decided to relax the *mamzer* restriction in this case and permit the marriage.

THE DOUBTFUL MAMZER: *SHE'TUKI*

What of the doubtful *mamzer,* a child whose exact parentage is not known? There are two categories of doubtful *mamzer.* The first is the *she'tuki,* "hush-child," which refers to the product of a promiscuous union, whose unmarried mother cannot or will not identify the man who fathered her child. If the mother is married and her husband did not sire the offspring, the child is a definite *mamzer* (unless the father is a non-Jew, in which case it follows the laws of interfaith marriage.) The *she'tuki* is a doubtful *mamzer,* because we cannot determine whether the natural father was himself a *mamzer,* or was related incestuously to the mother. Since the father's background is doubtful, so is that of his child.

When clarifying lineage, the mother is always believed in her testimony about the child who is, after all, an extension of herself—as the mother is of established legitimate birth so is her child. If she declares her child to be of pure lineage, he is so considered. If she affirms that the father is gentile, the child simply follows her ancestry.

The second type of doubtful *mamzer* is the *asufi,* an abandoned child discovered in a public place. In this case, neither of the parents is known. In a Jewish community of high moral standards, there is a strong possibility that the reason for abandonment is to remove from the child the shame engendered by the *mamzer* stigma. The child is therefore considered a doubtful *mamzer.* If the child is found in a predominantly gentile community, or even in a mixed Jewish-gentile neighborhood, rabbinic edict required formal conversion because the child is assumed to be the issue of a non-Jewish mother. If the child is found near an exclusively Jewish community, he is assumed to be of Jewish parentage, but he remains a doubtful *mamzer.*

This doubtful *mamzer* status depends also on the circumstances of abandonment. For example, if it is a time of war, famine, or depression the child is assumed to have been abandoned for economic or other reasons and is considered to be of legitimate parentage. Similarly, if the infant was obviously cared for by its parents—clothed, circumcised, or abandoned in a sheltered environment like a synagogue—it is considered legitimate. If the child was left uncared for, the legitimacy of his parents remains legally suspended and it is considered a doubtful *mamzer*. If *before* the child is declared by the courts to be *asufi*, someone declares himself a parent, or the doctor or an attendant at the birth offers to testify as to the status of the mother, the testimony is accepted at face value. However, once the child's *asufi* status has been established, the testimony must be in the nature of incontrovertible evidence. In the case of crisis, such as famine, if before or after a man or woman claims the child as his or her own, the statement is accepted even after the child is declared *asufi*.

The marital status of a doubtful *mamzer* is exacerbated because of legal technicalities. Because the doubtful *mamzer* may in fact be a *mamzer,* marriage to a legitimate Jew is not permitted. Ironically, because the doubtful mamzer might in fact be a legitimate Jew, marriage to a definite *mamzer* is also prohibited. There is even difficulty in marrying another "doubtful *mamzer,*" as either of them could be either a legitimate Jew or a definite *mamzer.* In the *very rare* cases of *she'tuki* or *asufi,* the law almost always determines a solution to the doubtfulness of the *mamzer*.

SEXUAL DYSFUNCTION

Is a marriage to one who is sexually incompetent a valid marriage? The ancient concept of the eunuch as recorded in Deuteronomy (23:2) is complicated today by sophisticated surgical procedures such as transexual operations and irreversible vasectomies. Is there a difference between willful castration and congenital sterility?

THE CASTRATED

Revulsion to the eunuch as a cultic functionary or royal social instrument is understandable in a religion that considers the chief blessing to be children, the first biblical command to "be fruitful and multiply," and the most sacred social act to be marriage. It represents the despicable way of life, the Canaanite way, which was the antithesis of the Torah ethic and that which Judaism was designed to overcome and eventually destroy.

Deuteronomy 23:2 says, "He that is crushed (*patzu'a dakka*) or maimed in his privy parts shall not enter into the assembly of the Lord." This verse implies that one who has willfully castrated himself may not marry a Jewish woman. The Amora Samuel establishes that only one who is castrated by "the agency of man" is prohibited to marry, but one who is castrated by "the agency of Heaven" (by illness or accidental injury to the genitals) has no marital restrictions. The intentionally castrated may marry a *she'tuki* or *asufi,* the child whose paternity is unknown and who is technically a doubtful *mamzer*.

THE HERMAPHRODITE

Unlike the willfully castrated, the sexually ambiguous may marry in certain cases because, by definition, the condition is a congenital sexual defect. Two types of people are considered in this catagory, the *tumtum* and the androgyne.

The *tumtum* has underdeveloped or ambiguous genitalia, and it is not possible to detect superficially whether the person is male or female. Thus according to law the *tumtum* is a "doubtful" male or female. The marriage of a *tumtum* to a man or woman is of questionable validity and a divorce is required.

The androgyne has both female and male genitals. This person is treated by most authorities as doubtful male, doubtful female. Since law had to classify technically, the androgyne is legally assumed to be a man who can marry a female. The marriage, nonetheless, has doubtful validity and there is question as to the nature of divorce in case of its termination.

THE AILONIT

The *ailonit* is a pseudo-hermaphrodite, a female with only primary female sexual characteristics. She has a masculine voice and is sterile. Although the law states that any marriage she contracts is void, a divorce is required by rabbinic decree lest others, unaware of her condition, consider Jewish marriage dissoluble without benefit of divorce. (This ruling applies *only* if the husband was unaware of her condition. If he knew of it and married her anyway, the marriage is valid.)

STERILITY

This refers to marrying a congenitally barren woman, or one who is barren as result of medication or surgery. Since the male is obligated by the Torah to procreate, he cannot fulfill his commandment with a sterile woman. However, in a polygamous marriage he could still have accomplished the commandment "be fruitful and multiply," hence the Bible does not prohibit a man from marrying a sterile woman. Once a man has fulfilled the minimum obligation (according to Hillel, siring one son and one daughter, and according to Shammai, two sons), it would seem that he could remarry a barren woman. There is some dispute on this among the rabbinic scholars and a competent rabbinic authority should be consulted on the matter.

PUBLIC MORALITY PROHIBITIONS

DIVORCED WIFE IN REMARRIAGE AFTER SECOND MARRIAGE

There was specific legislation against unions which, while the partners themselves were entirely legitimate, might cause a diminution of the public morality.

If something appeared licentious or promiscuous, it was considered *to-evah* (an abomination) and was prohibited. Such a case is cited in Deuteronomy (24:1–4): "When a man takes a wife and marries her, if then she finds no favor in his eyes because he has found some unseemly thing in her, and he writes her a bill of divorce and puts it in her hand, and sends her out of his house, and she departs out of his house, and if she goes and becomes another man's wife, and the latter husband dislikes her and writes her a bill of divorce and puts it in her hand and sends her out of his house, or if the latter husband dies who took her to be his wife, then her former husband, who sent her away, may not take her again to be his wife after she has been defiled; for that is abomination before the Lord, and you shall not cause the land to sin which the Lord your God gave you for an inheritance."

Ramban explains the biblical laws in this verse as intending forcefully and absolutely to prevent widespread immorality. "The reason for this prohibition is so that people should not exchange their wives with one another: he would be able to write her a bill of divorce at night and in the morning she will return to him. This is the sense of the expression, 'and thou shalt not cause the land to sin,' for this is a great cause of sins. And in the Sifre it is stated, 'And thou shalt not cause the land to sin'—this is intended to admonish the court concerning this." According to Ramban, the Torah's concern is to outlaw "sequential adultery" for those who would practice their immorality *within* the strict confines of the laws of marriage and divorce. If, while ostensibly observing the law, you indulge in something as low as wife swapping, you have brought down the whole exalted concept of the family.

Jeremiah refers to this law as a self-evident illustration of immorality: "If a man sends away his wife and she goes from him and becomes another man's wife, may he return to her again? Will not the land be greatly polluted?" (3:1).

This pertains only if both unions were valid marriages. If one was in harlotry, or in a cohabitation arrangement which authorities decided required no divorce, their subsequent "remarriage" would be permitted. Even if she committed acts of random fornication after her first divorce, if she did not marry anyone else she would be permitted to remarry her husband.

Such questions are both sensitive and complicated and should be referred to competent rabbinic authority for halakhic ruling.

UNFAITHFUL WIFE IN REMARRIAGE

The protection of public morality that inspired the first law inspired another that the Rabbis derive from Deuteronomy 24:1–4, cited above, and is considered by authorities as biblical: A wife who was faithless may not continue to live with her husband. If he divorces her because of her adultery, he may not remarry her, even if she did not remarry another in the meantime, "since she has been defiled." Ramban takes this to mean "defiled to him, because she knew another man."

KOHEN MARRIAGES

The *kohen,* or priest, was historically the chief religious functionary of the Jewish people. He served in the Temple and concerned himself exclusively with the study and practice of the Law, the spiritual development of the Jewish people, and the tenacious preservation of the tradition. His ancestry spans all of Jewish history from the Exodus to this very day. It is also the most distinguished family, having been assigned by Divine election to succeed the firstborn in the religious leadership of the Jews. Together with the king and the Prophets, the judge and the scholar, he was in the top ranks of communal leadership. The king provided national stability, the judge social stability, and the *kohen* religious stability and continuity.

The *kohen* generally had four functions. The first was ceremonial, the offering of sacrifices and the delivery of God's blessings to the people (Numbers 6:22–26). He also cared for the Temple and carried the Ark. His second function was to make decisions. The high *kohen,* during the time of the First Temple, consulted the *Urim* and *Thummim* (the breastplate) in order to obtain a "yes" or "no" answer to questions presenting contradictory possibilities. The third duty was the ritual treatment of disease and *tzaraat* (leprosy) resulting from violations of the moral or religious code. Fourth, the *Kohen* was a judge and a teacher. He participated with the elders in judging (Ezekiel 44:24) and also taught Torah (Deuteronomy 33:10). In the era of the two Temples, these functions were preserved in the expectation that the Sanhedrin would contain *kohanim.* At the destruction of the Second Temple, this function was taken over by the Sages.

The *kohen* priests were *not* similar in function or status to pagan priests. There were no orgiastic elements, no cultic funerary rites, no dramatic pagan symbolizing of the life-and-death cycle. The Torah dramatized this difference by placing certain restrictions on the *kohen:* He is forbidden any contact with the dead, except for his own immediate family and the abandoned dead; he is not permitted to marry a divorcee. The *kohen's* integrity sprang from his purity of birth, belief, and action. His Torah was no esoteric lore of cosmic magic; he dealt with laws and morality and taught them to the community at large.

The *kohen* had a unique mission among Jews, which is clearly distinguished from that of the *navi,* the prophet. The prophet, whose spirit can be traced to the shepherd, primarily stressed inwardness. He was an individualist who had sudden visions of God and exhorted his fellow Jews concerning severe matters such as idolatry, adultery, and murder. The *kohen* was also concerned with inwardness, but he insisted that it be outwardly manifested. His pattern can be traced to the farmer. As the farmer is concerned with rows of seeds, the *kohen* was concerned with the details of his vestments, the measurements of the Tabernacle, the accurate timing of the sacrifices—with order and design. He was not an individualist living outside the community, but one who stayed with the people even in times of the lowest degradation. Despite their differences, the prophet and the priest were considered brothers, as Moses the Prophet and Aaron the Priest were *brothers.*

Though the prophet was recognized as the highest religious type, it was understood that Judaism could not survive without the *kohen* and the detailed laws of tradition. The *Halakhah* embodied prophetic ideals in physical acts, which were administrated by the *kohen*.

Since the laws required meticulous concern for tradition, the stability of an hereditary priesthood was indispensable. The purity of the *kohen's* heredity has guaranteed the purity of his heritage. New scholars arose in every generation and many visionaries were born during the prophetic era; but only the *kohen's* ancestry of service remained intact and unshakable in the flux of history. Perhaps because of this, the Jews are referred to in the Bible as a *mamlekhet kohanim ve'goy kadosh,* a kingdom of *kohanim* and a holy people (Exodus 19:6).

The Bible (Leviticus 21:6–8) records the relationship of the *kohen* and the Israelites. Verse six states that *because of their exalted function,* "they shall be holy unto their God, and not profane the name of their God, for the offerings of the Lord made by fire, the bread of their God, they do offer; therefore shall they be holy." Verse seven emphasizes the *strict requirements for their family purity:* "They shall not take a woman that is a harlot (*zonah*), or profaned (*chalalah*); neither shall they marry a divorced woman (*ge'rushah*); for he is holy unto his God." In Verse eight the Israelites are instructed to honor the *kohen:* "Thou shalt sanctify him therefore; for he offereth the bread of thy God; he shall be holy unto thee; for I the Lord, who sanctify you, am holy."

While the primary functions of the *kohen* have been suspended since the destruction of the Temple—the sacrifices, the consultation of *Urim* and *Thummim,* the treatment of impurities, and the teaching of Torah—some functions remain. He delivers the priestly blessing in the synagogue on holidays in the Diaspora and daily in Israel; and he officiates as the representative of the Temple in the Redemption of the First-Born at the ceremony thirty days after the birth of the first-born male.

Because of his historic association with the Temple and his hereditary position of religious leadership, he is accorded distinguished honors. He is called first to the Torah (only if there is no *kohen* does an Israelite receive that honor), and he has the privilege of leading the grace after meals. If he forgoes the honor, the leader must recognize his permission.

Just as the *kohen* has certain honors, he also has certain restrictions. He may have no contact with a corpse or be within seven feet (four cubits) from it, be it in a chapel or a grave in the cemetery, or be under the same roof with a corpse unless there is a permanent partition between them. Even today this restriction is enforced. The main highway from Jerusalem to Jericho was built by the Jordanians over a portion of the Mount of Olives cemetery. Since halakahically the *kohen* may not use the road, signposts indicate an alternate route for *kohanim.*

A major set of restrictions concerns marriage. As the sacrifice he offered could have no blemish, the *kohen* himself could have no blemish. Thus to maintain the purity of his lineage he was kept to stricter marriage standards than his Jewish brothers. In addition to prohibitions that apply for all other Jews, the following partners are specifically prohibited to the *kohen.*

A *kohen* may not marry *ge'rusha* (a divorcee); or *chalalah* (a woman of defective *kohen* status); or *zonah* (a woman whose sexual relationships violated the law); or *giyoret* (a convert) or *chalutzah* (a Levirate widow). If he does marry any of them, his wife becomes a *chalalah,* unfit for a future marriage to a *kohen,* and their children likewise become *chalalim.*

The law of the *kohen* is essentially concerned with the pure status of the sons. The children follow the status of the father in terms of "tribe"—*kohen, levi,* or Israelite—unlike the determination of Jew or non-Jew, which follows the mother. The son, then, inherits the *kohen* status and bequeaths it in turn to his son. The offspring of a marriage between an Israelite male and a *kohen's* daughter would be an Israelite and not a *kohen.* The reference in the Bible is to *be'nei Aharon,* the *sons* of Aaron. Therefore, a *kohen* daughter may marry any of those prohibited strictly to the *kohen;* she is subject solely to the laws that inform all Jewish marriages.

DIVORCEE (GE'RUSHAH)

The *kohen* may not marry a divorcée, regardless of the cause of the divorce, the circumstances, or the duration of the previous marriage. If a Jewish divorce was issued for any reason, even though the couple never lived together as man and wife, she may not be married to the *kohen.* This is true even if a divorce was not biblically necessary, but was required by the Rabbis to prevent public misconception. The issuance of a divorce always precludes marriage to a *kohen.* While it is a virtue for an Israelite to remarry the wife he divorced (if she had not married another man in the meantime), the *kohen* may not even remarry his own wife.

If the *kohen* marries a divorcée despite the restrictions, he has violated the law and is under constant obligation to terminate the marriage even though it is technically valid. Any offspring of the marriage are *chalal,* of defective *kohen* status. If the child is a girl, she is not permitted to marry a *kohen;* if it is a boy, he is prohibited from functioning as a *kohen*. The *kohen's* wife becomes a *chalalah* as well. If he married a divorcée who was already pregnant, her child is not a *chalal,* regardless of who the father was. Since she was not married at the time, the child was not conceived in sin (*lo ba mi-tipat aveirah*).

LEVIRATE WIDOW (*CHALUTZAH*)

The Levirate marriage is commanded by the Torah for widows whose late husband was childless. The husband's brother is required to marry her in order to perpetuate the family of his late brother. In later years, however, the Rabbis saw this as a negative factor and required the ceremony of *chalitzah* to terminate the requisite marriage to her brother-in-law.

A rabbinic dictum holds that *chalitzah* is similar to divorce in regard to a *kohen* marriage, hence a *chalutzah* is not permitted to marry a *kohen*.

If a widow who is a doubtful *chalutzah* marries a *kohen,* no defect is ascribed to their children. Because it was a rabbinic decree, and she is only technically a doubtful *chalutzah,* her offspring are considered full-fledged *kohanim* and no divorce is necessary.

DEFECTIVE KOHEN STATUS (*CHALALAH*)

Chalalah is defined as a defect resulting solely from a specifically *kohen* violation. It pertains either to the offspring of a prohibited *kohen* marriage, or to a woman permitted to marry an Israelite but not a *kohen,* and who has married the *kohen* in disregard of the law. Technically, it signifies one who is "profaned" from the priesthood.

If the male offspring of the prohibited *kohen* marriage (the *chalal*) marries an Israelite woman, she becomes a *chalalah*. Thus the *chalal* male offspring continues to pass on the defective *kohen* status. The female offspring, when marrying Israelites, terminate the defective status. The children of that marriage may marry *kohanim* because the children follow the father's lineage.

The *kohen* himself cannot have his priesthood removed. If he terminates the prohibited marriage, by death or divorce, he may resume his *kohen* privileges. There is no such thing as the "defrocking" of a *kohen.*

ZONAH

The term *zonah* popularly conjures up the image of the harlot. Indeed, in the Bible, a *zonah* was a woman who sold herself to men for gain or lust (except in specific cases where *zonah* may imply an "innkeeper" who serves food) (Joshua 2:1), and this was the view of Rabbi Akiva expressed in the Talmud. Rabbi Elazar considered that any contact between unmarried singles brands the woman a *zonah* and she is therefore prohibited to a *kohen;* Rabbi Huna included lesbians under this category. Maimonides, following a different talmudic opinion, limits *zonah* to incestuous relationships and those with non-Jews. The definition of *zonah* in the later codes and commentaries follows the opinion that *zonah* refers to a technical legal parameter not directly related to harlotry.

The Jewish people fought an incessant and ultimately successful battle against professional immorality. There was no carnality in religion and no religion in carnality, according to contemporary scholar Louis Epstien. David Shapiro, a Jewish philosopher, notes that the Torah did not technically command the *woman* to "be fruitful and multiply," in order to remove her sexual status from religious law and to create as much distance as possible from the *ke'deshah* orgiastic rites of idolatry.

In the *Halakhah,* a *zonah* is simply one who enters into a sinful union. It is not like the sinful union of the *chalalah* which violates the specific *kohen* legislation, but one which violates the basic moral prohibitions (general illicit relations) that apply to all Jews.

There are two schools of thought as to which illicit unions are included under this term. Maimonides, Rashi, Rashba and others hold that all biblically-prohibited unions render the woman a *zonah.* These prohibitions include those which violate general negative laws (*chayyvei lav*) such as marriage to a *mamzer;* violations of positive laws, such as marriage to a Moabite convert; transgressions of those laws that incur the punishment of death or excision, such as incestuous relations; or the marriage of a *kohen* to a widow who had been guilty of adultery. (An adulterous wife may marry another Israelite even after compulsory divorce from her husband or his death, but she may not marry a *kohen.*) Each of these women is considered a *zonah.* There are exceptions to this rule: Prohibited unions, such as those with an animal, are considered criminal and punishable by death, but they do not brand the participant as *zonah* in a way that would prevent her marriage to a *kohen.*

Another school of thought was that of the Tosafists, Raavad, Rosh and Tur. They held that only violations of prohibitions that incur death and excision, such as incest and adultery, brand a woman *zonah.* But violating general negative or positive commandments does not categorize the woman as *zonah,* although she is nonetheless prohibited from marrying the *kohen.* But if she is prohibited to a *kohen,* what difference does it make if she is technically a *zonah* or not? The answer is that the child of a *zonah* may not marry a *kohen,* while the child of a prohibited but non-*zonah* marriage may marry a *kohen.*

The following are additional instances of *zonah:* (1) A Levirate widow who marries without the necessary *chalitzah* is considered a *zonah,* since her marriage was not valid, and she may not marry a *kohen.* (2) A woman, divorced from her husband, who marries another man who then dies or divorces her, and she subsequently remarries her first husband. She has violated a biblical law but she is not a *zonah,* and her child is permitted to marry a *kohen.* (3) A woman who has committed secondary (rabbinically-legislated) incest is not a *zonah,* and she is biblically permitted to marry a *kohen.*

FEMALE CONVERT *(GIYORET)*

Converts, because they come from diverse cultures, are all classed in the category of *statutory zonah.* This is no reflection whatsoever upon the integrity of the convert; on the contrary, righteous converts were held in great personal esteem. But the law had to pronounce on converts as a group, because no investigation could prove totally reliable. Also, one must remember that the boundaries of the *zonah* category were not those of the harlot, but were related to the peculiar *kohen* requirements.

The codifiers disagree as to whether the classification of *giyoret* as *zonah* is biblical or rabbinic. Indeed, according to Raavad, it reflects only the *kohen's* concern with the purity of his lineage. Thus a child of parents who were both converts before they married is technically permitted to marry a *kohen* because *horatah ve'ledatah bi-kedushah* (she was conceived and born in sanctity as a Jew). But the *kohanim* took upon themselves an extra stringency and did not permit it. The blemish here is not *zonah,* as one can become a *zonah* only as a consequence of a willful act—one is not born a *zonah.* It was then decided that the *kohen* should preferably not marry her but, having done so, he need not be compelled to divorce her. Such a marriage is legal and their child is not a *chalal.*

RABBINIC ENACTMENTS

The Sages enacted stringent laws to protect the integrity of the family, to prevent assault from unsuspected sources, and to isolate causes of potential disruption.

SECONDARY INCEST

Rabbinic law concerned itself primarily with extensions of biblical incest in the ascending and descending lines. The specific forbidden relationships in this category were mentioned in Chapter Four.

Biblical and rabbinic incest are legally quite different: A marriage that violates biblical incest laws voids the marriage; a rabbinic incest violation does not impugn the validity of the marriage, the legitimacy of the children, or their fitness to marry a *kohen.*

BIGAMY

Judaism's lifelong concern for the protection of the family as the core functional unit of society required that its stability be ensured, and its responsibility for raising the next generation be encouraged. To accomplish these goals, parentage had to be unmistakably established. *Maternity* is usually biologically provable—a woman gave birth to a specific child, and witnesses were present (or could have been present) to prove it. Because of the nine-month hiatus between conception and birth, however, *paternity* must be established by law.

Thus, in order to ensure correct identification of the father, a woman could not be married to more than one husband. The presumption of the law, in the absence of contradictory evidence, is that her husband is the father of her child. If it is legally established that another man fathered the child the woman is guilty of adultery, her paramour is an adulterer, and both are biblically to be punished by death. The child is considered illegitimate (*mamzer*) and may not marry a Jew of legitimate paternity.

The term *kiddushin* (marriage) implies exclusivity; hence there can be no valid *kiddushin* between a woman and her second husband if her first husband is still alive and they are not legally divorced. Biblically, if an adulterous marriage is performed it need not be dissolved by divorce since it is not recognized as a marriage in the first place. The Rabbis, however, instituted the requirement for divorce in most such cases so that unknowing outsiders would not assume that a Jewish marriage may be dissolved simply by agreement or abandonment. Indeed, a woman must be divorced by her first husband (*mi-de'oraita*) according to biblical law because a husband may not remain with a provenly adulterous wife; and, many authorities hold, also by her adulterous paramour (*mi-de'rabbanan*) according to rabbinic law, to prevent public confusion.

While polyandry (more than one husband) is regarded as abhorrent by the Bible, polygamy (more than one wife) is technically permitted. The Jewish tradition, however, subsequently banned polygamy. In a polygamous marriage, both maternity and paternity are clearly established. Hence a man's marriage to another wife is biblically valid, and can be dissolved only by death or divorce. The children are considered legitimate.

Domestic peace was equally significant to the life of the family as it was considered the only environment in which to raise children and encourage human happiness. The second wife of a polygamous marriage was termed *tzarah,* (troublesome rival) to connote a natural and destructive competition between two women married to the same man. Indeed, the talmudic Sage Rav said: "Marry not two wives. But if you marry two, then marry a third." The rivalry inherent in polygamy jeopardizes the peace of the home and threatens the happiness of the children. In time it became obvious that the Torah's permission for a man to have more than one wife could *not* be handled by most men; psychologically, economically, and in every other way, it became an unmanageable burden.

Accordingly, polygamy was rare even as early as the prophetic period. In the

Talmud, the Sages legally circumscribed polygamy by declaring that it was permissible only if the husband could properly fulfill his marital duties toward each of his wives. One early opinion held that upon taking a second wife, a man must divorce his first wife if she so desires. Similarly, he may not marry a second woman if he promised his first wife at their marriage that he would not do so. Moreover, he may not do so if local custom favors monogamy; where such custom prevails a girl marries with the implied understanding that she will be treated like all the other married women in the community. By the year 1000, the leading authority in the Ashkenazic Diaspora, Rabbenu Gershom, invoked the overriding ethical principle that one must at all costs prevent matrimonial strife. Accordingly, he decreed a one thousand-year ban (*cherem*) against all those in his jurisdiction (excluding Sephardim and Yemenite Jews) who commit polygamy. This ban was renewed for all Jews by Israel's Chief Rabbi when it expired in 1950. Known as "Cherem de Rabbenu Gershom," it is in force regardless of the wishes of the husband or the consent of the wife.

If a man violates this decree and marries a second woman while he is still married to his first wife (e.g., if he did not get a Jewish divorce), the second marriage is rabbinically prohibited but legally valid. However, the first wife can require the Jewish court to compel her husband, in communities where the courts have such powers, to divorce the other woman. Since the first wife cannot be forced to live under such conditions, she may also ask that the court order her husband to divorce her and indemnify her according to the provisions of the *ketubah*. If he gives his first wife a divorce, he may remain married to the second wife even though he married her in violation of the ban.

MARRIAGE WITH CO-RESPONDENT IN PREVIOUS DIVORCE

The protection of the family required not only the prohibition and punishment of adultery and other forms of immorality, but the enactments of laws depriving the parties to the sin from enjoying the consequences of their immorality—especially in light of the fact that biblical punishment could not be executed. Thus if a man's intimacies with a married woman were the cause of her divorce, and adultery can be proven, their subsequent marriage is prohibited. If adultery is rumored but not proven and despite the warnings of her husband (before two witnesses) she is found in a compromising situation, the subsequent marriage is biblically prohibited. If it is only rumored, it is a matter of rabbinic restriction. In this case, if marriage was contracted in violation of the decree and there are no children from this second marriage, divorce is compulsory. If there are children, the overriding consideration is their protection and their good name, and the marriage may continue in force.

To prevent collusion, this applies not only to a co-respondent (for whom this is a form of punishment as well) but also to anyone who is solely responsible for the execution of a previous divorce. Thus the same law holds for a man who is the only witness to the disappearance of the husband and whose testimony enables the woman to remarry. If she remarries the witness, the law may well have been compromised. Similarly, a judge who ruled in favor of an annulment may not marry the woman involved.

MARRIAGE BETWEEN A JEW AND A CONVERTED GENTILE LOVER

Marriage between a Jew and a gentile lover who converts to Judaism is not rabinically permitted. The Sages had no interest in sanctioning marital relations that began in sin. However, if the couple marries in defiance of rabbinic law they may remain married, even if they have no children.

JEWS WHO COHABITED BEFORE MARRIAGE

Premarital sexual relations between a Jewish man and a Jewish woman are considered improper but have no legal impact on their future marriage. This holds true as long as they were not prohibited partners at the time of their cohabitation. Indeed, the Bible (Exodus 22:15) considers their marriage, though not their premarital cohabitation, entirely proper. If he decides not to marry her, he is also prohibited from marrying the woman's sister, mother, or daughter. The Rabbis forbade this to protect the woman and to stabilize the family; they believed that the visits of his former lover would be a constant temptation for the man and remind him of his exciting past. If the marriage takes place despite the law, it is valid.

REMARRIAGE AFTER A SEXUALLY-MOTIVATED DIVORCE

The following prohibitions were enacted to protect public welfare:

A man may not remarry his wife if he divorced her because (1) she was an *ailonit* (pseudo-hermaphrodite), but not if she was childless for other reasons; (2) she had no regular menstrual cycle; or (3) her conduct caused him to suspect her of unfaithfulness.

Since all of these conditions may have been temporary, it was feared that the husband might entertain the possibility of remarriage when the temporary disabilities corrected themselves, and would try to annul his divorce. If his former wife had married someone else in the meantime, the marital confusion would be intolerable.

TEMPORARY DISQUALIFICATIONS

Certain days of the calendar, such as those for remembrance of historic grief or days of festive joy, are not considered auspicious for marriage; however, a marriage contracted on these days is valid.

In addition, the law does not permit marriage under the following circumstances:

MOURNING

A mourner for any one of the seven relatives for whom the laws of mourning are obligatory (i.e., father, mother, sister, brother, son, daughter, mate) may not marry for thirty days from the time of death. This rule has the following exceptions which are designed to alleviate specific family problems.

A man may marry after seven days of mourning if he has not fulfilled the law of procreation. Women should wait thirty days before remarrying.

After the death of his wife, a man may not remarry until after the three festivals, Passover, Shavuot and Sukkot, have passed. This waiting period was designed for good psychological reasons and should not be arbitrarily waived. A husband's memory and the experience of two wives should not be easily intermixed; moreover, a significant hiatus between marriages is a sign of respect to both women. However, if the husband is childless, or has young children to whom he cannot give adequate care, or if he is personally helpless without a wife, he may remarry earlier.

HAVCHANAH: NINETY DAYS FOLLOWING DIVORCE OR CHALITZAH

A woman may not remarry until after ninety full days have passed, a period that serves to separate the sexual experience of two husbands. This is true for all women, old or young, widowed or divorced, fertile or sterile, and even for a woman who miscarried after her husband's death, or whose husband had been in prison for years before dying. The only exception to this rule is remarriage to the same mate.

The purpose of the delay is to determine whether the woman is pregnant, so that we may know whether the child born after the second marriage has the first or the second husband as father—"to distinguish between the seed of the first and the seed of the second husband." This clarity of paternity is so morally compelling that the law covers all contingencies and is applied in all cases, even when it is known that the first husband could not have impregnated her.

A gentile couple converting to Judaism must wait ninety days after conversion before marrying, so that it can be determined whether their child is conceived as a Jew or a gentile. In urgent circumstances, however (e.g., when the husband must go immediately to war), the Rabbis relax the time limit if reliable medical testing verifies nonpregnancy. (This is in contrast to their unbending stance in instances where a child's paternity is in question. In such cases, the Talmud avers, the Rabbis would not compromise even if the Prophet Elijah appeared and confirmed a woman's nonpregnancy.)

There is no required waiting period for an unmarried woman after previous sexual contacts. The Tosafists hold that the law gives permission to a rape victim to marry immediately, if she so desires, in order to protect the reputation of the child.

PREGNANT AND NURSING WOMEN

Pregnant women who are widowed or divorced should not be remarried until they give birth. The Talmud fears that the new husband may be somewhat reckless in his sexual association and thus harm the child, or simply not provide properly for it during that period.

The Talmud, in a profound play on words, derives this law from the Bible (Proverbs 23:10): "Remove not the ancient landmarks which they of old have set, and enter not into the fields of the fatherless." There also may be an added dimension of confusion—that is, conflict in the woman of the intermixing of her present husband and the father of the child. If a couple marries despite this stricture the law considers the marriage valid, but they are to remain separated for the duration of the pregnancy.

A nursing mother should ideally wait twenty-four months before marrying (so that if she becomes pregnant again, she is fit for nursing), though rabbinic authorities today consider fifteen months an acceptable minimum. A number of factors may contribute to a possible further relaxing of the time requirement: if the mother was not able to nurse at the time of the divorce or her husband's death, if she had not nursed for three months prior to that, or if she is poor and marriage would help sustain her and the child. The Sages did not wish to tempt a well-meaning mother into giving the child to a nursemaid in midterm, or to start the child with a nursemaid. They believed that no woman hired for a fee is as reliable as the natural mother. If a nursing mother marries anyway, the *Halakhah* requires that she divorce and then remarry at the end of the weaning period.

SUMMARY OF ALL PROHIBITED MARRIAGES

The following summary of marriages prohibited by Jewish religious law details specifically whom one may and may not marry.

A MAN MAY NOT MARRY:

1. Anyone not of the Jewish faith.
2. The daughter of an adulterous or incestuous union (*mamzeret*).
3. A married woman, until the civil *and* Jewish divorces have been completed.
4. His own divorced wife after her remarriage to another man and the latter's death or divorce.

5. A widow of a childless husband who is survived by a brother, until after the *chalitzah* ceremony has been performed.
6. A married woman with whom he committed adultery.
7. A *kohen* may not marry a divorced woman, a *chalutzah*-widow, a convert, a *zonah*, or a *chalalah*.
8. Relatives (primary and secondary incest):
   (a) His mother, grandmother and ascendants; the mother of his grandfather; his stepmother, the wife of his paternal grandfather, and of his ascendants; and the wife of his maternal grandfather.
   (b) His daughter, granddaughter, great granddaughter and her descendants; his daughter-in-law; the wife of his son's son, and descendants; and the wife of his daughter's son.
   (c) His wife's daughter or her granddaughter and descendants.
   (e) His sister, half-sister, his full or half-brother's wife (divorced or widowed) except for Levirate marriage with the widow of a childless brother, and the full or half-sister of his divorced wife in her lifetime.
   (f) His aunt, and uncle's wife (divorced or widowed), whether the uncle be a full or half-brother of his father or mother.

A MAN MAY MARRY:

1. His step-sister (a step-parent's daughter from a previous marriage, even though they were raised together as brother and sister from their earliest youth).
2. His stepfather's wife (divorced or widowed).
3. The daughter-in-law of his brother or his sister.
4. His niece. In American and English civil law, a man may not marry a niece who is the daughter of *his* brother or sister, but *may* marry a niece who is the daughter of *his wife's* brother or sister. The halakhic permission—even encouragement—to marry the daughter of a brother or sister is superseded by the civil law's prohibition in this case.
5. His cousin.
6. His stepson's wife (divorced or widowed).
7. His deceased wife's sister, but not his divorced wife's sister.
8. A woman with whom he had relations in their unmarried state.
9. A *kohen* may marry a widow (who was never divorced).

A WOMAN MAY NOT MARRY:

1. Anyone not of the Jewish faith.
2. The son of an adulterous or incestuous union (*mamzer*).
3. A married man, until the civil *and* Jewish divorces have been completed.

4. A married man with whom she committed adultery.
5. Her divorced husband, after the death or divorce of her second husband.
6. The following relatives (primary and secondary incest):
   (a) Her father, grandfather and ascendants; her stepfather; and the husband of her grandmother and of her ascendants.
   (b) Her son, grandson, great grandson; her son-in-law, and the husband of her granddaughter and descendants.
   (c) Her husband's father, or grandfather, and the father of her father-in-law and ascendants; and the father of her mother-in-law.
   (d) Her husband's son or grandson and descendants.
   (e) Her brother, half-brother, her full or half-sister's divorced husband in her sister's lifetime, and her husband's brother.
   (f) Her nephew.
7. A convert may not marry a *kohen*.

A WOMAN MAY MARRY:

1. Her step-brother (a step-parent's son from a previous marriage, even though they were raised together as brother and sister from their earliest youth).
2. Her step-mother's former husband (divorced or widowed).
3. The son-in-law of her brother or sister.
4. Her cousin.
5. Her sister's husband (after her sister-s death, not divorce).
6. Her uncle. In Jewish incest law, an aunt-nephew marriage is prohibited, but an uncle-niece marriage is permitted even though the state prohibits it. A man may marry his deceased wife's sister, but a woman may not marry her deceased husband's brother. Even a childless widow, whom the Bible commanded to marry her husband's brother, must today receive *chalitzah*, enforced separation.
7. A man with whom she had relations in their unmarried state.
8. A *kohen's* daughter does not have the restrictions of a male *kohen*.

CHAPTER 6

Preferred Partners

Prohibited partners are defined in detail in the Torah, but no clear guidelines are given as to the qualities one *should* seek in a mate. Scripture offers law, not marriage counseling. To marry a Jew is an unquestioned requirement, but beyond that one must seek a Jewish mate with good character who is suitable in terms of goals and background.

Me'iri cautions: "The goal [in analyzing a mate's qualities] is not to look for a *pe'sul* [a defect]. But if, for example, one learns of a mate's parents that they are evil, that they reject the 'fear of Heaven,' and are personally and financially corrupt, even though he finds no obvious legal defect in them, it is a sign that there exists a hidden defect." The *Sefer Hasidim* emphatically says: "The offspring of a Jew who married a bride *converted* to Judaism, but who was a woman of good heart and modesty and charity, must be preferred to the children of a *Jewess* by birth who is, however, devoid of the same good qualities."

In Jewish literature, the Sages refer to the qualities in a *woman* that a *man* should seek. This is because throughout history it was the man who went forward to seek out and woo the woman; as the Rabbis say, "to look for the rib God took from man to form woman." Of course, a *woman* should seek similar qualities in a *man*. What follows is a cursory glance at the values in prospective mates that the Rabbis considered most important in marriage.

Two observations must be made at the outset: First, the list is not exhaustive. Moreover, it consists of generalizations that obviously cannot apply to every individual. The complexities of matchmaking are so great that it is considered to occupy all of God's time since creation. But because these observations were made by renowned scholars and saintly men endowed with great insight and wisdom, they must be taken seriously.

Second, the Rabbis never tired of warning against making precipitous decisions in so important and consequential a matter. The author of *Menorat ha-Maor* suggests an analogy: "When a person wants to sow seeds, he looks for the choicest field that he can find and buys it for much money so that the produce will be good and beautiful. And if that is what a person will do for a crop to eat or sell, then it is surely appropriate to do whatever one can for the seed that comes from his loins in order to give birth to a child who is right and proper." The Talmud cautions: *meton nesiv itetah* (wait before marrying the woman), to which Rashi comments: "Wait until you can look into her actions, to be sure that she is not wicked and argumentative." Even in an age when marriage was arranged by parents, the bride and groom had to see one another and give mutual approval before the wedding. This practice was even agreed to by Maimonides, the strictest interpreter of the sex laws. Should they fail to do so, only to learn later of mutual revulsion, they would be in violation of the commandment, "And thou shalt love they neighbor as thyself." In *Avot de'Rabbi Natan,* Rabbi Akiva says: "One who marries a person who is not right for him violates five commandments: 'Not to take revenge,' 'Not to bear a grudge,' 'Not to hate thy brother in thy heart,' 'Love thy neighbor as thyself,' and 'Thy brother shall live with thee.' Moreover, because of mutual hatred, he will cause the nullification of the *mitzvah* of 'be fruitful and multiply.' "

QUALITIES OF THE IDEAL MATE

The first prayer in the Bible is uttered by Eliezer, Abraham's servant, as he sets out to seek the ideal wife for Isaac. He is the first person of whom it is expressly recorded that he prayed for divine guidance at a critical moment in his life; not a formal prayer, but a "prayer of the heart," uttered spontaneously. He did not pray for divine intervention, but that his criteria for selecting the ideal mate be in accordance with God's will. The confident assurance of Abraham that Eliezer will succeed in this venture are the last words scripture records of the Patriarch: "He will send His angel before you, and you shall take a wife for my son from there" (Genesis 24:7).

The image of an ideal wife (Genesis 24:12 ff) projected by the servant is fascinating. He notes Rebekah's beauty and he stresses her chastity, but the dominant criterion that emerges is that she is generous, hospitable to strangers, and kind to animals. These qualities of compassion in the Jewish character remained the most important of all virtues throughout the millenial history.

Compassion is one of the three qualities considered the hallmark of all Jewish women, indeed, of all Jews. If a person does not exhibit at least one of these three qualities—modesty, compassion, and kindness—one should investigate further, as their absence indicates the possibility of an alien intrusion into the family tree. The *Shulchan Arukh* states that, "It is improper to marry one who lacks these distinguishing characteristics. . . . So whoever is arrogant, cruel and hates people and does no kindness is suspected of being a Gibeonite [not a Jew]." Every discussion of good marriage, peace in the home, or good children refers to one or more of these qualities.

COMPASSION (*RACHMANUT*)

Authentic Jews are "compassionate children of the compassionate;" if one shows no compassion, one is not a child of Abraham. God is referred to in the Talmud as *Rachmana* (The Compassionate). The word for compassion, *rachmanut,* derives from *rechem,* womb, calling to mind the warmth and care of the mother for her child. The Sages held that women are especially gifted with this quality, and they humanize society by subjecting all actions to the criteria of compassion.

Eliezer taught the world that one of the crucial tests is whether a person exhibits this compassion to animals. Causing pain to living beings is a sin and a sure sign of curelty, the antonym of compassion. Hence ritual slaughter is designed to be as humane as possible; hunting is a crime; one is not permitted to take the eggs from a bird's nest in the presence of the mother (Deuteronomy 22:10); and the ox is not to be muzzled while plowing (25:4).

The blessing of God for new garments (*shehecheyanu*) is not to be made over leather shoes because an animal's life had to be taken to provide them. This is one of the reasons for the prohibition of wearing leather shoes, one of the five "afflictions" observed on Yom Kippur. It is not proper to pray to God for compassion for oneself while wearing an article of clothing that testifies to one's lack of compassion to animals.

Compassion must be shown especially for the anguish of the disadvantaged—the orphan, the stranger, the widow. Visiting the sick and comforting the bereaved are especially highlighted because they require a great deal of extra concern and enthusiasm, but compassion does not mean wallowing in pity or perpetually sobbing for all the ills of the world. It must be founded in reason and mature understanding, and it must be constructive and imaginative in its application. Rabbi Hayyim Soloveichik, the "Brisker Rav," once remarked that a local do-gooder loved charity too much to be really charitable in the sense that is beyond dispensing funds.

MODESTY (*TZE'NIUT*)

Modesty is the foundation of Jewish values and is one of the fundamental underpinnings of the Jewish family. It is popularly thought to apply primarily to women, but it is a desirable quality in men as well. Although the term is generally used for relations between men and women, it is meant to apply to people in all situations.

Tze'niut means modesty, simplicity, a touch of bashfulness, and reserve. But perhaps above these, it signifies privacy. It is the hallmark of Jewish marriage, and the Rabbis refer to it as the specific quality to look for in the ideal mate. The classical symbol of *tze'niut* is the veil. It bespeaks privacy, a person apart; Isaiah (3:18) calls it *tiferet* (glory). The Assyrians ruled that a harlot may *not* wear a veil, to imply that she is on *public* exhibit. The veil was instinctively donned by Rebekah as soon as she observed her future husband in the distance (Genesis 24:65). That is one reason why the ceremony immediately prior to the wedding celebration is the *bedeken,* or the veiling of the bride by the groom, who blesses the bride with the ancient words spoken to Rebekah.

The principle of *tze'niut* rejects all nudity, not only in public, but also before family members at home. (thus one must not pray or recite the *She'ma* prayer while one is naked or standing in the presence of a naked person). The rejection of nudity recalls Adam and Eve who, after committing the first sin, realized they were naked and instinctively felt ashamed and hid (Genesis 2:25). The same attitude reappears when Noah curses Ham, who saw his father exposed (Gen.9:21–27).

Tze'niut also implies modesty in dress. Traditionally covered parts of the body should not be exposed, although one can dress stylishly. This attitude issues from a very highly refined sense of shame, an emotion often denigrated today in the name of freedom. Not only did the Bible prohibit removing all clothing, it did not permit wearing any garments belonging to the opposite sex (Deuteronomy 22:5) as this might lead to unnatural lusts, lascivious thoughts, and a freer intermingling between the sexes.

Tze'niut means discreet habits, quiet speech, and affections privately expressed, and infers the avoidance of grossness, boisterous laughter, raucous behavior, even "loud" ornaments. This is not merely a series of behavioral niceties, a sort of bible's guide to etiquette, but a philosophy of life.

This concept of modesty does not imply a rejection of the body. On the contrary, the Jewish people are taught to respect the body. Hillel did not bathe solely for hygienic reasons, but to care for the body—the most magnificent creation of God. Rabban Gamaliel, on seeing a beautiful person, praised God. One consequence of this concept is the emphasis on the need for marriage and on healthy sexual relations between husband and wife.

Tze'niut was intended to preserve the sanctity of the inner human being from assault by the coarseness of daily life. The Bible (Psalm 45:14) says *Kol ke'vudah bat melekh penimah* (the whole glory of the daughter of the king is within— some translate it playfully as, "the whole glory of the daughter is the royalty within"). Dignity comes not from exposure and indecent exhibition, but from discretion and the assurance that the human being will be considered a private, sensitive being, not merely a body.

The antonym of *tze'niut* is *hefkerut,* abandon, looseness, the absence of restraint and inhibition. In its extreme, it is gross immorality, *gilui arayot* (the uncovering of nakedness). *Tze'niut* is *covering, vulgarity* is *uncovering.* Vulgarity that is repeated ceases to astonish us or to shock our moral sensibilities. Thus the canons of taste have degenerated as immorality has increased. Those who would rather be clothed than exposed are considered square and puritanical, victims of the centuries-old repression of healthy instincts.

Privacy, in contemporary parlance, refers primarily to property. Sarah Handelman observed that "privacy refers to 'property,' not to 'person.' Our homes are our inviolate castles: 'Private Property—No Trespassing.' Our gems, stocks and bonds are hidden away in vaults. But our bodies, and the precious inner jewels of our personalities, are open to all comers. Nothing is inviolable there. God forbid that someone should know your bank balance, but a casual meeting with a stranger at a bar is warrant for immediate sexual intimacy." The Talmud has an interesting comment on privacy as it relates to persons and property: Privacy was required for women who did their laundering in a brook, because they had to uncover their legs. The Talmud ruled that private *property* rights had to be violated to protect the privacy of persons, "because Jewish women cannot be expected to humiliate themselves at the laundering brook." Because of such legal decisions, moral principles are still relevant to Jews. It is said that *Ein be'not yisrael hefker,* (the daughters of Israel are not in a state of abandonment, available for every public use). The vulgarities of society can be symbolized by the biblical phrase *Nezem zahav be'af chazir,* (A gold ring in the swine's snout). That which is pure gold, the God-given ability to reproduce, is so often used for wading through the public mud.

"A man should always be watchful of the possibility of moral abandonment . . . for it will cause all he owns to go to waste . . . as a worm in a sesame plant who eats everything within, without anyone noticing it, and all that is left is the shell." The gradual abandonment of *tze'niut* has proceeded virtually unobstructed and undetected, until all that remains is only an outer shell of morality.

SCHOLARSHIP (*LIMMUD TORAH*)

The study of Torah is Judaism's highest ideal. Nobility in Jewish society was limited to the wise men of the community who studied Torah "by day and by night," not for the sake of gain or for prestige, but *lishmah,* for itself. The very first petition to God in the Silent Devotion prayed three times a day is a petition for intelligence. The Rabbis gave it such a high priority that they declared, "A Torah scholar of illegitimate birth takes precedence over a high priest ignoramus."

Accordingly, a parent's greatest achievement is the marriage of a daughter to a *talmid chakham* (scholar) or a son to a *bat talmid chakham* (the daughter of a scholar). The Talmud urges, "One should sell even everything he owns in order to marry a Torah scholar's daughter, and one should likewise marry his daughter to a Torah scholar." The reason for marrying a scholar is self-evident in light of the hierarchy of Jewish values. The Talmud says the reason for marrying a scholar's daughter is "so that in case he dies or is forced into exile, his children will be scholars" (because their mother, as well as their father, has espoused the ideal of Torah study). Today, one may add, the ideal wife to seek should *herself* be scholarly, not necessarily only the *daughter* of a scholar.

The Talmud turns to hyperbole to emphasize the exalted goals one should seek in a marriage mate: "All the Prophets prophesied only so that a person should marry his daughter to a Torah scholar"; and, "whosoever marries his daughter to a Torah scholar, the Torah considers him as though he cleaved unto the *Shekhinah* (the indwelling of God's presence)." This emphasis on scholarship, translated to a secularized form, probably accounts for the disproportionate number of Jews on the list of Nobel Laureates and on faculties and campuses of American colleges. Torah scholarship has thrived in all the countries of the Jewish dispersion and in every century of the Jewish millenial history despite the condition of the Jew, the degree of persecution, the lure of alien temptations, or the abject poverty of society. Ludwig Lewisohn ends his little book on the Jewish heritage with this story:

> After the great martyrdom and the small liberation in 1946, a little group of surviving Jews made their way westward from Siberia whither the Soviet authorities had deported them. After many months of desperate hardships, they reached the little Polish town that had been their home and their fathers'. The town was a mass of rubble. They did not find even graves. All their kith and kin had been burned alive in the crematoriums. The synagogue was in ruins. But a stair to a cellar had been saved. Descending that stair, these Jews found a few talmudic volumes, charred and water-soaked but still usable in part. And they procured then a few tallow candles and sat down to read a page or two. There came one running then and cried: "Jews, do you forget that you are fleeing for your lives? The Soviets are closing the frontiers. The American zone is still far off! Flee!" And one of the group waved the messenger aside: "Shah!" he said gravely. "Be still. *M'darf lernen!* One must 'learn.' "

The emphasis on learning, the selective genetics involved in marrying the scholar—even to the extent of giving of one's fortune for it—and the insistence on having children imbued with that value is reason enough for the superb development of the Jewish mind.

But what if there was no scholar to marry? The Rabbis urge coming as close to it as possible: "If one does not find a daughter of the learned, he should marry the daughter of a *gadol ha-dor* [a man great in wisdom and charity and leadership]. If one did not find such, he should marry the daughter of a communal leader. And if not her, the daughter of the keeper of the charity fund. And if not her, then the daughter of the children's teacher. But on no account should he marry the daughter of an *am ha-aretz [one ignorant of the law to the extent that he is not sufficiently knowledgeable to be careful with the observance of its details].*

The history of the *am ha-aretz* cannot adequately be discussed in these pages. Rif mentions two types of *am ha-aretz:* "*The am ha-aretz* of Babylon ('here') is not like the *am ha-aretz* of Israel ('there'). 'Here' he may not understand the Bible and the Mishnah [the codified Oral Law], but he is a gentleman [he has *derekh eretz*] and is observant of the *mitzvot.* He is not suspect of giving false testimony or of theft and so on. But 'there,' the *am ha-aretz* is not only ignorant but also suspect of unethical behavior, including bloodshed and immorality." With such a wide span in definition, it is well-nigh impossible to define such a person precisely for any given age. However, according to *Chavvat Yair* it is widely agreed that technically there is no *am ha-aretz* today that accords with the definition of the talmudic Sages. As commonly used today, the term erroneously refers to ignorance rather than to unethical or nonobservant behavior. As such, *am ha-aretz* is still a term of opprobrium. According to the medieval codifiers, Rif and Maimonides, while these suggestions regarding marrying the scholar are in the nature of good advice, the talmudic dictum, "Sell everything . . . ", was required only in regard to marriage to the learned or the daughter of the learned. In fact, the author of *Birkei Yosef* suggests that if there is a choice between the daughter of a *gadol ha-dor,* one of the greats of the generation, with whom one will have no peace of mind, and the daughter of a simple but God-fearing man, with whom one will be able to live at peace, he should choose the latter.

In sum, one should strive to marry as intelligent and intellectual a person as possible, and to do so, it is proper to spend one's whole fortune. But even that great goal must be secondary to peace in the home.

PIETY (SHE'MIRAT HA-MITZVOT)

Tradition teaches that a good person is not necessarily a good Jew. In addition to ethical values one needs a faith in God and the observance of religious practices. This is not the place for a general discussion of the value of religion to the individual, but we can identify some of the values of marriage and home promoted by personal religious observance.

First, it provides a continuous opportunity for celebration. Man is *homo festivus,* a "celebrating person." Religious observance brings joy and conviviality and meaning to life. Such celebration is not a festive occasion like a birthday party, but the rejoicing of an idea, a historical moment, a religious encounter.

The observance of the Sabbath, for example, celebrates an idea—God's creation—and a historic event—exodus from Egypt. It does not simply encourage
good feeling and a party atmosphere, it teaches specifically and directly via the
law that instructs us in the method of celebration. This specific, unchanging
form of the law guarantees that observance of the Sabbath will endure and will
not eventually be compromised or omitted altogether.

The traditions combine pursuit of religious ideals with family unity. The
prohibited work activity grounds the family and enforces te'chum Shabbat, the
physical proximity of family and community members. Oneg Shabbat, the
positive delights of the Sabbath, the festive meals, communal prayer, and singing, and Torah study assure a leisurely holiday spirit. Indeed, as Ahad ha-Am
said, "More than the Jews have kept the Sabbath, the Sabbath has kept the
Jews." It works as a positive, functional good for people in the development of
their interpersonal relations and the closeness of the family .

Religious observance also fosters a sense of discipline. Historian John Mac-
Murray once said, "Anything that can be done anywhere and at anytime will
be done nowhere and at no time." The requirement that the Sabbath begin and
end at specific times, and that it be celebrated in specific ways, imposes a sense
of objective discipline upon a potentially fluid situation. The time and method
of observance is not left for casual, personal decision; rather, tradition provides
an ancient framework and clear ideals beyond selfish needs and impulsive desires.

Attending religious and communal events also strengthens a family's ties to
the community. The needs of unknown Jews come alive; Israelis are felt as
personally related; Soviet Jews are seen as brothers and sisters. In addition, it
inspires a relationship with history. Through the celebrations we wander
through the desert and reach a promised land, or storm the Sea of Reeds, or sit
at the feet of Moses. It establishes a common future in freedom and redemption,
a goal of peace and honor, and a sense of mission to strive for the achievement
of these goals.

The married couple shares something more than fun and furniture; they share
a whole people and ideals beyond their immediate interests. Such a couple
touches deep, common, historic roots, and begins to attain a glimpse into
matters of cosmic significance. They gain pride, stability, community and a
celebration of life.

Marrying one who is sensitive to the beauty of religion is to enrich one's
family and to strike roots deep in the soil of ancient tradition. We achieve
meaning by association with meaning. We survive because Judaism survives.

It is true, nonetheless, that marriage with a mumar (a heretic) is valid because,
"a Jew, though he has sinned, is still a Jew." But it is surely undesirable, and

the Rabbis pronounce against it in unmistakable terms, as they sing the glory of the *bayit ne-eman be'yisrael* (the faithful house of Israel).

The great teachers of the Jewish people also taught that religion should be practiced softly and should not become a cause of contention. No man or woman should dogmatically instill fear into the household. He or she should mold kindly though firmly, with love and not with threats. The love of God should inspire and strengthen the love of one's lifelong partner.

A ROLE MODEL

One of the most important questions a person should ask in considering a prospective spouse is what kind of parent will this person be to our children? The great teachers in the Jewish tradition firmly believed that this focus is especially significant in considering a wife because the mother has more influence on the character of the children than the father, the teachers, or any other person. *Seder Eliyahu Zuta* notes, "There are four motives in marriage: physical pleasure, material advantage, social prestige, and rearing a family. Only those prompted by the last, the divine motive, will find satisfaction: they will have children who will redeem Israel." A person may be willing to marry spontaneously out of love-struck emotion, but is that person willing to choose a father or mother for future children just as spontaneously? A role model for children must have unmistakable integrity, honesty, and honorableness. Children imitate not only words, but qualities of character.

FAMILY (*YICHUS*)

Alongside its emphasis on the need for investigating the qualities of character and soul of an intended mate, the Jewish tradition placed great importance on the family as a reliable indicator of a person's temperament and moral quality. When planting, one tests both the plant and the soil, and in preparation for marriage one tests not only the person but the family background. After Rebekah passed the test of kindness, Eliezer's first words to her were (Genesis 24:47), "*Bat mi at?*" (Whose daughter are you?). This is the oldest indication that a person must inquire after the family of the spouse.

The Sages held that the family has the greatest influence over the child. Without debating the relative importance of heredity and environment, it is clear that the family is the sole environment of the child during the formative years. The Mishnah teaches, "A father endows his son with looks, strength, wealth, wisdom and longevity" Like father, like son. Maimonides explains that if he looks like his father, a son will tend to approximate his father's longevity. However, Rabbi Bahya says: "Sons will follow, in their values, the maternal family, for such is the nature of wine that after a while it tends to take on the taste of the vat." Some say that the daughter follows the father, others that she more closely resembles her mother. A popular saying of the talmudic Rabbis is that, "before marriage, one should pay close attention to the wife's brothers, because her children will probably be like them."

The Rabbis believed that the influence of family, which is absorbed subconsciously, is the strongest determinant of the child's behavior, style, expectations, integrity, and honor. That is why, although the law could not formally be invoked against it, they urged people not to marry the children of immoral women and they urged the prospective bride and groom to look for decent, upright in-laws. Rashi says: "Seek for yourself a quiet family. Generally, an argumentative family is not of authentic Jewish descent. Because of their spiritual defect, which they try to live down, they implant hatred in themselves, and become quarrelsome. The legitimate Jewish families of Babylon are the quiet ones, because they are confident of their nobility."

Family has always counted more than beauty, more than wealth. In the festivities on Yom Kippur and Tishah Be'Av at which new matches were formed, "The beautiful women said: 'The most important aspect of a woman is her beauty.' . . . The daughters of reputable families, *me'yuchassot,* said, 'Pay attention to the family for the most important aspect of a woman is her children.' "

The concern for family values serves as a rational balance to decisions based on romance. The ability and desire to sustain true love through many years of marriage can best be judged by the background and training of the partners. Today, as in ancient times, it is likely that unless there is a rebellion against the family upbringing, the child will fit the parents' expectations and values.

What if there is a choice between personal values and family values—a person of fine character who comes from a family with little integrity? The Rabbis agreed unanimously and unequivocally that personal virtue took clear and absolute precedence. Using the plant-soil analogy, they said, from the soil (the family background) you still do not know about the tree (the individual growth). But if the tree is good, that is a positive indication the soil has some good quality.

In ancient times the concern for family issued not only from the desire to provide a determination of the prospective spouse's value system, but also as a test of the family's halakhic legitimacy. Was there an interfaith marriage? Was there a conversion, and if so, was it valid? If the suitor is a *kohen,* was there a relative who would cause a defect in that *kohen* status? Was there a possibility of a *mamzer* in the family?

The principle laid down by the Rabbis is clear: "All families are assumed to be kosher." Therefore, in normal circumstances, no one need investigate or demand proof of the purity of the family.

The Rabbis were vehement against those who gratuitously cast aspersions on families. The Talmud says, "He who declares others unfit is himself unfit and never speaks good of anyone. And Samuel said, "He stigmatizes others as unfit with his *own* blemish." People see their own failings in everyone else.

The law today follows the general principle of the Talmud. Rashba says that any family that declares itself Jewish is considered kosher without further investigation. However, we find incorporated in the regulations implemented by the Jewish community of Lithuania that a person from a totally unknown family must have proof that he or she is Jewish and some witness as to marital status.

In the twentieth century, with its unusually large number of interfaith marriages, unacceptable conversions, and general neglect of Jewish divorce, the rabbinate (of the Jewish community in Israel and the world over) often requires that unknown families from distant communities provide a statement of a rabbi attesting that the family is Jewish, and, that the prospective bride or groom is single, widowed, or has had a Jewish divorce.

In the discussion of marriage laws in his book *Horeb,* Rabbi Samson Raphael Hirsch gives these words of advice to the Jewish man. They apply equally to the Jewish woman with regard to her husband:

> When you choose a wife, remember that she is to be your companion in life, in building up your home, in the performance of your life task, and choose accordingly. It should not be wealth or physical beauty or brilliance of mind that makes you decide whom to marry. Rather, look for richness of heart, beauty of character, and good sense and intelligence. If, in the end, you require money, and your wife's family freely offers it to you, you may take it; but woe to you and your future household if you are guided only by considerations of money.
>
> Study well the character of your future wife; but since character is first revealed by contact with real life, and since the girl usually first comes into contact with real life only with marriage, look well at her family. If you see a family in which disputes and quarreling are rife, in which insolence and evil talk are common, in which you behold hard-heartedness, hate and uncharitableness, do not attach yourself to it. According to the view of our Sages, even the Jewish descent of such a family is considered doubtful. That you should keep aloof from all marriages, forbidden by Torah and the Rabbis goes without saying. Our Sages recommend that one should always look for the daughter of a learned man; of a man in whom the public has shown its confidence by entrusting him with communal office; above all, of a man whose daughter can be expected to have learned practical wisdom from the example of her father.

LOOKS

The Bible and the Sages considered physical beauty a noble attribute, and one to be praised. The Bible goes out of its way to describe Sarah, Rebekah, and Rachel as beautiful in form and in appearance, and the Talmud says, "There were four very beautiful women in the world: Sarah, Abigail, Rahab, and Esther." In another vein, the Sages said: "It is written in the book *Ben Sira* (25, 26): 'A good wife is a gift to her husband. A bad wife is a plague to her husband ... a beautiful woman has a fortunate husband, the days of his life are doubled ... but turn your eyes from a coquettish woman lest she catch you in her net!' " Indeed, an unmarried woman in mourning is ordinarily not permitted to wear cosmetics. But if a prospective husband may visit the house of mourning, she may attend to her cosmetic needs and do whatever is necessary to appear attractive.

While they praised beauty, the Rabbis cautioned that it should not be the dominant quality, surely not the only one, that a man should seek. Beauty, they note, may quickly disappear. For example, the author of *Avot de'Rabbi Natan* says: "For the first three months of pregnancy, a woman's face may become pale and distorted, and if beauty is her only virtue, what will become of the relationship?"

WEALTH

The Rabbis also considered wealth to be desirable. Judaism does not consider poverty noble; indeed, poverty is regarded as an unfortunate condition. Because of the time consumed in struggling for a livelihood, it is debilitating to the desire for study; because of its immobilizing effect on the mind and the person, work depletes the desire for higher spirituality. The Jew prays for *parnassah,* a respectable income. It is the *absence* of money, not money itself, that may be the root of evil. The possession of wealth is no transgression, but sin may be committed when the accumulation of riches excludes other more worthy goals, or if the funds are hoarded selfishly rather than shared with the poor.

Marriage to a well-to-do person of good character and family is not condemned, especially if that wealth enables one to devote time to valuable activities. Indeed, it is commendable for the in-laws to support a scholar. Long before contemporary society invented grants, fellowships, and other institutionalized forms of assistance to allow aspiring young scholars to continue their advanced education without undue hardship, Jewish tradition had already anticipated them by counseling comfortably situated parents to support a poor but talented son-in-law in his scholarly ambitions.

Conversely, the Rabbis spared no words in condemning one who married solely for economic reasons. In the case of the bride whose father contracted to give *naddan* (a marriage gift) but could not deliver it because of a financial setback, the groom legally had the right to renege and refuse to be married. But even though this decision is the strict legal interpretation of the law, the Rabbis declared that it is wholly improper for such a groom to leave his bride or even to quarrel with the family. To obtain a dowry from one's in-laws under duress, legal or otherwise, is not the way of *yosher* (righteousness or fairness). One who causes his bride anguish over such matters will reap the whirlwind: "He will have unworthy children, his marriage will not work, and he will never personally prosper." On the contrary, if he accepts the situation and does not quarrel, he will be blessed by God and his marriage will succeed handsomely. Of course, they note that neither should the father of the bride make any promise that he knows he cannot fulfill. Joseph Ibn Caspi said in the fourteenth century, "Marry a wife of a good family, beautiful in form and character. Pay no regard to money, for true wealth consists in a sufficiency of bread to eat and clothing to wear."

Ethicists were fond of saying, "Do not marry a woman only for beauty or wealth, for all of that will disappear and only the damage will remain." *Ritba* reports that it was the Sephardic custom on the Sabbath of the wedding to read an additional portion from the Torah scroll, namely the story of Abraham and Eliezer and the search for a bride for Isaac. Rabbi Bahya provides the reason for the custom: "To caution the community not to marry for beauty or for money, and to stay close to their families. . . . One who marries an unworthy person for good looks or money will have children who are unworthy, *and* the money will not last."

A curious, almost comical, incident is reported in *Sefer Hasidim.* A man married a woman he did not really like, but because he agreed to marry, he received a handsome amount of money. After the wedding, he recited *two* blessings: The first was *ha-tov ve'ha-metiv* (Who is good and who does good), the blessing of gratitude one offers on occasions of joy and good fortune. The second was *dayyan ha-emet* (Blessed is the true Judge), recited upon hearing bad news! The first he recited for becoming a wealthy man, the second for the prospect of living with someone he didn't like.

NEGATIVE QUALITIES

The Rabbis also urged the investigation of a prospective mate's negative attributes, which are not likely to disappear after marriage. Me'iri, a medieval rabbinic scholar, says, "Even though there are many things one has to search for in selecting a mate in terms of family, it is more important to look for character and principled conduct, because a bad mate can cause pain for a lifetime until, at last, one acquiesces and relinquishes every desire to do good himself. . ."

Some of the qualities to beware of, according to the Talmud, are the austere perfectionist and the perpetually angry. Tur warns against one who is bad tempered and augumentative; it is even a *mitzvah* to divorce such a person.

A woman who was divorced because of her licentiousness is not suitable for marriage with one who is moral, although the law does not technically outlaw such a marriage. There is question as to whether one may marry the daughter of an immoral woman. The Babylonian Talmud says, *Yissa adam bat dumah ve'al yissa dumah* (A man may marry the daughter of a woman of ill repute, but not a woman of ill repute herself).

The Talmud lists the necessary marital qualifications as "a gentle temper, modesty, and industry." But when a choice must be made between temper and modesty, *Sefer Hasidim* asserts that the much-cherished value of modesty, considered by many the highest value in family life, must give way: "Even if she is *tze'nuah* (modest), he should not marry her if she is bad-tempered." A contentious wife would disrupt *she'lom bayit,* the peace in the home.

SIMILAR AND OPPOSITE QUALITIES

The question is often asked whether the preferred partner should be opposite or similar to oneself. ? While there are no rules in these highly individual personal matters, the tradition unmistakably considers marriages to have a much better chance for success if both mates have similar background and experience. It is for this reason that despite the stringency of the prohibited incest laws, a preferred marriage appears to be one between uncle and niece. It is always referred to as *tiv-it,* natural. First cousin marriages are also considered more natural, although civil law in most states bans such marriages. The Midrash records that at uncle-niece marriages one can echo the words of Adam at the discovery of Eve, "This time she is bone of my bones and flesh of my flesh." These comments are valid, of course, only if there are no counter-indications.

Rabbi Bahya notes the success of relatives marrying by citing the cases of Abraham ("Go unto my country and to my kindred, and take a wife for my son," Genesis 24:4), and Amram, the father of Moses, Aaron, and Miriam ("And there went a man of the house of Levi, and took to wife a daughter of the tribe of Levi" Exodus 2:1). Me'iri says that the similarity of two natures will promote greater love and fewer instances of friction. In addition, he notes, since tradition indicates that children often take after the mother's brothers, the marriage of a woman to her mother's brother assures some degree of similarity between husband and wife. While the tradition lays stress on heredity and lays no claim to scientific accuracy or to the absolute relevance to every individual of this generalization, that is how the Sages saw the linkage of the generations.

The Talmud refers to age differences as follows: "He is a young boy, and she an elderly person... He is elderly and she a young girl. We say to them, 'What do *you* want with an old person? What do *you* want with a child? Look for someone like yourself and don't introduce quarrels into your home.' "

It is curious that later rabbis, while they believed that husband and wife should have similar natures, also felt that opposite natures are preferred in sexual relations. Rabbi Ezekiel Landau notes that often when both have very "hot" natures, conception will be impeded, but when one is more active and the other more passive, sexual relations are facilitated. Always citing the Bible for support, reference is made to the description of Eve as *ezer ke'negdo,* (a helpmeet opposite him)—she is considered in some respects as "helpmeet", in others opposite.

THREE TYPES OF GREAT WOMEN

Modesty, compassion and humility, the preferred values, should not be confused with weakness, lack of self-confidence, or lack of self-worth. On the contrary, *tze'niut* is found in its genuine state primarily in people who are strong, self-willed, and committed. Rabbi Joseph B. Soloveitchik identifies three types of great women:

1. *Ishah Chakhamah,* the wise woman: One whose intelligence and alertness leave no doubt as to her superiority. *Chokhmah* implies three levels of wisdom—innate intelligence, erudition, intellectual curiosity.
2. *Ishah Chashuvah,* dignified woman: A person who is not petty or garrulous. One who is a spiritual aristocrat with a sense of inner pride, who can ignore the coarse and the vulgar and convey a sense of internal honor.
3. *Ishah Ge'dolah,* the great woman: This refers to a woman who approximates the spirituality of the biblical woman. She combines two characteristics that appear to be mutually exclusive. On the one hand the biblical woman was humble and shy, while on the other she demonstrated an iron will and unshakable determination. She was both simple and stubborn, meek and fearless, quiet and forthright, a devoted follower and an indomitable leader. One quality was at the foundation of both aspects—strength. She had the strength to be fearless as well as the strength required for genuine meekness. *Oz ve'hadar le'vushah* (strength and dignity are her clothing) (Proverbs 31:25). A mere superficial glance at the history of heroic Jewish women will furnish abundant testimony to this truth.

The Midrash sums it all up. "Says Rabbi Acha: Whoever marries a proper wife, it is accounted him as though he fulfilled the whole Torah from beginning to end. That is why it is all included in the *Eshet Chayil,* the last chapter of Proverbs, whose first verse begins with *aleph,* the first letter of the Hebrew alphabet, and whose last verse begins with *tav,* the last letter of the alphabet."

Part Three

THE IDEA OF JEWISH MARRIAGE

CHAPTER 7

The State of Marriage Today

A TESTIMONIAL AND A CONDEMNATION

The institution of marriage stands serene and firm amidst the buffeting winds of change. The greatest pleasure of which the human being is capable is best attained within the boundaries of monogamous marriage, not in a world of unbridled sensuality and multiple lovers. Rooted in loyalty and integrity, nurtured by true love, and immortalized by children, marriage has been the locus of love and beauty and happiness for too many centuries to be written off because of periodic historic malaise.

What other human institution can provide so much warmth and intimacy? What other setting allows one generation to bestow the care needed to raise the next? Where else can one find such readiness for self-sacrifice? Where else can pain be so effectively divided and contentment so magnificently multiplied? Is there another harbor as welcoming and protective in the storms of daily life as marriage? No other relationship can so surely guarantee the survival of the human species and perpetuate morality. And where else but in marriage can we find the mystery, the dignity, and the sacredness of life?

Monogamy is designed to unify society. A breakdown in the sexual code, no matter how cogent the alternatives or options may seem, can bring social ills of a far more grievous nature than those of which monogamy is accused. Judaism, despite isolated instances, is based on monogamy. The fundamental marriage narrative of Adam and Eve presupposes it; Noah, intent on preserving human and animal life, had only one wife, and the animal survivors arrived in pairs. The Prophets use the monogamous metaphor of man and wife for God and Israel: As Jews had one God (*ha-shem echad*), God chose only one people (*am echad*);

thus in marriage there is a union of one wife with one husband (*basar echad*). The "woman of valor" glorified in the Book of Proverbs is not "*women* of valor;*" and rare was the rabbi, of the thousands of sages of the Talmud, who in polygamous times had more than one wife.

Polygamy was sanctioned in biblical times, although it was not explicitly commanded. It was considered a preliminary social form and was allowed to self-destruct. The formal termination came as a ban on polygamy by Rabbenu Gershom of Mainz, the "Light of the Exile," in the tenth century, fifteen hundred years after monogamy became the way of life for all but a few Sephardic communities. It is true that the biblical and rabbinic system of law, the *Halak-hah,* incorporates the biblical legitimacy of polygamy into the law of marriage. Here it is the source of legal decisions, especially in regard to marriage, divorce, and the nature of adultery. Morally and ideologically, however, there can be no doubt that Judaism strongly upholds an exclusive, monogamous marriage and a single standard.

A host of people, including ancient and modern philosophers and social scientists, decry the entire institution of marriage. Marriage, they tell us, is a "towering inferno"—you may have high hopes, but in the end you'll get burned. Indeed, it is true that many marriages either erupt in divorce or internalize the rage and hatred. Marriages built with thoughts of love, fulfillment, and family collapse in bewilderment, leaving lonely women, fatherless children, and homeless men.

For many, marriage has been a bitter disappointment made all the more bitter because of exaggerated romantic expectations. These people have been oppressed by failure as lovers and as parents, overwhelmed with dirty diapers and dirty dishes, complaints and sickness, and endless unfulfilled needs. Where were the satisfactions of marriage that people talk about—and what happened to the love that was supposed to conquer all?

A million people trapped in troubled marriages scramble for the nearest exit. They justify the failure of their own marriage by condemning the institution, and earnestly seek new alternatives. Some adopt the popular philosophy of the singles—they "don't want to tie themselves down," they "care about different people in different ways," and thus "get beyond monogamy." They may explore such "new" options as nonformal cohabitation, casual sex, or open relationships, but they have one goal in common: the rejection of binding commitments.

These experiences have been repeated in every community. It is understandable that urban philosophers and radical thinkers have lost no time in administering the last rites to the dying institution of marriage. They defend such worthy ideals as freedom, personal fulfillment, openness, and universal kinship, and present themselves as embattled liberals confronting the powerful and reactionary establishment of repressive paranoiacs who believe in traditional marriage.

Like sex, marriage can generate extremes—love and hate, intolerable prison and expanding universe, and the familiarity of family life that may breed contempt as well as children. The apparent contradiction between Proverbs 18:22, which says, "Whoso findeth a wife, findeth a great good," and Ecclesiastes 7:26, which says, "And I find more bitter than death the woman, whose heart is snares and nets," is reconciled by the talmudic Sages: "A good wife is man's best find, a bad one is worse than death." It often seems that there is no middle ground in love and marriage.

If marriage tends to either extreme, however, it is not the institution that has failed or succeeded, but the people involved in the marriage. But how can we know what kind of person will grow in marriage, and be able to sustain the experience of permanent closeness, life-long caring, and concern? These qualities are difficult to determine, and most people marry whether or not they are prepared. Romantic love is a barely adequate preparation for marriage; indeed, it often proves to be a *negative* factor in achieving marital happiness. The exhaustive exploration of sex techniques serves no real purpose, and living together with no binding commitment is not a good way to judge the success of a future marriage.

Marriage is people. Like sex, marriage cannot be abstracted from character. Good people make for good marriages, just as good children generally make good parents. Selfishness, immaturity, and an undisciplined, instinctual lifestyle are early indicators of possible failure in marriage.

CHAPTER 8

Jewish Insights into Marriage

The marital integrity of the Jewish people was legendary in ancient and medieval times, and Jewish family life is idealized even in these days of upheaval. What qualities make Jewish marriage so stable?

Jewish marriage is not designed for the ethical management of the sexual drive, nor is it a concession to human weakness. Jewish marriage makes its appearance within the natural order of creation, not as a law promulgated by Moses nor as a legal sanction, but as a blessing from God. Just as woman was created as a separate being, "a helpmeet opposite" man (Genesis 2:18), the purpose for the creation of marriage is stated in five words: *lo tov he-yot ha-adam le'vado*—It is not good for man to be alone.

Marriage was created at the beginning, at the same time the principals of marriage were created. It was not an afterthought, designed to control their passions, but part of the natural order of human society. The moment we are born we are destined for marriage. When a newborn child is named, the prayer is *le'chuppah u'le'maasim tovim* (to the marriage canopy and a life of good deeds). Marriage is thus grounded in the primeval relationship of the sexes in order to perpetuate the species and enhance personal growth.

Marriage is seen as a blessing because it enables us to overcome loneliness. According to Rabbi Joseph B. Soloveitchik, Genesis 2:18 reads *"heyot" ha-adam le'vado* rather than *"li-he'yot,"* which implies *not* that "it is not good for man to be *alone*," but that it is not good for man to be *"lonely."* Being "alone" means being physically alone, wanting company, needing assistance; being "lonely" means spiritual solitude, as one can feel lonely even in a crowd.

God seeks to remedy that with the creation of woman as *ezer ke'negdo,* a helpmeet opposite him. Now if *le'vado* (alone) means simply needing company or requiring assistance, then woman is *ezer,* a cook and bottle washer, a real helper. But if *le'vado* means lonely, then *ezer* is not just a partner to lighten the burden, she is *ke'negdo,* part of a spiritual union of two souls. The basic God-created human unit is man and woman, one flesh, completing one another. Man alone or woman alone constitutes only half of that unit, as the Zohar says: *Bar nash be'lo iteta peleg gufa.* Rabbi Samson Raphal Hirsch says that the word *kallah* (bride) means completion, as in *bayom kalot ha-mishkan* (the day the tabernacle was completed). In marriage, the partners complete and fulfill themselves. This is their natural state and a blessing from God.

This theme is repeated at every Jewish marriage. The seven nuptial blessings speak of paradise regained, the miracle of God's creation, and the creation of man and woman, so that mankind might endure. The sixth blessing refers to marriage in the scheme of creation: "Make these beloved companions as happy as were the first human couple in the Garden of Eden." The joy of the Creator's blessing is invoked at the inception of every Jewish home.

If God created man, woman, and their marriage relationship; and if the creation of man and woman is good and marriage a blessing; then God is a conscious, albeit silent, partner in the marriage. Thus the ideal Jewish marriage is a triangle composed of two human beings and their Creator.

Rabbi Joshua ben Korha said that man at first was called *Adam* to indicate his natural constitution—flesh and blood (*dam*). But when woman was created, the two were referred to as fiery (*esh*)—living, dynamic beings. God insinuated Himself into the marriage, then added two letters of his own name, *Y* and *H,* to the names of man and woman. He inserted the *Y* into man's name, turning *esh* (fire) into *i-Y-sh* (*ish,* man); and *H* into woman's name, making *i-sha-H* (*ishah,* woman). The Chronicles of Yerahmeel (6:16) comment on this: "If they walk in My ways and observe My commandments, behold My name will abide with them and deliver them from all trouble. But if not, I will take the letters of My name from them, so that they will revert to *esh* and *esh,* fire consuming fire." Hence with God as a partner, marriage is a blessing, *ish* and *ishah.* Without God, it can become *esh,* an inferno where man and woman devour each other.

Jewish marriage is therefore naturally sanctified by God. From this concept of God's involvement in marriage, there flow new insights and obligations that married people often ignore. For example, if one partner is unfaithful it is not just a marital problem, it shatters the fundamental unit of creation. In most cases of adultery, the religious court is instructed to issue a divorce even against their will. The couple may forgive a violation of their personal integrity, but they have no right to forgive their assault upon God's integrity and His participation in the marriage.

The moral conscience of the Jew was sometimes strict to the point of grief, and the Rabbis were painfully reluctant to pronounce the harsh decree, but no whisper of scandal was permitted to besmirch the name of marriage, or any of its three partners. Accordingly, the Sages ruled that lewdness was not allowed even in the privacy of the bedroom, because such behavior offends the presence of God.

This code of behavior based on the appreciation of the divine creation of marriage and God's active presence within it keeps the strict purity of the Jewish home. It is a code that originated in Jewish law, was hallowed by centuries of Jewish observance and is based upon the very real premise of God as a partner to every Jewish marriage.

The non-Jewish practice of celibacy reflects a philosophy of withdrawal from the real world. Jewish marriage is the decision to confront the challenge of the real world. The Jew, when he marries, enters not only marriage, but the world— the world of the Jewish community, of concern for the survival of the Jewish people, and of care and responsibility for total strangers. As a man-wife unit, the married couple has a new voice. Historically, the family-oriented Jewish community, which experienced very few divorces and virtually no abandonments, gave little consideration to the opinions of single people. When God became a partner at the wedding, and a new Jewish home was created, an overriding significance was added. In some communities this is still demonstrated by the groom's donning, for the first time, a *tallit* (prayer shawl).

The requirement of a *minyan* at the wedding (the quorum of ten which is the smallest unit of the Jewish social structure), is an important indication of the social significance of marriage.

Rabbi Joseph Soloveitchik describes how Maimonides differentiates three friendship categories (*chaver,* companion, associations) within marriage. First is *chaver le'davar*, a utilitarian association that depends on reciprocal usefulness. When the usefulness disappears, the bond of "love" dissolves (*batel davar, batel ahavah*). Second, is *chaver le'daagah,* someone with whom to share sorrows, troubles and also joys. We need this in order to lighten our load. Joys are multiplied and sorrows are divided when they are shared. Third is *chaver le'-deah,* a joint dedication to common goals. Both dream of realizing great ideals, with a readiness to sacrifice for their attainment.

Marriage must at least partake of the first and second friendship levels, the physical and psychological aspects of joint partnership. But if the partners are truly *chaverim* and their union is *chibbur* (a joint partnership), they form a community of commitment.

Love seeks eternity, sanctity, rootedness in a transcendent power. True lovers cannot endure in a hastily-put-together arrangement. Love will not be fulfilled until it reaches that ultimate moment, the total commitment of marriage.

Love is a sacred trust. The description of the relationship of bride and groom preserved in the blessing at the wedding service is *reim ahuvim* (beloved friends).

The secular sanction of a civil marriage is not sufficient to motivate love to rise to its highest level; it needs the sanctification of an almighty and eternal God. Love so desanctified cannot long withstand the daily frustrations, angers, and hurts. To flourish, love needs an intimation that it originates in the plan of the Creator; that the world could not exist without it; and that an all-knowing God delights in it.

Marriage is the natural home of love. Here it can grow and enrich itself, and leave something worthy in its wake. Love that is not able to express itself in the cares of married life is frustrated love. "It is not good that man should be alone" says Rabbi Jacob Zevi Meklenburg, "means that man's inner capacity for goodness can never be realized unless he has someone upon whom to shower his affections." Mature love is expressed through giving, and through giving comes even greater love.

To have a child is a flesh-and-blood connection with the future, and the birthplace of humanity's future is the home. The future of the whole Jewish people depends upon marriage, the covenantal relationship of husband and wife. Marriage is not simply a private arrangement designed solely for mutual satisfaction; it's importance rests in how the couple perceive their bond, the love they demonstrate, and the constellation of virtues they bring to the home. Every marriage covenant must partake of the original covenant. Jewish values thrive not as ephemeral theories, but as they are lived daily. This means that the Jewish couple needs a religiously-oriented home, an investment in the Jewish community, and a concern with the fate of God's world.

The eternal Jewish future depends on the old Jewish past, which gives ample evidence that Jews who relate to God survive. The words of the betrothal blessing are important in this context: He forbade relations for the betrothed, and permitted it for the married. These are declarations of God who created man and woman and ordained marriage. Given true love and a man and woman who follow religious and ethical precepts, life holds the possibility of being as close to paradise as is possible in this world. But if they violate God's commands, they must repeat the experience of Adam and Eve in paradise lost. Judaism teaches that every bride and groom must go back to Adam and Eve, and reenact that physical and spiritual drama of community as "one flesh."

Jewish marriage serves many purposes, but the phrase that incorporates all of these purposes is central to the wedding service: "You are hereby sanctified unto Me. . . ." But the covenant requires more than this declaration of sanctity. It is the remainder of the marriage formula that is crucial to Jewish survival: ". . . according to the laws of Moses and Israel."

CHAPTER 9

The Purposes of Marriage

COMPANIONSHIP

The years of romance and intense sexual activity are shorter and less enduring than the years of sustained, lifelong friendship. Companionship must precede true *yichud* love in marriage, it is a necessary component during the peak years of sexual involvement, and it is the sweet, mellowed, and blessed gift of married life in old age.

The Sages of the Talmud were referring to companionship when they said, "It is better to remain coupled than to be widowed." This parallels the wisdom of Ecclesiastes (4:9), which says, "Two are better than one." It is signified by the description of the relationship as the wedding blessing refers to them: *reim ahuvim,* (beloved *friends*). The idea of friendship between husband and wife was not a component of non-Jewish religions until the Protestant Reformers maintained that companionship should actuate a marriage.

As an illustration of this emphasis in Jewish tradition, two of the seven blessings under the wedding canopy are joyous celebrations of companionship: "Cause beloved friends to rejoice greatly, as of old You rejoiced Your creatures in Paradise. . ." and "Who has created joy and gladness, bridegroom and bride, mirth and exaltation, pleasure and delight, love, fellowship, peace and companionship. . . ." That companionship is stressed in these blessings is evident from the response of Rabbi David Abudarham to the question of why these nuptial blessings did not include the benediction over the *mitzvah* of procreation. His answer was that these blessings, because they were recited at every wedding, had to relate to the sterile as well as to the fertile. Thus the subject of companionship was an appropriate blessing, but procreation was not.

It is true that in the Bible's first account of creation (Genesis 1:28) the very first command is, "Be fruitful and multiply." In terms of the *law*, procreation is the major purpose of married life. In terms of *life*, however, the Torah does not consider it primary and certainly not exclusive.

Genesis 1 is the record of physical creation. Adam and Eve were natural beings, akin to the animals that surrounded them. But in the second account of creation (Genesis 2:7–24), Adam and Eve were endowed with spiritual dimensions. They rose above that natural environment, had metaphysical yearnings, and could relate to God. In Genesis 1, man and woman were simply *ha-adam* (undifferentiated hermaphrodites), while in Genesis 2 they were marriage partners. Humanity traces its history to the second chapter of Genesis, where God provides the motivation for the creation of woman: "It is not good for man to be lonely."

While it is true that a progressively larger group of people can endure life alone today, and some even thrive on it, loneliness is a tragedy for those who are not built to bear it. Sociologists have determined that it is particularly devastating for single men, whom society views as ideally free, swinging, and successful. Ramban says of Genesis 2:18 that *tov (good)* in Genesis refers only to permanent features of creation, whereas *lo tov* (not good) indicates the ephemeral. Therefore "It is not good to be lonely" implies that loneliness could not endure, and God had to relieve it by the creation of a companion.

Rabbi Isaac Breuer notes that with respect to His other and earlier works of creation, God speaks the word of approval, "good." Only at the creation of man does He utter the negative judgment, "not good." Loneliness is not felt by animals; only man can experience existential loneliness, the fragmentary and incomplete nature of this world. It is the genuine companionship of Adam and Eve that humanity requires, and which is the stated purpose for marriage in the scheme of creation.

Recently, a tendency has developed toward emphasizing companionship as the chief value, and sometimes the sole value, of marriage. In a Louis Harris survey on American men, eighty-four percent of the men said they consider family life "very important." Out of fourteen reasons to marry, two received majority votes: "Having another person to share one's life", and "to have someone to share important life experiences with." Only two out of five cited the desire to have children, and only one out of four the desire to have a stable sex life.

What, in Jewish philosophy, is the nature of companionship? "Therefore shall a man leave his father and mother, and shall cleave to his wife, and they shall be as one flesh" (Genesis 2:24). "One flesh" is the symbol not only of sexual union but of the intimacy of companionship. In the twelfth century, Raavad noted that verse 18 of Genesis 2 records God's intention to create a helpmeet for man, and in verse 21, He does so. But verses 19 and 20 interrupt with a story of Adam's reviewing and naming of the animal kingdom. How are these two events related? With profound insight, Raavad comments, "God says to man, 'It is not good for man to be alone,' like animals who copulate . . . yet the female does not become exclusively intimate with the male." The animals may come in pairs, but in fact they are alone. It is not good for human beings to be in pairs but still be alone. Therefore, a man shall cleave to his wife and they shall be "one flesh"—she shall be exclusively intimate with him and he with her. Elsewhere, Raavad continues: "Therefore, 'it is proper that a man should love his wife as he loves his own being, and respect her more than he does his own self,' and be compassionate with her, and watch over her, as a person would watch over one of his own limbs; and she should love him, for she was taken from his side. That is why the Creator commanded man regarding his wife that he should never diminish that which is her due—namely, food, clothing, shelter —in addition to the marital relations which must include joy and intimacy."

Thus a physical relationship alone is animalistic. Human beings also need intimacy, an exclusive, warm, personal relationship of care and concern. As there is a "oneness of flesh," there must also be a "oneness of soul."

Distinguished psychologist Erik Erikson, in defining the ages of man and the dominant psychological theme of each age, notes that the twenties are dominated by the need for intimacy. Seeking marriage or other unions during that age is an expression of this need. But becoming intimate is not a simple matter. Talent and maturity are needed to share intimacies, to have trust, and to risk vulnerability.

Many of the failures in marriage undoubtedly result from the extended childhood given young men and women today. Emotional dependence on the parent becomes an obstacle to forming adult emotional associations. Jewish marriages, which form traditionally closely-knit families, often display this syndrome. Hence the emphasis of the original prescription for companionship recorded in Genesis, "Therefore, shall a man leave his father and mother and cleave unto his wife. . . ." The formula is *leave and cleave.*

One must exercise intelligent independence before uniting with another soul. The Bible surely did not imply an end to the child-parent relationship upon growing up; but the quality of that relationship has to change in order to accommodate emotional growth. Part of the wisdom required of concerned parents is to know when to hold on and when to let go.

Jewish law, which places so much emphasis on honoring parents, applies this theme in legal fashion to a case of conflict between parent and child regarding the child's marriage. It affirms that a daughter or son must personally desire the mate he or she chooses. The Talmud says that "a minor daughter may not be married until she matures and specifies: 'Him do I desire.'" To a formal question as to whether a son must obey his father who protests his marriage to *ishah ke'sherah* (an upright Jewish girl), Maharik responded that the son should marry the girl he desires providing she is morally, religiously, and otherwise suitable. Until the child learns independence, there is no chance of learning intimacy.

Intimacy, according to Jewish tradition, requires yet another stage of independence—independence in the very midst of intimacy. Ramban notes that the Bible goes out of its way to say not only that a helpmeet (*ezer*) was provided Adam, but that the positioning of that helpmeet opposite (*ke'negdo*) him was important. "Perhaps man was created bisexual . . . but God saw it would be good for the helpmeet to be opposite him. He would then be able at will to separate from her or join her. . ." A contemporary scholar, Gerhard von Rad, believes that in a circumstance of intimacy, "opposite" implies a mirror image of oneself, in which one recognizes oneself in the other. That is certainly desirable and very often true of long and successful experiences of intimacy. But Ramban, and with him a host of other commentators, reads the biblical *ke'negdo* as literally opposite, as some popularly refer to the "opposite sex". Opposite, to Ramban, implies not a reflection of one another, but one distinctly different from the other—independent, yet intimate. Kahlil Gibran said, "Let there be spaces in your togetherness." A deeper understanding of the nature of nonsexual, mature relationships will reveal the requirement of both components—*ezer* as help, and *ke'negdo* as opposite. Perhaps this depth of understanding is behind the Yiddish folk saying that husband and wife are like *lulav* and *etrog*, the palm and the citron, two vegetable growths totally unlike in appearance that achieve meaning only when held together for the blessing on the Festival of Tabernacles.

In Jewish family law, no sexual congress is allowed between husband and wife during the period of menstruation and for seven days afterward. These are days when nonsexual intimacy can develop, and which also prepare the young, vibrant couple for the marital relationship of old age when sexuality, while still important, is no longer dominant. Companionship thus gets constant practice in Jewish family living.

There is an immature form of love called symbiotic union, which is a biological pattern of two entities that live together as one, such as a pregnant mother and her fetus. The fetus is part of the mother and receives everything it needs from her, and the mother's life is also enhanced by the fetus. In a psychic symbiotic union, the two bodies are independent but the minds feed upon one another. When such a fusion exists, no integrity remains for the individual.

Mature intimacy requires a deep, interpersonal relationship in which both people retain their individuality. Mature love enables one to merge with the other, but not to become submerged. Erich Fromm points up both the beauty and the paradox of love: "Two beings become one and yet remain two."

The Torah, in requiring the end result of *basar echad* (one flesh), requires *ezer*, an overcoming of loneliness, a mutual completion of the selves, and also *ke'negdo*, an opposite, independent person with whom one chooses to side at will. True *yichud* love embraces, never stifles, one's individuality.

Poet Rainer Maria Rilke once said of marriage that it is not a matter "of creating a quick community of spirit by tearing down and destroying all boundaries . . . once the realization is accepted that even between the closest human beings infinite distances continue to exist, a wonderful living side by side can grow up, if they succeed in loving the distance between them."

To further our understanding of the intimacy of Adam and Eve, it is necessary to note that the merging of the two beings was a merging not only of two *independent* partners, but also of two *equal* personalities. Sforno interprets *ke'negdo* as the opposite balance of a scale: equal in value and in dignity. Adam and Eve, *ish* and *ishah*, have equal worth, though different qualities and functions. *Ezer* signifies a "giving" quality that woman has always symbolized in Jewish history, not only as a giver of love, security, encouragement, and advice to her husband, but also as mother to the growing child within her, to its nourishment and development.

When dealing with religion, most people tend to assume that principles and values are intended as important but vague preachments. Judaism used values as action-determining ideas, and they sometimes become actionable in strange ways in practical legal considerations. An apt illustration may be found in the laws of evidence: A person is not permitted to bear witness regarding close relatives, up to those three times removed. The Talmud asked whether a man was permitted to testify about his *wife's* grandson, not his own. The difficulty revolved around a simple question: Is the grandson considered three times removed? The fundamental principle at work here is *ishto ke'gufo* (a man's wife is to him as his own body). What does that mean exactly in terms of law? Maimonides interprets it to mean that they are *once* removed from each other. *They are as close as can be, but they are still not identical.* Therefore, if his wife is once removed, her son twice removed, then her son's son is three times removed. Hence, he may testify for his wife's grandson. But Me'iri holds that *ishto ke'gufo* means that they are identical, *guf echad*, one body. If that is so, *he and his wife are the same,* her son is considered his son and hence only once removed, and his son's son is twice removed; he therefore would not be permitted to testify. The law was eventually decided according to Maimonides. The lesson of this decision and of the accepted laws of testimony should not be lost: man and wife are as close as possible, but they are not identical. For that is the nature of companionship and intimacy—*oneness is not sameness.*

In Malachi (2:14), a wife is referred to as *chaverte'kha*, your *chaver*, companion, as *Chatam Sofer* explains: one who is involved in a *joint* venture, or a "*joint* partner," as in the Aramaic translation. Not "one body, one thought," but one joined body retaining two thoughts. This is also reflected in the Kabbalistic term for sexual relations referred to earlier as *chibbur* (joining), from the same root as *chaverim*. *Chibbur* refers to a joining of equals, a mutuality, a reciprocal love.

Successful marriage requires the practice of the art of intimacy. It is a joint life venture not only in the passion of brief sexual excitement, but in the profound blending of personalities.

The growth of intimacy is a growth of personal sanctity and a sublime goal of Judaism.

CREATION OF A FAMILY

The Jewish people was first a family. The influence of the family model is so great that it casts its shadow on all of Jewish history. We still refer to Abraham, Isaac, and Jacob as *fathers,* rather than leaders or founders, and to Sarah, Rebekah, Rachel, and Leah as *mothers.* And the Jewish people are called after Jacob's family, the *children* of Israel. The allusion to family extends even further. The contemporary Catholic philosopher Jacques Maritain, struggling with a definition of Jews who are neither race nor religion, calls them *Beit Yisrael,* the *House* of Israel.

The relationship to God is also constructed on the family model. God and Israel are referred to in mystical terms as husband and wife; the Prophet Hosea considers Jews' lusting after other gods as the treachery of adultery in the celestial marriage. The Jewish people are called children (*banim atem la-Shem*), and God is called Father. The relationship to the patriarchs is embodied in the principles *be'rit avot,* the (covenant of the fathers) and *ze'khut avot* (merit of the fathers). The *covenant* remains firm regardless of the behavior of the Jews; the unconditional contract God made with our fathers is simply inherited by their children. But the *merit* of the fathers extends to the children only if they act as God taught them to act. When the child patterns his conduct after his father, he is amply rewarded by the Father in Heaven.

Fellow Jews are considered brothers, as in the prayer *acheinu be'nei yisrael* (our brothers, the children of Israel), while non-Jews, our fellow human beings, are referred to as *reim* (neighbors). Internal communal disputes among Jews, were considered "all in the family" and kept from public scrutiny.

The family spirit of the Jewish people has never been lost to most Jews who feel personally hurt when a fellow Jew commits a crime, and who feel family pride when Israel scores a victory in the international arena. So long as the Jew continues to believe in and pray to "the God of Abraham, the God of Isaac, and the God of Jacob," Jews will survive as a family.

We may think it obvious that the family should be considered a natural sociological unit, but the family has had its detractors in every age. When utopias are dreamed of, the family unit is usually disposed of. Plato's program for the ideal state includes total absorption of the family by the state. In trying to create a classless society, Karl Marx also abolished the family, a feat the Soviets tried to accomplish by state edict. Divorce was made very simple and children were taken from their families at a very early age, freeing the mother to join the labor force.

"Progressive" thinkers everywhere proclaim that the family's usefulness is vanishing. They argue that its primary function was economic, while the modern family no longer works or produces as an economic unit. As for social need, the state will educate children, provide doctors, and find homes for the aged. Further, they say, the family has become a psychological prison for superior children, and is often a menagerie of mismatched temperaments, talents, intellects, and goals that have nothing in common except an address and a last name.

Just as there are detractors, the family has always had supporters. Plato was succeeded by Aristotle, who refuted him. Karl Marx's classless society was found to be a disaster, and the Soviet Union set about the restoration of family life on a grand scale. Even Sigmund Freud, after his devastating criticism of traditional family relationships, conceded the family's indispensable role in the development of the child; a father and mother are necessary psychologically as well as biologically as the child matures and assimilates the moral ideals of his ancestors and of society.

Like marriage, the family has been part of the world since the dawn of civilization. Like marriage, the family may cause pain and tragedy, but most often it is the primary source of blessing for humankind. Is there a school in which one can learn love as well as one can in the family? Here ordinary people love others even more than they do themselves, and children receive unqualified love merely because they are there. Where else in our society will young people learn trust, the cement of interpersonal relations, if not in a family setting? It is in the family that children become socialized, and develop the ability to live with and understand two and three generations. The family teaches young people the axioms of the moral life, how to handle joy, and how to celebrate. Where else in this turbulent world will they learn the meaning of "Home, Sweet Home" to which, after travelling long distances, they may come back to find a light at the door, a warm meal on the table, and the welcome embrace of loving parents? The Latin word for womb is *hysteria,* named for the physical convulsion before birth. The Hebrew word for womb is *rechem:* compassion.

For human life to endure, it is clear that the primary order of business for marriage must be procreation. Isaiah said, "God did not create the world to be chaos. He created it to be inhabited" (Isaiah 45:18). The Talmud records that "one who does not participate in 'be fruitful and multiply' causes God's presence to vanish. For Genesis 17:7 reads, 'For you and your children *after you.*' When there are to be children after you, the Presence dwells amongst you. If there are to be no children after you, on whom will the Divine Presence dwell? On sticks and stones?"

"Be fruitful and multiply" is not simply one of the commandments, it is everywhere in the Torah and it is always a blessing. On the sixth day of creation, having blessed the fish and birds with fertility the day before, "God blessed [man and woman] and said unto them, 'Be fruitful and multiply and replenish the earth and subdue it' " (Genesis 1:28). After the Flood, mankind is reborn and Noah is blessed with fertility (Gen. 9:1). Through Isaac, Abraham is to be blessed with progeny as numerous as the stars (Gen. 15:5). Through Jacob, Isaac is to be blessed "with seed . . . as the dust of the earth" (Gen. 28:14). The biblical personalities confer blessings on children that are chiefly fertility blessings. The blessing Rebekah receives from her family before she leaves to marry Isaac is, "Our sister, may you grow into thousands of myriads" (Gen. 24:60). This blessing is the very one pronounced to this day as the groom veils his bride before the wedding ceremony.

The actualization of these blessings is reported after the Jews leave Egypt. "The children of Israel were fruitful and increased abundantly, and the land was filled with them" (Exodus 1:7). When God threatens to destroy Israel for its sins, Moses pleads with Him to remember His blessings of fertility and survival to the Patriarchs. The two words *pe'ru u-re'vu*—be fruitful and multiply—are the code words for the perennial regenerative force of humanity.

Procreation is the principal reason for sex, and therefore the primary, though not exclusive, purpose of marriage. God has written it into creation, and nature has ordained it by withholding complete satisfaction in copulation until the seeds of reproduction are brought forth. If we consider sex objectively, we see that it was created for the production of children, as lungs are for breathing and intestines are for digestion. The fact that we can use sex for other purposes does not alter childbearing as its primary purpose. The heart was not created for throbbing with excitement, but for pumping oxygen. The ears were not created for fun, though they may hear funny stories. We can use sex for our own purposes, but clearly God intended it for the business of human survival.

This does not mean that when two people decide to marry, their motive is solely to have children. If a man proposes marriage because of the declining birthrate, the woman would be well-advised to refuse him; this type of "love" is much too practical. People marry, obviously, because they want each other— and that is quite all right according to the Torah. It is when the two frustrate the procreational purpose of sex that they thwart the blessing of God.

It is extraordinary that sex should be used for childbearing. By the function of these bodily organs, one cooperates with God Himself in the production of a new human being. Sex is, therefore, man's greatest glory in the physical order. It is also astonishing that sex should be the instrument to produce a family. Of all the drives of the human being, sex is surely the most turbulent and unpredictable. Of all of the duties of the human being, the bearing and rearing of children requires the most order, stability, and tranquility. It is only in marriage that these two contradictory forces can be reconciled—enormous power channeled into enormous good. In marriage, sex loses none of its strength, but serves life; family love loses none of its stability, but is powered by zest and excitement. It is a blessing of the first magnitude.

Because procreation is the purpose of sex, the wanton wasting of seed (*hashchatat zera*) was prohibited. There are three principal forms of this wasting. The first is onanism, which refers to *coitus interruptus*. Onan (Genesis 38:9) "went in unto his brother's wife and spilled [seed] on the ground." The Rabbis call this "threshing within and winnowing without." The second is contraception, which is permitted only in limited circumstances, as will be discussed later in this chapter. The third is masturbation. Although current psychological literature almost unanimously endorses this practice as natural, useful, and even desirable, Jewish law and tradition look upon it as wrong. The blessing of God is not to be wasted for any reason; it must retain its naturalness and its integrity. Thus the blessing may be spent only within the legitimate moral confines of marriage.

Because people might excuse themselves from the blessing with a "thanks, but no thanks," Judaism declared procreation a religious duty—a positive commandment. Maimonides states, "God has commanded us to be fruitful and multiply *with the intention* of preserving the human species, and this is what the Torah says: 'As for you, be fruitful and multiply.' " Maimonides' use of the term "with the intention" probably means "binding insofar as it contributes to the preservation of the species in accordance with the demands of the law." Presumably, once one has done one's share in maintaining the population of the next generation, one may no longer be obligated to fulfill the command. "Be fruitful and multiply" is not only good advice, "a blessing on your head," it is law for every Jew.

Some very well-intentioned and highly idealistic people shun the idea of bringing children into a society that is shot through with violence and rife with injustice. They believe that the evils of poverty, prejudice, hatred, and corruption, and the mind-boggling inequities of colonialism and capitalism are unremitting and essentially irrevocable. They refuse to make their child heir to a certain destiny of sorrow.

It is unfortunate but true that this sentiment has been expressed in virtually every generation, surely in every century of Jewish history. It is a reflection of the indomitable character of the Jew that despite every indication of doom, every legitimate, substantiated, obvious reason for pessimism, the Jewish response was optimistic: "It will get better." And, incredibly, it *did* get better. Perhaps it is not so incredible—Is there no God? Have we no trust? Is trust only for sure bets or is it for when there is no other avenue of hope? Has not God assured us that we are an eternal people? Can He not interfere in history to save us? Is anyone who is familiar with history prepared to dispute this?

Things have been blacker, much blacker; but children were born even during the Holocaust. It is because of one such child, born during a much earlier holocaust, that we have the commandment to "be fruitful and multiply." The Midrash relates that Moses' parents did not want to have a child and so decided to divorce. What moral imperative could demand that they bring a child into the world when Pharaoh had decreed death for every male child? If by some utterly remote coincidence he could remain alive, he would become a bricklaying helot, whipped daily by sadistic guards in the slave stables. But Miriam, their daughter, convinced them that they were wrong. Why?

Because resignation as a response to challenge is the sign of spiritual failure. It would not have been difficult for Miriam to throw up her hands and resign the next generation, and with it all hopes of redemption. Miriam said to Amram, her father, "Pharaoh declares death only in this world. You decree death in the world to come." Some resolution to the crisis would come, and perhaps the cumulative effect of all those children who survived could bring a change in the prevailing conditions. It was this blind unreasonable faith, this struggle for redemption hidden in the heart of a young daughter, that effected the miracle for the whole people. A Moses is born not by strategy or by accident, but by an act of faith.

We have no right today to resign the future. Withdrawal will bring us no solution, only certain demise. Even if the analysis of present evils were correct, and that is by no means certain, our response must be, "Let us raise a new generation that will continue the struggle against injustice. Even the slight diminution of evil will be a major conquest on behalf of God."

There is another response that is characteristically Jewish: obstinacy. "You want us to submit? Never. "Everything looks hopeless? We will survive. How? *Davka*. In spite of everything." Jewish survival is not only a matter of faith. How did we survive? *Davka*—despite everything. That is why procreation is not only a blessing, it is a commandment for every age.

Some people cite the population explosion as a more severe threat to human survival than nuclear holocaust or urban crime and blight. As worldwide medical advances make possible a diminished death rate and a wildly increasing birthrate, the world's available supply of food and energy is at a critical point.

There is no shred of doubt that the crisis is very real and potentially disastrous. Thomas Malthus, who anticipated the problem in 1798, theorized that war, famine, pestilence, and poverty would eliminate the "unwanted population." He recommended late marriage and premarital continence, but he had little hope that restraint would be exercised. Others, among them Marx and Engels, insisted that overpopulation was a matter of production and distribution efficiency. Only one-fourth of the arable world is cultivated, the oceans have not been tapped, and even the soy bean has yet to yield its full potential. There is, however, universal agreement that contraception must be used extensively if the geometric progression of births is to be halted.

The Jewish community has demonstrated its very sensitive moral conscience in this regard. To halt overpopulation, as well as for other personal reasons, many young Jews have accepted a regimen of birth control that stands to bring the Jewish community to utter catastrophe. Everywhere in the United States, the Jewish birthrate is far smaller than that of the non-Jewish community in which it resides. We have exceeded zero—the Jews are at *negative* population growth. The Arabs inside the State of Israel are producing two to five times as rapidly as Jews. Simple arithmetic will demonstrate that this is the gravest threat to Jewish survival. In a few years, we will have contracepted our way to the loss of millions of unborn souls—a self-made holocaust. The Jews now number approximately thirteen million worldwide. Professor Salo Baron, a Jewish historian, estimates that without pogroms and crusades, the population of the Jews would now be two hundred million. Together with assimilation and interfaith marriage, the Jewish community seems hell-bent on suicide.

Every Jewish birth today is a commitment to the Jewish future. It is a resounding response to the Hitlers of history that the Jews will survive. Today, bearing children is more than just fulfilling the religious duty to "be fruitful and multiply"—it is an act of faith in the God of Israel and the destiny of the Jewish people.

Far more Jews today are limiting family size because of pressing personal reasons such as unstable early marriage, insufficient income, psychological unreadiness, or career objectives that have yet to be accomplished. One must assess these matters with great compassion. People are sincere, intelligent, and idealistic, and the weightiness of their concerns should not be easily dismissed. Yet one must also ask disturbing questions, because the violation of this first blessing-commandment strikes at the roots of our very survival. If the couple is not yet prepared psychologically, why did they marry so young? Shall we allow ourselves to enjoy the privileges of marriage without accepting the obligations? If the question is economic, we must ask ourselves what will we have to do without. Is it a question of a larger car, a newer convenience or a bigger apartment versus a larger family? Can we equate a material good with a new life? Is the limiting of the family to two children a question of ideals or convenience? Do we not sometimes underestimate our capacities? We may be living in a "new" world but, after all, we are only a generation or two away from those twelve-children families that enjoyed somewhat fewer conveniences.

The *Zohar* declares, "When is the person called complete after the supernal pattern? When he is joined with his mate in unity, in joy and in affection, and there issue from their union a son and a daughter. Then the person is complete below, like the Holy Name above."

THE LAW ON BIRTH CONTROL

The foremost scholars of the Talmud have debated the question, "How large a family must one have in order to fulfill the religious obligation?" Considering the crisis proportions of the problem today, an appropriate reply would be "as large a family as possible!" The Sages, however, discuss the minimum acceptable fulfillment of the *mitzvah*.

The Mishnah states, "A man shall not abstain from the performance of the duty of the propagation of the race unless he already has children." How many children? The school of Hillel ruled "one boy and one girl," to imitate God's creation, "male and female He created them." The school of Shammai ruled "two sons," as Moses had two sons before he separated from Zipporah. Conjecturing, one could postulate that the Shammaites take Moses as their paragon and emphasize two males because they hold that a family must provide men who can study Torah and defend the borders of the homeland. The Hillelites take their cue from creation and concern themselves with the propagation of the race, which requires a balance between men and women. While the *Halakhah* accepts the Hillelite view as normative, and a man has indeed fulfilled his basic obligations if he has sired one son and one daughter, that is not sufficient to provide all the guidance that is necessary for the implementation of the *Halakhah*. First, the *Halakhah* is concerned with the means of contraception used after the basic family unit has been established. Second, the national Jewish need for survival in this post-Holocaust period places upon each of us special requirements to avoid the disappearance of Judaism and all it stands for.

Technically, two commandments are focal when considering questions of birth control. First the duty to have children, based on the positive commandment "Be fruitful and multiply." Second, the prohibition against "wasting seed" (*hashchatat zera*). This does not refer to intercourse with a sterile woman, but to conception prevented by artificial means. The legal literature discusses circumstances in which these two principles may be disregarded.

Several ground rules should be stated:

1. Since extramarital relations are prohibited, there is no permission for the use of any contraception, under any circumstances, outside of marriage.

2. The "wasting of seed" refers *primarily* to the male, thus contraception for the man is ruled out.
3. If pregnancy will cause death or injury to the woman, there is every indication that the rabbi will permit the use of contraceptives. This question should be presented to the rabbi for his ruling.

A halakhically-competent and authoritative rabbi will ask the following *questions:*

1. What is the reason for wanting to control birth?
2. What means will be used? (Mechanical and chemical means are less satisfactory than oral contraceptives, which do not directly cause the "wasting of seed.")
3. How many children do you already have?
4. Is there any threat to the mother or to the unborn child?

Birth control is not a matter of "individual conscience." These words may sound like the ultimate heresy in the context of our individualistic American democracy, but religious law, like civil law, is not made by decisions of individual conscience. (There is a proper area for decisions of conscience—in areas *beyond* the law, but this volume is too short for a protracted consideration of this sensitive issue.) The crisis of Jewish survival is implicit in the birth control question. It is difficult to be objective about our problems. It is tempting to decide on the basis of what is convenient rather than for what is right.

Jewish law concerns itself in a comprehensive manner with matters of utmost private concern. These, too, as all of life, come under the aegis of the Torah.

SEXUAL RELATIONS WITHIN MARRIAGE: BEYOND PROCREATION

We have discussed the two central purposes of marriage in the Jewish tradition, lifelong companionship and the creation and nurturing of a family. There is also a third purpose, negatively-worded but of vital positive significance to the welfare of society: the constraint upon sexual adventurism. Marriage creates a framework where sex can function to unite two people and help to make their lives meaningful, rather than be squandered in successive, isolated experiences. Marriage provides strong banks within which sex can course at the utmost of its power for the service of life, and enables each person to turn to the business of life beyond the sexual, to grow closer to God and more compassionate to humanity.

Thus one purpose of marriage is the avoidance of illicit sexual relations. The Talmud says, "He who reaches the age of twenty and has not married, spends

all his days in sin. Sin actually? Say better: All his days in the *thought* of sin."
God is described as waiting for people to marry so that they may not succumb
to temptation and to erotic fantasies, which are obstacles to holiness. Marriage,
in which temptation is satisfied and sex given expression, is called holiness
(*kiddushin*).

Holiness, then, is part of the *mitzvah* of marriage. The presence of the wife,
the husband's tie to the family, will keep society ordered and the sanctity of life
maintained. For this reason, the Torah ordained the *mitzvah* of *onah:* conjugal
relations that are positively required, separate and distinct from the need for
procreation.

Sexual relations within marriage have a value and life all their own. Sex is seen
not merely as a means for perpetuating the species, but as part of the human
personality. It is not only a channel of life, but a channel of love. Judaism teaches
that God did not plan the reproductive organs as strictly mechanical means for
the production of new life; God constructed the human being to appreciate the
physical and soulful ecstasy of the sexual act. Saadiah Gaon notes the view of
some of his contemporaries (which he believes is one-sided), that "sexual intercourse holds the most remarkable of pleasures. It increases the soul's gladness
and gaiety, it drives gloomy thoughts from the mind and serves as an antidote
to melancholy. And there cannot be anything reprehensible about the sex act
since God's holy men in the Bible engaged in it with His approval. ..."

The sex act that does not symbolize love is only physical and is a meaningless
acrobatic. Menahem Me'iri said in the thirteenth century, "Had relations
been only physical, the Bible would not have referred to them as *ye'diah*
[knowledge]." Physical joys subside with mechanical repetition, and the sheer
vacuity only intensifies the lack of love.

The marital sexuality that is beyond procreation is called by the Bible *onah*.
Healthy, proper sexuality as an act of love in marriage can bring new value into
ordinary life. It adds a renewed hope of permanence and an ever-deeper fusion
of personalities. It precludes the certainty of ultimate boredom, for while one
soon comes to the end of what a body can give, there is no limit to the
exploration of a personality. This *mitzvah* of *onah,* quite distinct from the
mitzvah of procreation, serves the children already born by making the marriage
a firmer, warmer, and more loving partnership. Even if no children can be born,
the couple will serve the primary purpose of sex by adding one more strong and
happy marriage to the whole institution of marriage on which each generation
depends. The law of conjugal rights, and the quality of relationship which it
fosters, is essential to the understanding of love and marriage.

Literally, *onah* means "time." It refers to sex that takes place during the
portion of the month following the *niddah* period (abstention during the menstrual cycle).

Though it takes place only during fertile times of the month, *onah* does not relate to sex that serves the procreative functions (e.g., in the case of a pregnant woman, sterility, or a woman who has passed menopause). This sexual activity, far from being considered useless because it is nonproductive, is a religious duty. Indeed, there is substantial opinion that it may be encompassed by both a negative *and* a positive biblical command. The negative: Exodus 21:10, which is applied by the Rabbis to every Jewish wife, states that a man "may not withhold her conjugal rights." The positive: Deuteronomy 24:5 states, "When a man takes a new wife, he shall not go out to the military, neither shall he be charged with any business; *naki yiheye le'veito,* he shall be free for his house one year, *ve'simach et ishto,* and he shall rejoice his wife whom he hath taken." During the first year of marriage, the husband was considered to have only begun to fulfill the *onah,* and he was exempt from the military draft. This applied even if his wife was pregnant, so that intercourse would not serve the purpose of procreation. Raavad says that only these two motivations for the sex act, procreation and *onah,* bring sanctity and purity to the family.

The Bible conceives of sex within marriage as the woman's right and the man's duty. (Until quite recently, the western concept of marital duty was that it is man's right and woman's duty). The woman's right is assured by the Bible; she may not waive it, and her husband may not preclude it as a condition of the marriage contract.

Woman's duty to man is specifically described in the Talmud, though it is not recorded in the Bible. The basic idea of the woman's right does not originate in an act of kindness, but is an essential component of marriage. No man may marry a woman and then simply ignore her or her sexual needs. It is remarkable that it has taken western thought so long to come to the conclusion that was evident in ancient biblical times, namely, that women have sexual needs just like men. The Victorian idea that a "lady" has no such feelings is a piece of prudery that never appeared in the long Jewish tradition.

Jewish law goes so far as to state that if either partner to the marriage refuses to participate in conjugal relations, (under certain conditions) that person is considered rebellious (*mored*) and the other spouse can sue for divorce. The Bible records three fundamental, unqualified rights of the woman in marriage—food, clothing, and conjugal rights—but only a refusal of the last dubs the husband a *mored.* That surely is because *onah* is the essence of the marriage. Food and clothing can be handled in court, but a withdrawal from *onah* is a functional termination of married life.

The husband's refusal to cohabit with her entitles a wife to a divorce, and if necessary he is compelled to issue one. As long as he refuses, her *ketubah* clause of financial guarantee is increased from week to week, thus adding to the settlement he must grant her upon termination of the marriage. The husband will not be considered a *mored,* however, if he can adduce proof that he finds his wife repulsive. In that case, he must be prepared to grant a divorce. The wife, on her part, is considered rebellious (a *moredet*), if for twelve months she persistently refuses to cohabit with her husband. Anger or strife is not considered legal justification for a refusal to cohabit, and her *ketubah* is lessened by the courts from week to week. If she claims revulsion the husband is entitled, according to her own wish, to divorce her. Maimonides says, "A wife should not be urged to have sexual relations with a person whom she finds repulsive."

The frequency of conjugal relations was of concern to the law, although the regulation of passion was obviously difficult. While the law here applies to the complex desires and needs of the human being, it must make a minimum quantitative assessment in order for marriage laws of *onah* to be enforced. If it did not, the law would be rendered ineffective. Rights and duties must be defined, or they will be ignored as merely sentimental platitudes. While it does seem paradoxical to define love by law, it is an effective, minimal safeguard that enables love to continue to function satisfactorily in society. Of course, in regard to the frequency of copulation, the law cannot deal in absolute numbers. Raavad says, "The *onah* frequency ordained by the Sages refers to the satisfaction of the individual woman's desires." According to Maimonides, it is also relative to the man's potency and to the nature of his work.

In addition to normal *onah*, the husband is expected to respond to his wife's needs whenever that may be (outside of the menstrual period) and even anticipate her desire (e.g., before leaving on an extended trip).

The Sages who stipulated the once-per-week *onah* for scholars recommended that it take place on Friday night. This talmudic prescription can help us to understand the nature of *onah*. There are two well known interpretations in medieval Jewish literature. One is that of Rashi who said, "Friday evening: for it is a night of delight, rest and physical joy." The joy of sex is not vulgar and merely tolerated. It is a joy appropriate to the holiest day of the week, a physical joy that is not merely the delight of the spirit.

The second appears in the mystical document *Iggeret ha-Kodesh.* "Friday night: for it is the secret of the turning of the 'wheel of time' in the seven-day period." It is a highly spiritual moment, when we celebrate the end of the six-day physical creation and the beginning of the day of *olam ha-ne'shamot* (the world of souls). Sexuality is raised to the level of spiritual heights. *Onah* is not God's indulgence for the weakness of the flesh, it is God's elevation of humanity through loving union on the most spiritual of days. It is special, as the Sabbath is special.

The Sabbath suggestion is even more instructive in light of an ancient Christian stricture regarding the frequency of copulation. In that literature, we find an opposite tradition: on Friday, one is to abstain from conjugal relations in memory of the death of the savior; Saturday, abstain in honor of Mary; Sunday in memory of the Resurrection. In this tradition, holiness and sexuality appear contradictory.

The *onah* experience may not be mere mechanical fulfillment, for as such it does not conform to the biblical requirement to rejoice one's wife. Rejoicing means satisfying needs, and it signifies a sensitive and caring involvement of the whole person and a genuine sense of intimacy, (*kiruv*). Therefore, Maimonides teaches that one may not have intercourse without being mindful, sensitive, and alert. "One may not have intercourse while either intoxicated or sluggish or in mourning; nor when [one's wife] is asleep, nor by overpowering her; but only with her consent and if both are in a happy mood." The act must be capable of expressing devotion. Thus one may not have intercourse if husband and wife are not committed to one another and are thinking of divorce, nor if they quarreled during the daytime and have not resolved it by nightfall. Raavad refers to this as exploitation, using one's partner as a harlot. One should not perform the conjugal act while imagining some other partner. The physical *onah* must be expressive of love; otherwise, it is simply animalistic.

Great sensitivity is a basic requirement in the Jewish attitude toward sex. No excuse of superior religiosity on one hand, or of rough-and-tumble masculinity on the other, may justify a less than delicate approach. The Midrash asserts, "The groom may not enter the bridal chamber without the specific permission of the bride." The Talmud counsels, "*Ishte'kha gutza* [if your wife is short] bend down and whisper." In an insightful and instructive passage, the Talmud reaches the epitome of delicacy: "The intimation of desire will usually come verbally from the husband, but Jewish women will hint only with the heart." Rabbi Hananel elucidates, "She hints by dressing up, prettying herself, and speaking softly in order to encourage her man to perform the *mitzvah*." Me'iri notes, "Her 'hinting' is not forwardness, but praiseworthy for its modesty . . . and she will be blessed with good children."

In addition to being delicate and gentle, *onah* requires the couple to design an erotic atmosphere. Sweetness and respect must permeate the darkened room. *Iggeret ha-Kodesh* says:

> Therefore you should begin with words that will draw her heart to you and will settle her mind and will make her happy, to unite your mind with her mind and your intention with her intention. Tell her things, some of which will produce in her desire, attachement, love, willingness and passion. Tell her words which will draw her to fear of Heaven and to piety and modesty [*tze'niut*]. Tell her of pious and modest women and of how they bore proper and pure children. It is fitting to win her heart with words of charm and seduction and other proper things, so that the intent of both of you will be unified for the sake of Heaven. Similarly, one should not have relations while his wife is sleepy for their minds will not be unified. Arouse her instead with pleasing words of desire as we have explained.

In summary, when you are ready to have relations, ensure that your wife's mind agrees with yours. Do not hasten to arouse her desire, so that her mind may be serene. Begin in a pleasing manner of love, so that she will be satisfied first [i.e., the woman should achieve satisfaction before the man].

Ramban added a nuance to these requirements. In the three obligations of marriage, the husband's duty is to provide food, clothing, and conjugal relations. Special clothing appropriate to sexual activity is not part of the *clothing* obligation, but part of the *onah* obligation. Of course, the *onah* obligation is more critical to the marriage in the eyes of the courts, hence we see that clothes and linens are obligatory for the enhancement of amorous relationships. The reasoning of Ramban is also significant: "A wife is not to be treated as a concubine. . . The bedroom atmosphere must have honor."

Maharam of Lublin writes that these sensitivities should prevail at all times, not only when sexual activity occurs. ". . . Even for the bride who is a menstruant during her wedding and for the seven days of celebration thereafter. . . . Know that not only is conjugal intercourse a *mitzvah*. All forms of closeness by which man rejoices his wife are *mitzvot*. . . . Thus one who is starting on a trip and his wife is about to have her menses, must pay special loving attention to her with words of kindness, and care, and closeness."

In our age of commercialized sex and the fear of sexual repression, it is necessary to recite and repeat the simple standard of decency to every married couple: The bedroom door must stay locked—physically during erotic encounters, and symbolically at all times. It is no one else's business, and surely should not serve as living room banter. The only times these matters may be spoken of is in therapy. If we do otherwise, we vulgarize that which is beautiful and make coarse that which should be delicate. The Hebrew word we have used for sexual intimacy is *yichud*, privacy.

The acme of the cultic experience in ancient Canaan was public fornication, orgies of the fertility cult with their temple prostitutes. When the Bible commands "Therefore shall you keep my charge, that you do not any of the abominable customs which were done before you" (Leviticus 18:3), it refers to the Canaanites and Amorites whose hallmark was the public display of sex, "the abominable practice" of the nations. Exile is the punishment for its violation. We may not tolerate the Canaanite barbarism of today's X-rated society. Jewish love is discreet, modest, intimate, private, quiet. The Talmud says: "There is no one so loathsome as one who walks naked in the street." *Onah*, surely, is the very personal province of husband and wife.

Perhaps the most devastating destroyer of marriage is boredom. To avoid that distasteful eventuality, the physical act must be a fusion not only of bodies, but of personalities. An expression of mature love doesn't dull, it gets deeper and richer. An act of muscles and glands easily becomes routine, with the sense of mystery diminished by constant closeness, total availability, and a "business-as-usual" attitude. The fire that transformed *Adam* into *esh* with the creation of Eve, and into *ish* with the recognition of the divine component of marriage, reverses when only bodies unite.

The physical act must be sensitively appreciated. The *Halakhah* understood this crucial matter and provided for the widest latitude and the fullest expression, with the constant qualification that the act retain the potential for reproduction and that there be total consent and an abiding sense of human dignity. The law comprehends the human need for variety in the conjugal act, but it has only disgust for *pe'ritzut,* the obscenities of the Playboy ethic. The Talmud makes bold decisions on these matters, and Rabbi Huna even advised his own daughter in the method of conjugal relations with the goal of keeping awareness alive.

When conjugal relations are the result of compulsion, sexual intimacy is robbed of its essential holiness. It makes the blending of bodies and personalities inhumane. True, the tradition does counsel the spouse to yield if at all possible, but if that does not occur, the *Halakhah* has no tolerance. It is nothing less than "domestic rape." The Talmud says, "He who coerces his wife will produce unworthy children." The Rabbis go so far as to say that in such ugly exploitation of his wife, a man is considered morally, though not legally, to have cohabitated with a harlot and to have produced a child who is akin to a *mamzer.*

Maimonides declares, "You must not have relations with her against her will. In such relations, because they are not done with great desire, love, and willingness, the Divine Presence does not rest; for your intents are different and the mind of your wife does not coincide with your mind. You must not fight with her or beat her in regard to conjugal relations." The Talmud, in a precise and graphic analogy, says that "just as a lion tears his prey and devours it and has no shame, so an *Am ha-Aretz,* a boor, strikes his wife then cohabits with her and has no shame." Fortunately, wife-beating has virtually no history in the traditional Jewish community.

The use of sex as a weapon by a manipulating mate is a desecration. Indeed, the negative phrasing of the duty of *onah* implies this rejection of its misuse: *lo yigra* (a man may not diminish her *onah*) *ke'dei le'tzaarah* (in order to pain her). Rabbi Isaac of Trani complained, "Some men go on business trips and stay overly long, well into the period of her *onah."* There is a large body of rabbinic opinion that insists, for this reason, that the husband does not violate the duty of *onah* if he "diminishes it," providing his wife voluntarily concurs with him on its need. Maimonides adds that the wife is also not permitted this manipulation: "The Sages commanded the woman that she not withhold herself from her husband in order to hurt him or even to increase his love for her. . . ."

Cynics like to say that the world is a marketplace and we must barter to get what we want. However one may feel about this, surely people ought to be sensitive enough to consider conjugal sex beyond trade. Such manipulators only put their mates in the position of "in-house" prostitutes. May their spouses one day not find it more attractive "*out* of the house"?

The sexual act is not something invented by man's lust and tolerated by an indulging God. It is ordained by God Himself as the means for the perpetuation of the human race and for the ultimate expression of human love. There is nothing shady about the sexual appetite legitimately expressed. The Tenth Commandment says "Do not covet *another man's* wife." It is not said about desire for one's *own* wife.

The positive duty of the *mitzvah* of *onah* is *simchah*, the rejoicing during sex that is literally a religious duty. The Talmud says, "R. Joseph said that 'clothing' [one of the three obligations that husband owes to wife] really implies 'the closeness of the flesh'—as clothing is placed on the flesh, so the conjugal act must relate directly to the flesh. So as to tell people not to conduct themselves as the ancient Persians did who cohabited fully-clothed." If husband or wife insist on doing this, it could constitute cause for divorce. Ritba comments, "Even if they insist on this for the sake of religious modesty . . . for this is not the way of love."

The sexual aspect of marriage does not fall under the shadow of sin or shame, and this is evinced in many statements in Jewish literature. The beauty, character, and even the health of children is held to be influenced by the nature of the act. The act itself, ideally, should not be perfunctory and dutiful, but as fresh as the first union on the wedding night. The wife is urged to use cosmetics and to wear jewelry so that she should always continue to be attractive to her husband. Maharam Rotenburg went so far as to say, "Let a curse descend upon a woman who has a husband and does not strive to be attractive." Being religious means fulfilling the goals of Torah, it does not mean being "more religious" than one's neighbor. "Do not be overly-righteous," Ecclesiastes says. Judaism is not Puritanism.

"My beloved is like a gazelle" (Song of Songs 2:9). This is a symbol of the beloved as beautiful, graceful, dainty, nimble—the very perfection of erotic refinement. In Proverbs (5:19) a comely and beloved woman is called a "loving deer, a graceful roe." She is the picture of modesty: "Knowest thou the time when the goats gave birth?" asks Job (39:1). And like the mountain goat, the male should be strong, self-contained. able to retain his balance while climbing on rocks and negotiating the tall peaks. One can still see this picture in Ein Gedi in Israel: the mountain goat stands motionless, statuesque, his excitement and power molded in self-control, waiting only for his mate. She is modest and beautiful; he is strong and self-controlled. Solomon's Song is the Jewish way: "My beloved is like the deer."

Part Four

THE STRUCTURE OF THE MARRIAGE COVENANT

CHAPTER 10

"According to the Laws of Moses and Israel":
Ke'dat Moshe Ve' Yisrael:
The Jewish Marriage Ceremony

Jewish marriage law consists not only of *ishut,* the determination of prohibited and permitted partners, but of *kiddushin,* the legal *process* of establishing the marriage bond. The Bible has no single word for marriage, as it has none for religion. But the codes define it by these two categories: *ishut* and *kiddushin,* persons and process.

Maimonides begins his code on marriage with the Torah's unconditional requirement that a man and a woman may live together only with the formal sanction of *kiddushin.*

> Before the revelation (at Sinai), a man would meet a woman on the street and if both desired marriage, he would bring her into his home and have intercourse privately [without the testimony of witnesses] and she would become his wife. When the Torah was given, the Jews were instructed that in order to marry a woman, the man should "acquire her" in the presence of witnesses and then she would become his wife. As the Torah says, "when a man *takes* a woman and has intercourse with her." This *taking* is a positive commandment and is performed in one of three ways—with money, by contract, or by cohabitiation . . . and it is everywhere called *kiddushin*

or *erusin*. And a woman who is "acquired" in one of these three ways is called *me'kudeshet* or *arusah* [a betrothed woman]. And as soon as she is "acquired" and becomes betrothed, even though she has not cohabited and did not even enter the groom's home, she is a married woman. Anyone, other than her husband, who cohabits with her, is guilty of capital punishment. If he wishes to separate from her, he requires a divorce.

Maimonides tells us that a Jewish marriage consists of two stages. The first is betrothal, *kiddushin*. The second is the nuptials, *chuppah*.

Kiddushin (a rabbinic term) is accomplished by *kichah* (a biblical term), the "taking" of a woman by a man, in one of three ways (in ages past):

1. Money (kessef).   The man gives the woman money, even a low denomination coin, or the equivalent of money—today a ring is customary—before two witnesses and says, "You are hereby betrothed unto me with this ring in accordance with the laws of Moses and Israel." The bride, by her acceptance, indicates her willingness to be married to the groom.

2. Contract (she'tar).   The man gives the woman a deed, before two witnesses, which contains the names of the couple and the groom's marriage formula. This deed is not in the nature of evidence of the marriage, but is for the purpose of effecting the bond of marriage. It is not to be confused with the *ketubah*, which is given as protection of the woman *after* the *kiddushin*.

3. Intercourse (bi'ah).   After the man has addressed the marriage formula to the woman before two witnesses, the couple retires to a private place with the intent of effecting the betrothal through intercourse. The Sages considered this to be gross, virtually an act of prostitution, and in the third century Rav decreed flogging for those who chose this manner of betrothal. Nonetheless, if the marriage was performed in this way it was legally valid.

Only *kessef* is performed today; both intercourse and contract as forms of betrothal are obsolete.

Kichah ("taking," the formal acquisition) approximates the economic term *kinyan* and seals the marriage. Because this is the first stage in the process of creating a covenant of partnership, unions that are prohibited and void, such as incest, are never referred to in the Torah by the term *kichah*, but as *she'k-hivah* (sleeping together). In regard to almost all *valid* marriages, even those that are prohibited, the Torah makes specific reference to *kichah*.

This first stage of marriage is not a *preliminary* agreement to contract a marriage at a future date (like the western concept of engagement), but an integral component of the two-step marriage process. The betrothal portion is a sort of inchoate marriage; from that point onward, the couple is considered married. Until the second step is taken, however, the bride may not cohabit with the groom (or any other man). In this social suspension that marks the difficult transition from the single life to the married state, the couple is together yet apart. Until the twelfth century, this first stage of marriage lasted up to one year in order to make preparations for the final step. The second stage of the marriage process is the consummation. It is alternatively termed *nissuin,* meaning elevation of status, from *nassa,* coming by carriage from the father's home to the groom's; or *chuppah,* wedding canopy.

The Bible begins to use the term *kichah* as a preliminary to marital intercourse only *after* the Torah is received at Sinai. From this time forward, all Jewish marriages must have *both* components in order to be valid. The Rabbis, in order to make this perfectly clear to the couple, framed the betrothal blessing to read: ". . . who has forbidden us the betrothed [*arusot*], and permitted us those who are married to us by *chuppah* and *kiddushin.*"

By the twelfth century in Germany and France, the two elements were no longer separate but were fused into one ceremony and that is how marriage is performed to this day. The wedding ceremony begins with the betrothal, which consists of the blessings; the *kinyan* (the formal acquisition by means of the giving of the ring); and the recitation of the marriage formula. This is followed by a reading of the *ketubah* (the marriage contract). The marriage is finalized by the *chuppah* ceremony, which consists of the seven blessings, and *yichud,* when the bride and groom are brought together in a private room to symbolize the consummation of the marriage.

The reasons for combining the two ceremonies offer interesting insights into the moral concern of the Rabbis, the history of the period, and the economic plight of the Jews of the Middle Ages. Rashi, the classic commentator, offers the simple explanation that the costs were too burdensome. The families would be shamed if they could not afford a sumptuous all-day banquet in honor of the betrothal, and still another banquet in celebration of the nuptials. Putting the ceremonies together eliminated the need for two banquets. This also helps to explain the ancient custom of holding the betrothal on Friday afternoon. The Shabbat dinner of Friday night doubled as the betrothal celebration, and the nuptials were held on Saturday night after sundown.

Conditions for medieval Jews were unstable and hazardous. During the year between the betrothal and the nuptials, families might be compelled to flee to distant shores. That would leave the betrothed woman an *agunah,* (literally, a chained woman) married yet not married, unable to live with her fiancè and not permitted to marry anyone else without a divorce, which, considering the distance and lack of communications, was often quite difficult to arrange. Holding the two ceremonies in quick succession offered a practical solution to this distressing situation.

Morally, the fusion of the two ceremonies accomplished the removal of temptation from the betrothed couple, who were not permitted to cohabit during the year of betrothal. Indeed, we have seen that the betrothal blessing in talmudic days is worded precisely to prevent that eventuality. In the era when the idea of romantic love spread wildly throughout Europe, the temptations must have been great to relinquish the ideal of chastity in the expectation of the forthcoming marriage. This problem was not confined to the romantic era. In the third century, preventing these intimacies became a widespread problem in Judea, where poor grooms were housed by wealthier in-laws in the home of the prospective bride. The law took recognition of this problem when it refused to allow the complaint from a groom on the day after the *chuppah* that the bride deceived him because she was not a virgin. Because he and the bride lived in the same house, the groom could not be presumed innocent; in fact, it raised the possibility that it was he who deflowered the bride. In the very first chapter of the talmudic tractate of *Ketubbot* we read: "If in Judea a man boarded with his father-in-law but had no witnesses, he can not institute virginity proceedings against her, because he had already been alone with her."

THE BETROTHAL (*KIDDUSHIN*)

The Betrothal portion of the ceremony consists of a preliminary benediction, the marriage proposal, and the giving of the ring. Fundamentally, it is a ceremony of acquisition. "When a man *acquires* a wife" (Deuteronomy 24:1) are words that fall harshly on contemporary ears. We blush at retaining ancient modes and terms that offend our sensitivities and egalitarian sentiments—acquire, indeed! But the wisdom of the Torah, the insightfulness of the talmudic teachers and the sense of balance of the religious tradition, which has experienced thirty-five centuries of marriage, deserves comprehension, not apologies. For all its apparent incongruity with modern thinking, the ancient ways express enduring values. If we dig beneath the deceptively simple surface, we find that these values have surprising relevance for the twentieth century.

THE NEED FOR FORMAL ACQUISITION

As noted earlier, it is remarkable that love and sex, which are so unpredictable and explosive, should serve as the foundations of family life. The concept of marriage as acquisition was the first step in domesticating, channeling, and making productive the passion and romance of love and desire. The key word in the Bible, note the Rabbis of the Talmud, is *kichah*. It is mentioned twice, both times in different contexts. One refers to marriage, *ki yikach ish ishah,* when a man *takes* a woman. The other refers to Abraham's purchase of a field from Ephron, which he buys for the burial of Sarah (Genesis 23:13). What is the common denominator? According to the Talmud, we learn the significance of the *kichah* of marriage from the *kichah* of the field of Ephron. *Kichah* signified a transfer of money for the field, thus in marriage *kichah* means that a wife is "acquired" by her husband through a transfer of money (the groom gives the bride an object of value worth not less than a *perutah,* an insignificant coin). Ramban noted long ago that in making the analogy to money for purchase, the Sages of the Talmud did not intend to equate marriage with property, but only to define a mode of legal conveyance.

The *Halakhah* insists on a technically legal *kinyan* in order to create the new relationship. The woman now becomes *eshet ish* (a married woman), permitted to no other man, and the husband and wife become subject to the prohibited incestuous relationships with each other's closest relatives. Society could not create marriage out of what was merely a well-intentioned promise, or an agreeable arrangement, or a statement of shared goals, however noble these were. It required a formal, binding *kinyan.*

When Maimonides sketches the history of marriage from the primitive meeting on the street to formal marriage and, possibly, formal divorce, he is saying that the "acquisition" formalizes and crystallizes an otherwise amorphous relationship. Marriage is established through its framework: a formal beginning, a formal ending, and an acknowledged and accepted period of changed status and obligations. For example, betrothal by contract is derived from the need of formal divorce; in Hebrew this is expressed, *ve'yatze'ah ve'hayeta* (she goes out of one marriage and into another). As the "going out," a divorce, is accomplished by written document, her "coming in," marrying, is by written document (referring to the second mode of *kinyan*). There must be in that formal beginning and ending, whether it is expressed in writing, or in action, a moment when society declares a change in the new relationship. The marriage formula declares the woman prohibited to all other men, the divorce formula that she is permitted to all other men. What "clinches" the formula's capacity to create a new reality is the *kinyan,* a physical act designed specifically to seal the idea of the word and formalize it before witnesses, the representatives of society.

The use of the purchase of property as the model of marriage "acquisition" is carefully developed. People readily understand the responsibilities of land ownership, but may not appreciate the responsibilities of marriage and family. The headiness of love and shared hope cloud the realities of the couple's new situation. Young couples often feel that a love relationship is informal and should be celebrated festively, not with contracts, acquisitions, and other legalities. This hazy, undefined togetherness, however, makes for casual arrangements and hit-or-miss relationships. By using the word *kichah* in two different contexts, the Rabbis associated marriage with property transfer and thus insisted that marriage be initiated formally and seriously as a permanent bond.

A permanent bond means specific laws that do not by themselves take into account the prevailing individual sentiment. No amount of love, for example, can lawfully permit a bride to contract a marriage by agreeing to accept as a marriage gift an object worth less than a *pe'rutah*. The reverse is also true. A *pe'rutah* is a minimum legal unit, not one instituted for her honor or to serve as a gift of love. If it were, the bride could insist that her honor and love require an exorbitant sum. Like the daughters of the talmudic sage, Rabbi Yannai, she could assert that her honor deserves much more than a lowly *pe'rutah*—perhaps a barrelful of *dinarim*. The marriage gift is designed not to express personal worth, but to fulfill the technical legal requirements of formal acquisition.

Judaism must protect the family from the tempestuousness of sex, the alternating patterns of love, the sudden ups and downs of very close relationships. Just as the buyer of property intends to protect it, develop it, make it productive, and cherish it, this must also be the plan of those who undertake marriage. Because he bought the land, Abraham returned to it. Of course, he also returned to it because he buried his wife there, but the purchase of property was his investment in the Promised Land—it rooted him in a land to which his only tie had been spiritual. Jeremiah purchased property to demonstrate to his fellow Jews that despite impending destruction, a Jew must be tied to his land (32:6–16). So, indeed, the bond between man and woman—though qualitatively different from man's relationship with his property—must be responsible, firm, intelligent, and able to weather the most unfavorable conditions.

As the formal acquisition transferred the property from someone else's proprietorship, or from *hefker* (a state of abandonment and ownerlessness) to his personal care and protection, so the establishment of formal *kinyan* in marriage rescued family life from *hefker*. In this way, the formalizing of the marriage bond made it possible for the family to become the foundation of all society and the pattern for all government as well as the governance of the "family of nations."

Before Sinai, married life was a loose, voluntary arrangement, a sort of *ye'duah be'tzibbur* (common law) situation. If two people wished to live together, they did. If a woman desired another man, she could not be accused of adultery. If she wanted to move out, she did. Just as in our "living together" situations of today, there were no binding ties. Under such conditions, the legal protections of the family, such as the husband's obligation of support, honor, and fidelity, are at best fond hopes. At the drop of a shoe or a loud snore, children can be orphaned from one parent for life. It is abundantly clear that this can and does occur, and couples who cohabit undergo "premarital divorce" in our day. The informal arrangement was the old institution of concubinage (*pileggesh*), which Maimonides affirms was the relationship of a man and his exclusive girlfriend, without benefit of a formal marriage and marriage contract.

By formalizing marriage, Judaism saved marriage. By stamping it "legal acquisition," it made firm that which was vague and inchoate. It held the family fast—so fast that the family eventually held together the whole exiled and hopelessly dispersed Jewish community. This is surely hinted at in the betrothal blessing, when God is praised as *me'kadesh ammo Yisrael al ye'dei chuppah ve'kiddushin,* "He who sanctifies his people Israel through marriage and betrothal." Through the laws of marriage, God enhances family life, personal morality, and Jewish survival. Rabbi David Abudarham, a medieval liturgical commentator, said, "When we recite in our prayers 'God who sanctified us,' we may interpret it 'God who married us,' " for the Hebrew root of both "sanctified" and "married" is k-d-sh.

ACQUISITION IS NOT OWNERSHIP

We can understand the talmudic Rabbis' concept of marriage not only by what they *derived* from the comparison between property acquisition and marital acquisition, but also by what they *rejected* in it. Generally speaking, there are two concepts of property ownership: (1) an owner has the right only to *use* the property to achieve his ends; and (2) an owner exerts total *power* over the property. Philosopher Morris Raphael Cohen once defined property as nothing more than the sovereign *power* to exclude others.

While one could make a good case for the *use* concept of property, which ultimately belongs to God, there is nothing in Judaism that would not permit espousal of Cohen's power theory. We own property during our tenure on earth and, even if our ownership is not metaphysically absolute, politically we have exclusive sovereignty over that property. That is how society understands "private" property. One interpretation of *kichah,* therefore, implies exclusivity. When a man "takes" a wife, he chooses one woman and, with her consent, makes her his life-long partner. She has no other husband. This idea of exclusivity is derived from the concept of property ownership.

More specifically, the Talmud derives its interpretation of exclusivity from the acquisition of *temple* property, rather than from *secular* property acquisition. (The Talmud uses two terms for betrothal, which appear, respectively, as the titles of the first two chapters of the tractate *Kiddushin.* The first is *Ha-ishah Niknet,* [A Woman Is *Acquired*]; the second is *Ha-Ish Me'kadesh* [A Man *Sanctifies*]. The Talmud continues: "At the beginning the author uses the biblical term *niknet,* 'acquired,' while he later employs a rabbinical one, *me'-kadesh,* 'sanctifies.' What is the meaning of the rabbinical term sanctify? He forbids her to all other males, like something *hekdesh,* dedicated to the sanctuary, which is *exclusively* its property." Thus in marriage a wife is permitted to her husband but not to any other man; she is exclusive to this partnership.)

The rabbinic application of *kichah* to temple property is basic to an understanding of Jewish marriage. If we were to derive the lesson from civil property transfer alone, we could say that exclusivity is a result of *ownership.* A man owns property and no one else may trespass on it. Transposed to marriage, this would imply that the wife is exclusive to her husband as a *consequence* of his *ownership* of her person. Such an idea is repugnant to Judaism. The Jewish husband does not *own* his wife.

The lesson we learn from *hekdesh,* however, provides a fresh insight. In *hekdesh,* when a man dedicates an object to the temple, it is not a change in *ownership,* from owner to temple that is effected, it is a change in the *status* of the object. It becomes a sanctified item that cannot be used for secular purposes. The reason it is exclusive to the temple is not a consequence of temple ownership, but rather because its inherent status is sacred. Hence, in marriage there is no transfer of ownership—*no person owns another person*—instead the woman receives a new status as *eshet ish* (a married woman). It is not a *consequence* of her betrothal, it is the very *definition* of her betrothal.

The personal status inherent in *eshet ish* sets the character of Jewish marriage. The exclusive nature of the married woman may never be compromised, diminished, or voluntarily contracted out. A number of examples of her exclusivity are mentioned in different tracts of the Talmud:

1. If a man fulfills all the requirements of the betrothal ceremony except that he wishes to marry only "part of" the woman, the marriage is void. A woman must retain her integrity. She is exclusive and cannot be shared.

2. "If a man says to a woman, 'Today you are my wife, but tomorrow you will not be my wife,' will she be free without a divorce and the marriage void?" No. Personal status (*ke'dushat ha-guf*) is not terminable in advance; the duration of the status cannot be limited beforehand. The law states that the marriage is valid, but the condition is void; and she may not cease to be a married woman without a divorce or the husband's death.

The Jerusalem Talmud comments, "If someone says: You are betrothed to me for thirty days, she is betrothed forever" (that is, until divorce or death). Commentators note that the very nature of Jewish marriage implies that once a woman has this status conferred upon her, it is as though her husband said, "You are betrothed to me forever."

3. The termination of *eshet ish* is also absolute. A woman is either totally *out* of the status of "the married woman" or totally *within* it. If a husband hands a divorce to his wife and says, "You are now free to marry anyone except a certain man," the divorce is not valid and the woman is not divorced. There is no such thing as partial divorce.

All of the variations of marriage that compromise the integrity of a woman's married status are violations of the sacred Jewish concept of marriage. Commune marriages, planned serial monogamy, and wife-swapping, are modern reflections of ancient attempts to undermine the institution of marriage. The

Torah disqualifies these options when it likens marriage to acquisition of sacred property.

ACQUISITION BY CONSENT

In Jewish law, taking a wife can *never* mean taking by force. Perhaps it was to insure against the slightest possibility of this primitive interpretation that the tradition associated the "taking" of marriage with the "taking" involved in Abraham's purchase of the field of Ephron. Just as mutual consent is required for a property sale, it is an unqualified prerequisite for marriage.

An important part of the marriage service is the assurance of the woman's consent. Indeed, the emphasis on the consensual nature of the Jewish marriage contract is an ethical value that Judaism has taught the world. Contract law in England and America derives, to a large extent, from the talmudic law on marriage contracts and its persistent emphasis on the voluntary participation of both parties.

The focal phrase regarding consent in the Bible appears in Genesis (24:58) when Rebekah's brother and mother ask her if she is willing to marry Isaac. The Talmud refines and develops the concept in halakhic terms. The Talmud asks,"Why does the *Mishnah* begin with [a woman is acquired] *ha-ishah niknet,* rather than *ha-ish koneh* [a man acquires]?" The Talmud responds that the latter might imply to the uninitiated in Jewish law acquisition in *any* manner, even against the woman's will. The emphasis on *her* acquistion indicates—in the very first word of the first *mishnah* of the first chapter of the talmudic tractate on marriages—that the acquisition is dependent upon her consent.

Rashba, a noted thirteenth-century Spanish talmudist, asks why this emphasis was necessary, since *no* other contract could ever be made without consent. The answer is that a commercial transaction, entered into with only grudging consent made under duress, is valid. He quotes Maimonides who holds that in civil contracts, if we are sure that both parties consent, even though one of them does not specifically articulate "I agree," the contract is nonetheless valid. Rashba says that while this is true in commercial transactions, it does not hold for the marital procedure. In regard to marriage, consent made under duress invalidates the whole process. The Jewish tradition will not permit a marriage to begin on this basis; it will not allow any circumstance at all to reduce the woman's freedom to select as she desires.

Further, Kalman Kahana establishes that, with regard to property, only rights are being transferred. Rights, of course, also require consent; but even consent under duress is sufficient for the acquisition of a right. In regard to marriage, however, we are creating a new status, initiating a lifelong binding relationsip that requires wholehearted, clear-headed, unflinching consent. For property acquisition we require only *haskamah* (consent), even though it be unwilling. For marriage, the law requires *daat* (*willing* consent). Rabbi Hayyim of Volozhin, a nineteenth-century scholar, holds that the primary purpose of the presence of witnesses is to testify to the woman's *willing* consent.

Because clear consent is required, the ring given by the man must be of easily determined value. What appears to be a diamond might in fact be costume jewelry; the woman might be deceived. Perhaps she would have given consent to the marriage, but not *willing* consent, had she known its true value. She therefore has grounds for rescinding the marriage.

Because the betrothal could be executed with only a ring, a statement, a consenting nod, and witnesses, a problem arose around mock marriages. If the ceremony contains all the rudimentary components, but is done in jest at a party, without *willing* consent, is the couple required to get a formal divorce? There is a serious possibility that marriage might have been halakhically triggered!

Many such curious incidents are recorded, and many complicated Responsa were written on this subject. It is one of the reasons for the betrothal becoming a more "official" and public occasion. Originally, the betrothal was performed in the presence of only two witnesses in the privacy of the home, (while only the nuptials required the *minyan* of ten). Leading rabbis received questions about young girls who had been betrothed as a trick or joke; and girls who were still minors were being proposed to and given the ring without their parents' knowledge. Men often proposed to very young girls only in order to blackmail their fathers! In the year 810, to remedy this situation, Rabbi Ahai Gaon, of eighth-century Babylonia, instituted the requirement of the presence of ten adult males for the blessings at every betrothal. Subsequently, the marriage contract was required to be written and formally witnessed at the betrothal. Young girls were taught to take vows not to accept betrothal without parental consent. If instances of mock marriages occur today, a rabbi competent in halakhic decision should be consulted immediately. Marriage is far too serious a matter to become a subject of jokes, however well-intentioned. Hence the Rabbis were quite severe in their judgments. They strove to discourage a light-hearted attitude, and to keep marriage on an exalted level.

The concept of *daat* (willing consent) had many ramifications. A woman might withhold consent until she had negotiated numerous conditions in the contract; conversely, she might be so blinded by love or desire that she would agree to virtually any conditions in order to marry her suitor. If the loneliness of single life had become intolerable, she might be prompted to accept the lesser of two evils and marry under very difficult contractual conditions. For example, she might agree never to visit her mother. If she did so, even many years later, her husband could claim she violated the contract. The contract might then become void from its inception, requiring the marriage to be rescinded. Her children could then become functional orphans, and she would lose the monetary portion of her *ketubah*.

In order to defend women against unscrupulous men who might insist on intolerable preconditions to marriage, the Rabbis slowly eliminated all but the standard conditions of the marriage contract. Gifts of money continue at times to be included as conditions, so long as they do not bear adversely on the possibility of starting a family under favorable circumstances.

The law moved gradually from *contract*—the ability to negotiate *everything* independently which, as noted, often worked against women—to *status*, which by itself was a sort of guarantee of minimum livable conditions. Her new status was designed to enable her to make a success of marriage and family, without specific negotiations. Willing consent was not only consent to marry a specific individual, but to enter into this new personal status.

Rabbi Shimon Shkop, a twentieth-century Head of Yeshiva, notes that with property there is a change of owners (*baalut*), but obviously no change in the status of the land. In marriage, there is *no* change of owners (*be'alim*): the father did not own his daughter (he had only certain legally defined rights over a minor daughter, as he had responsibilities for her), and the husband does not own her as a wife. It is her status that changes. Previously, she was permitted to all men; now consorting with another man is subject to the laws of adultery. Previously, her cohabitation even with this chosen man was branded immoral; now it is a loyal following of the laws of Torah and considered a great *mitzvah*.

The very word *kinyan* is used in rabbinic literature for acquiring friends in general. The Sages say *ke'neh le'kha chaver* (acquire a close friend for yourself). Similarly, the sixth chapter of the Ethics of the Fathers is called *Perek Kinyan Torah*, "Acquisition of Torah"; Ben Sira (6:7) says *kanita ohev be'nisayon konehu* ("If you want to acquire a friend, take him on trial, and be in no hurry to trust him"). This implies that you must extend yourself to win good friends. In this sense, too, *kinyan* is surely an appropriate term for "acquiring" a wife.

WOMAN'S INDEPENDENCE

No individual can acquire possessive rights of another individual. Judaism believes in the sacredness and hence independence of the human personality, and it acts on that belief. Owning another human being could be a form of slavery. *Be'nei Yisrael avadai hem ve'lo avadim le'avadim*—"For the children of Israel are My servants, and not servants of servants." Children are not the servants of their parents, wives are not the servants of husbands, nor husbands of wives.

It cannot be overstated that acquisition in marriage is absurdly construed by some to mean ownership of a mate. This is nothing short of a calumny. The Torah speaks of woman's rights (*ishut*); it says nothing of a man's rights, only of his obligations. It says nothing of a wife's obligations, although the talmudic Sages developed scripturally-implied mutual obligations and rights. Biblically, men had obligations because they had the funds and the power, while women's influence, though often considerable, was at that time exercised indirectly.

Legal insight into Jewish commercial law is revealing. If acquisition of *kichah* were identical in marriage as in property, the executor of the contract would not be the man but the woman. In Jewish commercial law, whereas the consent of both parties is required, the buyer is passive and only accepts the transfer instrument and acquires title. It is the seller who prepares the contract and delivers it to the buyer. By all reasonable standards, if marriage were considered just another form of purchase the husband would be the buyer, the wife the seller. But in Jewish law the wife does not write the contract. There is also no discussion in any of the Jewish sources of the possibility of *chazakah*, another mode of property acquisition. When the Talmud asks whether barter (*chalippin*) might be used as a mode of acquisition in place of money, the commentators are quick to point out that there was never an assumption that marriage is to be equated with property, and it cannot be construed as another form of *kessef.*

The wife cannot remotely be considered the property of her husband. The husband never had the power of compulsion over his wife, as was true of English law until the end of the nineteenth century. In Jewish law, the husband is not responsible for his wife's crimes or her sins. Except when she is involved in irrational behavior or starkly immoral displays, the husband had no right to interfere in her life. Similarly, the particular heinousness of adultery is not that it is an invasion of the husband's private property, it is a sin against God that threatens the whole structure of family and society.

Indeed Maimonides writes that "If a woman says: 'My husband is objectionable to me, I cannot live with him. . . . I hold him in contempt and cannot willingly agree to be intimate with him,' we compel him to divorce her forthwith, for she is not a captive to be compelled to intimacy with one she hates." Rabbenu Tam, of twelfth-century France, and Rosh, of thirteenth-century Germany, two leading authorities, disagree because they fear this kind of reasoning may come to be used indiscriminately as an excuse for obtaining a divorce. However, we may infer that if it were humanly possible to be certain of the genuineness of the objection in each case, it would constitute grounds for compelling a divorce.

A married woman is considered legally and actually to be in her own possession. In reference to different subjects in the laws of marriage, two medieval authorities make pointed statements. Rashba: "The woman's person is not acquired by the husband and this marriage ceremony is not a property transaction." Ramban: "She has never been the property of her husband and is in her own possession."

A woman cannot be willfully compelled by her husband to lower her social status or economic level. Furthermore, if she and her husband are living in her mother-in-law's home and a quarrel develops between the two women, the wife can insist that the couple move out at the pain of compelling him to divorce her.

In classic Jewish literature, relations between husband and wife were based on mutual trust and respect, not on threats and browbeating. Wife-beating, so common in the western world, is considered to be utterly reprehensible by Judaism. Historically, it has occurred very rarely in Jewish families. If a man was found to be a wife-beater, he had to pay damages and provide her with separate maintenance. Failing that, the wife had valid grounds for compelling a divorce. By and large, men were prevented from such brutality by the force of public distaste. Jewish men were commanded to love and honor their wives by the words of the marriage contract, *ke'hilkhot guvrin ye'hudain*—as Jewish men are *accustomed* to do.

According to the Torah, the husband also has no legal rights to, or power over, his wife's personal finances. In every period of Jewish history, including the early patriarchal era and the Middle Ages, the wife had an independent right to property. Technicalities concerning the wife's property fill many folios of the Talmud. The rabbinic laws concerning use and maintenance of the property were designed for the furtherance of domestic tranquility (*she'lom bayit,*) which they considered superior to all other considerations.

Throughout the history of Judaism, women have had the right to work. In fact, during the Middle Ages, Jewish women often earned the major portion of the family budget. They engaged in a wide variety of commercial occupations, especially moneylending, a business often forced upon the Jewish community by the restrictive policy of the State regarding ownership of real estate. Community organizations frequently appointed women as trustees with the right to invest funds at their own discretion. Impeding a wife's right to work, which is a complicated legal issue, is considered by the Talmud to be legitimate grounds for compelling divorce. Such laws are not actionable outside of Israel today, as no divorce can be compelled by a Jewish court in the Diaspora.

The Rabbis guaranteed a married woman the right to work, but in the name of healthy family unity they decreed that her earnings must go to the family fund, just as her husband's earnings go to support her and the family. If she relinquishes her husband's support she may keep her wages. (The law does not give the husband the opportunity to refuse to support his wife when she works.) For the sake of domestic peace, the Rabbis ruled that there should be a household division of labor; (e.g., if the husband works the wife has to keep house or, if they are wealthy, at least manage the house. The wife, however, can refuse to do housework if she herself works and pays someone else to clean house in her stead).

These legal decisions clearly and unequivocally reflect the ideal of the independence of Jewish women. Rabbi Johanan said, "Thou shalt call Me *ishi* (my husband) and shalt call me no longer *baali* (my master)" (Hosea 2:18). The technical formal name for the husband after betrothal may be *baal* [master] and the process of acquisition *kinyan*. The true title for the married man is *ish,* and for betrothal, *kiddushin* [sanctification].

DIFFERENT ROLES

The woman has the last, albeit silent, word at the wedding service. It is the man's role to pursue, woo, and propose to her, but she must give positive willing consent to the proposal in order for the marriage to be legal. The witnesses have to be conscious of that *daat;* it is central to the entire service. Furthermore, she must receive the ring with the understanding that despite her acknowledged prior consent, this specific act is considered to clinch the betrothal, and therefore requires positive intent. The moment she receives the ring, she undergoes the momentous change in personal status.

The groom's role of initiator places him in a busy, hovering position at the wedding. *Natan hu, amar hu*—he must give the ring and he must propose marriage by enunciating this formula. In return for her consent he presents her with a *ketubah,* in which he records his binding obligations.

The tenor of the ceremony is an accurate reflection of the halakahic drama that is the core of the wedding. The bride's role is both veiled and central, she remains seated while attendants care for details. Similarly, the procession places the bride in the final and climactic role, as the groom and his escorts (*shushvinin*) anticipate the final arrival of the queen bride.

A clear understanding of the nature of the marriage contract is required to understand the delicate sense of balance in the wedding ceremony. In American law a contract is bilateral, and both parties participate in its signing. In Jewish law the contract is also bilateral, but the formal instrument is unilateral. Consent is required of both parties, but only the groom gives the contract, and only the bride receives it. All Jewish contracts take this form. The seller's role may be *physically* passive, but it is *legally* active, since the *kinyan* is concluded not in the act of *giving,* but in the act of *receiving.* When the bride receives the ring she closes the circuit. That is the dramatic gesture that signals "willing consent" to the witnesses.

Noble and well-meaning attempts have been made to give the bride a more active role in the wedding ceremony by the exchange of rings or an innovative recitation. These changes may not invalidate the marriage, but they can obfuscate the authentic message of the tradition, and introduce artificiality into the beautiful, profound, sacred, and historic wedding ceremony. Modern woman has indeed suffered some disabilities from legal ordinances and local usage or ancient custom, but her personal integrity and worth have always been maintained.

An unsurpassed insight into woman's role comes from the medieval Rabbi Isaac Arama. The Bible reports that Rachel was deeply distressed over her inability to bear Jacob children, while her sister Leah was able to bear children easily.

"And when Rachel saw that she bore Jacob no children, Rachel envied her sister; and said unto Jacob: 'Give me children, else I die.' And Jacob's anger was kindled against Rachel; and he said: 'Am I in God's stead, who had withheld from thee the fruit of the womb?' " (Genesis 30:1–2).

Rabbi Arama says that Rachel's cry indicates that she did not fully appreciate her role in life. Woman has two names given her in the Torah, which represent two aspects of her personality and her goal on earth. One is *ishah,* woman, a person of integrity who stands opposite and equal to *ish,* man. This is what she was called by God when she was created out of Adam's rib. She was given another name just before she gave birth to the first child. This name was *chavah,* which means "mother of all living things." A woman is both *chavah,* a mother, and *ishah,* a woman. She is *ishah* in terms of her own personality, the integrity of her thoughts, and her relationship with God and with man. Because she is able to reproduce a human being, she is also *chavah,* an additional glory that man can never know.

A woman who is barren and cannot fulfill her *chavah* role remains an *ishah,* a female person—alive, aware, concerned, and creative in other spheres. When Rachel says, "Give me children, else I die," she denies the value of *ishah.* Man and woman have the same value before God. Placed at opposite ends of the scale, unlike in terms of temperament and organic structure, each balances the other. Man and woman, bride and groom, Jacob and Rachel, *ish* and *ishah.*

TAKING IS GIVING

A man *takes* a wife and begins a life of *giving.* Only in the intimacy of marriage can one reach the higher levels of the ethical life, levels at which one can rejoice in supporting, helping, and strenghtening others without expectation of reward. The *taking in marriage cannot survive without the commitment to give.* This "taking-giving" moral lesson is best described by Rabbi Eliyahu Dessler, a twentieth-century ethicist. "Is the giving a consequence of love, or is perhaps the reverse true: the love a result of giving? We usually think it is love which causes giving. But the truth is that giving often brings about love, for the same reason that a person loves what he himself created or nurtured: he recognizes it as part of himself. . . . On this basis, we can understand yet another remarkable fact. Why do we find so often that this husband-wife affection does not seem to last? . . . People are generally 'takers' not 'givers.' . . . Each begins to demand from the other the fulfillment of his or her obligations. When demand begins, love departs."

Rabbi Moses Sofer, the nineteenth-century Hungarian author of *Chatam Sofer,* refers to the analogy of Abraham and the field of Ephron. "Husband and wife, at the outset of their marriage, are each 'buyers' and 'sellers.' The husband 'buys' a wife and writes her a marriage contract. The wife 'buys' a husband, who is obligated by the Torah to love, honor and support his wife. She is his 'field.' Her field stands *le'avdah u-le'shamrah* [as the Garden of Eden], to be 'worked and watched.' . . and he is her 'laborer'. . . ."

The field is not acquired in order to be abandoned or abused. *Kichah* implies an intention on the part of the buyer to give to it of himself, to produce, make an investment in the future, strive for a fullfillment of dreams. The wife is the field, to be tended and cared for; the husband is the laborer, "implanting the seed." From their interaction comes the great good of family living, a home for companionship and the birthplace of future generations.

THE NUPTIALS (*NISSUIN*): ACQUISITION BECOMES UNION

Once the couple has made a firm, formal commitment to a lasting bond, they are prepared for the concluding stage of the marriage service, *nissuin,* and the beginning of their life together as man and wife.

The nuptial ceremony is quite simple: the couple stands under the *chuppah,* the officiant recites the seven marriage blessings, and the bride and groom retire to the privacy of a room for some eight or nine minutes (*yichud*). Two witnesses stand outside the door to testify that the couple have symbolically accomplished the *chuppah.*

The differences between *kiddushin* and *nissuin* reveal the essence and spirit of the Jewish marriage service. While *kiddushin* evokes the image of the field, reflecting acquisition, the scene of *nissuin* is the home. *Chuppah* symbolizes shelter, the privacy of a home which bride and groom enter. The field is a place for business—real estate investment, sowing, and harvesting. The home is a place for children, parents, mate, and friends, for love and celebration. Traditionally, the dominant person of the field is the man—Isaac goes out to commune with God in the fields (Genesis 24:63), Esau is called "man of the fields" (Gen. 25:27), and Jacob's sons plot against Joseph in the field (37:15ff.). Woman traditionally has been the central figure at home. The Sages said *beito zu ishto*—a man's house is his wife.

The basic transaction of *kiddushin* is contractual, and has associations of the larger world—commerce, legalities, and economic arrangements. It must have precise legal formulations of words, precise minimum and maximum values given and received. Betrothal deals with a marriage formula, the value of the ring, the validity of the contract. The whole process is called *kichah* (acquisition) —a business term: unadorned, but transparently clear. In contrast, the transformation of *nissuin* is accomplished in a private room. No negotiations over conditions are associated with *chuppah,* only testimony to the couple's togetherness. The term for this is lovely, warm, and personal—*yichud,* together in private, an end to the solitary life and the beginning of family, shared promises, and the whisper of long commitments.

The *kiddushin* is in the nature of *hakhanah,* a preparation for the final *mitzvah* of "be fruitful and multiply." That is why one is permitted to effect this contractual stage of betrothal via messenger, performed, of course, with all of the technicalities required for establishing agency. The *nissuin,* the object of which transaction is personal and intimate, obviously cannot be effected by agency even if the sexual consummation of marriage were to be delayed until they meet, as no *mitzvah* requiring *personal* pariticipation (such as the donning of tefillin) can be legally accomplished through messenger.

Kiddushin is the first stage of the two-stage change of personal status. It prohibits the woman to her fiancè and to all other men, and it prohibits, by rabbinic decree, the man to all other women. The woman now has the status of *eshet ish,* a married woman, but thus far it is only *negative* in import. The blessing at the *kiddushin* speaks strictly of prohibited and permitted categories and of caution against immoral relations.

The second stage, *nissuin,* positively permits—indeed commands—sexual intercourse between bride and groom. The blessings speak of rejoicing, of God and paradise, and the idyllic first marriage of Adam and Eve.

The *kiddushin* celebrates a new *legal* bond in the community; the *nissuin* celebrates a *personal* tie. Betrothal is a *civil* procedure endowed with a special sanctity by the Rabbis; the nuptials are essentially a *religious* ceremony. Together they provide religious sanction for a previously prohibited act. The nuptials do not include proposals or gifts, only feelings.

The betrothal is called *kiddushin* (sanctity) because its primary purpose is to set aside. The nuptials are called nissuin, a term derived from the word *nassa* (to carry), which recalls the days when the townspeople carried the bride on a carriage from her parents' home to her new home with the groom. *Kiddushin* connects two equals, man and woman, in a relationship as husband and wife. *Nissuin,* which also means elevation, connects husband, wife, and God in a permanent commitment.

MARRIAGE IS COVENANT

"Holy matrimony" is a common phrase. But what is "holy" about matrimony? Outside of Judaism there are conflicting concepts of marriage: One holds that marriage is a sacrament; the other, that it is simply a social contract involving civil law.

Those who believe in its sacramental nature assert that the union of man and woman is essentially sinful, but in a concession to the weakness of the flesh, it was redeemed by the grace of God and transformed into a divine institution, holy matrimony. What God put together, man is not permitted to tear asunder, even if the marriage was a disaster and the home a prison. Only a moral offense such as adultery may be grounds for divorce; otherwise the marriage is dissoluble only by death.

Judaism holds that the holiness of marriage is the relationship, not the contract. Marriage can be ended by mutual consent; the reason need not be supplied. This indicates that marriage is arranged by man, and if it doesn't work, it can be terminated without religious penalty. The makers of the contract can become the breakers of the contract. The question was asked of Maharshal in the sixteenth century, "May the husband be coerced to grant a divorce on the ground that he is treating religion with scorn?" The rabbi answered, "He cannot be forced to divorce. Even if the charge were true, or even were he converted to another religion, if he still cared for his wife as the law required of a Jewish husband, she could not compel him to divorce. But she can also not be compelled to live with him. . ." (Maharshal was concerned in this instance with a trumped-up charge; no halakhic decisions of this serious nature should be assumed from this material.)

Because of the fundamentally social nature of the marriage contract, we can understand the category of prohibited and valid. Even in violation of religious laws (excluding adultery and incest), a marriage contracted is a valid marriage.

The *secular* view proposes that it is sufficient for marriage that two people want to have each other and are willing to live together. It requires nothing from religion, neither sanctification nor sanction.

Judaism cannot hold this view because it would ultimately destroy the moral life of the entire community. Adultery is not simply a social crime, such that if the offended mate forgives, it is forgotten. It is a sin against God and it stands to destroy the family. Incest is a heinous moral crime; producing a *mamzer*, or marrying one, matters very much to the Jewish people. Jewish survival and integrity depend on such concerns. That is why two people who, in certain situations, must prove that they are married but have no witnesses, will not be believed simply on their word. Because their marriage is not merely a personal arrangement, but affects all their close relatives, it cannot be legally determined by their simple statement of admission.

The Jewish concept of marriage can be summarized as follows: *The form, the contract and the process are* contractual. *The content, the bond, and the resulting relationship are* covenantal.

The covenant is the purpose and essence of all Jewish marriage. Malachi (2:14) speaks of "the wife of my covenant," and Ezekiel (16:8) says, "Yea, I swore unto thee and entered into a covenant with thee."

The contract is an agreement to abide by certain rules, but a covenant has a metaphysical dimension. By contract we share duties; by covenant we share destinies. The story of Creation, as told in the first chapter of Genesis describes how man and woman help relieve each other's burdens. In the second chapter, a spiritual element is added to their lives. They enter a covenant with God—and are enabled to relieve each other's existential loneliness in the world.

The paradigm of man's marriage covenant with woman is the *be'rit,* the covenant of God and His people, Israel. The covenant transforms Israel's historic destiny into God's destiny as well. When Israel is in exile the *She'khinah,* God's Presence, is also in exile. In His covenant with the Jews, God promises land and eternal posterity. The marriage covenant also promises posterity, along with home, growth, love, and companionship. Thus the blessing ends with God's sanctification of Israel through this couple: *me'kadesh ammo Yisrael al ye'dei chuppah ve'kiddushin.* Because marriage is covenantal, both components, *kiddushin* and *nissuin,* are initiated with the blessing over wine, as are the covenants of the Sabbath and circumcision.

The form is contractual, but the resultant relationship is covenantal. According to Maimonides' three-tiered classification, the relationship grows from *chaver le'davar,* a companion for help, to a *chaver le'daagah,* a companion for burdens. It is capped by *chaver le'deiah,* a companion for destiny. This signifies a sharing in the covenant, in the whole meaning of life, in those ideals which stand forever.

THE MINIMUM LEGAL REQUIREMENTS

CONSENT

Consent is the fundamental requirement of the wedding. There is no valid marriage without the total *willing consent* of the bride. In commercial transactions, a person may be compelled to agree to a contract even though the contract is unsatisfactory. Nonetheless, the sale is valid. Since marriage involves a formal contract, it might be assumed that it is bound by the same law of consent. The Sages, however, ruled otherwise. They held that if the groom would stoop to do something so uncomely as to "pressure" the lady to agree to marriage, the marriage should be annulled. Since the groom proposed marriage according to "the laws of Moses and Israel" (meaning the laws as the Sages had developed them), the Sages could determine whether it was performed according to their view of what constitutes proper marriage. If the bride later claimed that she felt forced to accept that which she did not desire, she would be free without divorce. The Sages were much more concerned with guaranteeing the woman's willing consent (*daat*) than the man's, because of man's traditionally greater independence. Consent, as indicated in Chapter 9, was not simply a condition of the agreement, it was central to it.

The consent required of man and woman is expressed in different ways. The man recites the betrothal formula upon presenting the ring, and the woman silently accepts the ring. Both acts imply consent.

LEGAL CAPACITY

It is a law of Torah that both partners must be mentally competent and sufficiently mature to understand the significance of the marriage act and the change of personal status that it effects. Three categories of the legally incapacitated are enumerated: *cheresh* (the deaf-mute, or retarded person), *shoteh* (the deranged), and *katan* (the minor).

The Retarded and Deaf-Mute (Cheresh and Chareshet)

This category refers to deaf-mutes or to those who are mentally retarded. (The ancient law usually considered deaf-mutes to be of arrested intelligence, which is why they are grouped here with the retarded. Deaf-mutes of normal intelligence are simply considered adults and are not included here.) They are considered generally unmarriageable by the Bible, but the Rabbis ruled that, if their capacity for peaceful domestic relations indicated the possibility for successful marriage, they were permitted to marry. Thus a retarded person or a deaf-mute married to a normal mate has contracted a valid marriage, and if the marriage fails, divorce is required to terminate it. If the groom's sounds would not be comprehensible to the bride and witnesses, the marriage formula should be done in sign language. A rabbi should be consulted on this matter.

The Deranged (Shoteh and Shotah)

Those judged to be deranged are not permitted to marry either others in this category or those who are manifestly "normal." It is felt that they lack the required awareness for marriage and will only cause harm, disruption, and lifelong suffering to themselves and their families. The Bible prohibits such a marriage, and the Rabbis did *not* enact laws enabling them to marry, as they did with the retarded, who can have an appreciation of domestic peace. If a person is adjudged by competent professionals to be merely of lesser wit, but with full self-awareness, that person is not considered incompetent to marry.

A Minor Male (Katan)

The Bible did not permit a boy under the age of thirteen years and one day to be married (Deuteronomy 24:1), and the Rabbis did not relieve this stricture.

Some rabbis conjectured that since the estate of marriage is one of bliss, we should invoke the principle of *zachin le'adam shelo be'fanav*—that one can do meritorious acts on behalf of another, even if he is not present. In that case, the court or the boy's father should be permitted to "marry him off" without his formal acquiescence. The final law denied this arrangement, however, since the husband has serious obligations laid upon him by the Bible. The court surely cannot accept these obligations for him without his full, mature willing agreement.

A Minor Female (Ke'tanah)

Historically, an under-aged girl found herself in difficult circumstances. She was frequently in danger of abduction by an enemy people if she was unmarried, and if her family was poor she was considered a drain on the family expenses. Girls therefore were brought into marriage at a very early age. (Even today Yemenite Jews emigrating to the modern state of Israel bring daughters married at age ten). For these and other reasons, the law permitted this marriage with the permission of her father, although the Talmud considered it a *mitzvah* not to marry her until she is prepared to say *le'ploni ani rotzah,* "him I want." Maharam Rotenburg, in a famous Responsum, advises the Jewish community to follow the rule of the Talmud, as he himself had done with his minor daughter.

In 1950 the Israeli rabbinate passed a law that made it illegal to marry a girl under the age of sixteen.

WITNESSES (EDIM)

A marriage must be witnessed by two qualified people in order to be considered valid. A hundred legally unqualified witnesses do not validate a marriage, according to Jewish law, even with the self-admission of the bride and groom that they are married. Where only one witness is present, the law is complicated and rabbinic authority will have to be consulted.

The Need for Witnesses

While the requirement for the presence of witnesses for marriage is derived from commercial transactions, their function in marriage is very different. In fiscal matters, the witnesses *testify;* in marriage, they *attest.* Attesting witnesses on a document are part of the event that transpired, an integral component. Without them, the event is not legally considered to have occurred. Testifying witnesses stand as evidence, *if* called upon, that a transaction was agreed upon.

Thus in commercial transactions, if both sides agree—even though there were no other witnesses—the integrity of the event is not called into question. In marriage, the lack of witnesses constitutes an invalidation of the essential contract. The witnesses recorded on the marriage contract are the actual authors of the *ketubah* and they virtually become the central functionaries. If there were no witnesses, the testimony of the bride and groom that a marriage took place is not valid because, according to the Talmud; "In the case of money matters, his admission does not involve others; in the case of marriage, self-admission would involve others." How would it involve others? Rashi says that "each party would now be prohibited to marry each other's consanguinous relations."

The author of *Ke'tzot ha-Choshen* explains that the witnesses to a commercial transaction may never be needed because the law is content with the admission of the parties to the act and that is *equivalent* to the testimony of witnesses. The law, however, will pay no attention to the admission of the parties to the marriage; thus the witnesses need to stand always as an essential part of the act.

Another purpose is cited by the author of *Or Same-ach*. He holds that unlike commercial transactions, which requires only *haskamah* (grudging consent), marriage requires *daat* (willing consent). The witnesses are required to judge this sensitively. Their presence for this purpose will help avert the possibility of a future denial of the validity of the marriage.

A third purpose cited by the Tosafists is that since a new status is effected wherein the woman becomes *davar she-be'ervah* (an incestuously-prohibited relation), it calls into being the law that no such *davar she-be'ervah* can be accomplished with fewer than two qualified witnesses. It cannot be effected by self-admission, as in commercial acts, or by one witness, as in purely ritual, nonmarital matters.

Their Place in the Service

In order for witnesses to fulfill their function as integral components of the marriage ceremony, they must be seen by the couple during the service. Further, the couple should be conscious of the fact that the witnesses are serving in that capacity. If they are not specifically aware of the witnesses, it is feared that bride or groom might consider it a casual custom, not a required need. Because the witnesses validate the ceremony, the law requires that the two witnesses must appear together, must see each other, and must be seen by—and their presence as witnesses recognized by—the couple.

It is proper that they be specifically appointed for this purpose. This should be done ideally by the groom, but the rabbi can also choose witnesses. Preferably, selection should be made by speaking their names and announcing that they are selected to the exclusion of everyone else in the room. There are several reasons for this specification. First, most people surrounding the couple under the *chuppah* are relatives, who are not permitted to serve as witnesses. According to many authorities, the inclusion of even one improper witness disqualifies all witnesses. Hence the groom or the officiant consciously excludes them. Second, those closest to the action are usually those responsible for the entire wedding. They may be so concerned with other matters at the celebration that they cannot give proper attention to their function as biblically-required attesting witnesses. Third, those who are not related (and therefore potentially able to serve as witnesses) will probably be standing outside the close huddle under the *chuppah,* which will obstruct the action that must be clearly seen. Their specification as witnesses brings them to the center, concentrates their attention on the marriage about to be effected, and consciously eliminates relatives and other invalid witnesses from inclusion in the formal aspects of the ceremony. It is generally preferable to have the rabbi and cantor, who are standing close by, act as witnesses. This also helps to avoid the interminable arguments over which friends should be honored to serve as witnesses.

Their Function

The witnesses must clearly see the groom give the ring to the bride, and they must distinctly hear the groom's recitation of the marriage formula. Most difficult—but most important—they must be able to discern, by the actions of the bride and by her looks, that she *willingly consents* to the marriage and that the groom intends not merely a gift but the functional enactment of marriage.

Their Qualifications

Witnesses must be practicing adult, male Jews who are not relatives of the bride or groom. The following persons are considered *invalid* as witnesses in Jewish law.

1. Relatives: Father; brother; uncle; brother-in-law; stepfather; father-in-law; sons and sons-in-law; nephews; first cousins; the husband to a wife's relatives; and witnesses who are related to one another.

2. Women: It was determined by derivation from scripture that in most cases, women may not serve as witnesses. There is no doubt that the *Halakhah* recognized the religious strivings of women. It surely did not intend the slightest denigration to the soul of women, whom they considered the first in the Sinaitic community to receive the Torah. In fact, Rabbi Saul Berman points out that the Sages were concerned that the religious spirit of pious women might move them to pay less attention to their role in the home in preference to their role in the temple and religious community. Thus women are consistently exempted from obligations of participating in communal worship and public events.

3. Minors: The witness must be older than thirteen years and one day. One day, according to most authorities, means just a few moments into the day of birth—a portion of a day is equal to a full day.

4. The deaf and dumb: Even though they may have good sight, witnesses must have mature intelligence and be able to articulate clearly and hear precisely the words of the court.

5. The blind: Even though they may recognize voices and people by hearing, the Torah says that only one who can see may testify.

6. The mentally deranged

7. The "wicked":   Exodus 23:1 cites the "wicked" as invalid witnesses. This category includes those who have committed capital offenses; those who have had flogging administered to them; those who are liable for any other punishment (by rabbinic edict); professional gamblers; and those who once committed perjury. Also included are those who act in uncivilized ways; heretics and agnostics; and those who violate the law with malice (*le'hakhit*), or even out of passion (*le'te-avon*).

The later rabbis go so far as to exclude from witnessing those who are *pe'rutzim be'eizeh averah, afilu aveirah kalah*—consistent though minor violators of the moral law.

In sum, an honest man who is a Sabbath-observant Jew is presumed to qualify as a witness under this category. Great sensitivity must be exercised not only to choose proper witnesses, but also to avoid personal inquisitions into the nature of their character or religious observance, remembering the rabbinic adage, "One who shames his neighbor has no share in the world to come."

Not "According to the Laws of Moses and Israel": Shelo Ke' dat Moshe Ve' Yisrael: Non-Jewish Ceremonies

Jewish marriage, as we have seen, must follow the process ordained by "the laws of Moses," which he received on Mount Sinai, and "of Israel," the Oral Law as developed by the teachers in the Talmud, Codes, and Responsa. As early as four hundred years ago, however, there arose the problem of Jews marrying in violation of that ordained process, rejecting or ignoring Jewish marriage. In those early days, non-Jewish marriages were often compelled by unfriendly host governments. Today, unfortunately, many Jews consciously choose to have one of these "alternative," non-Jewish ceremonies. Whether it is a civil, church, or cult ceremony, or no ceremony at all, it contravenes "the law of Moses and of Israel."

The following discussion is a simplification of a very complicated problem, and should not serve in place of rabbinic decisions in specific cases. Rather, it is intended as a guide to ways in which you may frame questions when consulting an authority.

CIVIL MARRIAGE

The first public Jewish confrontation with civil marriages occurred in Holland at the end of the sixteenth century; the second took place after the French Revolution, at the end of the eighteenth century. Most of the Responsa literature on this subject was produced in reaction to the large numbers of civil marriages performed during the last remnants of Jewish self-government in Germany in 1875, and in Austro-Hungary, (including Galicia) in 1891. Civil marriages were required by the governments of these countries. While most Jews went through this as an *addition* to the Jewish ceremony, others ignored the religious ceremony altogether.

It is clear that a civil marriage is not in accord with Jewish law. The basic questions are these: If a man and woman were wed in a civil ceremony, and if their intention was for marriage, not licentiousness, and if they are known to the Jewish public as husband and wife, are they considered to be married in accordance with Jewish law? If they wish to terminate the marriage, will a Jewish divorce be required? If they realize their error, should they undergo a Jewish marriage ceremony? The Halakhah is concerned with three problems when judging cases of civil marriage:

1. *Kavanah:* Intention to get married. Was the marriage based on the intention of the man and woman to live together formally as husband and wife, or were they married for other reasons? The halakhic question is this: Must the required intention be focused specifically on effecting *Jewish* marriage or is a general intent to live a *married life* sufficient to give the marriage Jewish validity?

2. *Chazakah:* The presumption made by the *Halakhah* is that people are "not wont to cohabit licentiously" when they can do so in accordance with Jewish law. Is this true for all people, regardless of their observance of the law? This presumption is usually invoked for a person only after marriage. For example, when a man is alone with his former wife, whom he has just divorced, it is presumed that they have remarried because he would not needlessly cohabit licentiously. Can this presumption also be applied to civil marriage?

3. *Bi'ah:* Cohabitation: Are witnesses required for the couple's specific statement of intent to marry by the mode of intercourse before they retire to privacy, or is it sufficient for it to be known in the community that they are living together as man and wife? Is it possible that, although there was no proper intent and no presumption, they might in any case, by cohabiting, have fulfilled the basic requirements of the law?

The halakhic response comes from many sources, and occupies a number of books, but the authorities agree that civil marriage is a violation of the law. *It is not a Jewish marriage.* The couple's participation in civil marriage is taken as a statement that they do not believe in "the laws of Moses and Israel." It is assumed that their concept of "licentiousness" is not that of the *Halakhah*. (N.B. It is possible that, if the marriage was originally contracted in a country that did not tolerate Jewish marriage, the intention was proper. This factor must be adjudged separately. The rabbi must decide whether or not the issuance of a *get mi-chumra* (a rabbinically-ordained divorce), is necessary, because the community might have assumed they were married Jewishly and that their separation without a divorce implies that religious divorce is no longer required. When a mate refuses a divorce, a rabbi should be consulted as to whether the *get mi-chumra* may be set aside).

If the marriage is to be continued, the couple should be encouraged to be married with a Jewish ceremony. A *civil divorce,* which the government requires, is of no value whatsoever to the *Halakhah* and will not be acceptable to the law and to the traditional community as a *Jewish divorce.*

CHURCH OR CULT MARRIAGE

The history of such marriage goes back at least to the Spanish Inquisition at the end of the fifteenth century. Today we very rarely find two Jewish people being married in church, but all too many young Jews have been converted to cults of all varieties. As a Jew cannot be considered by the law to be a non-Jew under any circumstances, only to be a sinning Jew, the problem of cult marriage is a difficult one.

The *Halakhah* takes note of two differences between cult marriage and civil marriage. First, in civil marriage the "laws of Moses and Israel" are *ignored;* in cult marriages, they are openly *rejected.* Second, church or cult marriage is a contradiction of Jewish marriage, but civil marriage is not.

The clear intent of the couple married in a church or cult ceremony is to defy Jewish marriage law. The *Halakhah,* therefore, does not consider it a marriage at all. In order to be considered married as Jews, such a couple must be married according to halakhic standards. A corollary of this law is that two Jewish apostates married according to Jewish law have a legal marriage, since they are full, if less than good, Jews; but two identified Jews married in an alien religious faith are not considered married.

LIVING TOGETHER ARRANGEMENT

Many couples decide to live together without benefit of marriage. This is akin to common law unions, called *yadua be'tzibbur,* the history of which goes back to the institution of concubinage. In the fifteenth century Rabbi Israel Isserlein, author of *Te'rumat ha-Deshen,* responded to the question of those who lived together but wished to separate. He dealt simultaneously with this question and with another regarding a church marriage, indicating that he believed there was no legal difference between them.

The *Halakhah* shows no concern in this situation for the possibility that the couple contracted marriage by *bi'ah*. In addition, since there is no legitimate intent to be married, there is no halakhic presumption that this concept is operative. This enables those who are living together not to require a religious divorce if they decide to separate. (In individual cases, this must be checked with authoritative scholars). Chief Rabbi Herzog considered such a situation to be a nonmarriage.

Couples who wish to write their own personalized, often moving, additions to the marriage ceremony must first consult with religious authority. The new words may be permitted according to Jewish law, but they must be written so as to conform with the traditional marriage *process* of "Moses and Israel." The fundamental components of the marriage service as outlined below must be followed, and a rabbi should be consulted well before the ceremony.

Part Five

CELEBRATING THE MARRIAGE COVENANT

CHAPTER 12

Planning the Wedding

DIGNITY AND EXTRAVAGANCE

The style of the wedding celebration is a reflection of the personal values of the couple and their families, and of their perception of communal standards.

The tradition calls for dignity, simplicity, and integrity. Coarseness, loudness, exhibitionist display, and revelry are not the hallmarks of a people who were taught the ways of modesty (*hatzneia lekhet*). A religion that considers the quality of *pe'ritzut* (licentiousness) despicable, and whose highest encomium is reserved for those who are *tze'nuim* (modest and humble), cannot abide the grossness and vulgarity of weddings designed for show rather than for genuine rejoicing.

Many medieval Jewish communities wrote limitations on wedding expenses into their statutes. In fifteenth century Castile, officials legislated against the imitation of the colorful excesses of their gentile neighbors. In Forli, it was noted that Jews expended on sumptuous banquets "more than they could afford and more than the wealthy Christians among whom we live." In the eighteenth century, the rabbis of Fuerth clearly delineated limitations on expenses—only one soup could be served, no more than four musicians could be hired, and they were not permitted to play after midnight. In Constantinople, the community restricted the amount of dowries even wealthy people were permitted.

The dangers of conspicuous consumption were many. First, it unnecessarily excited the envy of non-Jewish neighbors. Second, it emphasized competition in spending to keep up with others. Third, it underscored the distinction between the haves and the have-nots. (This problem arose at funerals as well, where limitations were also imposed. Rabbi Gamaliel in the Talmud therefore ordered the use of standard shrouds for all deceased.) Even worse, the extravagances of a wedding often bankrupted families and thereby undermined the economic structure of both the family and the communal treasury. This is presently occurring at an alarming rate in the state of Israel among traditional families.

There is no reason why one who has the funds should not spend them on a sumptuous wedding—it is an expression of joy. But ostentatious overspending is gross. Those who cannot afford large weddings need not feel that they must sink into a decade of wretched indebtedness to pay for one truly magnificent moment.

A great Jewish wedding consists of the genuine rejoicing of the guests. The wedding should reflect the deepest and most sensitive feelings of the bride and groom. This atmosphere can be achieved by the tone of the service, the presence of true friends, and the communal dancing of the guests who are expected by *Halakhah* to "rejoice the bride and groom" at the occasion of their most serious life decision.

Historically, a wedding was not necessarily a closed family affair. Many of the city's poor were customarily invited, even though they were not relatives or close friends. How often would they have the opportunity to celebrate in this fashion otherwise? Contributions were often made to charities by the two families. If charities were to receive the equivalent value of one extra course that could be eliminated at every Jewish wedding, they would all thrive. A wedding, as Rabbi Eliyahu Dessler noted, should signal a life of giving, not taking, and that is the chord that should be struck at the very beginning of marriage.

TE'NAIM: AGREEMENT TO MARRY

Te'naim—conditions—is the popular term for the *shidukhin,* a mutual agreement between two sets of parents for the date and financial conditions of the forthcoming marriage of their children.

In the times of the Mishnah at the beginnings of the Common Era, betrothal was preceded by the *shidukhin,* which then was an informally negotiated agreement. The third century authority, Rav, used the following formula: "How much do you give your son? So much and so much. How much do you give your daughter? So much and so much." Whereupon, they proceeded to carry out the betrothal.

The *shidukhin* was a necessary preliminary to the marriage that gave both families the opportunity to arrange for the material welfare of their children's union. It also served to discourage hurried and haphazardly arranged weddings, which could make a mockery of marriage and vulgarize the entire institution. This was so important that Rav, with the concurrence of his colleague Samuel, ordered corporal punishment for anyone who did not take the trouble to make these preparations. By the fifth century the orally-negotiated agreements, while still not formalized and reduced to writing, were entered into with such concern and sincerity that although they were only words they were nonetheless binding and considered promises, *de'varim ha-niknin be'amirah* (matters that are "acquired" by words).

When the betrothal and the nuptials were combined into one ceremony in the eleventh century, there arose an even greater need for preliminary family negotiations, similar to the western concept of "engagement." The agreements were now reduced to writing, and a ceremony was developed that gave it an official character and was enforced through bans and edicts. Breaking the negotiated promises was considered legally objectionable and morally reprehensible.

Standard forms were developed by Sephardim in the eleventh century, and Ashkenazim in the twelfth century. The written document was called *te'nai shidukhin* (conditions of the engagement) and subsequently *te'naim* (conditions). They were considered *te'naim rishonim* (first conditional agreements), while the *ketubah* was referred to as *te'naim acharonim* (last conditional agreements). Included in these conditions were all or some of the following items: date; place; dowry; financial obligations of both sets of parents to their children; clauses assuring the efforts of the groom's father to have his sons provide *chalitzah* in case the groom died before bearing children; inheritance rights; and penalties for failure to comply with the conditions. The Rabbis strongly disapproved of young men who broke engagements because of dowry disputes, and considered repugnant those who diminished their duties within marriage because of in-law defaults.

The consequences of violating the conditions of *te'naim* were often harsh. Jewish law did not look kindly upon those who cavalierly broke promises made in public ceremony, and such a breach was nothing less than a criminal act. It was considered not only a violation of law, but a moral transgression; at times the courts not only levied fines, they excommunicated the culprits. If an individual's word was not sacred, the social fabric of the entire community was threatened. Legal penalties included enforced payment for the elaborate preparations, the return of the betrothal gifts, and the payment of stipulated penalties for the disgrace caused a "precious daughter of Israel."

Of course, punishment was never meted out indiscriminately in Jewish life. Any reasonable argument regarding the complex area of interpersonal relationships was considered as a legitimate defense against this liability. The law did not want a couple to go into marriage in order to avoid a scene or a court hearing or public disapproval; indeed, this would be a constraint on the willing consent that Judaism required of bride and groom. But to break the engagement compact on the basis of information known to the parties prior to the *te'naim* was intolerable.

Because the consequences of broken *te'naim* were so harsh, they were eventually mitigated by modification of the document and the process. The ceremony was moved as close to the wedding date as possible. Today it is often performed moments before the marriage contract is written on the wedding night, and it is virtually impossible to violate. The legalities were made nonspecific. For example, the dowry sum to be provided in the *te'naim* is most often filled in with the term *ki-me'dubbar* (as agreed). The penalty for violating the contract is also stipulated as *ki-me'dubbar*. The date is followed by, "before or after this date as the parties agree." At the present time, outside of Hasidic circles and certain European families, the *te'naim* is frequently sidestepped altogether. As there are really no conditions left today, the *te'naim* is virtually devoid of substance and meaning. Those who prefer to use it do so primarily out of sentiment and family custom.

When it *is* used, it must follow the proper halakhic form; if it is broken, a rabbi must be consulted. The view of the Gaon of Vilna in this regard should not be forgotten. He held that it is a crime to break the contract, and that it would be better to marry and then divorce than to violate the word of the contract. The Gaon's view was actually written into the ceremony of the *te'naim*.

Like the wedding, at which a glass is broken, at the conclusion of the *te'naim* a plate is broken. This teaches the severity of cavalierly breaking *te'naim:* Like the piece of crockery, the *te'naim* can never be mended—when it is broken, it is discarded.

THE CEREMONY

The ceremony is very simple. It includes the writing of the *te'naim,* the *kinyan* (the formal acceptance of the contract), the signing, the public reading, and the smashing of the plate enclosed in a cloth napkin. The document should then be given to a third party who represents both sides or, if there are two copies made, one should go to the groom's representative and one to the bride's.

THE READING

This should be done in Hebrew and in English translation. Both sets of parents and the witnesses should be present.

THE BREAKING OF THE PLATE

It is customary for the two mothers to wrap a plate in a cloth and together break it over a table corner or chair. In addition to the symbolism described earlier, some commentaries conjecture that the plate-breaking is a symbol of the verse, *ve'gilu bi-re'adah,* (rejoice in trembling) balancing the joy of the occasion with its seriousness. Others say it is reminiscent, even in the midst of joy, of the destruction of the Temple. Possibly it was designed simply to serve as an auspicious beginnng of ceremonies that will conclude with the breaking of the glass at the end of the wedding ceremony, thus bracketing the wedding ceremonies and evoking a chorus of *"mazal tovs,"* beginning and end.

DESIGNING THE WEDDING

THE RABBI

The wedding, as we have seen, is not simply a beautiful ceremony—it is an intricate web of laws and customs that the Torah has ordained and society has developed for the protection of the family and social morality. These traditions are far too complicated to be implemented by a novice. Countless legal difficulties can beset this otherwise magnificent event if it is not overseen by a rabbi who is a scholar of the law.

The Talmud insisted that *Kol she-eino yodeia be'tiv gittin ve'kiddushin, lo ye'hei lo esek imahem*—whoever does not know the niceties of the divorce and betrothal procedures should not engage in supervising them. Maimonides instructed the Egyptian Jewish community that no marriage may be arranged without the supervision of an ordained rabbi. The presence of the rabbi gives the wedding the character of an official act. This was part of the historic Jewish effort to transform marriage from an unstructured, casual arrangement to a formal, officially approved, legal transaction, which carefully spelled out the responsibilities attendant upon the new status.

The rabbi has no part in effecting the marriage itself. He ascertains only that the partners are legitimately permitted to marry one another and that the marriage process is executed according to the laws of Moses and Israel. His primary value is not as a public speaker or a master of ceremonies, but as a scholar, able to assure that all the actions meet the centuries-old halakhic standards of the Jewish people.

Cantors who are not ordained as Rabbis should not perform marriages (though they perform *at* marriages.) The fact that the state may authorize them is irrelevant; the Jewish religion does not. A wedding should be postponed if there is no ordained rabbi available on the date selected.

Marriage is too important, the law too complex, and the Jewish family too essential to be left in the hands of those who, however well-intentioned or talented, have no knowledge of the intricacies of the marriage laws.

THE DATE

In the past, certain dates were considered auspicious for marriage. For example, some proposed that marriages be held only during the first half of the lunar Hebrew month because love and good fortune should increase as the moon increases. The last word on the numerous "good days" and signs, however, was an endorsement of all days except those the law banned because they would violate the spirit of either mourning or joy.

Judaism protects the integrity of our two most extreme emotions, love and death. It does not permit a wedding, which the *Halakhah* considers the epitome of joy, to interfere with mourning, the paradigm of sadness. Conversely, it does not permit two joyous experiences to take place simultaneously—we must be able to separate them and handle these experiences with uncompromised concentration. Thus there are specific times when no marriage may take place.

Never on the Sabbath

The Sabbath, a day of joy and rest, is not a day for weddings. The Talmud states that no formal agreement, written or verbal, is permitted on the Sabbath. In the early Middle Ages, although the betrothal and nuptials were regularly fused into one ceremony, the Jews sometimes separated them by one day, celebrating the betrothal on Friday afternoon and the nuptials on Saturday night, after the close of the Sabbath.

Maimonides, however, prohibited weddings on Friday afternoons and on Sundays because he found that preparations were so time consuming and demanding of effort that they caused unwitting violation of the Sabbath. The restriction was ultimately set aside by later authorities who assumed that, by the time the day of the wedding arrived, the extensive preparations had been completed and the Sabbath would be fully observed.

Saturday night weddings are a western innovation. On late summer days the food is often prepared, and the wedding families and musicians often arrive, before the Sabbath is over. To enter the Jewish covenant of marriage by violating the Jewish covenant of Sabbath, even by those who are generally not observant of the Sabbath, is both ludicrous and sacrilegious. In such instances, Saturday night weddings are to be discouraged. However, if meticulous care is taken not to violate the holiness of the Sabbath, there is no reason to avoid scheduling weddings on this night.

Not on Days of Joy

No weddings may be scheduled for Rosh Hashanah, Yom Kippur, Sukkot, Passover, and Shavuot, or on the Intermediate days. According to the Talmud there are two similar reasons: the first is (Deuteronomy 16:14) "And thou shalt rejoice in thy holy days," implying "but not with thy wife"; the second is *ein me' arvin simchah be' simchah;* "one should not intermix rejoicing with rejoicing." In this way, the integrity of the occasion remains intact. Because of the specific halakhic criteria for the concept of "joy," weddings may be held on Purim and Hanukkah.

Private joyous occasions must also be unsullied. Thus two brothers or two sisters should not celebrate their weddings on the same day; in fact, some authorities require waiting a whole week.

Not on Days of Sadness

A wedding may not contravene a day of public mourning or sadness. Therefore, it should not be held on fast days such as the Tishah be-Av, the fast of Gedaliah, the tenth of Tevet, the fast of Esther, and the seventeenth of Tammuz. In urgent circumstances, the wedding itself may be held on fast days (other than Tishah be-Av), but the meal and celebration should begin after nightfall.

Likewise, the period of semimourning for the Temple's destruction—the three weeks from the seventeenth of Tammuz through the Tishah be-Av—are days of public sadness on which a Jew should not celebrate a personal happiness. The law held it forbidden from Rosh Chodesh until after Tishah be-Av, but custom has extended the ban from the seventeenth day of Tammuz until Tishah be-Av. Therefore, engagement announcements and gatherings are permitted, but without music, dancing, and elaborate foods. Weddings are legally permissible, under similar restrictions, especially for those who have no children, but only for urgent reasons. In all cases a rabbinic authority should be consulted.

The same principles apply to the thirty-three day period from Passover to before Shavuot, a time for mourning the death of Rabbi Akiva's students and followers. There is a division of custom regarding the counting of these thirty-three days. Sephardim hold these days of semimourning from the second day of Passover through Lag ba-Omer. Many Ashkenazim, according to the decision of Rabbi Moses Feinstein, may hold weddings until after Rosh Chodesh Iyyar, and on Lag ba-Omer, evening and day, and from Rosh Chodesh Sivan and forward. The most common usage among American Jews seems to have been the prohibition of marriage until Lag ba-Omer, following the decision of the Bach, a seventeenth-century authority. This custom has the additional advantage of having specific, easy-to-determine parameters for the Jewish public. As there are many local customs and some leniency in cases of exigency, local competent rabbinic authority should be consulted before the planning proceeds too far.

THE MOURNER AND MARRIAGE*

1. When Marriages May Take Place.

(a.) Mourners should not be married during *sheloshim* [the thirty-day period following burial], and certainly not during *shivah* [the seven days of mourning

---

*This section is extracted from my previous book, *The Jewish Way in Death and Mourning* (Jonathan David Publishers, Inc.)

following the burial of certain relatives], even without pomp and music and sumptuous reception. Engagements may be contracted or announced during this period.

(b.) *After* the *sheloshim,* the wedding may proceed with all the adornments, the music and the food, and the bride and groom and their parents may dress for the occasion, without showing any evident signs of mourning.

(c.) During *sheloshim* (after *shivah*), there are exceptional circumstances when marriage may be contracted:

—If the groom is the mourner:

If he is childless, and preparations had been made, such as: the date set, the arrangements contracted for, and the food bought, so that postponing the wedding would incur a severe financial loss, or cause a large group of people to be absent.

If the date had *not* been set, but for some cogent reason such as military draft, it must be held during *sheloshim,* the couple may marry, but not live as man and wife until after *sheloshim.*

—If the bride is the mourner:

The marriage may take place during *sheloshim* only if she had already been engaged, the preparations made, and the groom is childless.

2. When Remarriages May Take Place

(a.) *If the wife died:*

The husband must wait for the passing of the three major festivals (Passover, Sukkot, and Shavuot) before he remarries. Rosh Hashanah and Yom Kippur do not count as festivals for this purpose. Shemini Atzeret may be counted as a festival in certain cases involving the family's urgent personal circumstances. The ostensible reason for this delay is the hope that the duration of three separate holidays and the cycle of seasons would temper his despair, and he would not enter a second marriage with the first love still fresh in mind. This time span may be as long as a year if death occurred soon after Sukkot, or only a few months if death occurred immediately prior to Passover.

There are notable exceptions to this general rule:

—If the husband did not sire children, marriage may be held after *shiva* and they may live as husband and wife.

—If he has small children who need to be cared for, marriage may be held after *shiva,* but marital relations must be postponed until after *sheloshim.*

—If he cannot bear to live alone, for whatever reason (this is not an infrequent occurrence), he may be married, but may have no marital relations until after *sheloshim.*

(b.) *If the husband died:*

The wife may remarry after three months, a considerably shorter time than the three-festival duration for a man. Evidently, the wife was considered better able to control her emotions, having to be more concerned with the rearing of her children than with her own feelings. The reason for the three-month delay is that it must be evident that she is not bearing a child from a deceased mate. Under exceptional circumstances to be judged by competent rabbinic authority, if it is known medically that she could not possibly be pregnant, and if her fiance is childless, she may be granted permission to remarry after *shiva*. . . .

3. Becoming a Mourner after the Ceremony

(a.) If one of the seven close relatives of the bride or groom died after the ceremony, but before the marriage was consummated, the couple must live apart until after *shiva,* [when they formally begin their seven days of rejoicing].

(b.) If the relative died after the consummation of the marriage, the mourning is postponed until after the full week of wedding celebration. During this time, the mourner may care for personal hygiene and grooming, and may experience all the joys of living. When the week is over, however, the garment of the mourner is rent and *shiva* begins in full, as noted above.

THE LOCATION

The Groom's Home

Marriage is dramatically symbolized when the bride leaves her parents' home and sets up house with her husband. In ancient times, the groom's father built special quarters in the family home for the married couple (the *chuppah* represents that chamber in the wedding ceremony). It is this private room that *yichud*—the togetherness that declares to the community that the bride and groom have been chosen by each other above all others—takes place and the marriage is effected. Ran holds that the process of the bride moving in with her husband is enough of a statement to effect the marriage, even without the immediate ceremonious privacy of *yichud.*

The Bride's Home

If the groom's family was too poor to afford a gala celebration, the bride's parents made the wedding at their home. Indeed, the groom often lived in their home for the first several years of marriage, especially if he was a student. In this case, however, no move took place, and there was no "recognizable" change in the bride's living conditions. In ancient times, therefore, the bride's home was not a desirable location for the wedding. (Today the wedding can be held at the bride's home if desired, though it is not only proper but also technically preferable that the groom give the bride's family some small gift—not only in gratitude, but as a symbolic lease for the *chuppah*.)

The Synagogue

To remedy this problem, according to the Gaon of Vilna, the wedding was held in the synagogue. Since the synagogue was considered community property, the community could cede the area where the *chuppah* would stand to the groom, as though it were his own room. A refinement in the law was added which transformed the fee customarily paid a synagogue for its use for a wedding into a lease of that property for the groom. This became an attractive alternative to holding the ceremony in the bride's home.

Outdoors

The community could not abide placing the *chuppah* directly in front of the Ark because the Chuppah is, after all, a public representation of the bridal chamber. Hence the *chuppah* was kept on the syngogue grounds, but it was held in the *chatzar beit ha-ke'nesset* (the synagogue patio), or the *schulhauf* (the courtyard) rather than in the sanctuary. Rema, in the sixteenth century, who was the first to record the use of a portable room in the form of the *chuppah,* was also the first to record the outdoor wedding. For Rema, the outdoor ceremony was a reminder of the stars that symbolized to Abraham the multitude of his progeny. A practical reason, of course, was the ability to accommodate a large number of guests at the service. In addition the generally hostile gentile environment made a home religious service undesirable.

Halakhically, it is preferred to hold the wedding service on the synagogue premises, but sensitivity should be shown in placing the *chuppah* in the inner sanctum of the synagogue. Historically, it was the presence of a symbolic bedchamber near the Ark. Despite this concern, weddings today are frequently held in the sanctuaries of orthodox synagogues. It is felt that the positive qualities of a synagogue wedding outweigh the negative connotations.

The Hotel or Catering Hall

Because the *chuppah* is portable and can represent the groom's home, the wedding may be held at a hotel or wedding hall (the fee for the wedding may also be counted as the groom's lease).

Where Then Is It Preferable?

Technically, the wedding may be held anywhere. It is preferable to hold it at the synagogue, which has its own *ke'dushah* (sanctity) and which therefore is the appropriate environment for *kiddushin,* the sanctification of marriage. In addition, the couple is associated at the beginning of married life with the institution of the synagogue, to which it can look for help and to which it will return in nostalgia for a replay of the most glorious moment of life.

If at all possible, the wedding should be held in the general area of the synagogue, "under the canopy of heaven." It is beautiful and meaningful to hold the wedding in a natural setting, where one can feel closer to God. It also provides a historical connection with what must have been the original setting for the wedding before the Babylonian exile of the sixth century B.C.E.

Preferences for wedding locations are rabbinic and customary in nature, not mandatory. The traditionally preferred location should not cause family strife—quarreling is prohibited by the Bible. It is better to follow the biblical edict than to marry in a rabbinically optimal location! The Sages noted in the Talmud that weddings are usually marred by family dissension: "there is no *ketubah* that is signed without quarreling." One wonders if parents, in their zeal to "do the best" for their children, ever realize how much harm is done by quarreling at a time when the lesson should be family solidarity and cooperation?

THE MINYAN

The requirement that a congregation of at least ten adult Jewish males be present for the wedding service was evolved gradually. In talmudic times, when the nuptials and betrothal were two distinct ceremonies separated by up to a year's time, the nuptials were emphasized; betrothals were most often held informally at home. There was no stated need for an authorized rabbi, or a *minyan*.

As a consequence of this loose structure, many "doubtful" marriages resulted from boyish pranks or the desire to blackmail the fathers of unsuspecting young girls. Numerous responsa were written in reference to this problem, "so that the daughters of Israel may not be considered as unprotected property" to be treated with careless abandon. As a result, the betrothals required an ordained rabbi, the *minyan* was considered desirable at betrothals for the public pronouncement of the blessings, and the *ketubah* was read publicly. In this way, the community placed its official stamp on the marriage.

According to the *Halakhah,* the nuptials require a *minyan* of ten men, which includes the groom and his two witnesses, (the *minyan,* unlike the witnesses, may be related to the groom). The presence of the *minyan* during betrothals, considered "desirable" in the Talmud, was made a requirement in the eighth century by Rabbi Ahai, author of *She'iltot.* If no *minyan* is present and the betrothals cannot be delayed, the betrothal blessing may be pronounced. The blessing is valid, as the presence of a *minyan* is only a post-talmudic precaution.

The blessings of the nuptials, however, may not be recited if there is no *minyan.* In addition, the same seven nuptial blessings, which are recited on each of the seven days following the wedding, require a *minyan.* If there is none, only the last blessing (*asher bara*) may be recited at the table—but even this blessing requires the presence of at least three people. The last blessing may not be recited even in the presence of three under the *chuppah,* as the seven blessings must be treated as a single unit at that time.

The need for a quorum in both these ceremonies is somewhat unusual. The *minyan* was ordained for a prayer of sanctity such as the *kaddish*. The nuptials, technically, are not prayers of sanctity, but there are other reasons for the presence of a quorum of ten.

First, in respect to the blessing of God, *Shehakol bara li-khe'vodo* ("who created all things for His honor") and to the mention of the Holy City of Jerusalem, it would appear disrespectful to affirm them without the presence of a congregation of ten. The marriage is so important that even though its blessings are not in the technical category of sanctity, they are treated as such. Homiletic support for this was derived from the marriage of Ruth and Boaz (Ruth 4:2ff), when Boaz summoned ten men to witness the event.

Second, it teaches that a wedding is not just a celebration of the establishment of interpersonal relationships. An announcement is made to the world, represented by the community of ten, that two people are about to enter upon a special relationship that will redefine the expectations of other men and women toward them in other relationships.

The *minyan* also speaks to the couple, underscoring the idea that Jewish marriage must be integrated into the Jewish community, as symbolized by the community of ten. Finally, it declares to all who are present that the marriage is celebrated before God, that this union has cosmic significance, and that God's will will be realized through it.

WEDDING APPAREL

The *Halakhah* is concerned not only with the souls of Jews, but with their appearance. They must be modest as well as attractive. A normal amount of ornament and color in daily life are considered both innocent and proper, but excess ornamentation and loud clothes are offensive. (Admittedly, there is a fine line between good taste and bad taste.) The Talmud teaches that a woman gives her husband proper cause for divorce if she takes a vow not to wear colorful apparel or ornaments.

The bride and groom are considered as king and queen at the time of their wedding and should dress accordingly. The Talmud reports that in ancient times the bride and groom wore crowns—the rich wore gold, the poor wore braided wool. The Rabbis later ruled that, in respect to the war and bloodshed during and after the Second Temple's destruction, such pomp and show were inappropriate.

The bride, at her first marriage, traditionally wears white as a sign of purity on the wedding day, which is considered to be a day of repentance and forgiveness. It also indicates that she has practiced the purification rites of *mikvah* before the wedding.

Some grooms choose to wear a *kitel,* a white linen robe, which is donned over the clothes as the groom arrives under the *chuppah,* and is removed at the end of the service. Two reasons are offered by the tradition. One is that the *kitel* represents a shroud, reminding the groom that though he is a king and center of attention, he is only a mortal and should repent and see to it that his actions are sensitive rather than haughty and vulgar. Second, it symbolizes forgiveness and purity to demonstrate that all the sins of bride and groom are forgiven on their wedding day. Support is derived from Isaiah 1:18: "Though your sins be as scarlet, they shall be white as snow." The western idea of the bride wearing "something old and something new, something borrowed and something blue" is apparently not rooted in the Jewish tradition.

The bride also wears a veil, reminiscent of the matriarch Rebekah, which the groom ceremoniously places over her face. The groom wears a head covering as well, as should all the male guests; indeed, all men and women who take part in the procession should do so.

The Rabbis saw danger in needless extravagance. They were especially sensitive at occasions such as weddings to the fact that such display could cause grief to the poor side of the family. Lack of jewelry on such an occasion is a sober reminder of the destruction of the Temple. Traditionally, therefore, only discreet jewelry or other ornaments are worn.

CHAPTER 13

The Week before the Wedding

SEPARATION OF BRIDE AND GROOM

The custom of separation is of recent vintage, and its source is not known. Rema indicates that the bride and groom require chaperonage to enhance their honor, as do members of the royal family. A second reason for chaperonage may also be a primordial fear of propitious moments—that some accident may occur at this very sensitive moment in life and therefore more protection is needed. (This reason should not prevent the couple from meeting under the chaperonage of parents and friends.)

Another reason may be that the meeting of two lovers so close to the wedding may psychologically stimulate even a slight menstrual stain, and thus prohibit them from cohabiting on their wedding night. This theory, however, was proposed in the Talmud only in regard to the bride's having been *proposed to* within seven days before the wedding date, not merely seeing her fiancè within the week. Even Rosh, who holds that psychological tension is heightened the closer one gets to the wedding date, makes no mention of the separation of bride and groom. It has been suggested that the tradition of separation is only applicable to the day before the wedding to enhance the joy of their meeting as partners. This is similar to the custom of not eating matzah on the day before Passover so that it may be savored more fully on Passover night.

Because the reasons for separation are obscure, it is difficult to establish clear guidelines. It is this custom which determines that a bride not be present at the synagogue when the groom is called to the Torah on the Sabbath prior to the wedding. It also serves to prevent many couples from posing for photographs before the wedding guests arrive. Questions as to how many days of separation, under which conditions, and how firm is the custom, are difficult to determine. Therefore, if any exigency regarding marriage preparations or arrangments for future living quarters requires both partners to be present, they may meet, but they should preferably be accompanied by chaperones.

THE *AUFRUF*

It is a centuries-old tradition to initiate the round of wedding celebrations by having the groom called to recite the blessing over the Torah at the Sabbath service before the wedding. After the Torah reading and the groom's concluding blessing, the congregation often supplements their chorus of *mazal tovs* by throwing nuts and raisins at the groom. If that Sabbath proves especially inconvenient, it may be held on the previous Sabbath or on a weekday when the Torah is read.

The purpose of the synagogue appearance is to publicly announce the forthcoming nuptials. This custom probably originated from legal requirements in medieval France and Germany when community leaders were responsible for ascertaining that there were no impediments to the validity of the marriage before permission could be granted to the couple to hold the wedding in the marriage halls. The most effective way of accomplishing this was the synagogue announcement.

Another and more obvious purpose is the association of the wedding with the Torah. When the celebration is begun with a call to the Torah, the mood is set for sanctity and sobriety. At the time of the First Temple, Solomon had two special gates built: one for grooms, the other for mourners. The public sat between the two. When mourners came, they spoke words of consolation. When grooms entered, they greeted them with the blessing: *Ha-shokhen baba-yit ha-zeh ye'samechakha be'vanim u'vanot*—"May He whose Presence dwells in this house rejoice you with sons and daughters."

The *aufruf* also defines the religious boundaries of the marriage ceremony which, as has been noted, is essentially a civil function. It also gave the entire community, even those not invited to the wedding, the ability to participate in the festivity by attending the usual *kiddush* (Sabbath refreshments) immediately after the service.

The pre-wedding Sabbath has a venerable history. *Mahzor Vitry* records that the groom entered the synagogue with his ushers as a retinue, donned his *tallit* (prayer shawl) and sat down beside the Ark surrounded by his attendants. During the service, the cantor inserted special prayers into the regular service in honor of the couple, and a special reading was recited (Isaiah 61). On the Sabbath after the wedding, in a custom celebrated mostly by the ancient Sephardic community, a reading from a second Torah was specially arranged for bride and groom. This was the Genesis narrative of Eliezer and Rebekah, which, according to Rabbi Bachya, emphasizes that one should marry for right values and not for money, prestige, or beauty alone.

It appears from historical records that grooms traditionally donated the cover used to place over the Torah between readings. This reinforces the opinion that the groom's *aliyah* to the Torah was the special event of the Sabbath. The requirement of the community to extend this honor is in the nature of a *Chiyyuv* (obligation), equivalent to and, according to some, superseding that of the *bar mitzvah* boy. A special hymn, *echad yachid,* was sung for grooms if it was their first marriage, but not for the marriages of widowers or divorcées.

In eighteenth-century Frankfurt, it was customary to extending the celebration back to Friday night, reminiscent of the *shalom zakhar* ceremony for a newborn son.

The celebration at the synagogue on Saturday morning characteristically included the *bevarfen*, the throwing of nuts and raisins. This was undoubtedly a fertility blessing. The Talmud records that at a wedding, the guests passed wine by the couple and then threw wheat, grain, and nuts at both bride and groom. The Maharil, a fourteenth century architect of Ashkenazi custom, records that the groom was brought to greet the bride at the synagogue courtyard door before the wedding began. The groom took her hand, and all assembled threw wheat grains at them and said three times, *pe'ru u-re'vu,—*"be fruitful and multiply!"

One author cites a homiletic reason for throwing the nuts, almonds and raisins. The Hebrew word for nut is *egoz.* The *gematria* (numerical value) of those letters is seventeen, which is also the value for *chet* (sin) and for *tov* (good). A marriage can be very good or very bad, depending on how married life is conducted. So, almonds can be either sweet or very bitter, and wine can be used for purposes of intoxication or for sanctification. Marriage can be lived with drunken abandon or it can be gloriously sanctified.

FAMILY PURITY

An appreciation of the concept of family purity, *taharat ha-mishpachah,* is fundamental to a deeper understanding of Jewish marriage. Because it offers new and fresh insights into the sexual aspects of marriage, it is important to consider it *before* one enters marriage. The law, indeed, requires that a bride begin the practice of family purity within four days before the wedding, as she stands at the threshold of creating her family. Special attention should be paid to the personal preparations, specifically for brides. In case of doubt, a properly ordained rabbi should be consulted.

A superbly written account of the concepts of "family purity" appears in the

book *A Hedge of Roses* by my brother, Dr. Norman Lamm. What follows are
excerpts from that small but important book. (A clear and detailed description
of the *laws* of family purity can be found in another excellent English-language
work on the subject, *Pardes Rimonim: A Marriage Manual for the Jewish
Family,* by Dr. Moses Tendler.)

THE CONCEPT OF FAMILY PURITY

Jewish law forbids a husband to approach his wife during the time of her menses,
generally from five to seven days, and extends the prohibition of any physical contact
beyond this period for another seven days, known as the "seven clean days." (That
is why one will always find, in observant Jewish homes, two beds for husband and
wife, never a double bed.) During this time husband and wife are expected to act
towards each other with respect and affection but without any physical expression
of love—excellent training for that time, later in their lives, when husband and wife
will have to discover bonds other than sex to link them one to another. At the end
of this twelve to fourteen day period (depending upon the individual woman), the
menstruant (known as *niddah*) must immerse herself in a body of water known as
a *mikvah* and recite a special blessing in which she praises God for sanctifying us
with His commandments and commanding us concerning immersion (*tevillah*).

The *mikvah* itself—along with its prescribed dimensions and source of the water
—is an ancient institution. It was in wide use during the times of the two Temples,
for in those days anyone who had contracted any of various kinds of "impurity" was
forbidden to eat of sacrificial meat or the tithe, or to enter the sacred precincts of
the Temple. The way of effecting purification was through immersion in the
mikvah. Most of these forms of impurity have fallen into disuse today, simply
because of the historical circumstance of the destruction of the Temple in 70 C.E.;
today there is neither sacrifice nor Temple. Only the law of the impurity of *niddah*
remains intact, for it affects not only the right to enter the Temple in Jerusalem,
but also the intimate marital relationship of every couple. (One might add, as a
historical note, that Christianity took over from Judaism the institution of *tevillah,*
or immersion, as the rite of initiation into the Christian communion; but that in
the course of time it modified it so that most sects define baptism as the sprinkling
of water upon the communicant rather than the full immersion in the pool.) *Mikvah*
is used today not only for family purity, but also for the initiation of proselytes, both
male and female, into Judaism. In addition, some pious male Jews immerse themselves before prayer and before Sabbath and Holy Days. The *mikvah* is a communal
institution, generally an inconspicuous building, and administered with the utmost
of modesty and delicacy. . . .

By thus preparing for their wedding and afterwards for their monthly marital
reunion—separating from each other and then, before joining each other, the wife
immersing in the *mikvah,* and reciting thereupon the blessing thanking the Almighty for sanctifying us through this institution—husband and wife acknowledge,
in the most profound symbolic manner, that their relationship is sanctified and
blessed, that it is pure and not vulgar, sacred and not salacious. Family purity has

a magnificent cleansing effect upon the psyche. It purifies and ennobles the outlook of man and woman upon each other and their relationships to each other.

Staying Married

That Judaism's view on these most intimate aspects of married life is worthy of consideration by modern young couples is indicated by the striking record of domestic happiness characteristic of Orthodox Jewish homes even in the midst of an environment where the breakdown of family life becomes more shocking with each year. . . .

This typical Jewish family cohesion is surely not the result of any indigenous ethnic or racial virtue of the Jewish people. Nor does it derive from some general, well-intentioned but amorphous "concern for religious tradition." It is, most certainly the product of the specific "Orthodox" tradition—Halakhah or Jewish "way of life." It is this codified tradition, this obligatory law, that has bestowed the gift of stability upon the Jewish family. . . .

Taharat ha-mishpahah is also crucial in protecting the marital bond from one of its most universal and perilous enemies which comes to the fore soon after the newness of married life has worn off: the tendency for sex to become routinized.

It is easy enough to get married. It is quite another thing to stay married. . . .

Familiarity and Boredom

Unrestricted approachability leads to over-indulgence. And this over-familiarity, with its consequent satiety and boredom and *ennui,* is a direct and powerful cause of marital disharmony. When, however, the couple follows the Torah's sexual discipline and observes this period of separation, the ugly spectre of over-fulfillment and habituation is banished and the refreshing zest of early love is ever-present.

There is so much insight in this comment of the rabbis! Familiarity does indeed breed contempt, and a little absence does make the heart grow fonder. . . .

With the institution of *taharat ha-mishpahah* . . . the drama of love-without-sexual-contact followed by the loving union of husband and wife and their being together is repeated every month. Thus the separation of husband and wife physically during the period of *niddah* and the "seven clean days," when they may express to each other feelings of tenderness without any physical contact, is equivalent to the period of engagement. Then, just as she did when she was a bride, the wife undergoes the immersion in a *mikvah,* recites the same blessing she did as a bride and comes to her husband, in purity and love, as she did on her wedding night. . . .

There are some people who imagine that voluntary separation will accomplish the same result, and that it is therefore unnecessary to follow the whole pattern laid down by Jewish law. But such voluntary separation ultimately proves inadequate. One partner may suspect coldness on the part of the one who proposes the withdrawal. Moreover, a lack of religious sanction means that the entire separation will no longer be elevating and ennobling as it can be only when it is informed by religious significance.

The Affirmation of Life

The institution of family purity possesses grand symbolic significance when seen in the context of all of the Torah's legislation concerning *tum'ah* and *taharah*, terms which are loosely and misleadingly translated as "uncleanliness" and "cleanliness" or "purity" and "impurity." The reason we term these translations as inaccurate is because they imply, or at least they allow the listener to infer, that there is some hygienic element involved in them. This, of course, as explained above, is simply not so. They are spiritual states, and have no relation to physical disgust or attractiveness. . . .

Each form of *tum'ah* has a specifically prescribed procedure to revoke it and allow the defiled individual to regain the state of *taharah* or purity. However, there is one element that is common to all forms of *taharah*, and that is immersion in a *mikvah*, which is the climax of every procedure of purification.

What, in the larger sense, is it that underlies all forms of *tum'ah*, and in what way, in the same sense, does *mikvah* neutralize the principle of *tum'ah*?

A Whisper of Death

The Torah is a "Torah of Life."

The Torah itself defines for us the purpose of all the commandments: "and he shall live by them"—"and not die" (Lev. 18:5; Sanhedrin 74a).

An analysis of the various species of *tum'ah* reveals that what they all have in common is the awareness of death. The most potent source of impurity is, indeed, a corpse, or a part thereof. The other kinds of *tum'ah* imply, directly or indirectly, fully or partially, the suggestion of death, even if only the loss of potential life. . . .

A man who suffers from "running issue" (a form of gonorrhea) is impure. The issue is semen, and therefore the loss of potential life. . . . Hence, the state of *tum'ah*. In the same manner, when a woman is *niddah*, during her menstruation, she loses an unfertilized ovum, and it is this loss of potential life, this whisper of death, that confers upon her the state of impurity. . . .

By the same token, *taharah* or purification is a reversal of the process of *tum'ah*. Just as *tum'ah* implies death, *taharah* implies life. And it is the *mikvah* above all that symbolizes the affirmation of life. For it is water that is the most potent symbol of life. "And the spirit of God hovered above the face of the water" (Gen. 1:2). Fresh water is itself called, in Hebrew, *mayyim hayyim*, "living water.". . .

All organized living matter, from protoplasm through man, is in itself essentially watery. The average early human embryo is 97% water, an adult man 60%. Body water continues to diminish slowly with age, "as though the water content of the body were a measure of its vital activity. It would appear that the flame of life is sustained by water." . . .

Freudian psychologists recognize that in dreams and myths the ocean or water is a symbol of life, for man is born from a bag of water, the amniotic fluid, of the mother. . . .

Similarly, when a non-Jew wishes to convert to Judaism and be received into the Covenant of Abraham, we require of him that he immerse himself in the *mikvah*. For the proselyte is considered a new individual, a new-born child, and the sense of birth, of new life, is emphasized by the *mikvah*. By emerging from the waters of the *mikvah*, a new Jew has been born to us.

So that *tum'ah*, the intimation of death, whether it be through *niddah* or any other form, is counteracted by immersion in the water of the *mikvah*, the symbol of life.

By means of this symbolism, we may understand the special requirements for a *mikvah*. The *mikvah* must be a gathering of *natural* water, such as a well or lake or rain-water, and not a pool or bath artificially accumulated by such means as plumbing. The question "what is the difference between (natural) water and (artificial) water?" already perplexed the ancients. According to what has been said above concerning the symbolic significance of water, we may begin to appreciate the difference between the two. By insisting upon the naturalness of the waters of the *mikvah*, we affirm that God alone is the Author of Life and to Him and Him alone do we turn for continued life for us and our descendants after us. Man is not the absolute master of his life and destiny; *mayim she'uvim*, water artificially accumulated, does not therefore possess the power of purification that appertains to natural water. Life is of God.

WEDDING PROCEDURE FOR THE MENSTRUANT BRIDE

If the bride is a menstruant on the wedding night, the wedding ceremony must be modified somewhat, but it will not be apparent to the guests. The seclusion of bride and groom after the ceremony (*yichud*) is omitted, or it may even be held, but with another person present. This wedding ceremony is called *chuppat niddah*.

Because there will be a great desire for sexual fulfillment, despite the restrictions, the couple should be chaperoned.

THE GROOM AND THE MIKVAH

It is a custom in some Jewish traditions that the groom is also immersed in a *mikvah*. The author of *Chuppat Chatanim* says, "It is a good support for the soul. He should silently confess his wrong-doings during the immersion, for it will help him shed the external trappings he heaps upon himself. If, for some reason, he cannot get to the *mikvah*, he should intensify his study of Torah. That will purify him."

FASTING ON THE WEDDING DAY

Although it is not recorded in the Talmud, an ancient tradition advises bride and groom to fast on the day of their wedding. (This applies both to those who are marrying for the first time and to those who are remarrying.) They fast from daybreak until after the *chuppah,* eating their first meal during their *yichud* seclusion at the end of the ceremony.

Two reasons are advanced for fasting. First, tradition records that the sins of the bride and groom are forgiven on their wedding day. Because it is a day of forgiveness, it is considered a day of spiritual inventory and of repentance, akin to Yom Kippur—as represented by the fasting, the wearing of white, and the recitation of the confession at prayers (*vidui* and *al chet*).

The second reason is more practical, and halakhically more functional. The Sages sought to avoid the drinking of liquor before the wedding, as guests and relatives toast the future—it is a long way from stag nights and prenuptial bacchanalias, customary the world over, to the fast day of the traditional Jew. Unlike a Yom Kippur-type fast, which would require observance until nightfall, the wedding fast lasts only until after the *chuppah,* even if it takes place in the afternoon. It is not necessary to "make-up" the fast (*hashlamah*) on another day, in the event of a midday *chuppah.* Even though it is a personal fast, there need be no formal acceptance or vow to fast. If the *chuppah* is delayed beyond nightfall, and fasting becomes difficult, bride and groom may eat, but not drink intoxicating beverages. If even during the day the fast becomes too burdensome, they should discontinue it rather than arrive ill at the *chuppah*.

DAYS OF NO FASTING

The following are days, as recorded in the Talmud, on which one does *not* fast. To do so would contravene the sense of public joyousness. When one does not fast, one should nonetheless not eat excessively, and surely not drink intoxicating liquids.

1. *Rosh Chodesh,* except *Rosh Chodesh Nissan,* when one should fast.
2. *Issru Chag,* the day following the final days of Passover, *Shavuot,* and *Sukkot.*
3. *Hanukkah*
4. *Purim,* both *Purim* and *Shushan Purim* (the day following)
5. Fifteenth day of *Av*
6. Fifteenth day of *Shevat*

One *does* fast on:

1. *Lag Ba-Omer*
2. The days between *Yom Kippur* and *Sukkot*
3. The days between *Rosh Chodesh Sivan* and *Shavuot*
4. All days of *Nissan*

THE PRAYERS ON THE WEDDING DAY

Anenu is a prayer for fast days recited during the silent *amidah* prayer at *minchah*, the afternoon service. It is found in the standard prayer books.

Vidui and *al chet* are prayers of confession. They are recited even on days when no fast may be held. They can be found in the service of the *minchah* before Yom Kippur. These prayers afford the bride and groom a thoughtful moment of spiritual cleansing from the long past and a fervent prayer for a creative and successful future together.

The admonition of the saintly Shelah is very appropriate: "The groom and bride need to sanctify themselves very, very much as they prepare to enter the *chuppah,* because of what the Sages said: 'God forgives them their sins,' and therefore they should repent on the day before the wedding. For all Jews are accustomed to fast, and are alert to the need to repentance and the examination of their deeds from birth to this very day. They should confess and seek forgiveness and pardon and atonement from God. Their regrets should be sincere, with broken hearts for their sins, and they should resolve from this day onward with great strength to serve God in truth and wholesomeness and to be sanctified and pure."

CHAPTER 14

The Day of the Wedding

There are two islands of activity surrounding bride and groom before the ceremony: *kabbalat panim* and *hakhnassat kallah*.

THE GROOM'S TABLE (*KABBALAT PANIM*)

The guests are customarily instructed to rejoice with the groom, although this is not equivalent to the *mitzvah* of honoring the bride. The Talmud established a bride's throne, where she is surrounded by the women, and the tradition of subsequent centuries established a groom's table (in Yiddish, *chosen's tish*). Before the celebration, the men gather at this table to sing and to toast the groom and one another. It is here that the *minchah* service is usually recited. Custom has it that at this time the groom, if he is able, delivers a brief lesson from Torah. But custom could not bear to impose upon an already burdened groom the responsibility of preparing a lecture before his peers, and therefore the groom is interrupted by community singing, after one or two sentences of the "lecture." Primarily, however, the groom's table is the place where the *ketubah* is written and signed.

THE MARRIAGE CONTRACT (*KETUBAH*)

The *ketubah* is a unilateral agreement drawn by witnesses in accordance with Jewish civil law, in which they testify that the husband guarantees to his wife that he will meet certain minimum human and financial conditions of marriage, "as Jewish husbands are wont to do."

It is not a ceremonial document of scripture or prayer. That is why it is written in Aramaic, the technical legal language of talmudic law, rather than in Hebrew, the language of the "Song of Songs." Neither is it a state document establishing the new relationship of man and woman. It makes no mention of the confirmation of God or of society. It is not an instrument of the privileged class, as in ancient societies, but one obligatory on every person. It is also not an affirmation of perpetual love. It is a statement of law that provides the framework of love.

The *ketubah* restates the fundamental conditions that are imposed by the Torah upon the husband, such as providing his wife with food, clothing, and conjugal rights, which are inseparable from marriage. It includes the husband's guarantees to pay a certain sum in the event of divorce, and inheritance rights obligatory upon his heirs in case he dies before his wife.

It is not a mutual agreement; the wife agrees only to accept the husband's proposal of marriage. It is assuredly not a bill of sale; the man does not purchase the bride. In fact, the *ketubah* represents the witnesses rather than husband or wife. Through this instrument they attest to the groom's actions, promises, and statements, and to the bride's willing acceptance of the marriage proposal.

It is a charter of woman's rights in marriage and of man's duties. The *ketubah* is designed for woman's protection, and every legal nuance in this matter was developed so that her husband shall not regard it as easy to divorce her. In a male-oriented society, the woman always needed more defense against the violation of personal rights than the man. The *ketubah* required money to be paid by the husband in case of divorce. This made it difficult for the husband to divorce his wife without appropriate reflection and consideration. The requirement of a scribe and a specially convened court and witnesses for a divorce also protected the wife from an arbitrary husband, especially when the Rabbis, in accordance with Hillel's dictum, were lenient with divorce. Moreover, the *ketubah* protected whatever property was to be hers at the termination of the marriage.

Because of this concern for the integrity of "the daughters of Israel," the Sages said that to live with a wife without a *ketubah,* or without specification of fair conditions, is regarded as concubinage—the difference between a wife and a concubine is that a wife has a *ketubah,* and a concubine does not. They considered that an unstructured marriage arrangement was fit only for a man and his concubine, that it placed the woman at an unfair advantage, and that it was beneath a Jewish woman to be so considered. When the Jews of France were robbed of all their possessions and expelled by Philip the Fair in 1306, they moved *en masse* to Provence. Rashba ordered that no married life be resumed there until every man give his wife a replacement *ketubah.* This *ketubah de'irkhesa* is required, even today, for everyone who has misplaced or lost the original *ketubah.*

In this manner, a strictly legal document with detailed monetary conditions was converted by the Rabbis into an ethical statement that would safeguard the wife and mother and serve as an anchor in turbulent marital seas.

Following is an outline of the *ketubah,* in English and Aramaic, and a descriptive commentary. The *ketubah* used is the standard form of the Rabbinical Council of America, New York. There are other new forms of the marriage contract, but only the traditional *ketubah* is considered here.

OUTLINE OF THE KETUBAH

The Date and Place of the Wedding

On the _____ day of the week, the _____ day of the month _____ in the year _____ since the creation of the world according to the reckoning which we are accustomed to use here in the city of _____ in _____.

ב _____ בשבת ב _____ לחדש _____
שנת חמשת אלפים ושבע מאות _____ למנין שאנו
מנין כאן _____

The Date. The law prescribes that the date appear at the beginning in *private* agreements, but at the end in court agreements. Though the *ketubah* has the status of a court decree, it is in the nature of a private agreement and so the date is placed first.

The Place. The same rationale is used for the place. A divorce document contains more geographical information (e.g., mention of a neighboring river). The Sephardim retained this custom, and Rema, in the sixteenth century, urged that the technicalities of the *ketubah* follow those of the divorce. But the Talmud simplified the *ketubah* and the Jews of Europe have followed that tradition.

The Groom, the Bride and the Proposal

_____ son of _____ of the family _____ said to this maiden _____ daughter of _____ of the family _____ "Be thou my wife according to the law of Moses and Israel."

איך החתן _____ בן _____
למשפחת _____ אמר להדא בתולתא
_____ בת _____
למשפחת _____ הוי לי לאנתו כדת משה וישראל

The Names. Their Hebrew names, their fathers' names and usually, though not always, their family names. The mother's name is given when praying for recovery from illness, as a symbol of mother's compassion. A father's name is used in legal matters, just as a father's family name has always been used in legal affairs. Added to their names is also the appellation for a rabbinic scholar, *Rav,* or priestly or Levitic descent, *kohen* or *Levi.*

The Proposal. "Be thou my wife according to the law of Moses and of Israel" is the marriage proposal. The *ketubah,* following in time as it does the betrothal and its oral proposal formula, "You are hereby betrothed unto me according to the law of Moses and Israel," is written by witnesses testifying that the groom in fact proposed to the bride. The formula has remained intact for some two thousand years. The Talmud considered variants, but this language of proposal endured.

The Groom Promised the Basic Support

". . . and I will work for thee, honor, provide for, and support thee, in accordance with the practice of Jewish husbands, who work for their wives, honor, provide for and support them in truth."

ואנא אפלח ואוקיר ואיזון ואפרנם יתיכי ליכי כהלכות גוברין
יהודאין דפלחין ומוקרין וזנין ומפרנסין לנשיהון בקושטא

Support. This is referred to as the alimentation clause. Providing support is elemental in marriage, and is considered so obvious that the Talmud makes no reference to it. But the phrase is so beautiful and appropriate that it appears in the *ketubah* not only once but twice, "honor, provide for, and support . . . honor, provide for, and support. . . ." Indeed, one authority described it as *le'shufra di'she'tara* (for the beauty of the contract).

Funds for the Wife, If and When the Marriage Terminates

"And I will set aside for thee two hundred silver *zuz mohar* due thee for thy maidenhood, which belong to thee according to the law of the Torah, and thy food, clothing, and other necessary benefits which a husband is obligated to provide; and I will live with thee in accordance with the requirements prescribed for each husband."

ויהיבנא ליכי מהר בתוליכי כסף זוזי מאתן דחזי ליכי מדאוריתא
ומזוניכי וכסותכי וסיפוקיכי ומיעל לותיכי כאורח כל ארעא

The Mohar. The funds, called *mohar,* are so important that this clause is called *ikkar ketubah*—the basic part of the *ketubah,* or simply the *ketubah.* *Mohar* is the cash gift the groom gives the bride, as Eliezer, Abraham's servant, gave "precious things" to Laban, Rebekah's father, and as Jacob gave seven years of service for the hand of Rachel. The great sage and the *ketubah's* most important author, Rabbi Simeon ben Shetach, decreed that this serve as protection for the bride rather than only a gift, and ordained that the funds were not given but set aside for the bride. During marriage, therefore, it was considered a debt which was paid only in case of death or divorce, and the *mohar* thus became a divorce or life insurance settlement rather than a mere marriage gift. This arrangement also enabled poor grooms to marry without any immediate monetary expenditure. The Talmud provides another reason, *mishum china,* to give the woman a secure financial position at the time of divorce so that she may remarry, and make the trials of marriage less poignant.

The Law of the Torah.   There is a running dispute between the Jerusalem Talmud and the Babylonian Talmud as to whether this settlement, which all agree is historically of biblical times, is biblically or rabbinically mandated. Today we generally take *mohar* to be rabbinically commanded, yet because of the gravity of the marriage bond we persist in using, "which belong to thee according to the law of the Torah." We also include "two hundred silver *zuz,*" the Tyrean coin used in biblical assessments, rather than the "current" coin used in rabbinically-ordained payments.

Mohar for brides previously married is one-half the total and is recorded as rabbinically-mandated.

Food, Clothing, and Conjugal Relations.   The obligations are basic to marriage and are obligatory even without specific contractual condition. They are the *rights* (including conjugal relations) of the wife, and are accounted *duties* of the husband.

The Bride Accepted the Proposal

And _____ this maiden, consented and became his wife.

וצביאת מרת ـــ בתולתא
דא והות ליה לאנתו

Willing Acceptance.   The proposal having been made in the traditional formula, the witnesses now assert that the bride accepted with *willing consent,* and therefore "she became his wife." *Ve'havat lih le'into* is an Aramaic translation of Ruth 4:13, *va-tehi lo le'ishah.*

And She Brings a Dowry

The dowry (*nedunya*) that she brought from her _____ house, in silver, gold, valuables, clothing, and household furnishings, all this _____ the said groom accepted in the sum of one hundred silver pieces.

ודן נדוניא דהנעלת ליה מבי ـــــــــــــــــــــــــــــــ בין בכסף בין
בדהב בין בתכשיטין במאני דלבושא בשימושי דירה ובשימושא

דערסא הכל קבל עליו ————— חתן דנן במאה

זקוקים כסף צרוף

The Dowry. *Nedunya,* (dowry), popularly referred to as *naddan,* is given the bride by her father for her use in the home she is about to build. This dowry includes the items listed plus any other valuables she may bring with her. In the Bible, Rachel and Leah are given servants Bilhah and Zilpah as dowry. It is the daugter's share of her parents' inheritance. The sons succeed their father, but the daughters leave him and therefore receive an equivalent in the form of dowry. The Sages make it compulsory for a father to give his daughter, as a start in married life, sufficient funds to buy a woman's wardrobe for one year.

The dowry is distinct from property or possessions that the bride owns and continues to own privately throughout marriage. Thus it serves as an inducement for suitors. The dowry is included in the *ketubah,* and is the property of the bride, technically "leased" to the groom for the duration of marriage. The bride's private property, called *nikhsei melog,* is given outright to the bride, the husband enjoying only the "fruit" (*usufruct*) during marriage. It is not part of the dowry and is not included in the *ketubah.*

The Groom Accepted. The *ketubah* originally listed all items in the dowry and tabulated the cost. In time, this was standardized under the general categories listed and estimated at a standard sum of one hundred silver pieces, one half of the *mohar* that the groom provided the bride for use of the dowry, but which, in reality, comes today to very much more than the half *mohar.*

The Groom, in Turn, Promised an Additional Gift

adding on his own, *mattan,* another hundred silver pieces, *kenegdan,* making a total of two hundred silver pieces.

וצבי ————————————— חתן דנן והוסיף לה מן דיליה

עוד מאה זקוקים כסף צרוף אחרים כנגדן סך הכל מאתים

זקוקים כסף צרוף

Tosefet Ketubah: The Mattan. The additional monies, known as *tosefet ketubah* or *mattan,* is the addition to the *mohar,* called *ikkar ketubah,* the basic contract. This is the gift that the groom makes and that matches the dowry sum (*kenegdan*)—one hundred silver pieces. The total of dowry estimate plus *tosefet ketubah* comes to two hundred silver pieces.

The *tosefet ketubah* has a parallel history to *mohar,* although the *mohar* was legal and compulsory and the *tosefet ketubah* social and voluntary. Both were designed to protect the woman. The latter was originally a wedding gift to the bride, and turned into a debt which was to be redeemed at the termination of marriage, by death of the husband or divorce. It had the same security advantage as did the *mohar* (although this was not instituted by Simeon ben Shetach).

And Secured the Promise with a Lien on His Property

And thus said _____, the said groom: "I take upon myself, and my heirs after me, the surety of this *ketubah,* of the dowry, and of the additional sum, so that all this shall be paid from the best part of my property, real and personal, that I now possess or may hereafter acquire. All my property, even the mantle on my shoulders, shall be mortgaged for the security of this *ketubah* and of the dowry and of the addition made thereto, during my lifetime and after my lifetime from this day forever."

וכד אמר _____ חתן דנן אחריות שטר כתובתא דא
נדוניא דן ותוספתא דא קבלית עלי ועל ירתי בתראי להתפרע
מכל שפר ארג נכסין וקנינין דאית לי תחות כל שמיא דקנאי
ודעתיד אנא למקנא נכסין דאית להון אחריות ודלית להון
אחריות כלהון יהון אחראין וערבאין לפרוע מנהון שטר כתובתא
דא נדוניא דן ותוספתא דא מנאי ואפילו מן גלימא דעל כתפאי
בחיי ובתר חיי מן יומא דנן ולעלם

The Surety of This Ketubah. Rabbi Simeon ben Shetach made the *ketubah* into a note of indebtedness to protect the wife. He also introduced a guarantee that it would not remain merely a promise made in the flush of love, but a contractual obligation. The *ketubah* therefore includes a lien on the groom's property to secure the satisfaction of the triple obligation of *mohar, nedunya,* and *tosefet ketubah,* or as the *ketubah* reads, *she'tar ketubta da, nedunya den, ve'tosefta da.* A lien on the debtor's property (the groom's) means that the law considers the property as a sort of mortgage. It is a *shibuda de'oraita,* a lien that is a biblical mandate, even more than a simple mortgage. The lien of the *ketubah* obligates the husband personally and it is therefore not only a mortgage on his real estate, but also on "property, the best part ... real and personal ... the mantle on my shoulders ... now ... or hereafter ... during my lifetime and forever."

And the Lien Is Fully Valid

And the surety for all the obligations of this *ketubah,* dowry and the additional sum has been assumed by _____ the said groom, with the full obligation dictated by all documents of *ketubot* and additional sums due every daughter of Israel, executed in accordance with the enactment of our Sages, of blessed memory. It is not to be regarded as an indecisive contractual obligation nor as a stereotyped form.

ואחריות שטר כתובתא דא נדוניא דן ותוספתא דא קבל עליו

חתן דנן כחומר כל שטרי כתובות

ותוספתות דנהגין בבנת ישראל העשויין כתקון חכמינו זכרונם

לברכה דלא כאסמכתא ודלא כטופסי דשטרי

Not a Stereotyped Form. To assure the legal effectiveness of the debt and
the lien made at a moment of exhilaration and romantic expectation, and to
prevent the *ketubah* from being considered a mere statement of love commitment, with no legal binding force, the Sages expressly affirmed, "It is not to be
regarded as an *asmakhta,* an indecisive contractual obligation," a sort of specula-
tion, or as a "stereotyped form," a routine rubber-stamp procedure.

Then Everything Was Sealed

And we have completed the act of acquisition from _____ son of
_____ of the family _____ the said bridegroom, for ____
_____ daughter of _____ of the family _____
this maiden, for all that which is stated and explained above, by an instrument legally
fit to establish a transaction. And everything is valid and established.

וקנינא מן _____ בן _____

למשפחת _____ חתן דנן למרת _____

בת _____ למשפחת _____ בתולתא דא

כל מה דכתוב ומפורש לעיל במנא דכשר למקניא ביה הכל

על שריר וקים

The Act of Acquisition (Kinyan). In order to seal all of the stipulated
obligations, and to assure that the document is not *asmakhta* (based on specula-
tion), the Rabbis required the legal formality of *kinyan,* the *act* of acquisition.
Because the bride cannot take possession of all the property, the groom affirms
it by a symbolic act called *kinyan suddar.*

Thus, at the wedding, the rabbi or one of the witnesses gives a handkerchief
or other article (but not a coin) in behalf of the recipient, the bride, to the
groom. The groom then returns it. Then they record in the *ketubah, ve'kanina*
("and we have completed the act of acquisition"). This symbolic act must be
seen clearly by the witnesses, who are the makers of the contract, before they
sign to its validity. If the *ketubah* is calligraphed by a scribe, or printed in
advance of the wedding, one letter of the word *ve'kanina* (or the whole word)
is usually omitted so that the *ketubah* is technically not completed before the
kinyan itself is made. If this custom is overlooked it does not alter the *ketubah*'s
validity, so long as the witnesses in fact witness the *kinyan*-transfer of the
handkerchief.

Everything Is Valid and Established. The Sages took precautions that legal documents not be tampered with or added to, and therefore instituted several procedures in concluding the document. First, the last sentence had to briefly summarize the contents: second, the formula *ha-kol sharir ve'kayam*, ("and everything is valid and established") must appear at the end of that line; and third, the witnesses must sign very close to the last line.

In the *ketubah*, the summary is "for all that which is stated and explained above, by an instrument legally fit to establish a transaction." The formula follows, "and everything is valid and established." And the witnesses sign immediately thereafter on the next line beneath the formula.

And the Witnesses Attested to It

Witness ————————————————————————————————————

Witness ————————————————————————————————————

עד ————————————————————————————— נאום

עד ————————————————————————————— נאום

The Witnesses. The witnesses must follow these guidelines, although today the preprinted *ketubot* usually prevent error.

1. The witness must write his first name, son of his father's first name, whether he is a *kohen* or *Levi,* preferably also the family name, and follow it with the word *ed* (witness).
2. It must be in his own handwriting, not that of the scribe.
3. It must be signed as close to the text as possible, so that no words can easily be inserted.
4. The signature should not begin in the middle of the line.
5. Ideally, the two witnesses should sign one name under the other, as they would on a *get* (divorce).
6. They should not sign before it is fully completed, including, if it is calligraphed, the omitted letter in *ve'kanina.*
7. They should have read the document, or have had it read to them.
8. They should have witnessed both the *kinyan* and each other's signing, as on a *get.*

The *ketubah* will be read aloud and formally presented during the wedding ceremony. The couple must always know where the *ketubah* is located. If they cannot locate it, they must see a qualified rabbi who will write them a replacement *ketubah, ketubah di'irkhesa.* This is a matter of law, not mere custom.

The *ketubah* must be filled out by a rabbi who knows the *Halakhah.* It cannot be done reliably by a well-meaning, knowledgeable friend, or by a Hebrew calligrapher, unless carefully instructed by a rabbi. The *ketubah* is a very complicated document, especially for widows, converts, and divorcees.

I have purposely omitted instructions for the proper completion of the *ketubah,* and the text of the *ketubah de'irkhesa,* to insure that the community heed the Talmud's words of caution: "He who does not know the nature of divorce and marriage should have nothing to do with them."

Once the *ketubah* is completed, the procession proceeds from the groom's table to the bridal throne, accompanied by singing and dancing. The groom is at the head, followed by friends.

ATTENDING THE BRIDE (*HAKHNASSAT KALLAH*)

The bride is a queen and deserves all the attention and respect due her station. It is a positive commandment, of rabbinic origin, to accord her honor, praise her, provide for her, and make her happy. The Talmud assigns her a *kisei ha-kallah* (bridal throne) and instructs all who can attend to act as her retinue.

The concept of *hakhnassat kallah* is three-fold. First, it signifies providing the bride, especially an orphaned and poor bride, with dowry, trousseau, and everything she might need for the wedding. It is subsumed under the general *mitzvah* of "Love thy neighbor as thyself," and is included by the author of the prayer book as among those things of which "the fruit is eaten in this world, but the principal remains in store for the world to come." Maharil notes that there is no greater charity than *hakhnassat kallah* for a poor girl. The Rabbis go so far as to say that the community must sell a synagogue item, even one that has a donor's name on it, and even a scroll of the Torah, in order to raise money for an orphaned bride. The Talmud also stipulates that all of this be done discreetly.

Second, *hakhnassat kallah* means to make the bride happy. That is done by helping her arrange her hair and jewelry, dancing before her, and complimenting her. The Talmud could not precisely define "complimenting" her—*Keitzad me'rakdin?* (How does one praise a bride?) The school of Shammai held that one must tell the truth under all circumstances, with no exaggeration. Thus if she is beautiful, say so; if not, say nothing. Or find a good quality to compliment, such as beautiful eyes or hands, for there is no one who does not have one good quality. But the school of Hillel held otherwise. They recommended, under all circumstances, calling her *kallah na'ah ve'chasudah* (a beautiful and gracious bride) and saying of her that "a thread of kindness is drawn around her," even if she does not happen to be pretty or kind. One should not even specify her virtues, because that would imply that her other qualities are less than praiseworthy. Hillel does not consider this a falsification, because one is permitted a slight, harmless compliment "for the sake of good will." Then again, even if it may be certain that the bride is not beautiful, is it so certain that she does not have a shred of kindness or graciousness? The law decided in favor of Hillel.

The third meaning of *hakhnassat kallah* is the most precise historically. It is *le'hakhnisah le'chuppah* (to lead her to the bridal canopy), to be part of her retinue. The Talmud declares that one is permitted even to sacrifice time from the study of Torah when helping with the burial of the dead or leading the bride to the canopy. The bride takes precedence over the funeral cortège in any conflict of time. The law also advises that when a funeral cortège and bridal procession are both to proceed on one street, the funeral is detoured because the honor of the living bride takes precedence over the deceased.

The purpose of this elaborate demonstration is to honor one who is performing so great a *mitzvah,* and also to impress her groom with her popularity. In line with these reasons, Me'iri says, *Be'rov am hadrat chatan ve'kallah*—"The greater the number of people, the greater the glory of groom and bride." As we say, "the more the merrier."

It is sad that the custom of joyously accompanying the bride to the *chuppah* is not observed today. In the past, the most important officials of the community often came to greet the bride. One of the reasons for the decline in this aspect of *hakhnassat kallah,* which surfaces in a review of rabbinic opinion, is the concern for the public mixing of the sexes and the ribaldry that might result. This must be the reason for the strange reversal in Jewish custom: the *groom* is now accompanied during his procession to the bride's throne to perform the veiling ceremony. That is now called, by some, *hakhnassat kallah;* but there is no doubt that it is far more in keeping with the sense of the tradition that the women form a jubilant entourage as they lead the bride to the processional. Indeed, Maharil performed both traditions: first he led the procession of the groom, who is supposed to appear under the *chuppah* first, and then he returned to lead the bride's procession. This does appear to be a custom that should be accepted by modern Jewry.

THE VEILING CEREMONY (*BEDEKEN*)

The veiling ceremony is held only for a bride's first marriage. When the two islands of activity for bride and groom are bridged by the procession from the groom's table to the bride's throne, the merging signals the beginning of the wedding celebration. The groom, the rabbi, the fathers and the whole entourage proceed to the bride (who is flanked by both mothers) for the veiling ceremony. The groom places the veil over the bride's face and recites the blessing given to Rebekah by her mother and brother before she left for her marriage to Isaac: *Achotenu: at hayi le'alfei revavah*—"Our sister, be thou the mother of thousands of ten thousands" (Genesis 24:60). The rabbi, then the parents, extend their words of hope and prayer. In some families, it is customary at this time for the bride's father to place his hands over her head and offer her the priestly benediction. The groom and his party return to their places and the wedding begins.

Historically, there were variants to the basic ceremony. In some, the bride was veiled in the morning before the evening wedding. In others the groom was not to be present, and the rabbi ceremoniously veiled the bride. In most ceremonies, however, the absence of the groom was not permitted.

The source of the veiling is the Bible. There are two instances of a woman veiling herself in the presence of a man. The first, obviously, does not apply— Tamar veils herself as Judah approaches (Genesis 38:14). The purpose there was not symbolic, but to hide her identity from her father-in-law. The second is most obviously the origin of the *bedeken*—Rebekah veils herself as she is told that Isaac is approaching. "And she said to the servant, 'What man is this that walketh in the field to meet us?' And the servant said, 'It is my master.' And she took her veil and covered herself" (Gen. 24:64).

According to several rabbinic authorities, the veiling was not a mere social formality, but had the force of law as it was legally considered the *chuppah,* which is the concluding step of the marriage. Most authorities today hold that it is a beautiful traditional ceremony, but that it does not have the significance of *chuppah.* Nonetheless, its performance assures that all theories of *chuppah* are observed, to guarantee the absolute observance of the law of marriage, without exception.

There are a number of interpretations of the veil's symbolism, all of which reflect truths that are worthy of being dramatically enacted before the wedding service.

1. *The veil is a symbol of the married woman.*   It expresses a dignity, which Isaiah (3:18) calls *tiferet,* and which was reserved for women of station. Ezekiel (16:20) speaks of "covering with silk" the woman he loves. Interestingly, Rebekah does not wear a veil while on the journey in the company of the servant, Eliezer, but instinctively dons it when sighting Isaac. This may account for the insistence of major authorities that the groom himself veil the bride, and that it should never be done without him—it is only his presence that makes her veil significant.

2. *The veil is symbolic of her new unapproachability to others, not only sexually, but as* hekdesh, *a sanctified object in the temple.*   The sacred objects of the tabernacle were "veiled" before being taken up to be carried by the Levites. The betrothal ceremony is likened, in a legal sense, to those sanctified objects of the temple. This is the significance of the term *kiddushin:* the groom, in marriage, sets the bride aside as *hekdesh.* The analogy strikes deeper if we compare it to the face of Moses, which radiated light after he received the commandments. Moses placed *masveh* (a veil) over his face as though to imply separateness, withdrawal, almost an other-worldliness.

3. The symbol of the veil most often referred to is "modesty." Although the Bible makes no requirement of women wearing veils for modesty, it is inescapable in this context. It is a sign of *tze'niut* par excellence—the retiring, discreet, quiet presence. The diametric opposite is arrogance, best symbolized by *azut panim* (barefacedness). It is given a remarkable expression in the law. According to Ibn Yarhi, the veil demonstrates that this was not a "betrothal in the market place," whose grossness, even though it is within the law, was condemned by the Rabbis, and whose perpetrators were flogged by the court of Rav in the days of the Talmud. The symbolic modesty of the veil teaches an important lesson: that "the glory of the princess is the interior" of the person. No matter her beauty and her charm, her inner qualities of soul and character are more important. The veil covers the externals in order to direct the attention of the inner person.

4. The veil also conveys psychological significance. Netziv notes that the instinctive action of veiling at the sight of Isaac symbolized Rebekah's married life with him. There was none of the open husband-wife communication so characteristic of Abraham with Sarah or Jacob with Rachel. Her veil symbolized that she was a private person, vigorously self-confident and not easily compromised. It was God's way of assuring that the patriarchal blessing would go to Jacob, despite Isaac's intent to confer it upon Esau. If she were less individualistic and self-assured, she might have been swayed by her husband. Although anthropologists conjecture that veiling indicates being possessed by someone else, here it implies self-possession. Her veil was the symbol of her capacity to be both a wife, sharing life goals and hopes with her husband, and a private person.

CHAPTER 15

The Wedding

The wedding celebration is composed of two distinct and successive ceremonies: betrothal (*kiddushin*) and nuptials (*nissuin*). The *kiddushin* includes the betrothal blessings, the proposal, and the giving of the ring before two witnesses. This is followed by a transition stage—the public reading of the marriage contract. Afterwards, the *nissuin* begins. This consists of the seven blessings, followed by the breaking of the glass, and finally by *yichud*, several minutes of seclusion after leaving the *chuppah*.

THE BRIDAL CANOPY (*CHUPPAH*)

The *chuppah* is a tapestry attached to the tops of four poles. The word *chuppah* means covering or protection, and is intended as a roof or covering for the bride and groom at their wedding.

The *chuppah* is not merely a charming folk custom, a ceremonial object carried over from a primitive past. It serves a definite, though complicated, legal purpose: It is the decisive act that formally permits the couple's new status of marriage to be actualized, and it is the legal conclusion of the marriage process that began with betrothal. Together these two *kinyanim* (acts of acquisition) are called *chuppah ve'kiddushin*.

Chuppah symbolizes the groom's home, and the bride's new domain. More specifically, the *chuppah* symbolizes the bridal chamber, where the marital act was consummated in ancient times.

The tapestry canopy that we know as *chuppah* was first identified by Rabbi Moses Issereles (Rema) in the sixteenth century, and we must assume that it was relatively new in his time. The concept, however, is ancient, and the Talmud considers it biblically required for marriage.

What exactly is *chuppah?* Although we do know that originally it was the groom's home, or an addition to his father's home into which the new couple moved, we cannot know, in precise halakhic terms, what the symbol of that *chuppah* is supposed to be today. (Psalm 19:6 speaks of the *bridegroom* emerging from his *chuppah,* while Joel 2:16 says, "Let the bridegroom emerge from his chamber [*chedro*], and the bride from her *chuppah.*")

According to several of the medieval scholars, notably Ran and Rif, chuppah was effected by the bride's mere entrance into the groom's home. That is why the symbolizing of the *chuppah* in a synagogue or hall, for example, can be done with only a canopy; if it had walls, then as soon as the couple stepped into it after the betrothal with the intent of marriage, they would change status. Maimonides held that it was only in seclusion, *yichud,* that the *chuppah* sealed marriage. *Tur* felt that the groom covered the bride with an article of clothing, and that was the legal *chuppah* act. *Nachalat Shivah* quotes the authoritative Ashkenazic custom that a *tallit* over both their heads was the definitive *chuppah.* The Tosafists stated that the covering of the bride's face with a veil finalized the marriage. Mordecai taught that the very process of leaving her father's home to enter the groom's home was itself *chuppah;* others, such as Rosh, held that the decorated hand-carried coach, which in the days of the Second Temple transported the bride through the city, was really the *chuppah.* The "Bach," therefore rules that we perform virtually all of these acts in order to cover all halakhic possibilities. The bride is veiled, and the overhead canopy is the groom's covering for the bride. The beautiful ancient Askhenazic custom of placing the groom's *tallit* on the couple's head for the nuptial blessings has been retained largely by Sephardim and German Jews.

The construction of the *chuppah* is simple: a cloth or *tallit* is spread over four poles. Care should be taken, if at all possible, that the cloth be fastened to the top of the poles (rather than to their sides), which serve as a legal separation and wall. Legally, this constitutes a private domain in regard to the laws of the Sabbath, and it transforms the *chuppah,* technically into the groom's private home.

What sort of cloth should be used for a *chuppah?* Historically, the *chuppah* was a desirable object of art, which everyone sought to decorate—after all, it also symbolized the covenantal marriage of God and His people. The medieval community often used a *parokhet* (an Ark covering), although it was felt to be inappropriate to apply an object of sanctity to the bridal chamber. Considering the suggestion that the cover be affixed to the *top* of poles, a floral *chuppah* is not desirable, although it is perfectly acceptable to cover and decorate the tapestry *chuppah* with a canopy of flowers. Perhaps genuine beauty resides in simplicity. How much more elegant is the symbol of a *tallit* attached at the top of four portable poles held by four friends!

The *chuppah* is required only for the nuptials, but with today's elaborate *chuppot,* one cannot help but have the *entire* service, even the betrothals, under the *chuppah.* That is perfectly acceptable, but it would be more significant, and also more instructive to an unknowing audience, to raise a portable *chuppah after* the reading of the *ketubah,* in time for the seven blessings of the nuptials.

The bride and groom must stand under the *chuppah.* It is not necessary for rabbi, cantor, witnesses, or parents to be under the canopy. If their presence were a requirement, the other symbols of *chuppah*—veil, *tallit,* clothing, privacy—would not be effective without them.

The *chuppah* is a legal instrument, but the fact that only this canopy symbol survived makes a statement to the couple. First, it teaches that this simple, fragile roof, which is now common to both partners, launches the marriage. In the words of William Henry Channing, it teaches them "to live content with small means: to seek elegance rather than luxury, and refinement rather than fashion, to be worthy not respectable, and wealthy, not rich." Second, it affirms the teaching of *Ha-manhig* that the *chuppah* sets the couple apart from the crowds, to avoid it appearing as though they were "marrying in the marketplace," which was considered gross and indelicate in the extreme. Marriage is the establishment of a home, an island of sanity and serenity "far from the madding crowd."

THE PROCESSION

The order of the procession, the people chosen, and the decor are varied and not important to the law. These arrangements should suit the taste of the couple, although traditions have developed over the centuries that may serve as guides.

The groom *must* arrive under the *chuppah* before the bride. After all, it is his symbolic home and legally he has leased it for the bridal chamber. The bride's transition from her parents' home to her husband's is demonstrated by this procession, and the *chuppah* affords the opportunity for that expression.

The selection of escorts (*shushvinin*) for the bride and groom is not explicitly described. The Rabbis playfully imagined the angels accompanying Adam and Eve, the first "bride" and "groom," at their wedding. At first, notes the Talmud, each had one accompanying person, to help them arrive properly under the *chuppah.* The tradition speaks of both fathers accompanying the groom and both mothers the bride; the Zohar tells of each being accompanied by the parents. There is no expression in all of Jewish tradition of the bride walking with her father only, as a symbol of the father "giving away" the bride.

In our times, complications arise from the large numbers of children of divorced parents. Arrangements are very rarely satisfactory. One possible method for parents who will not walk together at their child's side is to revert to the tradition of both fathers escorting the groom, and both mothers the bride. One major point must be kept uppermost in the minds of the parents: The children should not be used as instruments for revenge, or for parents to play out their anger. Traditional escorting is not sacrosanct; it does not have even the rank of rabbinic law. Quarreling, however, is prohibited by biblical law. It is foolish to allow such questions of mere ceremonial procession to cause controversy and mar the joy of bride and groom.

The importance attached by the tradition to accompanying the bride and groom derives, according to *Tashbatz,* from the idea that at this time they are king and queen, and royalty is never to be left alone. Another more practical consideration is *gemillut chasadim,* the simple kindness of being available to offer help and positive support, a steadying hand in a moment of tension and concern.

The wedding is the supreme definition of joy in Jewish life. The more people who share joy, the greater the joy felt by the couple.

CANDLES

Candles were often a common feature of the bridal procession and *chuppah,* although they were never mandated. At times they were thrown as torches (with safety in mind, of course). More frequently, they were held by the two people escorting the bride and groom. The numerical value of candle (*ner*) multiplied by two for the escorters of bride and groom equals the numerical value of "be fruitful and multiply"!

Light was always associated with celebration: "For the Jews, there was light and joy, *orah ve'simchah*" (Esther 8:16). Candles are lit at the beginning of major holidays, as on the Sabbath. Moreover, as with much of the ceremony, the wedding was likened to the covenant that married the Jew to God at Sinai. Just as there were bursts of thunder and lightning at Sinai, so here the lights announce the making of a covenant of Jewish marriage.

NEW CIRCLE

Custom has it that the bride, as she arrives under the *chuppah,* walks three times around the groom (in some communities, seven times). The tradition is both beautiful and meaningful, although it is not required by the *Halakhah.*

The reason for this unusual custom is shrouded in the mist of the past. One rabbinic author suggests that a woman is a "protective wall" for her husband, preventing him from foolishness and guarding him from harmful influences. As Jeremiah (31:22) says, "A woman encompasses a man." Another rabbinic author says that it symbolizes the light that now envelopes a man as he emerges from bachelorhood. There he was considered only *palga gufa* (half a person), now he is completed and encircled by his wife.

Another cogent and meaningful reason may be offered. The marriage canopy described by Rema is the marriage chamber with the walls removed, so that it may be the center of public ceremony. Thus there will be no question that *chuppah,* to be complete, will require seclusion in private. The bride makes *invisible walls* by drawing a circle with her own body and then stepping inside. This is both public declaration of togetherness, and a separation from the rest of society at this most awesome and decisive moment. It is a physical expression of the marriage proposal, "sanctified unto me," in which "sanctity" implies "*separated* unto me." It is a statement of the new status of the couple.

The exclusivity of marriage signifies more than just conjugal fidelity: it signifies to all others that no one may step into that circle to invade their privacy or interfere in their lives; and it signifies to the couple that they may not arbitrarily expose their personal marital concerns to anyone outside the circle.

The bridal circuit is also a demonstration of the fundamental verse of marriage in Genesis: "Therefore shall a man leave his father and mother and cleave to his wife and they shall be one flesh" (2:24). Both bride and groom leave their parents after the procession and station themselves under the *chuppah* which, for the duration of the wedding, is owned solely by the groom for the couple's use. When the bride draws the circle, she stakes out a new series of relationships: her husband is at the center, and her parents, still the objects of respect and loyalty, are now at the periphery. As she steps inside, she signals the beginning of "and he shall cleave unto his wife, and they shall be one flesh." It is a new family circle within society.

Carried further, the circle yields yet another truth of marriage. The Rema required a public symbol of the *yichud* seclusion in order to complete the nuptials, and so he removed the walls of the chamber. This openness is an expression that marriage, though exclusive and inviolable, is not a closed system. The family is part of a community, the community part of the world. The love that makes marriage beautiful must make life beautiful, and its influence must slowly spread to the larger circles of society, to bring to the outside world a spirit of selflessness, sanity, and warmth.

Why three circuits are made is a matter of conjecture. The number three occurs several times in the subject of marriage. The Bible mentions betrothal (*ki yikach*) three times; a man may legally betroth a woman in one of three ways; and his obligations to his wife are subsumed under three general biblical requirements of food, clothing, and conjugal relations. Another reason may be the threefold repetition of betrothal in Hosea (2:21–22), representing the marriage of God, the groom, to Israel, the bride: "and I will *betroth* thee unto Me forever. Yea, I will *betroth* thee unto Me in righteousness, and in justice, and in loving kindness and in compassion; And I will *betroth* thee unto Me in faithfulness." These sentences are recited by men donning the tefillin (phylacteries worn at weekday prayers) every day as they wind the tefillin straps three times around the middle finger. As the celestial betrothal is symbolized by a threefold circling, so the earthly betrothal is represented by the bride's encircling of the groom three times.

STANCE

All participants at the *chuppah* should stand, except the infirm and the aged. Some even hold that *everyone* at the wedding should stand either because of the reference to sanctity, *ke'dushah* (as one stands during the *ke'dushah* prayers during a religious service), or in respect for the bride and groom. The bride customarily stands to the groom's right.

Bride and groom may face in any direction. Rokeach suggests they face east as the blessings refer to "the cities of Judea and the streets of Jerusalem," and the breaking of the glass to the destruction of the ancient Temple. Some authorities say they face north, while Maharil counsels that they should face south. Ba'er Heitev holds that they face the Ark when in a synagogue. While contemporary opinion tends toward facing east, whatever direction is most convenient is perfectly acceptable. In most Hasidic weddings, the couple faces the wedding guests. In most American weddings, it is accepted practice that they face only the rabbi and witnesses, in a demonstration of the personal conponent of this public celebration. The rabbi, cantor, and witnesses customarily face the bride and groom. Where the other members of the wedding party stand is their own decision.

WINE

One blessing over wine precedes the betrothal ceremony, another the nuptials ceremony. Because the two ceremonies retain their own integrity even though united, two cups of wine should be used for the two blessings over wine. The Tosafists add that since in ancient times the betrothal took place in the bride's home and the nuptials in the groom's (at different times), the two separate cups recall that history. The law also holds that one should not recite two prayers of *ke'dushah* over one cup, for *mitzvot* should not be bunched together; each deserves respect. While two wine glasses are definitely preferred, one may be used and then refilled.

The source for the drinking of wine is not explicitly stated in the Talmud, though some rabbis presume that it is implied. *She'iltot* is the basis of the final halakhic decision that it is *preferred* at the betrothal, but that only at the nuptial ceremony is it definitely *required*. *Only* kosher wine should be used and placed, sealed, under the *chuppah* alongside the two wine glasses. If kosher wine is not available, whiskey, beer, or the equivalent should be used.

Who should drink the wine was a subject of much debate. Some authorities held that the person who reads the blessing, the rabbi, should proceed to drink that for which he recited the blessing, and then serve it to groom and bride. Others held that only the couple need drink the wine; still others maintain that the rabbi drinks, but the bride and groom should not. Today it is customary that only the bride and groom drink the wine, as they are in fact performing the *mitzvah,* and the rabbi's blessing is recited on *their* behalf. While it is not necessary for the bride and groom themselves to recite the blessing, it is entirely proper that they recite the *amen* after the rabbi's blessing.

The wine need not be drunk entirely, only tasted. An interesting innovative suggestion is that when the couple sips the wine after the nuptials, when they are legally married, the groom should himself present the wine to his wife as the first demonstration of his obligation to support his wife. These are nuances of custom, however, and there are many possible variations.

Wine, in the Jewish tradition, is closely associated with the Sabbath and with festivals. At the onset of the Holy Day, wine ushers in the spirit of sanctity, *kiddush,* and at the end wine closes it, *havdalah.* This accomplishes a significant task: It marks the boundary lines and separates the holiness of the Holy Day from the secular character of the ordinary day. At the wedding, the wine symbolizes both *kiddush,* sanctity, and *havdalah,* separation, as the blessing itself indicates: "... who has *sanctified* us with His commandments and commanded us about [some say '*separated* us from'] illicit relations. ...." As wine is used at the threshold of the Sabbath to sanctify it and to separate it, so it is used at the threshold of marriage to separate it from the prohibited and to sanctify the bonds of proper marriage.

Wine is associated in Jewish tradition with *shirah,* song and festivity. As such it is appropriate to joyous occasions like the Sabbath and marriage. Both are not only to be observed, but need to be celebrated. Marriage is very similar to the Sabbath. Both are covenantal, reciprocal love relationships. Abraham Joshua Heschel describes a rabbinic allegory:

"[Rabbi] Shimeon ben Yohai said: After the work of creation was completed, the seventh day pleaded: 'Master of the Universe, all that Thou hast created is in couples; to every day of the week Thou gavest a mate; only I was left alone.' And God answered: 'The community of Israel will be your mate.'

"When the people of Israel stood before the mountain of Sinai, the Lord said unto them: 'Remember that I said to the Sabbath: The community of Israel is your mate. Hence: *Remember* the Sabbath day to sanctify it' (Ex. 20:8). The Hebrew *le'kadesh,* to sanctify, means, in the language of the Talmud, to consecrate a woman, to betroth. . . . With all its grandeur, the Sabbath is not sufficient unto itself. Its spiritual reality calls for companionship of man. . . ."

This companionship is demonstrated anew every week: the custom of Rabbi Yanai was to put on special robes on the eve of the Sabbath and then address the day: "Come O bride, come O bride."

The Sabbath is a bride and its celebration is like a wedding. The Midrash makes many comparisons: "Just as a groom is dressed in his finest garments, so is man on the Sabbath; as a man rejoices all the days of the wedding feast, so does man rejoice on the Sabbath; just as man does no work on his wedding day, so does a man abstain from work on the Sabbath day; and therefore the Sages and ancient saints called the Sabbath a bride."

As the Sabbath was like a wedding, so the wedding took on characteristics of the Sabbath. Wine signaled the sanctification. As the Sabbath sanctified the day, investing the commonplace with the mystery and grandeur of holiness, calling activities such as eating and sleeping *oneg* (delight), marriage is able to sanctify the mundane routines of life with the sense of the holy and to endow personal relationships with the character of covenant. The sanctity of marriage means embracing life and elevating it to the level of the sacred. As the Sabbath made a sanctuary of time, marriage must make a sanctuary of a human relationship.

The saintly Shelah drew more specific comparisons: There are seven blessings in both the Sabbath silent devotion and in the nuptials. The central prayers are those of *ke'dushah*—the Sabbath devotion's *ata kidashta,* and the wedding's *kiddushin.* There is recognition of the quality of joy, *simchah,* in both—on the Sabbath the prayer *yismach moshe,* and the *same'ach te'samach* blessing at the wedding. As the Sabbath has an "additional" service, *mussaf,* the wedding contract prominently contains an "additional" commitment of support, *tosefet ketubah.*

BETROTHAL BLESSINGS

After the initial blessing over the wine, the rabbi recites the betrothal blessing, *birkhat erusin.* The groom does not recite this blessing according to our custom, because he is *tarud,* undoubtedly nervous and not able to concentrate. Moreover, because some grooms may not be fluent in the language, expecting them to recite it might cause them embarrassment, especially at so sensitive a moment. As the blessing is geared to *ke'lal yisrael,* the sanctity of *all* Israel, and not only to these people, the rabbi is in any case the proper person to recite it.

Praised be Thou, O Lord our God, King of the universe who has sanctified us with His commandments and has commanded us concerning illicit relations; and has prohibited us those who are merely betrothed; but has permitted to us those lawfully married to us by *chuppah* and *kiddushin*. Blessed art thou God, who has sanctified His people Israel by *chuppah* and *kiddushin*.

בָּרוּךְ אַתָּה יי אֱלֹהֵינוּ מֶלֶךְ הָעוֹלָם אֲשֶׁר קִדְּשָׁנוּ
בְּמִצְוֹתָיו וְצִוָּנוּ עַל הָעֲרָיוֹת וְאָסַר לָנוּ אֶת הָאֲרוּסוֹת
וְהִתִּיר לָנוּ אֶת הַנְּשׂוּאוֹת לָנוּ עַל יְדֵי חֻפָּה וְקִדּוּשִׁין.
בָּרוּךְ אַתָּה יי מְקַדֵּשׁ עַמּוֹ יִשְׂרָאֵל עַל יְדֵי חֻפָּה
וְקִדּוּשִׁין.

Who Has Sanctified Us.   God has not merely *allowed* human beings an erotic indulgence by the legal validation of marriage. God has *sanctified* us by giving us the institution of marriage. Through it we achieve a closer relationship with Him and a more intimate relationship with other people. Thereby we enrich the family and perpetuate the species, for God created the world with the specific purpose that it be inhabited and civilized.

With His Commandments.   The Rabbis pondered whether this blessing could technically be classified as *birkhat mitzvah* (a blessing that precedes the performance of a *mitzvah*), as the blessing over the *shofar,* for example. The predominant opinion held that it could not be so classified, since the *mitzvah* is not completed until *after* the couple had conjugal relations. In any case, the *mitzvah* did not depend on him alone, and the bride had not yet formally consented. Nonetheless, the Sages could not bring themselves to exclude such a *mitzvah* from having a blessing. Thus they instituted a special blessing for the sanctification of the Jewish people for practicing marriage that was properly authorized by the law.

Illicit Relations.   At the moment of betrothal, not at the nuptials, the extension of the incest laws to include a mate's relatives begins. Hence the reference is first and foremost to illicit relations. The new status brings in its train new limitations. The bridge between sanctity and illicit relations is very natural, as the two themes follow one another in Leviticus 18 and 19. Says Rabbi Judah: "One who separates from illicit relations is called holy."

Has Prohibited Us Those Merely Betrothed.   The sanctification of betrothal is not enough. We are prohibited conjugal relations even after betrothal, if the nuptials have not yet been held.

The blessing is unusual because of this phrase. There is no other blessing extant over that which is not permitted. Why then a negative blessing at this occasion? One answer, given by the author of *Ha-manhig,* serves to highlight and enhance the phrase, "but has *permitted* those lawfully married. . . ." It is also a way of emphasizing, in the very benediction over the sanctity of marriage, that the process of the marriage ceremony has yet to be concluded.

But Has Permitted Those Lawfully Married.   This aspect of *nissuin* is needed to conclude the marriage process. *Sedei Chemed* notes: We should not refer to the bride as one *permitted,* but as one with whom we are *commanded* to cohabit, since "be fruitful and multiply" is a commandment, not merely permission. But stylistically, since the language of the blessing refers to one *prohibited,* the opposite is one *permitted.*

Married To "Us."   The pronoun "us" was added by Rabbenu Tam in the twelfth century. The Talmud mentions only *ne'ssuot* (married), with the clear understanding that "married to *us*" is what is implied. But since in later generations *ne'ssuot* referred to *all* married women, the addition of "to us" specified without doubt that it means "we are permitted *our* wives" and not "we are permitted *all* married women"! It also serves to underscore the exclusivity of the marriage presently being performed, just as the word *li,* "betrothed unto *me,*" is the highlight of the marriage proposal.

By Chuppah and Kiddushin, Nuptials and Betrothal.   This phrase is problematic. It is in reverse chronological order—it should have read "*kiddushin* (betrothal) and *chuppah* (nuptials)." This traditional phrase led some to conclude that the Hebrew should be read *chuppah in kiddushin,* not *chuppah and kiddushin*—the nuptials as part of a whole process of sanctification. Our custom retains "and," not "in." It is likely that before the two ceremonies were combined, the Rabbis had to emphasize to the couple that though they are betrothed, they may not live as husband and wife until after *chuppah.* Precisely at the height of the ceremony of betrothal and in its special blessing, the second ceremony is emphasized and repeated after only six words.

The groom and bride now taste the wine. A modern custom that enables the mothers of the couple to participate is to ask each to lift the bride's veil when she drinks the wine after the betrothal blessing and after the nuptials. After the betrothals the veil is raised and then lowered; after the nuptials, it is raised and need not be lowered again—the bride is fully a wife.

THE MARRIAGE PROPOSAL

Before the groom places the ring on his bride's index finger, he recites the following marriage proposal in both Hebrew and English because it *must* be understood by bride and groom.

Harei at me'kudeshet li be'tabaat zo ke'dat mosheh ve'yisrael.
Behold, thou art betrothed unto me, with this ring,
in accordance with the Law of Moses and Israel.

Betrothed (Me'kudeshet).   Not only does *me'kudeshet* have the technical connotation of set aside, selected, but also the sense that the bride is dedicated to the groom, and the relationship is sanctioned and thereby sanctified.

To Me (Li).   This small word *li* defines the marriage proposal and makes the bride exclusive. The word is avoided by some rabbis, who recite the formula *soto voce* to the groom who repeats the Hebrew phrase verbatim, in order to assure to whom the *"me"* refers. I suspect the bride and groom have no doubt about whom they are marrying, and *li* cannot in one's wildest imagination refer to the rabbi who recites it.

The Law of Moses and Israel.   The phrase refers to the Torah and to the Oral interpretation of the Sages. It is not recorded in the Talmud and it is not found in Maimonides' code. There is no doubt, however, that it was used then as we use it today. The *ketubah* contains the phrase, but the written document serves only to attest to the oral statement. The phrase implies a very important foundation of Jewish marriage law: "Everyone who marries, marries in accordance with the rabbinic understanding of the law." The marriage is validated on the condition that it meet with the approval of the Sages who represent the law of Moses and Israel.

This proposal formula has long been the magic phrase of Jewish young people and their parents, and has attracted all sorts of interpretations. One is noteworthy for its unusual insight: The phrase has thirty-two letters, which represent the kabbalistically-conceived thirty-two ways that wisdom proceeds from God to man; and thirty-two is represented by *lev,* which means "heart."

THE MARRIAGE RING

While the marriage ring appears to have an ancient tradition, there is no specific reference to it in the Talmud. Saadiah Gaon cites as a possible origin the phrase in Nehemiah 7:46 *be'nei tabbaot* (children of the rings). He considered them to be children of those who cohabited while only betrothed (with the ring) but not yet married. Contemporary scholars believe that *tabbaot* was simply a family name. Maharshal cites references to indicate that the ring is a Palestinian custom that only later was accepted in Babylonia practice; one scholar posits that it was introduced into Palestine in the seventh century and into Babylonia in the ninth century. The author of *ha-Ittur* records a strange custom that may have been a transitional practice that ultimately led to the use of the ring: The groom performed the betrothal over a cup of wine with a ring *inside* the cup, saying, "You are hereby betrothed unto me with this cup and all that which is inside it." (This practice does not appear in the major medieval codes of Rif or Maimonides.)

The law, unlike history, is clear and unequivocal. The ring is a money equivalent, *shaveh kessef,* which is one of the original three legal acts of acquisition and the one that is exclusively practiced today. Rema writes, "It is the correct custom to betroth with a ring." The *Halakhah* established the following practices regarding this central object of the wedding ceremony:

1. The ring should be of plain metal, preferably gold, and with no precious stones. The reason for this is the avoidance of possible misrepresentation on the part of the groom—for example, using costume jewelry that the bride believes is genuine. This might invalidate the marriage because she accepted the proposal on false premises, and might not have willingly consented to marry under those conditions. The bride has to be aware only that the ring is worth a minimum of a *pe'rutah,* a low-valued coin.

2. The ring must belong to the groom. He may borrow it from someone on condition that he return it after the wedding, and if the bride knows about it, the marriage is valid. It is not good practice, however, to borrow his bride's engagement ring for the wedding!

3. The bride should not put the ring over a glove. To do so does not invalidate the marriage, but it is preferred that there be no obstruction between her finger and the ring.

4. The ring should be placed by the groom on the bride's index finger, not her "ring finger." Abudarham says the pointing finger is used so that she will more easily be able to show the witnesses that she received the ring. Maharam Mintz says that the index was once the ring finger; even though this is no longer so, we retain that custom. In any case, because it is the most active finger, it may serve as a symbol that the ring is not accepted as just another gift but as an act sealing the most important transaction in life.

5. The groom must first propose by reciting the marriage formula, and only after that may he place the ring on her finger. It is her silent consent after the proposal that clinches the matter. Silence after receiving the ring does not indicate her assent to marry.

6. The witnesses must be specifically assigned as witnesses, to the exclusion of everyone else. They must be assured that the ring has the minimal requisite value, and they must clearly see the action of the groom, hear what he says, and be satisifed that the bride accepts it with willing consent. There is a wise custom that at this moment the bride momentarily lifts her veil so that she may see the ring clearly and so that the witnesses may know with certainty that it is she who is the bride and that she accepts the groom's proposal. Some customs, notably Hasidic, insist that the veil remain lowered throughout the service until after the nuptials.

In summary, the procedure is as follows:

(1) The groom, or best man, gives the rabbi the ring;

(2) the groom specifies the witnesses;

(3) the rabbi shows the ring to the witnesses to ascertain minimal value;

(4) the rabbi asks the groom if the ring belongs to him and if it is of this minimal value;

(5) the bride lifts her veil, if it covers her eyes;

(6) the groom takes the ring and recites the proposal;

(7) he then places the ring on her index finger in the presence of the witnesses (she may place it on her ring finger after the ceremony); and

(8) the bride replaces the veil.

The mystical reason for the ring's use in the wedding ceremony is difficult to comprehend. Rema says, "It is the correct custom to betroth with a ring, and the reason is given in *Tikkunei ha-Zohar*, [the major work of Jewish mysticism]." *Arukh ha-Shulchan* refers the reader to *chokhmat ha-nistar* the "hidden wisdom" of the Kabbalah. The mystical reason quoted is: "From the secret of marriage there dawns on the woman the secret of *enveloping* light."

We offer one insightful comment of contemporary writer Kohren Arisian on the nature of the wedding ring. The circle was considered to be the most perfect of all forms in nature. The Greeks attributed such mystical qualities of perfection to the circle that when they discovered that this perfect form in its dimensional relationship produced an irrational number, they concealed this fact. Yet the Greeks knew that perfection implied imperfection; the rational, the irrational. Just so, the perfect marriage symbolized by the circle of the ring must always contain the imperfection of the parties to that marriage, since the parties to it are only human.

THE READING AND DELIVERY OF THE *KETUBAH*

The reading of the entire Aramaic marriage contract is an honored tradition. Maimonides said, "The custom of our fathers is law, and custom was to read the *ketubah* aloud."

The origin of the reading is probably the twelfth-century scholar, Rabbenu Tam. He indicates that it serves as a separation between the two distinct ceremonies of betrothal and nuptials. Because it is placed as a divider, the blessing over the wine can once again be recited at the start of the nuptial service.

The *ketubah* is written in the language of the Talmud. The Rabbis were careful even about the sounds of the phrases as well as their legal import. It is not respectful to play background music to the reading, which would detract from its special significance. The reading is difficult and unfamiliar to most people, and probably only rabbis and scholars will be able to read it creditably.

After it is read, the document is given to the groom for him to hand to his bride and for her to hold in her safekeeping for all the days of their marriage.

It is probably wise for the bride to pass it to her parents or maid of honor so that it should not be lost. As already indicated, Jewish law is clear that husband and wife may not cohabit without knowing the whereabouts of their *ketubah.* If the rabbi sees that the couple will not be able to care for the *ketubah* in the midst of the hectic celebration, he should hold it until a more sober time when he will give it to the wife. If the *ketubah* cannot be located, the rabbi must draw up a replacement contract.

There can be no nuptial service unless the *ketubah* is given the bride. Since the Rabbis forbade conjugal relations without it, the lack of the *ketubah* makes the ceremony *kiddushin she'einah re'uyah le'biah*—a marriage that cannot be consummated.

THE SEVEN BENEDICTIONS (*SHEVA BERAKHOT*)

The seven benedictions under the *chuppah* are recited by the rabbi or others who are given the honor. They should be read only in the presence of a *minyan,* which may include the rabbi, the groom, witnesses, and parents. The benedictions are not to be recited by the groom, although the tradition refers to them as *birkhot chattanim,* groom's blessing. Maimonides expressed shock that a groom should recite the blessings since the benedictions are designed to bless, congratulate, and pray for him and his bride. If no one else can recite them but the groom, he may do so.

The benedictions cover many themes—the creation of the world and of humanity, the survival of the Jewish people and of Israel, the marriage, the couple's happiness and the raising of the family. It puts the state of marriage into a dynamic relationship with the beginning and end of history—the Garden of Eden and the expectation of the Messiah. The first three blessings have nothing directly to say about the marriage itself, but they form the foundation of the nuptial benedictions that follow. The last blessing is the climax of rejoicing, with the chanting of ten synonyms of joy that reach a crescendo in the praising of God who rejoices the groom with the bride. The seven blessings are as follows:

1. "Blessed art Thou, O Lord our God, King of the universe who hast created the fruit of the vine."

בָּרוּךְ אַתָּה יי אֱלֹהֵינוּ מֶלֶךְ הָעוֹלָם בּוֹרֵא פְּרִי הַגָּפֶן

Under the *chuppah,* the blessing over wine is the first blessing read, although it appears to be more appropriate as the last, immediately prior to the drinking of the wine. It is read last only when the *Sheva Berakhot* are recited at the end of the meal on the seven festive days. Custom has it that when several people are honored with reading the blessings under the *chuppah,* the person who recites the wine blessing should recite it in conjunction with the one following it.

2. "Blessed art Thou, O Lord our God, King of the universe, who has created all things for His glory."

בָּרוּךְ אַתָּה יי אלהינו מלךְ העולם שֶׁהַכֹּל בָּרָא
לִכְבוֹדוֹ.

This is the only occasion at which this blessing is recited. It is a simple but eloquent tribute to God in the midst of a large assemblage and is equivalent, one might almost say, to *kiddush ha-shem,* the public santification of God's name. The question is why it was confined only to the nuptial service. Rashi answers that at this most important moment in life, it was considered appropriate to pay gratitude for divine kindness in enabling us to survive. Abudarham notes that the betrothal could have served as the setting for this blessing as well, but that the nuptials were considered the very peak of joy and the legal definition for the joy.

The Midrash records that God appointed angelic escorts for Adam and brought ornaments for Eve at their wedding, and that He arranged seven *chuppot* set up in Paradise, on which the Rabbis patterned the seven benedictions. The wedding, then, is the time to be grateful for His greatness. Rema remarks that the wedding, which is designed to increase God's creations and is a living demonstration of Isaiah's phrase that God did not create the world for it to be abandoned to chaos, is a testimonial to God's creativity. When is it more appropriate to sing of the glory of God than at the symbolic accomplishment of God's work? This moment also represents the miracle of the fusion of disparate natures, which the Sages considered as difficult a job as the splitting of the Red Sea. It is the basis on which all society exists.

It is also a reminder to the couple that there is no more profound suggestion than that life goals should not be selfish, but should be designed for the betterment of the world and the glory of God.

3. "Blessed art Thou, O Lord our God, King of the universe, creator of man."

בָּרוּךְ אַתָּה יי אלהינו מלךְ העולם יוֹצֵר הָאָדָם.

4. "Blessed art Thou, O Lord our God, King of the universe who hast made man in His image, after his likeness, and hast prepared for him, out of his very self, a perpetual fabric. Blessed art Thou, O Lord, creator of man."

בָּרוּךְ אַתָּה יי אלהינו מלךְ העולם אֲשֶׁר יָצַר
אֶת הָאָדָם בְּצַלְמוֹ בְּצֶלֶם דְּמוּת תַּבְנִיתוֹ וְהִתְקִין לוֹ
מִמֶּנּוּ בִּנְיַן עֲדֵי עַד. בָּרוּךְ אַתָּה יי יוֹצֵר הָאָדָם

Image and Likeness (Tzellem—Tavnit). "Image" (*tzellem*) is a term that can be used only for God, who has no corporeality. "Likeness" (*tavnit*), from *banoh* (which means "to build" and relates to a gathering of components into one whole), refers to a person. It therefore may not be used to describe God, only man. The Rabbis, in formulating the blessing, therefore referred to "His [God's] image," and in "his [Adam's] likeness." Our highest obligation is to develop the image of God in which we were cast. The human being occupies the physical form *tavnit,* that God specifically intended for Adam, in order to house the spirit which is cast in the image of God. At the moment of marriage, the message is unmistakable—not only man's soul, but his body, too, is of divine origin. Do not live like an animal; strive to live so as to enhance the image of God.

A Perpetual Fabric (Binyan Adei Ad). God created man and woman, and in their fusion He created a perpetual fabric. It is a structure (*binyan*) in which two people together can reach into the future, to create *banim* (children).

Creator of Man. Rashi tells us why we need two blessings of God the "Creator of man." The first of the two, he says, is for the first account of creation in Genesis, before woman was created, which apparently has no direct relevance to the marriage ceremony. It was included merely as an antecedent for the sake of the second blessing, which is for the creation of man *and* woman.

Celebrating the creation of man and woman equally conveys the sense of the dual destiny of the human being. Despite the difference in sex, both are created in the image of God and both are included in the covenant. Both together are accorded the title of "man"; Adam alone is not. Judaism, despite sometimes intemperate statements of scholarly individuals, does not consider woman an inferior sex.

Rabbi Joseph B. Soloveitchik analyzes the two blessings in great depth. The two blessings are of different formal structure. The first is a short form, as in the blessing over food. The second is a long form and contains a formal opening, "Blessed art Thou . . .", and a formal conclusion, "Blessed art Thou, O Lord, Creator of man." These structures represent two forms of creation—the "natural" man and the "transcendental" man.

The natural man, described in the first account of creation (Genesis 1:27–28), belongs to a biological category. On the day he was created, most animals were created, and he is subject to the laws of animate nature. "Transcendental" man, described in the second account of creation (Genesis 7:20–24), belongs to a higher religio-ethical-social category. Natural man is given the mission to be fruitful and multiply and conquer the earth—to civilize the world. Transcendental man is a spiritually-attuned being—he is given moral commands by God. The term "*ad-nai,*" God, is introduced here and, as Judah ha-Levi notes, that speaks of a mature relationship between God and man. Natural man is nonreflective;

transcendental man is self-conscious. One is physical, the other metaphysical.

The natural man of the first account of creation is outer-directed, at home with the society and with nature, never experiencing loneliness. Transcendental man is inner-directed, dreadfully alone, desperately needing a human partner. Woman in the first account of creation is *part* of man—a biological unity. Only in the second creation is she created *ezer ke'negdo,* a helpmeet opposite him, a spiritual human being. Together they form an ontological unity.

The first blessing is the short form. The laws of nature are unchanging, there is no individuality. Each being, man or animal, is only a representative of the whole species, nothing more. In this natural philosophy, marriage has no meaning but the perpetuation of the species. The short blessing is like a blessing over vegetables, "Blessed art Thou, o Lord, King of the universe, who created the fruit of the earth." So, here, for natural man, "Blessed art Thou O Lord, King of the universe, Creator of man."

The second blessing, which represents transcendant man, is the long form, as in the blessing at the Torah. It speaks of God's likeness, *de'mut tavnito*—a new image, a spectacular and exciting panorama, *tzellem elokim,* the image of God and the fusion of personalities that reaches into the future to create *binyan adei ad,* a perpetual fabric. Living on this level requires Torah teaching for the development of the religious and ethical dimensions of life.

> 5. "May she who was barren be exceedingly glad and rejoice when her children are united in her midst in joy. Blessed art Thou, O Lord, who makes Zion joyful through her children."

שׂוֹשׂ תָּשִׂישׂ וְתָגֵל הָעֲקָרָה בְּקִבּוּץ בָּנֶיהָ לְתוֹכָהּ
בְּשִׂמְחָה. בָּרוּךְ אַתָּה יי מְשַׂמֵּחַ צִיּוֹן בְּבָנֶיהָ

Her Children. The previous blessing refers to a "perpetual fabric," while this one addresses itself to the barren woman bearing children and of their subsequent uniting in joy.

Barren (Akarah). Rashi says that *akarah,* as in Isaiah (54:1), refers to Jerusalem, the symbol of Zion and, in a larger sense, to the entire Jewish people. In this sense, the blessing speaks of Jewish survival—the people, the Torah, the Hold Land. She may be taken for barren, but in fact her seed will grow and will return to her boundaries to repel foreign invaders and alien ideologies. Mother Zion, pictured as grieving for the loss of her children, is rewarded by God and rejoices as she sees her children return.

At every Jewish wedding, there is a special guest: Mother Zion, glorifying in her children as they gather in joy. Judaism is refreshed and renewed. *Am Yisrael chai*—the Jewish people lives.

6. "O make these beloved companions greatly rejoice even as Thou didst rejoice Thy creation in the Garden of Eden as of old. Blessed art Thou, O Lord, who makest bridegroom and bride to rejoice."

שַׂמֵּחַ תְּשַׂמַּח רֵעִים הָאֲהוּבִים כְּשַׂמֵּחֲךָ יְצִירְךָ בְּגַן
עֵדֶן מִקֶּדֶם.בָּרוּךְ אַתָּה יי מְשַׂמֵּחַ חָתָן וְכַלָּה.

Beloved Companions. Being in love is not enough to ensure successful marriage—this requires companionship. In the history of religious literature, it is only since the Protestant Reformation that friendship between husband and wife became a basis for marriage. Khoren Arisian notes, "This was actually a harking back to Judaic precedent (compare the Song of Songs 5:16: 'This is my beloved, and this is my friend') as well as to a medieval ideal. Inherent in the reformer's stress on friendship in marriage was the belief that love in the form of friendship between husband and wife should actuate a marriage. This emphasis became a new dimension in marriage which has continued into our own day."

Bridegroom and Bride. Commentaries pondered the meaning of the subtle difference in the concluding phrases of the last two blessings: "Bridegroom *and* bride" and "bridegroom *with* bride." It is obvious that the change was purposeful.

Rashi, the master commentator, says that the penultimate blessing, while recited at the wedding, was actually a prayer for the success, sustenance, and well being of the two as fiancès *before* the wedding. Hence the use of "and." They are two separate individuals who will only later come together. The last blessing refers to them at the *conclusion* of the wedding when they are already married. Hence "bridegroom *with* bride"—together in joy.

7. "Blessed art Thou, O Lord, King of the universe, who has created joy and gladness, bridegroom and bride, mirth and exultation, pleasure and delight, love, brotherhood, peace and fellowship. Soon may there be heard in the cities of Judah and in the streets of Jerusalem, the voice of joy and gladness, the voice of the bridegroom and the voice of the bride, the jubilant voice of bridegrooms from their canopies, and of youths from their feasts of song. Blessed art Thou, o Lord, who makest the bridegroom to rejoice with the bride."

בָּרוּךְ אַתָּה יי אֱלֹהֵינוּ מֶלֶךְ הָעוֹלָם אֲשֶׁר בָּרָא
שָׂשׂוֹן וְשִׂמְחָה חָתָן וְכַלָּה גִּילָה רִנָּה דִּיצָה וְחֶדְוָה
אַהֲבָה וְאַחְוָה שָׁלוֹם וְרֵעוּת מְהֵרָה יי אֱלֹהֵינוּ יִשָּׁמַע
בְּעָרֵי יְהוּדָה וּבְחֻצוֹת יְרוּשָׁלַיִם קוֹל שָׂשׂוֹן וְקוֹל
שִׂמְחָה קוֹל חָתָן וְקוֹל כַּלָּה קוֹל מִצְהֲלוֹת חֲתָנִים
מֵחֻפָּתָם וּנְעָרִים מִמִּשְׁתֵּה נְגִינָתָם.בָּרוּךְ אַתָּה יי
מְשַׂמֵּחַ חָתָן עִם הַכַּלָּה.

This last blessing is the only one of the seven that is cast in the form of a petition: "Soon may there be heard . . ." It is also the only one which may be recited at the table after the meal and during the "seven days of feasting" following the wedding, without the presence of a *minyan,* but with a minimum of three men. It is a summary of the themes of the previous blessings: creation, joy, bride and groom, Mother Zion.

In this blessing we reach the crescendo of joy, reciting no fewer than ten synonyms for happiness—"joy," "gladness," "mirth," "exultation," "pleasure," "delight," "love," "brotherhood," and "peace," and ending with "friendship" —for the bridegroom *with* the bride.

Following the seventh blessing, the bride and groom sip the wine. The rabbi's address, if there is to be one, is delivered either now, before the ceremony begins, or after the reading of the *ketubah.*

THE BREAKING OF THE GLASS

The end of the public wedding ceremony is marked by the breaking of a glass, usually a thin glass wrapped in a napkin to contain the fragments. It is smashed under foot by the groom after the seven benedictions, or after the rabbi's address if it follows the benedictions. Some customs placed it after the betrothals, but our western tradition is to perform it at the very end.

Ancient custom designated that one of the wine cups be broken, although there was a difference of opinion as to which of the two wine cups. Maharil held that it was the nuptials cups, because the breaking immediately followed the nuptial blessings. Rema and most others held that it was the betrothal cup, and for good reason: Breaking the nuptials cup, over which the seven benedictions were recited, is a gross symbol when great concern at this moment is for *making* the marriage, not *breaking* it. However, once the nuptials are recited the betrothal has been accomplished, and the breaking of that cup signifies that the nuptials have been satisfactorily completed. The author of *Match Moshe* held that it may be any glass at all. Originally, the blessing was recited over a glass cup which was then smashed. But when silver cups began to be used, any other glass was used for breaking. One commentator held that smashing *either* of the wine glasses was not an auspicious sign and that another glass should be used.

The general custom that prevails today at traditional weddings is the use of a prepared glass or bulb. However, this robs the ceremony of its historic beauty and significance. Therefore, it is preferable to use a glass goblet for the betrothals and a silver *kiddush* cup for the nuptials. Immediately after the seven benedictions, the rabbi can pour the remaining wine from the glass into a prepared bowl, wrap it in a cloth napkin and have the groom place it on the floor and crush it.

Some rabbis were bothered by the problem of *bal tashchit,* the formidable principle of not wasting material needlessly, and also of *bizayon kos shel berakhah,* the "shaming" of the "cup of blessing" by smashing it. But the response was that it is neither waste or shame because the very breaking conveys important moral ideals. What are these ideals?

First, we should note that much has been written on the mythology and also the psychology of the ceremony. Some of the scholarship is erudite, some is trivial popularizing, and little of it is of immediate relevance to the theme of this book. Many scholars find the roots of every Jewish observance or idea in an alien theology or primitive rite. We are concerned here with the symbol as it lives today, and the significance we can derive from its practice.

The source for the custom is related in the Talmud. Mar, son of Ravina, made a wedding feast for his son, and when he noticed that some of the rabbis became boisterous in their joy, he brought a precious cup worth four hundred *zuz,* and smashed it before them. This quieted them down immediately. Rabbi Ashi also made a wedding feast for his son, and when he noticed that the rabbis were boisterous, he brought a cup of white glass and smashed it before them and immediately they sobered. Rashi said the breaking was of a white wine cup and that only that kind of glass could be used for the ceremonial breaking; the Tosafists derived from this the prevalent custom of breaking any glass utensil at every wedding service.

What is the reason? From the Talmud it would appear that breaking the glass served to engender sobriety and balanced behavior. Psalms 2:11 says, "Serve the Lord with fear, and rejoice with trembling". Rabbi Ada ben Matanah, interpreted in Rabbah's name: *Bime'kom gilah, sham te'hei re'adah,* "Where there is rejoicing, there should be trembling." A wedding should not be sheer undisciplined merriment, and the breaking of expensive glass stunned the guests into tempering their gaiety. The ceremony serves, then, to moralize pleasure and attain tempered emotions.

In the fourteenth century, the author of *Kol Bo* offered another explanation. The broken glass represents the wreckage of our past glory, and the destruction of the ancient Temple in Jerusalem in the first century. It recalls, at the most joyous and momentous occasion of the life cycle, that there is a continuing national sadness. It is a memory of Zion that stands as a reminder that in life great joy can be cancelled by sudden grief. It enriches the quality of joy by making it more thoughtful and by inspiring gratitude for the goodness of God.

It is customary to recite the following words when breaking the glass: "If I forget Thee, O Jerusalem, may my right hand fail . . . at the height of my joy." Sephardic Jews, and also many of Ashkenazic descent, recite this phrase at the performance of an analagous custom during the wedding, the placing of a bit of ash on the groom's forehead. This sign of mourning is placed at the site of the tefillin—the ash of bereavement (*efer*), in place of the glory which signifies tefillin (*pe'er*).

Perhaps a deeper significance can be realized if, as the groom's action recalls the demolished house of God, the now-married couple takes it as an obligation upon themselves to rebuild the Temple in their own lives by building their own Jewish home, as every synagogue is a *mikdash me'at,* a miniature temple. The Sages say that all that is left of the Temple today are *dalet amot shel Halakhah,* (the four ells of Torah law). If the home we build will house the spirit and practice of these four ells, we will have contributed to the rebuilding of the Temple in our own way and in our own homes.

How unfortunate it is, therefore, that the phrase of Jerusalem's destruction is rarely recited and, instead, a chorus of *mazal tov's* greets the breaking of the glass. If the reason for the glass breaking is to temper joy, this is surely inappropriate; if the reason is to recall a national tragedy, it is vulgar. Often not only is a joyous *mazal tov* sounded, but a licentious sneer that it is a "good sign" if the glass is smashed at the first try. This elicits gross comments regarding the groom's prowess. The late Sephardic Chief Rabbi of Israel, Ben Zion Ouziel, wished that he could have abolished the custom for this very reason. In fairness, however, it should be noted that the *mazal tov* is not so much in response to the breaking of the glass, as it is to the end of the ceremony. In any case, it would be less than resonsible to eliminate a millenial tradition because of some people's untutored reaction to it. Perhaps we should reinstitute the reference to Jerusalem and move the glass breaking back to the middle of the wedding ceremony.

The two fundamental reasons lead us to another insight derived from this ceremony—the magnificent, sensitive balance within Judaism that testifies to its rich maturity and to its suitability to the whole range of human emotions. It connects the private moment under the *chuppah* with the public national event of the Temple, the ancient past with thoughts of a long future, heady joy with a tragedy bewailed for nineteen hundred years. The *breaking* of a glass at the symbolic moment that celebrates *making* a new home, is also reminiscent of the Talmud's assertion that "*joining* two people in marriage is as difficult as *splitting* the sea."

Through the ages, other homilies were derived from the ceremony. *Tzafenat Pa'neah* suggests the hope that the breach in the relation between God and Israel caused by the Temple's destruction will be repaired just as a broken glass can be repaired by melting under the glazier's fire. God's marriage with the Jewish people will be unbroken, as will the marriage of these children of God to one another.

Rabbi Bachya traces this custom, as so many other marriage customs, to the revelation on Sinai. What joy is greater than the wedding, in the private lives of this bride and groom? What joy is greater in the religious lives of the people

Israel than the *simchat Torah,* the exquisite moment at Sinai? At Sinai, there was the tragic breaking of the tablets of the commandments at the foot of the mountain; at the wedding *simchah* there is a symbolic breaking of the glass under foot. Every new family helps repair the breach at Sinai—the breaking, in joy, at every wedding overcomes the breaking of the tablets.

Contemporary preachers have suggested new meanings for this closing ceremony. The fasting in repentance before the wedding and the purification from the stains of the past in the *mikveh* is symbolized in the crushing of the glass, which represents a final, dramatic breaking with the past. A full life is the cup from which we drink. It is a "cup of blessing," one which we use to celebrate Sabbaths and festivals. A life that is filled to the brim with meaning is the life for which we strive.

PRIVACY (*YICHUD*)

The symbolic consummation of the wedding takes place in a private room after the ceremony. This is not custom, but a firm requirement of the law that must be testified to by witnesses. It is the final act of *chuppah* that seals the marriage. When the couple emerges from *yichud,* they are man and wife.

The *yichud* should be arranged for in advance. The private room should contain food, as the couple has been fasting. Eating together in private is one of the functions of this privacy. As noted previously, since the *process* of the bride's moving to her husband's home is itself a sign of marriage, Taz suggests that the bride and groom hold hands and proceed directly from the *chuppah* to the *yichud,* where they remain privately for approximately ten minutes.

The seclusion of the couple in the *yichud* room should be witnessed by two qualified witnesses waiting outside, specifically appointed for this task, much as the witnesses to the *ketubah* and the ring ceremony were appointed.

There are many demands on the couple's time at this juncture. Photographers want to take their pictures, a receiving line becomes impatient, an old aunt insists on showering them with kisses, and everyone wants to comment on the service. But this is their time. Bride and groom deserve this respite of privacy and togetherness at this unforgettable moment; it is wrong to deny it to them.

CHAPTER 16

After the Wedding Ceremony

THE FIRST MEAL

The first meal shared by the husband and wife with their guests has religious significance. It is considered by the law to be a *se'udat mitzvah,* a festive meal in fulfillment of a commandment, and serves an important psychological purpose: *le'same-ach chatan ve'kallah,* to "rejoice the groom and bride." The roots of this first meal reach far back into Jewish history, when Jacob's father-in-law, Laban, invited all of the local people to a party immediately after the wedding (Genesis 29:22).

The wedding is the peak of joy. The Rabbis of the Talmud said, *Ein simchah be'li chuppah* (there is no real joy outside of the marriage ceremony) and every *mitzvah* repast is traced to this prototype. Joy in the Jewish tradition is never self-contained; it reaches outward. For many centuries, it was customary to invite the poor to the wedding, in order to bring happiness into their often drab lives. While nowadays this is largely impractical, it does teach us to give charity as a sign of gratitude to God who gave us joy.

The purpose of the meal is to instill joy into the hearts of bride and groom. Superficially, it might appear that since this event in life is the very epitome of joy, there should be no need to make them rejoice. But beneath the laughter, the music, and the exchange of *mazal tovs,* there is often a tense concern for the future. The responsibilities and adjustments of living together and raising a family are not always anticipated during the dating game, and after the wedding the partners may wonder if they have made the right choice.

Hence when guests rejoice the bride and groom, they distract them and at least temporarily lift their burden and free their minds to concentrate on one another. To this end, the greatest and most staid of scholars would customarily dance with the bride, each holding one end of a napkin or handkerchief, in what is called a *mitzvah tentzel* (a *mitzvah* dance). One of the auxiliary purposes of this dance is to give the groom more confidence in his choice, and the bride in hers. Musical instruments, which were usually discouraged by the Rabbis in memory of the Temple's destruction, were not only permitted at a wedding but were considered an integral component of "rejoicing" the couple. Ran holds that not only at the *chuppah* are we instructed to rejoice them, but wherever they go they should find the community participating in their joy.

THE GRACE AFTER THE MEAL

A festive spirit is assured when joy is demonstrated through the observance of relevant religious symbols. For a married couple the repetition of the seven nuptial blessings after the *birkhat ha-mazon* (grace) every day of the first week is a reminder of their beautiful moment under the *chuppah*. Additional prayers are inserted as introductions to the grace.

The Introductory Prayers for the Grace

Two prayers are recited—one sad, one joyful—as part of the prefatory invocation at the first meal and thereafter during the first week.

The first element is a commemoration of the destruction of the temple.

דְוַי הָסֵר וְגַם חָרוֹן וְאָז אִלֵּם בְּשִׁיר יָרוֹן נְחֵנוּ
בְּמַעְגְּלֵי צֶדֶק שְׁעֵה בִּרְכַּת בְּנֵי יְשֻׁרוּן.

"Banish, O Lord, both brief and anguish, then shall even the mute exult in song. Guide us in the paths of righteousness. Accept the blessing of the children of Jeshurun (Israel)."

This four-line poem, prefixed to the grace proper, is attributed to a tenth century poet and grammarian, Dunash ben Labrat. The words "grief" and "anguish" (*devai* and *charon*) are key words of lamentations at the destruction of the two Temples. Chapter One of the biblical book of Lamentations includes *ve'libi davai*, "my heart is faint." "Remove the lamentations," prays the poet. Chapter Four speaks of the pouring out of God's wrath. "Keep it from us," our poet pleads, so that even the mute will rise in prayer.

This poem is recited while holding the wine goblet for the saying of grace, and only in the presence of a *minyan*. (If there are not ten, but there are three or more, the introductory prayer of grace used at a circumcision, *nodeh le'- shimkha*, which was also designed for this purpose, is read in its stead.) This prayer is recited even on the Sabbath, when petitionary prayers are avoided.

The second element is a two-word insertion into the introductory statement *she-ha-simkhah bi-me'ono*, "in whose dwelling there is joy."

בִּרְשׁוּת (כֹּהֵן) מָרָנָן וְרַבּוֹתַי נְבָרֵךְ אֱלֹהֵינוּ
שֶׁהַשִּׂמְחָה בִּמְעוֹנוֹ וְשֶׁאָכַלְנוּ מִשֶּׁלּוֹ

"Praised be our God, *in Whose dwelling there is joy,* and of Whose bounty we have partaken.

So high is the level of wedded joy that human beings can experience that God Himself is said to rejoice with the couple in His own abode. The two-word inclusion is suggested in the Talmud and receives more commentary and halakhic treatment than the rest of the introductory poem (which is post-talmudic).

Ma-on, (dwelling) is considered by the mystic Ibn Yarhi to be the fifth of the seven levels of Heaven, where the angelic hosts pour forth their lyric ecstasies.

Simchah, joy. Can we then speak of "God's joy"? One commentary cites a tradition that angels in the "dwelling" brought food for Adam and Eve's wedding. Another mystical interpretation is that these exalted words are recited only at a wedding because it is a new relationship that will produce children who will survive their parents' death. Parents are thus assured, as at no other time, that the children will survive them. Thus in His "dwelling" there will be complete joy, but in this world there can never be pure, consummate joy.

The words are recited wherever bride and groom have their meals during this one week, just as the seven blessings are recited at the end of the grace.

The Ceremony of the Wine Glasses

The bride and groom are king and queen, and wine is poured, mixed, and sipped in their honor. Tradition has made this legal requirement a whole joyous ceremony. Two glasses of wine are twice that normally used for *kiddush* to introduce the Sabbath. One glass is required for the grace, the other for the seven nuptial blessings. Rema requires two separate glasses, as under the *chuppah,* because one should not celebrate two sanctities with one cup.

After one cup has been filled, the grace, with its prefatory prayers, is recited. The full cup is held by the leader during the grace, then placed on the table.

Another cup is filled and someone (either the same leader or another person) is chosen to lead in the recitation of the *Sheva Berakhot,* the seven benedictions. He begins with the second blessing, leaving the first—over the wine—for last. The honor of reciting the individual blessings may be distributed to guests. After the sixth blessing, the leader of the *grace* recites the blessing over the wine (which serves for both the nuptial benedictions and the grace). The wine from the two cups is then intermixed in a third glass. This wine is then sipped by bride and groom, while the leader drinks from his original cup of wine. Hasidim and some other group have everyone at the table drink from this "cup of blessing."

If there is no *minyan,* the seven benedictions are not to be recited. If there are three or more, only the last blessing (*asher bara*) is recited, and the ceremony of the wine glasses is still performed.

THE FIRST WEEK

The law, with its profound insight into the human psyche, required that the couple stay together during the first week to continue to celebrate. They are not to go to work or otherwise to separate, unless there is an urgent need. This tradition harks back to Jacob, who celebrated seven days with Leah and then with Rachel. The custom became widespread and was not confined to Jews; Samson's marriage to his Philistine wife was also celebrated for seven days.

The law considers the seven-day rejoicing to have been formally instituted by Moses, much as he ordained the *shiva,* the seven days of mourning. Extreme moments of love, like death, are deeply emotional. It is difficult, if not impossible, for an individual to experience such traumatic moments and then continue life as though nothing out of the ordinary has happened. Moses ordained, therefore, that both celebration and commemoration be followed by a seven-day tapering-off period, during which one might ponder and accept the intensity of the event and allow it to be gradually integrated into the psyche. Both *shiv'at ye'mei ha-mishteh* (or simply, *Sheva Berakhot*), seven days of rejoicing, and *shiv'at ye'mei avelut* (or *shiva*), seven days of mourning, are not to be working days. The community is asked to participate in both events—to console the mourners in their home, and to provide a *minyan* for *Sheva Berakhot* every day for the newlyweds; and both are followed by special periods of one year: for *kaddish* for the mourners; for staying together at home (*naki yih'yeh le'beito*) for the new husband and wife.

The *Sheva Berakhot* are recited for only the seven days, beginning from the first meal after the *chuppah.* They are to be recited morning and night, if the halakhic conditions are met, on every one of those days. Since to do this there must be a *minyan* at each meal, honeymoons are not planned by many traditional Jewish couples until *after* the seven days. At the beginning, the new husband and wife must learn to accommodate each other in a familiar setting, not in some far-off place that has no relation to the anticipated reality of their future lives. They are part of a family and a community, and this should be their primary environment. The popular emphasis on the glories of the honeymoon period are so overrated and idealized that the newlyweds, busy adjusting to the demands of everyday life, begin to feel disappointed, let down, and unsuited for each other. Judaism says, wisely, that this is precisely the time to stay at home and to be surrounded with family and friends, familiar sights and sounds. It is a time for bride and groom to "rejoice one another" by being together simply and wholesomely in the environment in which they lived as singles.

NEW FACES (PANIM CHADASHOT)

The party atmosphere of the wedding must inform all of these festive *minyan* meals of the *Sheva Berakhot*. Therefore, the law requires *panim chadashot,* new faces. If everyone at the meal was at the wedding, the party would soon lose its spontaneity. The requirement for a *Sheva Berakhot* party is that at least one member of the *minyan* must be someone new. The law levies upon each person who was not at the wedding the requirement to "rejoice" the couple. Thus the *Sheva Berakhot* provided a marriage setting in which each new person could instill new *simchah*.

Newcomers who have not eaten together with the new couple, even though they attended the *chuppah* and heard the blessings, are considered to be "new faces." This also applies to those who came to visit during the seven days, but did not eat.

On the Sabbath or a festival, a "new face" is not necessary as part of the *minyan*. The Sabbath is what is "new."

If possible, the seven blessings should be recited on Friday night, Saturday afternoon and also at the third Sabbath meal, *Se'udah She'lishit.* It is customary, in order to endow the third meal with greater significance, for the groom to speak on a theme of Torah, if he is capable of doing so.

THE FIRST YEAR

The Bible requires time for adjustment at the very beginning of marriage so that love can grow quietly before the tornado of life sucks everyone into its orbit. "When a man takes a new wife, he shall be deferred from military duty, he shall not be charged with any business, he shall be free for his house one year, and shall cheer his wife whom he has taken" (Deuteronomy 24:5).

The purpose of this requirement was to free the husband from complex psychological concerns, which might divert his mind from the house the couple must build and the adjustment they must make. We should not dismiss this idea as an anachronism. This couple represents the survival of the Jewish people. Broken families will generate a broken people. Whatever obstacles can be avoided must be removed by the law. "Stay home," it says. "Learn to live together before you learn to live with others."

Appendix: A Note on Remarriage and Divorce

REMARRIAGE

Judaism discourages loneliness and recognizes the pain of solitude. It seeks to encourage those who are alone to seek meaningful and richer lives. Hence, whenever possible, it urged remarriage. *Tav le'metav tan du mi-le'matav armelo:* Better to remain coupled than a widow (single).

The Rabbis showed sharp insight into the difference between first and subsequent marriages, although there is an apparent conflict. Resh Lakish says, "One should match two people only on the basis of their deeds"; Rav says, "Forty days before the creation of a child, a heavenly voice calls out: 'So-and-so's daughter is destined for so-and-so.'" Is there a conflict between the opinions? According to Rashi, no. "Rav is speaking of a first marriage, Resh Lakish of a second." The first marriage expresses Rav's dictum—God makes the ultimate determination. The second marriage expresses the insight of Resh Lekish—it depends on the rational, planned blending of the qualities of the soul.

There is a positive value to the suggestion that divorced couples remarry one another (*machazir ge'rushato*). The Torah, however, forbids a man from remarrying a former wife who had married another man in the meantime.

Unlike other religions, the Torah expected remarriage, as a matter of fact: "Lest he die in battle and another marry her" (Deuteronomy 20:7); "Then this latter man . . . writes her a bill of divorcement . . . or the man who married her last dies" (Deut. 24:3). Just as divorce frees her to marry, so does death.

There are some differences in the ceremony between first marriage and remarriage. For example, the remarried *ketubah* substitutes for *be'tulta da* (maiden) the words *armalta da* for the widow, and *matarakhta da* for the divorcee, and the amounts stipulated are changed.

The first marriage requires seven days of rejoicing; the subsequent marriages, though they may be just as joyous, require only one day of *Sheva Berakhot*. However, if one of the couple had never been married, the full seven days of the *Sheva Berakhot* are to be observed.

The veiling need not be done for a woman's subsequent marriage. The *yichud,* which seals the marriage for a first-time marriage, is not necessary in a second or third marriage. Such marriages are sealed upon retirement to their home, when the couple can fully, not just symbolically, consummate the marriage. The elective elements of the ceremony—who walks down the aisle, who are the escorts, whether the children of the previous marriages should attend— are matters for intelligent and sensitive determination by the couple.

Several points should be remembered for remarriage:

1. If the deceased husband was childless and he has a surviving brother, a *chalitzah* ceremony must take place.
2. A divorcee may remarry a number of times.
3. A divorcee may not marry a *kohen.*
4. Jewish divorce must precede remarriage. This is an absolute requirement of Torah law. *A civil divorce is not recognized by traditional Jewish courts.* The child whose mother did not obtain a Jewish divorce from her former husband may very well be categorized as a *mamzer.*

PROCEDURE FOR OBTAINING A RELIGIOUS DIVORCE

Judaism discourages loneliness, but it also realizes that a bad marriage can be far worse than being alone. Thus Jewish divorce, when necessary, is condoned.

People familiar with civil court procedures in divorce matters are not aware of the simplicity, ease and relatively low cost of a Jewish religious divorce. What follows is excerpted from a document prepared by the Rabbinical Court of the Rabbinical Council of America.

"The prerequisites for a Jewish divorce are the consent of both parties and the husband's direct authorization for the writing, witnessing, signing, and transmission of the bill of divorce to his wife. . . .

"The divorce is written in the presence of a tribunal of three qualified persons, in accordance with specified regulations.

"The husband may deliver the divorce document personally to his wife or through an agent, properly appointed in the presence of a rabbinic tribunal of three rabbis, known in Hebrew as a *Beth Din.* The wife must receive the writ of divorce in her hands, either directly from her husband or from his duly appointed agent. Until this is done, the Jewish divorce is not consummated.

"Jewish religious law does not make it necessary for both parties to be in the same city. The husband in his community may authorize the writing and witnessing of the writ of divorce. He may then appoint his agent to deliver the document to his wife, who resides in another city. In such a case, the Rabbinic Tribunal prepares additional papers, certifying that an agent has been duly appointed. A specific procedure follows, with official delivery of the bill of divorce to the wife, in the presence of a Rabbinic Tribunal in the community in which the wife resides.

"A Jewish divorce may be sent to any Jewish community of any country. It is valid everywhere when prepared and delivered by recognized, ordained rabbis. It permits either party to remarry in accordance with Jewish law. The actual divorce proceedings are normally completed in about an hour and a half."

Compliance with this simple procedure may alleviate future suffering in consonance with the fundamental principles of justice.

Notes

Notes are listed by page and line number (e.g., the first note gives source information for the quotation in line one of page three). Works that are cited frequently appear in the notes by abbreviated title. These abbreviations can be found in the lefthand column of the bibliography; the righthand column provides full title and publication information. Abbreviations of talmudic tractates, divisions of the Shulchan Arukh, and the Midrash are explained below.

Talmudic sources are quoted according to tractates, which are abbreviated as follows:

Av. Zar.	Avodah Zarah	Meg.	Megillah
Avot	Avot	M.K.	Mo'ed Katan
B.B.	Bava Batra	Ned.	Nedarim
B.K.	Bava Kamma	Nid.	Niddah
B.M.	Bava Metzia	Pe'ah	Pe'ah
Bek.	Bekhorot	Pes.	Pesachim
Ber.	Berakhot	Sanh.	Sanhedrin
Betzah	Betzah	Shab.	Shabbat
Bik.	Bikkurim	Shevu.	Shevu'ot
Eduy.	Eduyyot	Sot.	Sotah
Er.	Eruvin	Suk.	Sukkah
Git.	Gittin	Ta'an.	Ta'anit
Hag.	Hagigah	Tanh.	Tanhuma
Hor.	Horayot	Tem.	Temurah
Kelim	Kelim	Yev.	Yevamot
Ket.	Ketubbot	Yoma	Yoma
Kid.	Kiddushin		

Shulchan Arukh (Sh.A.) is divided (and abbreviated) as follows:

OH	Orach Hayyim	HM	Choshen Mishpat
YD	Yoreh Deah	EH	Even ha-Ezer

Books of the Bible, when followed by "R.," refer to the Midrash Rabbah on each of the volumes.

PART ONE: FINDING A MARRIAGE PARTNER

CHAPTER 1. THE MATCHMAKER

Page	Line	
3	1	Gen. R. 68:4 and elsewhere.
3	21	Gen. R. 68:4 and elsewhere.
4	1	Sot. 2a.
4	12	M. Avot. 3:15.
4	23	SC *"Chatan ve'Kallah,"* chap. 14.
5	34	Kid. 12b.
6	10	Nathan Ausubel, ed., *A Treasury of Jewish Folklore* (New York: Crown Publishing Co., 1948), pp. 413–414.
6	11–12	B.K. Mordechai, Siman 172. See also: Sperling, p. 400 in regard to *Divrei Chayyim* and *Chatam Sofer.*
6	20	Tanh., *Ki Tissa.*
6	31	AH, HM 185.
7	16	*Chayyei Adam,* Introduction to *Zikhru Torat Moshe.* This is the only *legal yichus* relative to *Shiddukhin.*
7	29	Ned. 81a.
8	3–4	Lewis, p. 130.
8	19	Boll. See also: De Burger; Bulka, *Family and Marriage Newsletter.*
8	24–26	Quoted in De Burger.

CHAPTER 2. ROMANTIC LOVE AND THE JEWISH CONCEPT OF LOVE

11	1–2	L. in SH, pp. 13–44.
11	14–15	MEW, p. 316.
11	23–25	*The Descent of Man,* chap. 21.
11	26–29	Rougemont, p. 292.
12	5–7	S. Hasidim, no. 1289.
12	11	Rougemont, pp. 50–55.
12	35–36	*Poor Richard's Almanac,* 1738.
14	18–21	GRA to Prov. 31. See also: MHRM Schiff to Ket. 17a.
14	38	R. to Gen. 29:11.
15	1–2	Biur to Gen. 29:11.
15	41	Sanh. 76b. Love of wife is not explicit, but the Rabbis interpret "neighbor" to mean "wife."
16	7	Yev. 61a.
16	14	MHRK, *Shoresh* 164.
16	18	GRA to YD 240.
16	19	Meg. 27a; B.B. 151a.
16	21	Meg., chap. 1, end. See also: *Ne'tivot le 'Shabbat* to EH 1:8.
16	35	Kid., chap. 4, beginning.
16	37	Tem. 16a on Josh. 15:16–17.
17	1	M.T., *Issurei Bi'ah,* 21:3.
17	5 ff.	Pesik. R. Kah. 22.
19	27	According to Maim. REMA holds that if it was overlooked, it does not invalidate. See GRA to EH 61:8.
20	29–37	Ebreo, p. 28.
21	24 ff.	*"Playboy* Report on American Men." A Louis Harris Poll, reported in *New York Times,* 1979.
22	9	Sanh. 71a.
22	11–13	BCH to Sanh. 71a. See also: Me'iri ad. loc.

Page	Line	
23	7	Resp. MHRM Mi-Lublin (Meir ben Gedaliah Lublin, 1558–1618), chap. 53. Er. 102b. See also: TAz to YD 184:14; SHKH to YD 127.
23	8–9	BM 59a. Bending down to whisper to his wife during normal conversations certainly applies during moments of intimacy.
23	9–11	MHRM of Lublin, chap. 53, quoted in *Mitzvot ha-Bayit,* vol. 2, p. 8. (See notes p. 23, line 7.)

CHAPTER 3: THE SEXUAL COMPONENT IN LOVE AND MARRIAGE

Page	Line	
24	10	Thielicke, pp. 74 ff.
24	12	Ket. 13b.
24	13	Suk. 52a.
26	35	Sanh. 58a.
27	24–25	Philip Birnbaum, ed., *High Holyday Prayer Book* (New York: Hebrew Publishing Co., 1951), pp. 527–528.
27	31–35	Thielicke.
28	16	IK, pp. 138–146.
28	33	Yev. 63b.
29	2–4	Niebuhr, p. 73.
29	11–14	IK, pp. 40–47.
29	17–19	Vital, Intro. to *Etz Hayyim.*
29	19 ff.	*Sur Me-Ra* (Jerusalem: Keter Publishing House Ltd.), pp. 50. ff.
30	6	Gen. R. 9:9.
31	1 ff.	Thielicke. pp. 40–41.
32	35 ff.	These laws are incorporated under *Issurei Bi'ah,* which is in *Sefer Kedushah,* rather than in *Ishut,* which is in *Sefer Nashim.*
32	40	Yev. 20a.
33	7–8	Ket. 62b.
33	39	Kid. 2b.

PART TWO: PROSPECTIVE PARTNERS: THE PROHIBITED AND THE PREFERRED

Page	Line	
38	16	R. to Yev. 49b. But, not according to Tos. ad. loc.

CHAPTER 4: PROHIBITED AND VOID

Page	Line	
39	8	Diodorus 1:27. See: Raphael Patai, *Sex and Family in the Bible and the Middle East* (Garden City, New York: Doubleday & Company, 1959), p. 22.
39	21	For fuller treatment see: (1) MLBT; (2) *The Jewish Marriage,* (3) EJ "Marriage Prohibitions;" and (4) Judah Goldin, *Ha-Madrikh.*
40	33–34	MT, *Issurei Bi'ah,* 21:1.
40	34–35	RMBN, *Maggid Mishneh* on MT, *Issurei Bi'ah,* 21:1, who explains Maim. and RMBN. (This commentary is in most editions of MT.)
41	31 ff.	Ornstein, as quoted in *Likkutei Batar Likkutei* to Lev. 20:10.
43	15–17	MT, *Ge'zelah va-Avedah,* chap. 1.
43	17–18	See the beautiful essay by Nachshoni, vol. 1, pp. 363-367. See also: David Zevi Hoffmann (1843–1921, Germany) *Melamed Le'ho-il,* (Frankfort a. M.: Hermon, 1925/26, 1931/32. Reprints, New York: Frankel, 1954), end chapter.
43	22 ff.	S. Chin, no. 416.
43	29 ff.	Hirsch, as quoted in Nachshoni to *Yitro.*

Page	Line	
43	33 ff.	IB.E.on Ex. 20:14.
44	4	Kid. 7a. See also: R. *ad loc.*
44	20	H. Grodzinski, *Igge'rot Achiezer* (Vilna: 1922; New York: 1945), vol. 1, chap. 15, records the debate between RSHB who requires a divorce, and the *Sha'ar he-Mishpat,* with whom R. Hayyim Ozer agrees, that a divorce is not required from the second "husband."
44	27	Av. Zar. 3a.
45	25 ff.	TT to Lev. 20:10, paragraph 22.
45	30	Shab. 62b.
45	35 ff.	*Imrei Shefer,* as quoted in *Likkutei Batar Likkutei* to Lev. 20:10.
45	39	Hirsch, as quoted in *Likkutei Batar Likkutei.*
46	12	Shevu. 47b; see TT on Ex. 20:13, paragraph 89.
46	27 ff.	Sanh. 52b. and 46a.
47	2–4	EH 4:13.
47	6	Tam, on Ket. 3b; *"ve'lidrosh";* RSHB on Yev. 45b. See also: R. Elchanan Wasserman to Yev. 35, beginning.
47	12	Kid. 74a.
47	15	Deut. 17:15 and Tos. to Yev. 45b.
47	18 ff.	RMBN on Ex. 20:13.
49	6	Ruppin, pp. 317–332.
49	18 ff.	Egon Mayer and Carl Sheingold, *Intermarriage and the Jewish Future* (New York: American Jewish Committee, 1979).
51	32	Av. Zar. 26a.
51	33	Av. Zar. 20b.
51	34	Av. Zar. 21a.
51	35	Av. Zar. 2a.
51	37	Av. Zar. 8a.
52	3	MT *Ma'akhalot Assurot,* 11:7. See also: *Torat ha-Bayit.* 5:1.
52	5	R. and Tos. to Av. Zar, 57b, *"la-afukei."* See also: Tos., *"assur,"* to Sanh. 63b.
52	17	MLBT, p. 178.
52	22	MLBT, p. 181.
52	28	MLBT, p. 182, quoting Mielziner.
53	24	Kid. 68b.
54	5	An excellent analysis of these questions was presented in an unpublished paper before the Rabbinical Council of America by Rabbi David Silver, former president of its Beth Din.
54	13	Sanh. 47a; YD 362:5.
54	29	S. Esh, vol. 2.
54	35	Felder, YY, v. 2, p. 210, *"Divrei Hillel . . ."*
54	38	OH 55:11–12.
55	4–6	*S. Esh,* vol. 2, chap. 6.
55	9–12	IM.
55	28	*S. Esh,* vol. 2, p. 21.
56	23	JBS, *Shiu. Rav.,* "The Seder Meal."
57	10	YD 152.
57	11	YD 123.
58	34	Massarik.
58	37 ff.	*Moment Magazine,* March, 1979.
59	5	*Ibid.*
59	11	David Max Eichorn, *Conversion to Judaism* (New York: KTAV, 1965) and elsewhere.

Page	Line	
59	27	Irving Agus, Lectures, Yeshiva University, Bernard Revel Graduate School, 1962.
59	36	Suk. 8b; Yev. 24b.
60	22	CHP, pp. 270-296. This is a comprehensive statement on the reaction of contemporary scholars, as well as ancient Sages, representing the mainstream thinking of the Halakhah scholars of today.
65	25	EB, *Micropaedia*, vol. 5, pp. 107–108.
66	24	R. on Gen. 9:22.
66	31	Josephus, *Wars*, I, 24:7.
66	37	MT, *Issurei Bi'ah*, 22:2.
66	40	EH 24.
67	1	*Ibid.* See also: BCH to *Arba'ah Turim*.
67	6	*Sifra.* 9:8.
67	11	MT, *Issurei Bi'ah*, 21:8.
67	15	Shab. 65a; Yev. 76a.
67	17	Yev. 76a.
67	23	S. Chin, no. 209.
67	36	Ned. 51a.
67	40	RSG, EVD 3:1.
68	20	EJ'74, pp. 197–198.
68	24	Mehler.
68	27	Matt.
69	11 ff.	EJ'74, p. 200.
69	26–29	Lev. R. 18:9.
69	34 ff.	EJ'74, pp. 201–202.
70	9–16	EJ'74, p. 202.
73	2	Josephus, *Antiquities*, IV; VIII, 23.
73	8	Smith, C.R., p. 23.
73	27	Yev. 39b.
73	32	*Ibid.* "... *ba-rishonah* ..."
73	35	Louis Ginzberg, *Ginzei Schechter* (New York: Jewish Theological Seminary of America, New Ed., 1969), vol. 2, pp. 270-271.
73	36	MT *Yibbum* 1:2 and *Hagahot Maimuniyot, ad loc.*
73	36	R. and Tos. to Yev. 39b, *"amar."*
74	3	Chajes to Yev. 22b.
74	16	Yev. 41a.
75	11	HRB, chap. 83.
75	13	HM, pp. 97-98.
75	14	*Ibid.* quoting Smith, W.R.
75	23	MT, *Halitzah*, chap. 8 See also: *Hagahot Maimuniyot, ad loc.*
75	28	*Torah Mi-Zion*, vol. 1, chap. 25.
76	11	Yev. 18a-b.
76	13	Yev. 17b-18b.

CHAPTER 5. PROHIBITED BUT VALID

Page	Line	
78	1	MT, *Issurei Bi'ah*, 15:13.
78	13	JT, Kid. as quoted by RMBN to Deut. 23:3. See also: BT, Yev. 66b and R. ad. loc.
78	15	Engel to Kid., chap. 62.
78	19	S. Hasidim, chap. 377; see further on preferred mates.
78	31	Kid. 66b.

Page	Line	
78	39	Yev. 45b, unlike the version of RSHB to this.
79	9	Yev. 49a.
79	12	*Ibid.*
79	14	Kid. 72a.
79	31	Hor. 13a.
79	36	Kid. 66b.
80	4	Kid. 69a. See also: EH 4:24.
80	6	Kid. 72b.
80	8	Kid. 69a. See also EH 4:22.
80	12	MT, *Issurei Bi'ah,* 15:12.
80	18	EH 4:47.
80	21	See *Shev She'mate'ta,* vol. 2, chap. 19, relative to the opinion of *Nimmukei Yosef* that the child retains the *chezkat kashrut* of the mother. Another reason, given by *Maggid Mishneh,* is that the doubtful *mamzer* is biblically permitted to marry. Only the Rabbis prohibited it and only the Rabbis chose to confirm her statement in this matter. (See chap. 14, end, and note for p. 40, lines 34–35.)
80	28	EH 4:31-36.
80	31	EH 59.
80	39	EH 4:31, "*. . . ein bo mishum asufi . . .*"
81	31	Yev. 75b.
81	33	EH 5:10.
82	7	MT, *Ishut,* 4:11.
82	11	KM, *Issurei Bi'ah,* 1:15.
82	11	MT, *Ishut,* 4:11. RVD does not even require divorce in such a case. See also: EH 44:5; Ket. 100b; MT, *Ishut,* 24:2.
82	15	Tos. to Git. 46b, "*ha-motzi . . .*"
82	18	*Nimmukei Yosef* to Yev. 2a. See also: MT *Ishut,* 4:10.
82	25	Yev. 62a.
82	26	*Ibid.*
83	13	RMBN on Deut. 24:4, "*. . . acharei . . .*" (See Chavel, ed., p. 297.)
83	38	Deut. 24:4.
84	1	*Ibid.* See RMBN *ad. loc.*
84	13	EJ, "Priests."
84	15	Dispute between Maim. (*S. Mitzvot, Asei,* 34) and RMBN, *Shoresh* 3.
84	17	Yoma 71b; 73a.
84	23–24	*Sifrei.* Deut. 153.
84	26	Kaufmann (Greenberg, ed.), p. 304.
84	34–35	Eldad to *Sidra Va-yikra.*
86	9	YD, 371:5 and SHKH, 18 *ad loc.*
86	13	For detailed laws, clearly presented, see AH Hil., *Piryah ve'Rivyah,* chaps. 6 and 7.
87	3–4	AH, EH 7:37.
87	21–22	Tos. to Yev. 15b, unlike MT, *Issurei Bi'ah,* 18:5.
87	26–27	OH 128:40.
87	29–32	Yev. 61b.
87	35 ff.	MT, *Issurei Bi'ah,* chap. 18.
88	5–6	SLCJ, chap. 7.
88	6–10	Shapiro, "Be Fruitful and Multiply," p. 52 ff.
88	16 ff.	MT, *Issurei Bi'ah,* chap. 18. See also to Yev. 61a, "*. . . she-nevalah . . .*"; and RSHB to Yev. 68, "*. . . mina hanei mila . . .*"
88	28 ff.	Tos. to Yev. 61a; RVD to MT, *Issurei Bi'ah,* 18:1; Tur. to EH 3.
89	11	RVD to MT, *Issurei Bi'ah,* 18:3.

Page	Line	
89	20	Kid. 77a and 78b.
90	23	As above. It is a dispute between RSHB and *Sha'ar Efrayim*. R. Hayyim Ozer decided against requiring a *get* from the paramour.
90	34–35	Pes. 113a.
91	1	Yev. 44a.
91	3	Yev. 65a. EH 1:9.
91	5	EH 76:8.
91	13	Herem of Rabbenu Gershom, at Worms, 1030. See Louis Finkelstein, *Jewish Self-Government in the Middle Ages.* (New York: JTSA, 1924), reprint (New York: Feldheim, 1964). See also: *Otzar ha-Poskim,* EH 1:10, No. 61:2.
91	14	Schereschewsky, pp. 72 ff.
91	20	TUR to EH 44; *Darkhei Moshe* to EH 44.
91	21–23	EH 154.
91	24	EH 154. Eisenstadt, *Pitchei Te'shuvah,* 5.
91	35–37	Sot. 27b-28a; MT, *Sot.* 2:12-16.
91	38 ff.	Yev. Chap. 2, end.
92	9	Yev. 24b.
92	16	MT, *Issurei Bi'ah,* 2:11.
92	22	Ket. 100b.
92	23	Nid. 12b.
92	24	MT, *Ishut,* 24:15.
93	5	M.K. 23a.
93	17	EH 13:1.
93	25–26	Yev. 35a.
93	36	In the case of *giyoret,* we do not say *"lo plug"* (Maim.).
94	1	Tos. to Yev. 35a.
94	5–7	Yev. 42a-b.
94	8–10	Tos. to Sot. 26a, *"lo yissa."*
94	12–14	EH 13:12. See also: Yev. 36b and Tos. *ad loc., "ve'lo Katani."*
94	15–17	IM, quoting R. Shlomo Kluger, *Chokhmat Shlomo* (printed in many editions of Sh. A.), to EH 13:11, uses eighteen months as a minimum. R. Hayyim Ozer and others use fifteen months as the earliest time. See: *Achiezer,* vol. 3, chap. 16, as quoted in Braun to EH 145, p. 46.
94	17–21	For an exhaustive treatment of the subject, see *Resp.* of R. Shlomo Kluger, *Ha-Alef Le'Kha Shlomo, Resp.* 52 to 72.
94	24–26	Sot. 24a, 26a; MT, *Gerushin,* 11:28 and *Maggid Mishneh,* EH 13:12. (See note for p. 40, lines 34–35.)
95	6 ff.	Hertz, p. 559.
95	19 ff.	*Ibid.*
95	27–29	R. and Tos. to Yev. 62b.
96	3 ff.	*Ibid.*
96	15 ff.	*Ibid.*

CHAPTER 6. PREFERRED PARTNERS

Page	Line	
97	6	Me'iri to Kid. 70a.
97	10–13	S. Hasidim, no. 377. See also: Abrahams, p. 84.
97	16–17	Kid. 2b.
98	3 ff.	*Men. ha-Maor,* part 2:3, 6.
98	8 ff.	Yev. 63a. See also: R. ad. loc.
98	11–12	Kid. 41a.
98	13	MT, *Issurei Bi'ah,* 21:3.
98	15 ff.	ARN 26:4.

Page	Line	
99	2–6	EH 2:5.
99	7	Betzah, 32b.
99	11–13	Meg. 14b. See also: BB 104b.
99	16–17	Maim., MN III, 26 and 48.
99	20–21	REMA to YD 28:2; SHKH to YD 6; REMA to OH 223, end.
100	7–8	Code of Hammurabi 1:40.
100	34	Lev. R. 34:3.
100	34	JT, Ber. chap. 9, Halakhah no. 1 records the story of Rabban Gamaliel reciting a blessing upon seeing a beautiful non-Jewish woman on the Temple Mount. BT, Av. Zar. 20a records the same incident in the name of Rabbi Simeon, who responds with the phrase, "*Mah Rabu Ma'asekha*" rather than with a benediction. Maim. MT, *Hil. Berakhot* 10:13, curiously, decides with the JT. *Magen Avraham,* to O.H. 225, notes that while *histaklut,* "staring," is not permitted, *re'iyah,* simply "seeing" someone, is permitted (indeed, cannot be avoided).
101	11	Handelman.
101	16 ff.	B.B. 57b.
101	22–24	Yev. 107a.
101	28–31	Sot. 3b.
101	37–38	Philip Birnbaum, *Daily Prayer Book* (New York: Hebrew Publishing Co., 1949) p. 86.
101	38–40	Hor. 13a.
102	3–5	Pes. 49a.
102	6–9	Pes. 49a; MT, *Issurei Bi'ah,* 21:32. See also: *Yad ha-Melekh, ad loc.*
102	11–13	Ber. 34b.
102	13–15	Ket. 111b.
102	21 ff.	Lewisohn, pp. 47-48.
102	40 ff.	Pes. 49b.
103	9	RF to Pes. 49b.
103	16–18	*Chavvat Yair, Resp.* 70.
103	21 ff.	MT, *Issurei Bi'ah,* 21:32.
103	24 ff.	*Birkei Yosef* to EH 2:3.
104	12–14	Ahad ha-Am, "*Al Parashat Derakhim,*" *Ha-Shiloach,* 1898, III, p. 79.
105	13 ff.	*Seder Eliyahu Zuta,* chap. 3.
105	23	*Ein Ya'akov* to Kid. 70a.
105	27–28	*Mid. Ag.* on *Chayyei Sarah,* 24:47.
105	32–33	M. Eduy, 2:9.
105	33–34	Maim. to Eduy, 2:9.
105	35–37	Bahya, *Chayyei Sarah,* 24.
106	1–3	B.B. 110a.
106	6–9	Pes. 49a.
106	9–13	R. to Kid. 71b.
106	15–19	M. end of Ta'an.
106	17–19	Ta'an. 31a.
106	26–28	TAZ sub-chapter 3; *Birkei Yosef* to EH 2:3.
106	37–38	Kid. 76b.
106	41 ff.	Kid. 70b.
107	1–2	*Ibid.*
107	3–5	Tesh. RSHB, vol. 2, chap. 15.
107	14 ff.	HRB, pp. 96–97.
107	38 ff.	Ta'an, 23b.
108	14	AH, EH 61.
108	28–30	AH, YD, *Hil. Talmud Torah,* 246:1.
108	31–32	Kid. 60a.

Page	Line	
108	35–37	AH *"Piryah ve-Rivyah,"* chap. 2.
109	6–8	Abrahams, Israel, ed., *Hebrew Ethical Wills.* (Philadelphia: Jewish Publication Society of America, 1926), part I, p. 145.
109	9–10	Me'iri to Prov. 14:1.
109	10–13	RTB to Yoma 70a.
109	13–17	See SC quoting Rabbi Bahya, *Chatan ve'Kallah,* chap. 14.
109	18 ff.	S. Hasidim, quoted by *Magen Avraham,* OH 223:1.
109	27–32	Me'iri to Shab. 11a.
109	33–34	Me'iri to Yev. 63a.
109	34–35	TUR, EH 2:75. See also: MT, *Issurei Bi'ah,* 19:17 and MT *Hil. Teshuvah,* 2:10.
109	36–37	EH 119:5.
110	1–2	Sot. 27a.
110	4–5	Sot. 3b.
110	6–8	S. Hasidim, chap. 951. *Maggid Mishneh, Issurei Bi'ah,* chap. 2, end, quoting the Midrash. (See note, p. 40, lines 34–35.)
110	21 ff.	R. Bahya to Gen. 24:3.
110	25 ff.	Me'iri to Yev. 62b.
110	32–35	Yev. 101b.
110	38 ff.	*Noda bi'Yehudah,* vol. 1 to EH 69.
111	8 ff.	JBS:TRT.

PART THREE: THE IDEA OF JEWISH MARRIAGE

CHAPTER 7. THE STATE OF MARRIAGE TODAY

117	6	Ber. 8a.

CHAPTER 8. JEWISH INSIGHTS INTO MARRIAGE

118	14–15	Birnbaum, *Daily Prayer Book,* pp. 743-744.
118	19 ff.	JBS, AE.
119	11 ff.	Ket. 7b-8a.
119	21 ff.	Joshua, son of Korha, *Chronicles of Yerahmeel,* 6:16.
120	4–6	Shab. 33a.
120	23–25	Ket. 7a-7b.
120	26 ff.	Maim. CM, Avot, 1:6.
121	12–15	*Ha-Ketav ve'ha-Kabbalah* to Gen. 2:18.

CHAPTER 9. THE PURPOSES OF MARRIAGE

122	6	Yev. 118b; Kid. 7a, 41a; JT, Ta'an, 4:6.
122	13 ff.	Ket. 7b-8a.
122	19 ff.	Abudarham, *Birkhot Erusin,* p. 98a.
122	22–23	BCJL, pp. 33-36.
123	22 ff.	Isaac Breuer in *Moriah,* See also: Thielicke, p. 4.
123	41 ff.	RVD, *Ba'alei ha-Nefesh;* introduction. See also: *Mitzvot ha-Bayit, v. 1, p. 77.*
124	9	*RVD, Ba'alei ha-Nefesh.* See: *Reishit Chokhmah, Sha'ar ha-Kedushah,* chap. 16.
124	19 ff.	Evans, pp. 48-50.
124	40 ff.	Kid. 41a.
125	2	MHRK to Kid. 41a.

Page	Line	
125	19–20	Gibran, p. 19.
125	32 ff.	Fromm, pp. 18-19.
125	40–41	Fromm, p. 21.
126	5 ff.	Rilke, p. 28.
126	12–13	Mik. Ged. Sforno on Genesis 2:18.
126	23–24	Sanh. 27b and 28a. Because of the dictates of the law, and not because of prejudice, see B.B. 159a.
126	27–30	MT, *Edut*, 13:13. An even more apt illustration, but too complicated for this text, is the theory of RVD concerning *Palginan Dibura*. See: *Hid. RAN* to Sanh. 10a.
126	32–33	Me'iri to Sanh. 28a.
126	41 ff.	Chatam Sofer, *Resp.* OH, chaps. 54 and 55.
127	29–30	Birnbaum, *Daily Prayer Book,* pp. 125-126.
128	40 ff.	Yev. 63b.
130	1	Sheed, pp. 97-106.
130	13–14	Yev. 34b.
130	18	Nid. 13a, 13b; EH 23:1.
130	24 ff.	MT, *Ishut,* chap. 15.
131	10 ff.	Ex. R. to Ex. 2:1. See also: Ber. 10b.
133	12 ff.	M.Yev. 61b.
133	15–16	*Ibid.*
133	16–17	*Ibid.*
133	22–24	MT, *Ishut,* 15:4.
133	26–27	Yev. 12b, 100b; Ket. 39a; Nid. 45a; Ned. 35b; M. Eduy, 1:13; Yev. 62a, 62b.
133	27–29	Tos. to B.B. 60b, *"din hu."*
133	31–32	Genesis 1:28.
133	32–33	Yev. 34b; Nid. 13a.
134	35 ff.	Kid. 29b.
135	6–8	AH, EH 1:1.
135	15–20	RSG, EVD, 10:6.
135	22–23	Me'iri to Pes 49a.
135	33	Sheed, p. 119.
136	2–3	Ket. 61a. MT, *Ishut,* chap. 13, on *onah.*
136	6–7	According to SMK, chap. 285, R. Hirsh Melekh of Dinuv, *Derekh Pikudekha* to *Mishpatim,* quoting SMK.
136	14–15	RVD *Ba'alei ha-Nefesh,* p. 116.
136	16–17	Meiselman, p. 122; Feldman, p. 64.
136	18–20	EH 38:5, following R. and against RMBN to BB 126b and RTB to B.M. 94a.
136	21	Ket. 59b.
136	29–31	Ket. 63a.
136	33–34	*Ibid.*
137	2–3	According to REMA on EH.
137	6–7	MT, *Ishut,* 14:8.
137	16–18	RVD, *Ba'alei ha-Nefesh.*
137	18–19	MT, *Ishut,* 14:1-2.
137	23–24	Ket. 62b.
137	26–27	R. to Ket. 62b.
137	30–32	IK. pp. 68–71.
138	6–8 ff.	MT, *De'ot,* 5:4, 5.
138	13–14	RVD, *Ba'alei ha-Nefesh,* p. 121.
138	19–21	Lev. R. 9:6.
138	21–22	B.M. 59a.
138	22–24	Er. 100b.

PART FOUR: THE STRUCTURE OF THE MARRIAGE COVENANT

CHAPTER 10. "ACCORDING TO THE LAWS OF MOSES AND ISRAEL": THE JEWISH MARRIAGE CEREMONY.

Page	Line	
150	36–38	*Lechem Mishneh* and Radbaz to MT, *Melakhim*, 4:4.
151	1–4	Ket. 7b.
151	5–8	Abudarham as quoted in Jacobson, vol. 3, p. 109.
151	12–14	Rackman, pp. 226-230. Another equally masterful article is in Kahana, pp. 26-32. It is a very closely reasoned dissertation. Kahana and Rackman hold opposing views. Rackman says that the Halakhah bases itself on the fundamental comparison of marriage and property with certain notable exceptions. Kahana, apologetically, says the more fundamental analogue is marriage and *hekdesh,* the goods sanctified for temple use, with certain notable exceptions. The student with strong talmudic background would do well to study both.
151	14–15	Rackman, p. 234.
151	27–34	Kid. 2b. See Tos. for deeper understanding of this idea.
152	21–26	Ned. 29a.
152	27–31	As quoted by Kahana, p. 56.
152	32–36	Git. 82a-82b.
153	16–22	To Kid. 2b.
153	23 ff.	*Ibid.*
153	26–28	As brought down in Kahana, p. 43, note 3.
153	28–30	To Kid 2b.
153	35–36	See the excellent discussion on this point in Kahana, pp. 43-46.
154	2–4	Volozhiner, *Chut ha-Meshulash,* chap. 1, section 2. A contrary view is held by *Avnei Millu'im,* 27:6, and R. Hayyim Soloveitchik, *Beit ha-Levi,* vol. 3, chap. 27. They hold that it is not essential for witnesses to establish the woman's willing consent. See RAN to Ned. 30a, that it is man's willing consent that is of concern. The woman, in this case, considers herself momentarily *hefker,* "ownerless." But see Kahana, p. 44. He quotes insight of Shkop, v. 2, 7:12.
154	17–19	Ket. 7a-7b. Further on this see: Baron, v. 3, pp. 46-47.
154	23–25	*She'iltot,* 16.
154	27–28	Falk, pp. 51ff. He writes an entire essay on this subject.
155	14 ff.	Kahana, p. 44.
155	21–22	There are two terms of acquisition which clarify the difference between the transfer of ownership and the change of status. For this, see: Kahana, pp. 92-93, and Meiselman, pp. 96-98.
155	24	M. Avot. 1:6.
156	10–12	Meiselman, pp. 96-98.
156	14–18	Kid. 3a; 6b.
156	21–22	Belkin, pp. 183-184, for insightful and broad discussion of this point.
156	24–26	Reference in Sanh. 57a is to a non-Jew who singles out a female servant for his male servant.
156	27 ff.	MT, *Ishut,* 14:8.
156	31–33	Tam referred to in RSH; Siman 34 to Ket.
156	38–42	RSHB and RMBN to Git. 9b. See also: Kahana, pp. 28-30.
157	9–11	Tesh. Geon., *"Sha'arei Zedek"* p. 94. See also: *Ter. Desh.* no. 218.
157	24–25	MHRM *Rot.,* no. 48 (Lemberg). See also: Jung, p. 42.
157	29–31	Ket. 59b. See also: Ket. 61b, on refusal of conjugal rights; Ket. 71b, on cruel and inhuman treatment; Ket. 70a, on nonsupport.
157	40–42	RAN disagrees with this decision, but that is how it proceeded.
158	2 ff.	Ket. 71b.
158	24–31	Meiselman, pp. 96-102.
159	4 ff.	Arama to Gen. 30:1ff.
159	32 ff.	Dessler (Eng. ed.), pp. 126-133.
160	3 ff.	Moses Sofer., *Chatam Sofer,* Resp. to EH. vol. 2, Siman 74. See also: Genesis 23:3-18

Page	Line	
160	23	Witnesses to the function of *chuppah* and *yichud* are presently required, but actually were a matter of dispute among the later decisors. JBS (*Mah Dodekha Mi-Dod*) does not stress this requirement.
160	33–34	Yoma 2a, and elsewhere.
161	3–4	Ket. 48b.
161	9–10	AH, EH 35:1
161	17–19	R. to Ket. 7b, *"assei."*
162	14 ff.	MHRSHL. See: Simon Hurwitz, *The Responsa of Solomon Luria* (New York: Bloch Publishing Co., 1938), pp. 67-68.
163	26–27	MT, *Ishut,* 4:1.
164	9–11	Yev. 112b. See also: Sanh. 69a; Nid. 45b; Git. 70b, and AH, EH 68.
164	14	*Resp.* of *Zikhron Yosef,* EH, chap. 10, regarding the retarded and deranged. This is a fundamental view as evidenced by citations to this *Resp.* by other authorities. e.g., R. Akiva Eger and *Or Same'ach.*
164	18–20	Yev. 14:1.
164	20–22	EH 44:1.
164	25–26	Yev. 69b.
165	15–16	Kid. 41a.
165	20–21	Schereschewsky. p. 365; pp. 431 ff.
165	22–25	Kahana, pp. 34–39.
165	25–26	The question of one suitable witness is discussed by REMA and GRA to EH 42:2.
165	27–28	Kid. 65b.
166	4 ff.	*Ibid.*
166	6–7	*Ibid.*
166	8 ff.	*Ke'tzot ha-Choshen,* 241:1. See also: Kahana, p. 35.
166	14 ff.	*Or Same'ach,* to MT, *Edut,* 9:27, quotes R. Hayyim in *Hil. Yibbum ve'-Chalitzah.* See Kahana, p. 35.
166	19 ff.	Tos. to Yev. 88a, *"medai."*
166	25–28	AH, EH 43; 30:31.
166	30–31	The requirement of attesting witnesses appearing together is discussed by GRA to EH 133.
166	35	The custom of JBS and *Beit ha-Levi,* vol. 2, 39:10.
167	22 ff.	MT *Edut,* 13:3; HM 33:10.
167	29	See excellent article by Berman.
167	30–33	Shev. 30a.
167	34–36	See *Lechem Mishneh, Ishut,* 2:21.
168	8 ff.	HM 34:2.
168	12–13	HM 34:22.
168	14–16	AH, EH 42:50.

CHAPTER 11. NOT "ACCORDING TO THE LAWS OF MOSES AND ISRAEL":
NON-JEWISH CEREMONIES.

Page	Line	
169	7–10	The latest available and readable literature on this subject includes: (1) the halakhic sources in the *Resp.,* which can be found in *Otzar ha-Poskim,* vol. 10, p. 5 ff. Of primary interest is the *Resp.* of Rivash; (2) Schereschewsky; (3) EJ, numerous articles, (4) Elon, *"Ha-Kikah Datit"; "Ha-Mishpat ha-Ivri";* and others, and (5) Ellinson provides an excellent halakhic view.
171	15	Elon, p. 378; Ellinson, p. 175.
171	35 ff.	*Ter. Desh 5* Siman 209.
172	9–10	Herzog, 2:33.

PART FIVE: CELEBRATING THE MARRIAGE COVENANT

CHAPTER 12. PLANNING THE WEDDING

Page	Line	
175	10–11	Baron, vol. 2, pp. 301-306, 315.
176	22–24	Dessler (Eng.ed.), pp. 126-133.
176	25–27	Falk, pp. 86-112, develops the history of the institution of matchmaking.
176	30–33	Ket. 102b.
176	38 ff.	Kid. 12b.
177	2–6	Ket. 102b.
177	13	Judah ben Barzillai al-Bargelcni, *Sefer ha-She'tarot,* S. Halbertsam, ed. (Berlin: 1898; Reprint, Jerusalem: 1966), no. 72.
177	14	Finkelstein, *Jewish Self-Government,* p. 140.
178	15–19	GRA, *Sefer Sha'arei Rachamim.*
178	21–23	Sperling, p. 411, no. 970. See note by *Toledot Aharon, ad loc.*
178	33–35	Ber. 30b-31a.
179	11–13	Kid. 13a; 6a.
179	13–15	Maim., *Tesh Rambam,* nos. 155-156. See also: *Resp.* of Abraham, son of Maim., p. 182, as brought down by Falk, p. 57.
179	15 ff.	Falk, pp. 57-59.
179	34 ff.	YD 179; AH, EH 64:13.
180	12–15	*Sefer Ma'aseh ha-Geonim,* p. 55. See also: Falk, p. 44, note 1; LMA, p. 79.
180	16–18	MT, *Ishut,* 10:14.
180	19–21	TUR and RSH as referred to in AH, EH 64:11.
180	31 ff.	M.K. 8b.
180	33	AH, EH 64:18.
181	4 ff.	The idea of mourning on fast days follows the concept of JBS. The law, in times of urgency, follows REMA, OH 550:3; *Magen Avraham,* 559:11; M. Ber. 550:3.
181	17	Based on *Chayyei Adam,* 133:8, 11 and M. Ber. 551:15.
181	24 ff.	IM, OH 159.
181	32 ff.	This chapter is reprinted from WDM, pp. 184-186.
183	4–6	TAZ and SHKH on YD 342:1. See full discussion of the *Resp.* in Greenwald, p. 65, note 3.
183	7–11	Greenwald, p. 66, note 5. TOS. to Ket. 48b.
183	18–20	RAN to Ket. 2a. See also R. to "She-pirsa hiddah" and RF *ad loc.*
183	30–31	GRA to EH 55.
184	2–4	*Shulchan ha-Ezer* to GRA, *ibid.;* also quoted in Werdiger, p. 25.
184	10 ff.	REMA to EH 55:1.
184	15–16	Falk, p. 50.
184	18–19	See *Resp.* of Rabbi Elyah Gutmacher, in which he strongly opposes the use of the sanctuary. See also: Chatam Sofer to EH 98. Re: similarity to Christian custom.
185	7–9	Shab, 130a.
185	12 ff.	AH, EH 34:10; 62:11-12. See also: Falk, p. 51.
185	21–23	Git. 46a.
185	27–28	Ket. 7b-8a.
185	29–31	*She'iltot,* no. 16.
185	38–40	AH, EH 62:12.
186	5–8	AH, EH 62:11.
186	26–28	Ket. 71a-71b.
186	30–31	Sot. 49a.
187	2–5	Sperling, p. 407, no. 957, quoting *Kol Bo.*

Page	Line	
187	5–7	*Ibid.* Quoting *Matteh Moshe.*
187	17–18	Sot. 49a.

CHAPTER 13. THE WEEK BEFORE THE WEDDING

188	1	*Hagahot ha-Radal,* no. 58; as quoted in Werdiger, p. 6.
188	2–3	REMA to EH 64.
188	3–5	R. to Ber. 54b.
188	13–15	See whole analysis in AH, YD 192.
188	15–17	Immanuel Jakobovitz, *The Meaning of the Marriage Service.* London: n.d.
189	5–7	OH, *Hil. Ke'riat ha-Torah,* beginning.
189	9–11	Margolioth, Ephraim Zalman, *Sha'arei Ephraim,* (New York: 1952), p. 10.
189	12–13	Joshua Boaz Baruch, *Shiltei Gibborim* to M. Kid. 4:2; RSH. *Halakhot* to M. Kid. 4:4. See also: Falk, p. 37.
189	19 ff.	JBS explains that the groom has an obligation of *simchah*—not only for eating and drinking but to rejoice others, as *Peri Megadim* holds that giving charity must accompany *yizkor* on holidays by law, as the biblical portion of "and thou shalt rejoice on thy holidays, thou and thy house . . ." is read. The essence of rejoicing is rejoicing others, whether by acts of charity or the teaching of Torah. The groom's being called to the Torah is as though he himself read it aloud for others to follow. For this reason there arose the custom that the groom, if he is able, recites a Torah lesson at the table at the writing of the *ketubah.*
189	21 ff.	As quoted in Werdiger, p. 3, and Sperling, p. 402.
189	32 ff.	M.V. as cited in Werdiger, p. 3.
189	36	According to *Or Zaru'a,* as cited in Werdiger, p. 3.
190	2–3	According to Bahya, as quoted in Werdiger, p. 5.
190	16–18	Ber. 50b.
190	19 ff.	MHRL as quoted in Falk, p. 38, and Werdiger, p. 5.
191	6 ff.	HR, pp. 34-38.
192	3 ff.	HR, pp. 52-56.
192	19 ff.	HR, pp. 58-67.
193	1 ff.	HR, pp. 79-81.
193	16 ff.	HR, pp. 81-89.
194	34 ff.	One of the first references is *Rokeach,* no. 353.
195	4 ff.	REMA to EH 61:1; AH, EH 61:21. MHRM Mintz, as cited in Werdiger, pp. 6-9.
195	4–5	JT, Bik., chap. 3 from Gen. 28:9.
195	17–19	*Chokhmat Adam.* 129:2.
195	19–20	AH, EH 61:21.
195	25	REMA to OH, no. 573. See also: *Levush ad* loc.
196	8 ff.	Shelah, as cited in Werdiger, p. 8.

CHAPTER 14. THE DAY OF THE WEDDING.

198	19–21	Ket. 11a.
198	25–28	Neuman v. 2, pp. 42-46.
198	31–34	Sanh. 21a.
199	16–18	Git. 18a; *Hagahot Maimuniyot* on MT, *Yibbum,* 4:33.
199	21–22	*Nachalat Shivah,* 12:16.
199	23	Git. 27a; B.M. 18a, 20a.
200	19–20	So it appears in the *Ketubah* of Rav Hai. See JMC, p. 160, note 75.
200	20–21	Shitah, RTB to Ket. 63, *"be'omer."*

Page	Line	
201	1	1st century B.C.E.
201	7–9	Ket. 84a. R. Hananel, *"le'Ketubbot."*
201	9	R. and Tos. to Ket. 84a.
201	15–17	Bek. 50b, Rav; Kid. 11a.
202	9–10	Ket. 52b.
202	18–22	Worth more because *nedunya* and *tosefta* are measured in *kesef tzaruf*, unlike the *zuz* of *mohar*. See GRA to EH 66:22 and *S. Eidut.*
203	25–26	B.B. 175b.
204	33–38	Omitting the letter is only a *chumrah be'atzmah* to make it appear as *ma'aseh beit din,* but there is really no concern for *"mechze ke'shikra."* See: Git. 26b.
205	2–3	B.B. 161b, Rabbi Jonathan.
205	3–4	B.B. 160b.
205	5	B.B. 162a.
205	15–16B	*Kitzur Nachalat Shivah,* no. 2.
205	24–25	HM 45:11.
205	29–30	Git. 10b.
206	3–4	Kid. 6a, 13a.
206	9–10	*Sefer Haredim,* chap. 6, note 13, derives this from the language of MT, Er. 6:6. See also: ET, *"Hakhnassat Kallah."*
206	10–11	M. Kelim, 22:4., *Bartenura.*
206	14–17	The M. in Pe'ah does not include *"Hakhnassat Kallah."*
206	17–18	MHRL *Shoresh* 123.
206	18–21	Suk. 49b.
206	21	ET, *"Hakhnassat Kallah."*
206	22	ARN to Ket. 17a.
206	24 ff.	R. and Tos. to Ket. 16b and 17a.
206	27–29	RTB, quoted in Shitah, p. 175, col. 1.
206	29–31	*Baraita* to Ket. 17a.
206	31	R. to Ket. 17a, *"chasudah."*
206	32–34	Tos. to Ket. 17a, *"Kallah."*
206	34–35	RTB to Ket. 17a, *"Ye'shabhenu."*
206	37	EH 65:1.
207	1–2	Meg. 29a, 3b; Ket. 17a.
207	2–5	SHKH to YD 360:1.
207	10–11	Me'iri, p. 75.
207	18–22	YD 361, *"derishah";* E.H. 61.
207	23–26	MHRL, *Hil. Nissu'in,* as quoted in Werdiger, p. 54.
207	33–36	JBS, concerned with the theory of TAz (Y.D. 342) that the *bedeken* is *chuppah,* does not allow it to be done through the agency of others. Therefore, it is done solely by the groom.
208	3–4	MHRL, *Hil. Nissu'in,* as quoted in Werdiger, p. 54.
208	5	*Matteh Moshe* in *Chup. Chat,* p. 68.
208	10–14	MHRL, *Hil. Nissu'in.*
208	15–17	Tos. to Yoma 13b, *"le'hadah";* EH 65, *"de'rishah."* Opposed by TAZ, Ote 2.
208	30	BCH to TUR on EH 61.
209	1	Kimhi to Gen. 24:64.
209	6–9	*Sefer ha-Manhig,* pp. 91b-92a.
209	14–16	NTZV to Gen. 24:65.

CHAPTER 15. THE WEDDING

| 210 | 8 ff. | On this subject, see EH 61 and all the commentaries. See also: excellent historical essay by Solomon Freehof, in Daniel J. Silver, ed., *In Time of* |

Page	Line	
		Harvest (New York: Macmillan Co., 1963), pp. 187-193; Felder, SY, *Resp.* no. 35 on *chuppah.*
210	10	Abudarham to Kid. 19.
211	9–10	RAN and RF to beginning of Ket, *"o she-pirsa."*
211	14–15	MT, *Ishut,* 10:1.
211	15–16	TUR to EH 61.
211	16–18	Werdiger p. 23.
211	18–19	Tos. to Yoma 13b.
211	19–20	Mordecai to beginning of Ket.
211	21–22	RSH to Suk. 25b.
211	23–24	BCH to TUR; EH 61.
211	25–27	*Nachalat Shivah* and *Sefer ha-Manhig* on EH 61.
211	29–31	Felder, SY, *Resp.* 35.
211	31–33	*Da'at Kedoshim,* chap. 2. See also: EH 7, especially as GRA considers the primary *kinyan* to be *chatzer* rather than *chuppah.*
211	36	JT, Sot. 9:15.
212	15–17	Channing.
212	18–20	Felder, SY, *Resp.* 35.
212	33–35	Ket. 12b.
212	36–37	*Zohar,* Gen. 49a, although Braun says it is an American custom and he saw reference to it only once. *Resp. Levushai Mordecai,* v. 4, 22:2.
213	11–13	*Tashbatz,* following *Pirkei de'Rabbi Eliezer,* chap. 12.
213	14–16	MAHARSHA to Ber. 61a.
213	22–24	*Matteh Moshe* as quoted in Werdiger, p. 60.
214	2–4	Sperling, no. 539, *"Korban ani."*
214	6–9	See. Hid. RSHB to Ket. 4a.
215	11–13	*Ba'er Heitev* to Eh 62:1.
215	13–14	Werdiger. p. 63.
215	15–17	*Rokeach,* no. 353.
215	18–19	MHRL, *Minhagim.*
215	19	*Ba'er Heitev* to EH 61:7.
215	20	AH, EH 62:9.
215	20–21	*Ba'er Heitev* to EH 61:7, *Kenesset ha-Ge'dolah.*
215	30–32	Tos. to Pes. 102b.
215	34–35	Werdiger, pp. 30-31.
216	1	*Tashbatz,* vol. 3, chap. 65.
216	2	Werdiger, p. 32. The first mention of it appears in *Zohar* and *Masekhet Kallah Rabbati;* some (e.g., *Ha-amek She'eilah,* who cites approval of Tam to *She'iltot,* no. 16) trace it to R. Yehudah Gaon.
216	2	Gen. 16.
216	3	GRA to EH 34:2.
216	3–4	EH 62:62.
216	7–9	*Tesh. Geon.* 39. In the name of Rabbi Natronai ben Hilai Gaon.
216	10	*Tesh. Geon, Chemdah Genuzah,* chap. 118.
216	10–11	R. *Pardes,* p. 100.
216	11–13	*Tashbatz,* vol. 3, no. 379.
216	13	AH, EH 62:9.
216	14–15	Yavetz to *Siddur;* and others.
216	16–19	JBS at the wedding of my niece.
216	25–31	*Rokeach,* no. 329. *Sefer ha-Manhig,* chap. 111.
216	35 ff.	JT Hag. 77b. See: Heschel, pp. 51-52. See also: Gen. R. 11:8.
217	9 ff.	Ex. R. 41:6.
217	36–38	Jacobson, vol. 3, p. 111.
218	23–24	Rabbenu Nissim to RF on Ket. 7b.

Page	Line	
218	27–28	RSH to Ket. 7b.
218	31–32	JT, quoted in Jacobson, vol. 3, p. 113.
218	38 ff.	*Sefer ha-Manhig* as noted in Werdiger, pp. 30-31.
219	4–7	SC, vol. 18, chap 22, *Pe'at ha-sadeh, Ma'arekhet Berakhot.*
219	14–16	Werdiger, pp. 72-73.
219	19–21	*Ba'al ha-Ittur, "Birkhat Chatanim,"* Gate 5.
219	22–24	RSH to Ket. 7b.
220	15–16	Tos. to Ket. 3a, *"ad atah."*
220	24–25	It is first mentioned in the 7th century. See: Tesh. Geon. p. 30.
220	25–28	RSG commentary to Neh. p. 30.
220	29–30	MHRSHL, *Hiddushim,* to end of B.K.
220	31–32	Falk, p. 62. See also: LMA, pp. 196-200.
220	32 ff.	*Ba'al ha-Ittur,* vol. 2, p. 27, Tur 4. Quoted in Werdiger, pp. 38–41.
221	1–2	REMA to EH 27.
221	5 ff.	EH 31:2.
221	11 ff.	See RSH to Kid. chap. 1, no. 29, and *Beit Shmuel* to EH 28:19. For questions on borrowed rings, see series of *Resp.* in Braun, vol. 4, p. 57.
221	19–20	Abudarham in Chup. Chat., p. 66.
221	20–22	MHRM Mintz in Chup. Chat., p. 66.
221	27–28	Kid. 12b, 13a; EH 27.
221	32–35	Werdiger, p. 64.
222	9 ff.	REMA to EH 27.
222	11–13	AH, EH 27.
222	14 ff.	Arisian, p. 41.
222	23–25	*Hagahot Maimuniyot* to MT, *Ishut,* 3:60.
222	28–29	REMA to EH 62:9.
222	30–31	See RTB quoted in *Shitah* to Ket. 63, on the repeated alimentation phrase in the Ketubah, that it was done *"le'shufra de'Ketubah."* See also: *Tesh. RSHB,* Resp. 629 and *Hagahot Maimuniyot, Ishut* 10:7.
223	16–19	Chida, *Chayyim Sha'al,* vol. 2:38, 56 in the name of R. Abraham, son of Maim.
223	25–27	R. to Ket. 7b.
223	29	For some of the following interpretations, see these sources: (1) Jacobson, vol. 3, pp. 118 ff; and (2) Werdiger, pp. 74 ff.
223	35	E.H. 62:2.
223	36–37	*Darkhei Moshe, EH 62:2.*
224	12–14	R. as quoted in Jacobson, vol. 3, p. 125.
224	14–17	Abudarham, p. 362.
224	18 ff.	As noted in *Kol Bo,* chap. 75.
224	24 ff.	Jacobson, vol. 3, pp. 48 ff.
224	29–31	Breuer, pp. 55 ff.
225	4–5	Ket. 8a. See Radvaz in Shitah.
225	16 ff.	R. to Gen. 2:25.
225	27 ff.	Based on JBS: (1) "The Lonely Man of Faith" (*Tradition,* vol. 7, no. 2; Summer, 1965), pp. 5-67; (2) "Adam and Eve" and "On the Nature of Man" in JBS, Shiu. Rav; and (3) Primarily, reference to the blessings was incorporated in a wedding address in New York, October 10, 1961.
225	40–41	Ha-Levi, vol. 2, p. 106.
227	13–14	Arisian.
227	19 ff.	R. to Gen. 2:8.
228	10–11	Many prefer scheduling this after the *Ketubah* to provide greater separation between the two ceremonies. One minor problem with speaking after the

Page	Line	
		seven blessings is the interruption between the blessings and the *yichud.* See *Peri Megadim* to OH, 206. Few authorities have concern for this problem.
228	16–17	*Matteh Moshe,* as quoted in Werdiger, p. 36.
228	21–22	*Levush* to EH 64.
228	27	*Matteh Moshe,* as quoted in Werdiger, p. 36.
229	7	See: Lauterbach; Solomon B. Freehof, *Recent Reform Responsa* (Cincinnati: Hebrew Union College Press, 1960) *Resp.* no. 40 on this subject. Both are Reform scholars who build enormous structures on kernels of elemental truth. Citations from *Shelah* and interpretations read into the talmudic text serve to ignore the centuries-old persistence of the custom, despite the logic and science.
229	12 ff.	Ber. 30b.
229	22 ff.	*Ibid.* See: *Rokeach.*
229	30 ff.	OH on Tishah Be'av. See *Kol Bo, ad loc.*
230	17 ff.	Ouziel, part II; EH, p. 431.
230	33 ff.	Tzof. Pan. on *Matot.*
230	39–40	Bahya. *Shulchan Shel Arba.*
231	19–20	TAZ to EH 57.
231	21	*Shulchan ha-Ezer,* vol. 3, p. 10.
231	23–25	Felder, SY, p. 178, quoting Tos. to Kid. 10b, unlike RAN in Ket.

CHAPTER 16. AFTER THE WEDDING CEREMONY

Page	Line	
232	8 ff.	Suk. 25b.
232	10	*Chavvat Yair, Resp.* no. 1.
233	5–7	MHRL. *Laws of Eruvei Chatzerot.*
233	7–9	RAN to Ket., chap. 2, *"okhlin ve'shotin."*
233	30–31	*Levush,* but not according to TAZ. See: Werdiger, p. 87.
233	34	MHRL, *Minhagim.*
234	4	AH, EH recommends removal of *"vav"* before *"akhalnu mishelo,"* because the preceding phrase *"she-ha-simchah"* is only a description of God and not the subject of the blessing.
234	6–8	Ket. 8a.
234	9–10	Hag. 12b.
234	11–12	Ket. 8a. See: *Shitah, ad loc.*
234	13 ff.	MHRSHL to B.K. chap. 7.
234	24–25	REMA to EH 62:9.
234	34–35	According to Caro, a *"revi'it,"* According to TAZ, *"me'lo lugmo,"* a mouthful. He then recites concluding blessing.
235	9–10	Ket. 8b: MT Berakhot 2:9; EH 62:6.
236	3	Ket. 8a.
236	9–12	Chup Chat, second opinion of Sh. A.
236	15–16	AH, EH 62:6.
236	31	Zohar to *Ki Tetze,* no. 278.

APPENDIX: A NOTE ON REMARRIAGE AND DIVORCE

Page	Line	
237	3–4	Yev. 118b.
237	5–6	Sot. 2a and R. ad. loc.
237	21–24	REMA to EH, chap. 8, end. See also: R. and Tos. to Yev. 26a and IM to EH on this subject.
238	25 ff.	Rabbinical Court of the Rabbinical Council of America.

Bibliography

HEBREW LANGUAGE SOURCES

All Hebrew language sources in this bibliography are cited by the author's name. The generally accepted authority for all names, spellings, and dates is the *Encyclopaedia Judaica* (Jerusalem: Keter Publishing House, 1971) or the *Encyclopedic Dictionary of Judaica* (Jerusalem: Keter Publishing House, 1974). To facilitate use of the bibliography, every title has a cross-reference to the author's name. Where possible, the author's name is followed by dates and location of primary activity, and by acronym.

S. Chin   Aaron ha-Levi of Barcelona (14th century; Spain.) *Sefer ha-Chinukh,* attributed to Aaron ha-Levi of Barcelona. Edited by Charles B. Chavel. Jerusalem: Mossad Harav Kook, 1951/52.

RVD   Abraham ben David of Posquieres (called Raavad, Rabad, Ravad) (c. 1125–1198; Provence), *Ba'alei ha-Nefesh.* Warsaw: 1863.

————. *Hassagot ha-Ravad.* In *Mishneh Torah.*

————. *Hassagot ha-Ravad al ha-Rif.* In *Alfasi.*

Abraham ben Nathan ha-Yarhi of Lunel, France (c. 1155–1215). *Sefer ha-Manhig.* Jerusalem: Lewin-Epstein, 1966/67.

Abraham ibn Ezra. See: ibn Ezra, Abraham.

Abudarham, David ben Joseph (14th century; Spain). *Abudarham ha-Shalem.* Jerusalem: 1963.

Abudarham   *Abudarham ha-Shalem.* See: Abudarham, David ben Joseph.

RSHB   Adret, Solomon ben Abraham (called Rashba) (c. 1235–1310; Spain;
Hid. RSHB   talmudic commentator). *Hiddushei ha-Rashba.* Warsaw: 1902.
Tesh. RSHB   ————. *Teshuvot ha-Rashba.* 4 vols. (7 parts). B'nei B'rak and Jerusalem: 1957/58–1964/65.

She'iltot   Aha of Shabha (680–752; Babylonia). *She'iltot de'Rav Ahai Gaon.* Jerusalem: Mossad Harav Kook, 1975.

Ahai Gaon. See: Aha of Shabha.

Akedat Yizhak. See: Arama, Isaac.

RF   Alfasi, Isaac ben Jacob (called Rif) (c. 1013–1103; Algeria, Morocco, Spain). *Alfasi.* Vilna: Romm, 1911.

MM   Al-Nakawa, Israel ben Joseph (d. 1391, Spain). *Menorat ha-Ma'or.* New York: 1929–1932.

Amudei Golah. See: Isaac ben Joseph of Corbeil.

Arama, Isaac ben Moses (c. 1420–1494; Spain, Italy). *Akedat Yizhak.* Jerusalem: Haivri, 1961.

Arba'ah Turim. See: Jacob ben Asher.

Arukh ha-Shulchan. See: Epstein, Yehiel Michal

RSH   Asher ben Jehiel (called Rosh) (c. 1250–1327; Germany, Spain;

Tesh. RSH   talmudic commentator). *Te'shuvot ha-Rosh.* Zholkva: 1803.

Tos. RSH   ———. *Tos'fei ha-Rosh (Tos'fot ha-Rosh).* Leghorn: 1776; commentary on tractate Niddah may be found in later editions of the Talmud.

Shitah   Ashkenazi, Bezalel ben Abraham (c. 1520–1592; Eretz Israel, Cairo). *Shitah Me'kubbetzet.* Tel Aviv: Zioni, 1954–64.

ARN   *Avot de'Rabbi Natan.* Edited by Solomon Schechter. New York: Feldheim, 1967.

Azulai, Hayyim Joseph David (called Hida) (1724–1806; Jerusalem, Italy). *Birkei Yosef.* Vienna: 1860–1869.

Ba'al ha-Turim. See: Jacob Ben Asher.

Ba'alei ha-Nefesh. See: Abraham ben David of Posquieres.

Babad, Joseph ben Moses (1800–1874; Poland). *Minchat Chinukh.* New York: 1952.

BT   *Babylonian Talmud.* See: *Talmud Bavli.*

Bacharach, Jair Hayyim ben Moses Samson (1638–1702; Germany). *Chavvat Yair.* Jerusalem: 1968.

ibn Paquda   Bachya (Bahya) ben Joseph ibn Paquda (11th century; Spain). *Hovot ha-Le'vavot (Duties of the Heart).* Tr. to Hebrew by Judah ibn Tibbon. Tel Aviv: Mahbarot Le'sifrut, 1949.

Bahya ben Asher (d. 1340; Spain). *Midrash Rabbenu Bahya al ha-Torah.* Amsterdam: 1746.

Bayit Chadash. See: Sirkes, Joel.

Beit Yosef. See: Caro, Joseph.

NTZV   Berlin, Naphtali Zevi Judah (called Netziv) (1817–1893: Volozhin, Russia). *Ha-Amek Davar.* Tel Aviv: Dvir, 1961.

Beur ha-Gra. See: Elijah ben Solomon Zalman.

Birkei Yosef. See: Azulai, Hayyim Joseph David.

Braun   Braun, Zalman. *She'arim Me'tzuyanim be'Halakhah.* New York: 1949–1950.

Brisker Rav. See: Soloveichik, Hayyim.

Caro, Joseph ben Ephraim (1488–1575; Turkey, Safed). *Beit Yosef.* In *Arba'ah Turim.*

KM   ———. *Kesef Mishneh.* In *Mishneh Torah.*

Sh. A   ———. *Shulchan Arukh.* 10 vols. Vilna: Romm, 1911. (The Code

OH HM   is divided into four sections: Orach Hayyim [O.H.]; Yoreh

YD EH   Deah [Y.D.]; Choshen Mishpat [H.M.]; and Even ha-Ezer [E.H.].)

Chafetz Chayyim. See: Israel Meir ha-Kohen.

Chajes   Chajes, Zevi Hirsch (1805–1855; Ukraine, Poland). *Tiferet Zevi.* Drogobych (Drohobycz): 1889.

Chatam Sofer. See: Sofer, Moses.

Chavvat Yair. See: Bacharach, Jair Hayyim.

Chayyei Adam. See: Danzig, Abraham.

Choshen Mishpat. See: Caro, Joseph.

Chossen Yosef. See: Engel, Joseph.

Chuppat Chatanim (Huppat Hatanim). See: Meldola, Raphael.

Chut ha-Me'shulash. See: Volozhiner, Hayyim.

MHRK   Colon, Joseph ben Solomon (called Maharik) (c. 1420–1480; France, Italy). *She'eilot u'Te'shuvot Maharik.* New York: 1958.

Commentary on the Torah. See: Nachmanides, Moses.

Commentary to the Mishnah. See: Maimonides, Moses.

Danzig (Danziger), Abraham ben Jehiel Michal (1748–1820; Vilna). *Chayyei Adam.* Warsaw: 1899.

Darkhei Mosheh. See: Isserles, Moses.

TAZ   David ben Samuel ha-Levi (called Taz) (1586–1667; Poland). *Turei Zahav* (on *Schulchan Arukh*). Y.D.: Lublin: 1646; O.H.: 1692; E.H.: Zholkva: 1754; H.M.: Berlin: 1766.

Dessler   Dessler, Elijah (1891–1954; Russia, England). *Mikhtav me-Eliyahu.* London: 1955–74. (Selections translated into English by Aryeh Carmel. *Strive for Truth!* New York: Philipp Feldheim, 1978).

Dinei Mishpachah. See: Schereschewsky, Ben Zion.

RSHBZ   Duran, Simeon ben Zemach (called Rashbaz) (1361–1444; North Africa). *Magen Avot.* Leghorn: 1785.

————. *Tashbatz.* Amsterdam: 1739.

Eisenstein, Judah David, ed. *Otzar Dinim u'Minhagim.* New York: Hebrew Publishing Co., 1917.

————. *Otzar Yisrael-Encyclopedia.* Jerusalem: Shiloh, n.d.

Eldad   Eldad, Yisrael. *Hegyonot Mikra.* Jerusalem: 1958.

Rokeach   Eleazar ben Judah of Worms (called Roke'ach) (c. 1165–1230). *Sefer ha-Rokeach.* Warsaw: 1886. (See also: Judah ben Samuel he-Hasid of Regensburg).

GRA   Elijah ben Solomon Zalman (called the Gaon of Vilna and the Vilna Gaon) (1720–1797; Vilna, Lithuania). *Beur ha-Gra.* In *Shulchan Arukh.*

————. *Sefer Sha'arei Rachamim.* Vilna: 1876.

Ellinson   Ellinson, Elyakin G. *Nissuin She-lo Ke'dat Moshe ve'Yisrael.* Tel Aviv: Dv ir, 1975.

ET   *Encyclopedia Talmudit.* 15 vols. Jerusalem: Mossad Harav Kook, 1947– .

Engel   Engel, Joseph ben Judah (1859–1920; Poland). *Chossen Yosef.* New York: 1944.

TT   Epstein, Barukh ha-Levi (1860–1942; Russia; Torah commentator). *Torah Temimah.* New York: Hebrew Publishing Company, 1925.

Epstein, Joseph. *Mitzvot ha-Bayit.* 2 vols. New York: Balshon Press, 1966.

AH   Epstein, Yehiel Michal ben Aaron Isaac ha-Levi (1829–1908; Belorussia). *Arukh ha-Shulchan.* 8 vols. Warsaw: 1900–1912; New York: Pollak, Grossman, n.d.

Etz ha-Da'at Tov. See: Vital, Hayyim.

Etz Hayyim. See: Vital, Hayyim.

Even ha-Ezer. See: Caro, Joseph.

IM   Feinstein, Mosheh (1895–   ; United States). *Iggerot Mosheh.* 6
       vols. New York: Balshon, 1959– .

Felder, SY   Felder, Gedalia. *She'eilat Ye'shurun.* Toronto: 1954.

Felder, YY   _____. *Ye'sodei Ye'shurun.* 6 vols. New York: 1955–60.

Freiman   Freiman, Abraham Hayyim. *Seder Kiddushin ve'Nissuin.* Jerusalem:
            Mossad Harav Kook, 1964.

       Ganzfried, Solomon ben Joseph (1806–1886; Hungary). *Kitzur
       Shulchan Arukh.* Leipzig: 1933).

       Gaon of Vilna. See: Elijah ben Solomon Zalman.

Tesh. Rab. Gersh.   Gershom ben Judah, Me'or ha-Golah (Rabbenu Gershom) (c. 960–
                      1028; Germany). *Teshuvot Rabbenu Gershom Me'or ha-
                      Golah.* Edited by Shlomo Eidelberg. New York: Yeshiva Uni-
                      versity, 1955.

Greenwald   Greenwald, Leopold. *Kol Bo Al Avelut.* 2 vols. New York: 1947–
              1951.

       Ha-Amek Davar. See: Berlin, Naphtali.

       Ha-Emunot ve'ha-Deot. See: Saadiah Gaon.

       Hagahot Maimuniyot. See: Meir ha-Kohen of Rothenburg.

       Hagot be'Parshiyot ha-Torah. See: Nachshoni, Yehudah.

       Hai Gaon (9th century; Head of Pumbedita Academy, Babylonia,
       890–898). In *Te,shuvot ha-Ge'onim.*

       Hassagot ha-Ravad. See: Abraham ben David of Posquieres.

       Hassagot ha-Ravad al ha-Rif. See: Abraham ben David of Pos-
       quieres.

       Hayyim Brisker. See: Soloveichik, Hayyim.

       Hegyonot Mikra. See: Eldad, Yisrael.

       Heikhal Yitzchak. See: Herzog, Isaac ha-Levi.

Herzog   Herzog, Isaac ha-Levi (1888–1959; Chief Rabbi, Israel). *Heikhal
           Yitzchak.* 3 vols. Jerusalem: 1959/60.

       Hida. See: Azulai, Hayyim Joseph David.

       Hiddushei ha-Ramban. See: Nachmanides Moses.

       Hiddushei ha-Ran. See: Nissim ben Reuben Gerondi.

       Hiddushei ha-Rashba. See: Adret, Solomon.

       Hiddushei ha-Ritba. See: Yom Tov ben Abraham Ishbili.

       Hiddushei R. Hayyim ha-Levi. See: Soloveichik, Hayyim.

       Hirsch Commentary on the Pentateuch. See: Hirsch, Samson Ra-
       phael.

Hirsch   Hirsch, Samson Raphael (1808–1888; Germany; philosopher and
           commentator). *Commentary on the Pentateuch.* New York:
           The Judaica Press, 1971.

Shelah   Horowitz, Isaiah ben Abraham ha-Levi (called Shelah ha-Kadosh)
           (1565?–1630; Germany, Czechoslovakia, Israel). *She'nei Lu-
           chot ha-Be'rit.* Fuerth: 1764.

       Horowitz, Phinehas ben Zevi Hirsch ha-Levi (1730–1805; Germa-
       ny). *Sefer Hafla'ah.* Lemberg: Grossman, 1816.

Hovot ha-Le'vavot (*Duties of the Heart*). See: Bachya (Bahya) ben Joseph ibn Paquda.

IB. E. Ibn Ezra, Abraham (1089–1164; Spain; biblical commentator). In *Mikraot Ge'dolot*.

Ibn Yarhi. See: Abraham ben Nathan ha-Yarhi.

IK *Iggeret ha-Kodesh* (14th century). Berlin: 1793. Translated by Seymour J. Cohen. New York: KTAV Publishing House, 1976.

Iggerot Mosheh. See: Feinstein, Mosheh.

Isaac ben Joseph of Corbeil (called Semak) (d. 1280; France). *Amudei Golah* (i.e., *Sefer Mitzvot Katan*). Satmar: 1935.

"Ish ha-Halakhah." See: Soloveitchik, Joseph Dov.

M. Ber. Israel Meir ha-Kohen (called Chafetz Chayyim) (1838–1933; Lithuania). *Mishnah Be'rurah*. Tel Aviv: Pardes, 1955.

Isserlein, Israel (1390–1460; Germany). *Te'rumat ha-Deshen*. Warsaw: 1882.

REMA Isserles, Moses (called Rema) (1525?–1572; Poland). *Darkhei Mosheh*. In *Arba'ah Turim*. Warsaw.

———. *Mappah*. In *Shulchan Arukh*.

Tur Jacob Ben Asher (called Ba'al ha-Turim and Tur) (1270?–1340; Germany; codifier and commentator). *Arba'ah Turim*. Vilna: 1900.

———. *Peirush al ha-Torah*. New York: 1956.

Jacobson Jacobson, I. *Ne'tiv Binah*. Tel Aviv: Sinai, 1964–68.

JT *Jerusalem Talmud*. See: *Talmud Ye'rushalmi*.

Joshua Boaz ben Simon Baruch (16th century; Spain, Italy; talmudic commentator). In *Babylonian Talmud*.

S. Hasidim Judah ben Samuel he-Hasid of Regensburg (c. 1150–1217; Germany). *Sefer Hasidim*. Jerusalem: Lewin-Epstein, 1972. See: *Sefer Hasidim*.

Halevi Judah ha-Levi (c. 1075–1141; Spain; philosopher and author). *The Kuzari*. 2 vols. Jerusalem: Mossad Harav Kook, 1945.

Judah the Pious. See: Judah ben Samuel he-Hasid.

Kaufmann Kaufmann, Yehezkel. *Toledot ha-Emunah ha-Yisraelit*. 4 vols. Jerusalem: Mosad Bialik; Tel Aviv: Dvir, 1967. (*The Religion of Israel*. Translated by Moshe Greenberg. Chicago: University of Chicago Press, 1960.)

Kesef Mishneh. See: Caro, Joseph.

Kimhi, David (called Radak) (c. 1160–1235; Provence; biblical commentator and grammarian). In *Mikraot Ge'dolot*.

Kitvei ha-Ramban. See: Nachmanides, Moses.

Kitzur Shulchan Arukh. See: Ganzfried, Solomon.

Kol Bo. Anonymous, 13th century commentary. New York: Shulsinger Brothers, 1945/46.

Kol Bo Al Avelut. See: Greenwald, Leopold.

Kuzari. See: Judah ha-Levi.

Landau Landau, Eleazar ben Israel (1778–1831; Poland). *Yad ha-Melekh* (on *Mishneh Torah*). Parts 1, 2, and 4. Jerusalem: 1965.

MHRSHL Luria, Solomon ben Jehiel (called Maharshal) (1510?–1574; Poland). *Yam Shel She'lomo*. B'nei B'rak: 1959–60.

Magen Avot. See: Duran, Simeon.

Maharam Mintz. See: Muenz (Minz), Moses.

Maharam Rotenburg. See: Meir ben Baruch of Rothenburg.

Maharam Schick. See: Schick, Moses.

Maharam Schiff. See: Schiff, Meir ben Jacob ha-Kohen.

Maharshal. See: Luria, Solomon.

Maharik. See: Colon, Joseph.

Maharil. See: Moellin, Jacob.

MV   *Mahzor Vitry.* See: Simhah ben Samuel of Vitry.

Maim.   Maimonides, Moses (called Rambam) (1135–1204; Spain). *Com-*

CM   *mentary to the Mishnah.* In *Babylonian Talmud.*

MT   ———. *Mishneh Torah (Yad ha-Hazakah).* 5 vols. Vilna: Rosencrantz, 1899/1900. Reprint: New York: 1944/45.

MN   ———. *Moreh Ne'vukhim.* Jerusalem: 1959/60.

S. Mitzvot   ———. *Sefer ha-Mitzvot la-Rambam.* Jerusalem: Epstein Brothers, 1952/53.

Tesh. Rambam   ———. *Te'shuvot ha-Rambam.* Edited by Abraham Hayyim Freiman. Jerusalem: 1934.

Mappah. See: Isserles, Moses.

SC   Medini, Hayyim Hezekiah (1832–1904; Turkey, Crimea). *Sedei Chemed.* 10 vols. Warsaw: Piotrkow, 1890/91, 1911/12; Reprint: B'nei B'rak: Beth Ha-Sofer, 1962/63–67.

MHRM Rot.   Meir ben Baruch of Rothenburg (called Maharam Rotenburg) (c. 1215–1293; Germany). *Maharam Rotenburg.* Berlin: 1891.

Meir ha-Kohen of Rothenburg (13th century; Germany). *Hagahot Maimuniyot.* Berdichev: 1907.

Me'iri   Me'iri, Menahem ben Solomon (1249–1316; Provence). *Sefer ha-Midot le'ha-Me'iri.* Selections edited by Menahem Mendel Meshi-Zahav. Jerusalem: 1966.

Mekhilta   *Mekhilta de'Rabbi Yishma'el.* Edited by Jacob Lauterbach. Philadelphia: Jewish Publication Society of America, 1933–35.

Chup. Chat.   Meldola, Raphael (1754–1828; London). *Chuppat Chatanim (Huppat Hatanim).* Venice: 1937.

Menorat ha-Maor. See: Al-Nakawa, Israel.

Midrash Aggadah. Edited by Solomon Buber. New York: Mada, 1960.

Me'or ha-Golah. See: Gershom ben Judah.

Mid. Gad.   *Midrash ha-Gadol.* Edited by Margaliot. Jerusalem: Mossad Harav Kook, 1947.

Mid. Rab.   *Midrash Rabbah.* Vilna: Romm, 1921.

Midrash Rabbenu Bahya al ha-Torah. See: Bahyah ben Asher.

Tanh.   *Midrash Tanhuma.* 2 vols. Edited by Solomon Buber. Jerusalem: 1963/64.

Mikhtav me-Eliyahu. See: Dessler, Elijah.

Mik. Ged.   *Mikraot Ge'dolot.* New York: Pardes Publishing Co., 1951.

Milhamot ha-Shem. See: Nachmanides, Moses.

Minchat Chinukh. See: Babad, Joseph.

M.   *Mishnah.* 12 vols. Vilna Edition. Reprint: New York: Pardes, 1952/53.

M. Ber. *Mishnah Be'rurah.* See: Israel Meir ha-Kohen.

M T *Mishneh Torah.* See: Maimonides, Moses.

Mishpe'tei Ouziel. See: Ouziel, Ben Zion.

Mitzvot ha-Bayit. See: Epstein, Joseph.

MHRL Moellin, Jacob ben Moses (called Maharil) (1360?–1427; Germany) *Sefer Maharil.* Jerusalem: 1968/69.

MN *Moreh Ne'vukhim.* See: Maimonides, Moses.

Moses ben Maimon: See: Maimonides, Moses.

Moses ben Nahman: See: Nachmanides, Moses.

Muenz (Minz), Moses ben Isaac ha-Levi (called Maharam Mintz) (c. 1750–1831; Hungary). *Te'shuvot Maharam Mintz.* Tel Aviv: 1969.

RMBN Nachmanides, Moses (called Ramban) (1195–1270; Spain, later to
C T Israel; biblical commentator, philosopher, mystic). *Commentary on the Torah.* Edited by Charles Chavel. Jerusalem: Mossad Harav Kook, 1962. Also in *Mikraot Ge'dolot.*

Has. RMBN ———. *Hassagot Shel ha-Ramban.* Kushta: 1510.

Hid. RMBN ———. *Hiddushei ha-Ramban.* Jerusalem: 1928.

Kit. RMBN ———. *Kitvei ha-Ramban.* Edited by Charles B. Chavel. Jerusalem: Mossad Harav Kook, 1964.

———. *Milhamot ha-Shem.* In *Alfasi.*

Tesh. RMBN ———. *Te'shuvot ha-Ramban.* Jerusalem: 1967.

———. *Torat ha-Adam.* Edited by I. Z. Meltzer. Jerusalem: 1955.

Nachshoni Nachshoni, Yehudah. *Hagot be'Parshiyot ha-Torah.* B'nei B'rak: 1978.

Nachalat Shivah. See: Samuel ben David ha-Levi.

Natronai bar Hilai (9th century; Gaon of Sura in Babylonia). See: *Te'shuvot ha-Geonim.*

Nefesh ha-Hayyim. See: Volozhiner, Hayyim.

Ne'tiv Binah. See: Jacobson, I.

Netziv. See: Berlin, Naphtali Zevi Judah.

RAN Nissim ben Reuben Gerondi (called Ran) (c. 1310–1375; Spain;
Hid. RAN talmudic commentator). *Hiddushei ha-Ran.* New York: Feldheim, 1946.

———. *Ran* (on the Rif). In *Alfasi.*

Nissuin She-lo Ke'dat Moshe ve'Yisrael. See: Ellinson, Elyakim G.

Orach Hayyim. See: Caro, Joseph.

Ornstein, Jacob (d. 1839). *Ye'shuot Yaakov.* Zholkva: 1809.

Otzar Dinim u'Minhagim. See: Eisenstein, Judah David.

Otzar ha-Ge'onim. Edited by Benjamin M. Lewin (1879–1944). 13 vols. Haifa: 1928–43.

Otzar ha-Poskim. 9 vols. Jerusalem: Otzar ha-Poskim Institute, 1962–65.

Otzar Yisrael - Encyclopedia. See: Eisenstein, Judah David.

Ouziel, Ben Zion Meir Hai (1880–1953; Chief Rabbi of Israel). *Mishpe'tei Ouziel.* 3 vols. Tel Aviv: 1935–40.

Palestinian Talmud. See: *Talmud Ye'rushalmi.*
Peirush RaSag al ha-Torah. See: Saadiah Gaon.
Pesik. R. Kah. *Pesikta de-Rav Kahana.* Jerusalem: 1963.
RVD Raavad (Ravad). See: Abraham ben David of Posquieres.
Rabbenu Gershom. See: Gershom ben Judah, Me'or ha-Golah.
Rabbenu Tam. See: Tam, Jacob.
Radak. See: Kimhi, David.
Rambam. See: Maimonides, Moses.
Ramban. See: Nachmanides, Moses.
Ran. See: Nissim ben Reuben Gerondi.
Rashba. See: Adret, Solomon.
Rashbam. See: Samuel ben Meir.
Radvaz. See: Duran, Simeon.
R Rashi (Solomon ben Isaac; R. She'lomo Yitzchaki) (1040–1105; France; leading commentator on Bible and Talmud). In *Mikraot Ge'dolot* and *Babylonian Talmud.*
Recanati Recanati, Menahem ben Benjamin (13th–14th century; Italy). *Ta'amei ha-Mitzvot ha-Shalem.* London: Otzar Hahokhmah, 1963.
Rema. See: Isserles, Moses.
Rif. See: Alfasi, Isaac.
Ritba. See: Yom Tov ben Abraham Ishbili.
Rogachover. See: Rozin, Joseph.
Rokeach. See: Eleazar ben Judah of Worms.
Rosh. See: Asher ben Jehiel.
Tzof. Pan. Rozin (Rosen), Joseph (called "The Rogachover") (1858–1936; Poland). *Tzofenat Pa'neach.* Edited by Menahem M. Kasher. Jerusalem: 1964.
RSG Saadiah Gaon (882–942; Gaon of Sura in Babylonia; commentator
EVD and philosopher). *Ha-Emunot ve'ha-Deot.* Edited by Judah ibn Tibbon. Jerusalem: 1945.
———. *Peirush RaSag al ha-Torah.* Edited by J. Kapah. Jerusalem: Mossad Harav Kook, 1962.
———. *Sefer ha-Mitzvot le'RaSag.* Warsaw: 1914.
Samuel ben David ha-Levi (1625?–1681; Poland). *Nachalat Shivah.* Warsaw: 1884. Reprint: Jerusalem: 1969.
Samuel ben Meir (called Rashbam) (c. 1080–1174; France; Biblical Commentator). In *Mikraot Ge'dolot.*
Samuel he-Hasid of Speyer. See: *Sefer Hasidim.*
Schereschewsky Schereschewsky, Ben Zion. *Dinei Mishpachah.* Jerusalem: Reuben Mass, 1967.
MHRM Schick Schick, Moses ben Joseph (called Maharam Schick) (1807–1879; Hungary). *Maharam Schick.* 2 vols. Israel: 1971/72.
MHRM Schiff Schiff, Meir ben Jacob ha-Kohen (called Maharam Schiff) (1605–1641; Germany). In standard editions of the *Talmud.*
Sedei Chemed. See: Medini, Hayyim Hezekiah.
Seder Eliyahu Zuta. Zholkva: 1757.
Seder Kiddushin ve'Nissuin. See: Freiman, Abraham.

S. Eidut   *Sefer Eidut le'Yisrael.* Edited by Oscar Z. Rand. New York: Ezras Torah Fund, 1947/48.

Werdiger   *Sefer Eidut le'Yisrael.* See: Werdiger, Jacob.

Sefer ha-Chinukh. See: Aaron ha-Levi of Barcelona.

Sefer Hafla'ah. See: Horowitz, Phinehas.

Sefer ha-Manhig. See: Abraham ben Nathan ha-Yarhi.

Sefer ha-Midot le'ha-Me'iri. See: Me'iri, Menahem ben Solomon.

Sefer ha-Mitzvot la-Rambam. See: Maimonides, Moses.

Sefer ha-Mitzvot le-RaSag. See: Saadiah Gaon.

Sefer Hasidim. Although Judah he-Hasid was main author of *Sefer Hasidim,* it also contains works of his father, Samuel ben Kalonymus he-Hasid of Speyer (12th century) and his student, Eleazar ben Judah of Worms (c. 1165–1230). See: Judah ben Samuel he-Hasid.

Sefer ha-Yashar. See: Tam, Jacob.

Sefer Ma'aseh ha-Geonim. Edited by Abraham Epstein and Jacob Freimann. Berlin: Druck von H. Itzkowski, 1909.

S. MHRL   *Sefer Maharil.* See: Moellin, Jacob.

Sefer Mitzvot Katan. See: Isaac ben Joseph of Corbeil.

Sefer Sha'arei Rachamim. See: Elijah ben Solomon Zalman.

SMK   Semak. See: Isaac ben Joseph of Corbeil.

S. Esh   *Seridei Esh.* See: Weinberg, Jehiel.

Sha'arei Yashar. See: Shkop, Shimon (Simeon).

SHKH   Shabbetai ben Meir ha-Kohen (called Shakh) (1621–1662; Vilna). *Siftei Kohen* (on the *Shulchan Arukh*). Y.D.: Cracow: 1646–7; H.M.: 1663.

Shakh. See: Shabbetai ben Meir ha-Kohen.

She'arim Me'tzuyanim be'Halakhah. See: Braun, Zalman.

She'eilat Yeshurun. See: Felder, Gedalia.

She'eilot u'Te'shuvot Maharik. See: Colon, Joseph.

She'iltot de'Rav Ahai Gaon. See: Aha of Shabha.

Shelah ha-Kadosh. See: Horowitz, Isaiah

Shemen le'Minchah, bound with *Minchat Chinukh.* New York, 1952.

She'nei Luchot ha-Be'rit. See: Horowitz, Isaiah.

Shishah Sidrei Mishnah. 6 vols. Edited by Hanokh Albeck. Jerusalem; Mosad Bialik; Tel Aviv: Dvir, 1958.

Shitah Me'kubbetzet. See: Ashkenazi, Bezalel.

Shiurei ha-Rav. See: Soloveitchik, Joseph Dov.

Shkop   Shkop, Shimon (Simeon) Judah (1860–1940; Lithuania). *Sha'arei Yashar.* New York: Ha-Va'ad Le'Hotza'at Sifrei Ha-Gaon Rabbi Shimon, 1967.

Shulchan Arukh. See: Caro, Joseph.

Sifra   *Sifra de-Vei Rav.* Jerusalem: Sifra, 1959.

Sifrei. Sulzbach: 1802.

SHKH   *Siftei Kohen.* See: Shabbetai ben Meir ha-Kohen.

Simhah ben Samuel of Vitry (11th–12th century; France). *Mahzor Vitry.* Edited by Simon Hurwitz. Berlin: 1893.

Sirkes, Joel (called Bach) (1561–1640; Poland). *Bayit Chadash (Ha-dash)*. In *Arba'ah Turim*.

Sofer Moses (1762–1839; Hungary). *Chatam Sofer*. Responsa, 7 vols. Jerusalem: Makor, 1969/70.

Hid. R. Hayyim Soloveichik, Hayyim (called Rabbi Hayyim Brisker; "The Brisker Rav") (185 3–1918; Russia). *Hiddushei R. Hayyim ha-Levi*. Brisk: 1936.

JBS Soloveitchik, Joseph Dov (1903– ; United States; leading 20th century scholar; Professor of Talmud, Yeshiva University). "Ish

Ish Hal. ha-Halakhah". *Talpioth*. vol. 1.

Shiu. Rav _____. *Shiurei ha-Rav*. New York: Yeshiva University Press, 1974.

Sperling Sperling, Abraham. *Ta'amei ha-Minhagim*. New York: 1944.

Strive for Truth! See: Dessler, Elijah.

Ta'amei ha-Minhagim. See: Sperling, Abraham.

Ta'amei ha-Mitzvot ha-Shalem. See: Recanati, Menahem.

Talmud Bavli. 20 vols. Vilna: Romm, 1895.

Talmud Ye'rushalmi. 7 vols. Vilna: Romm, 1921/22.

Tam Tam, Jacob ben Meir (Rabbenu Tam) (c. 1100–1171; France; Tosafist). *Sefer ha-Yashar*. New York: Menorah, 1959.

Tashbatz. See: Duran, Simeon ben Zemach.

TAZ Taz. See: David ben Samuel ha-Levi.

Ter. Desh. *Te'rumat ha-Deshen*. See: Isserlein, Israel.

Tesh. Geon. *Te'shuvot ha-Geonim*. Edited by Abraham Harkavy. Berlin: 1887. Reprint: New York: 1959.

Te'shuvot ha-Rambam. See: Maimonides, Moses.

Te'shuvot ha-Rashba. See: Adret, Solomon.

Te'shuvot Rabbenu Gershom Me'Or ha-Golah. See: Gershom ben Judah.

Te'shuvot ha-Rosh. See: Asher ben Jehiel.

Tiferet Zevi. See: Chajes, Zevi Hirsch.

Toledot ha-Emunah ha-Yisraelit. See: Kaufmann, Yehezkel.

Torah Temimah. See: Epstein Barukh ha-Levi.

Torat ha-Adam. See: Nachmanides, Moses.

Tos. *Tosafot*. (12th–13th century Franco-German talmudists.) In *Babylonian Talmud*.

Tosef. *Tosefta* (Printed with Code of Rif, *Alfasi*). Vilna: Romm, 1911.

Tos'fei ha-Rosh. See: Asher ben Jehiel.

Tur. See: Jacob ben Asher.

Turei Zahav. See: David ben Samuel ha-Levi.

Tzafenat Pa'neach. See: Rozin, Joseph.

Vilna Gaon. See: Elijah ben Solomon Zalman.

Vital Vital, Hayyim (1542–1620; Safed, Jerusalem, Damascus; talmudic commentator). *Etz ha-Da'at Tov*. Tel Aviv: 1965.

_____. *Etz Hayyim*. Jerusalem: 1910. Reprint: Jerusalem: Mekor Hayyim, 1963.

Volozhiner Volozhiner, Hayyim ben Isaac (1749–1821; Russia). *Chut ha-Me'-shulash*. New York: 1965.

_____. *Nefesh ha-Hayyim*. New York: 1944.

Weinberg, Jehiel Jacob (1885–1966; Lithuania, Germany). *Se'ridei Esh.* Jerusalem: Mossad Harav Kook, 1961–69.

Werdiger, Jacob. *Sefer Eidut le'Yisrael.* B'nei B'rak: 1963.

Yad ha-Hazakah. See: Maimonides, Moses.

Yad ha-Melekh. See: Landau, Eleazar.

Yam Shel She'lomo. See: Luria, Solomon.

Ye'shuot Yaakov. See: Ornstein, Jacob.

Ye'sodei Ye'shurun. See: Felder, Gedalia.

RTB   Yom Tov ben Abraham Ishbili (called Ritba) (c. 1250–1330; Spain; talmudic commentator). *Hiddushei ha-Ritba.* Warsaw: 1902.

Yoreh Deah. See: Caro, Joseph.

Z   *Zohar* (Fundamental work of Jewish mysticism). 5 vols. edited by Reuben Margaliot. Jerusalem: Mossad Harav Kook, 1960.

ENGLISH LANGUAGE SOURCES

Abrahams   Abrahams, Israel. *A Companion to the Authorised Daily Prayer-book.* New Revised Edition. New York: Hermon Press, 1966.

LMA   ———. *Jewish Life in the Middle Ages.* Philadelphia: The Jewish Publication Society of America, 1896: Reprint. New York: Meridian Books, 1958).

Adler, Rachel. "Abortion—The Need to Change Jewish Law." *Sh'ma,* November 15, 1974, pp. 163–164.

———. "Tumah and Taharah: Ends and Beginnings." *Response,* no. 18 (Summer, 1973), pp. 117–124.

Agus, Irving A. *Rabbi Meir of Rothenburg.* 2 vols. Philadelphia: The Dropsie College for Hebrew and Cognate Learning, 1947.

Allan, Alfred K. "Newest Jewish Problem: Divorce." *The National Jewish Monthly,* December 1961, pp. 7–8.

Arisian   Arisian, Kohoren. *The New Wedding.* New York: Vintage, 1973.

Baron.   Baron, Salo Wittmayer. *The Jewish Community.* Volumes 2 and 3. 3 vols. Philadelphia: The Jewish Publication Society of America, 1942.

Banning, Margaret Culkin. "The Case for Chastity." *The Reader's Digest,* July, 1962, pp. 46–50.

Belkin.   Belkin, Samuel. *In His Image.* London: Abelard-Schuman Ltd., 1960.

Berkovitz   Berkovitz, Eliezer. *Crisis and Faith.* pp. 35–128. New York: Hebrew Publishing Company, 1975.

Berman.   Berman, Saul. "The Status of Women in Halakhic Judaism." *Tradition,* Vol. XIV, no. 2, Fall, 1973.

Bernard   Bernard, Jessie. *The Future of Marriage.* New York: World Publishing Co., 1972.

Bible. *The Holy Scriptures.* Philadelphia, Jewish Publication Society of America, 1917.

Bleich, J. David. "Abortion in Halakhic Literature." *Tradition,* Volume 10, no. 2, Winter, 1968, pp. 72–120.

CHP   _____. *Contemporary Halakhic Problems*. pp. 146–178. New York: KTAV Publishing House, Inc., Yeshiva University Press, 1977.

Blidstein, Gerald. *Honor Thy Father and Mother*. New York: KTAV Publishing House, 1976.

Boll, Eleanor Stoker. "Should Parents or Cupid Arrange Marriages?" *New York Times Magazine*, December 13, 1959, pp. 15ff.

Brav, Stanley Rosenbaum, ed. *Marriage and the Jewish Tradition*. New York: Philosophical Library, 1951.

Breuer   Breuer, Isaac. *The Jewish Marriage*. New York: Philipp Feldheim Publishers, 1956.

Bubis, Gerald B. "The Modern Jewish Family." *Journal of Jewish Communal Service*, no. 47, 1971, pp. 238–247.

Bulka, Reuven P. "Divorce: The Poblem and the Challenge." *Tradition*, Summer, 1976, pp. 127–133.

_____. *Family and Marriage Newsletter*, Vol 3. No. 1., New York, Rabbinical Council of America.

Channing   Channing, William Henry. *My Symphony*. New York: Barse and Hopkins, 1910.

Chipman, Jonathan. "Sex and the Tradition: A Rejoinder." *Response*, 34, vol. XI, no. 2, Fall, 1977, pp. 103–106.

Cohen, Boaz. *Law and Tradition in Judaism*. New York: The Jewish Theological Seminary of America, 1959.

Cox, Harvey. "Evangelical Ethics and the Ideal of Chastity." *Christianity and Crisis*, April 27, 1964, pp. 75–79.

DeBurger.   DeBurger, James E. *Marriage Today: Problems, Issues and Alternatives*. New York: Schenkman, 1977.

Denes, Magda. "Performing Abortions." *Commentary*, vol. 62, no. 4, October 1976, pp. 33–37.

Dresner, Samuel H. and Sherwin, Byron. "Before Marriage—Pre-Marital Fidelity." *Impact*, Winter, 1978, pp. 4–18.

Ebreo   Ebreo, Leone. *The Philosophy of Love* (*Dialoghi d'Amore*). Translated by Friedberg-Seely and Jean H. Barnes. London: The Soncino Press, 1937.

Elon.   Elon, Menachem, ed. *Principles of Jewish Law*. Jerusalem: Keter Publishing House, 1975.

EJ   *Encyclopaedia Judaica*. Edited by Cecil Roth. Jerusalem: Keter Publishing House, Ltd., 1971.

JMC   Epstein, Louis M. *The Jewish Marriage Contract*. New York: Arno Press, Inc., 1973. Reprint of the 1927 edition published by Jewish Theological Seminary of America, New York.

MLBT   _____. *Marriage Laws in the Bible and the Talmud*. Cambridge: Harvard University Press, 1942.

SLCJ   _____. *Sex Laws and Customs in Judaism*. New York: KTAV Publishing House, Inc., 1967.

Evans   Evans, Richard I. *Dialogue with Erik Erikson*. New York: Harper & Row, Publishers, 1967.

Falk   Falk, Ze'ev W. *Jewish Matrimonial Law in the Middle Ages.* London: Oxford University Press, 1966.

BCJL   Feldman, David M. *Birth Control in Jewish Law.* New York: New York University Press, 1968.

Feldman, David M. "Woman's Role and Jewish Law." *Conservative Judaism,* vol. 26, no. 4, Summer, 1972, pp. 29–39.

Friedman, Theodore. *Letters to Jewish College Students.* pp. 167–182. New York: Jonathan David Publishers, 1965.

Fromm   Fromm, Erich. *The Art of Loving.* New York: Harper & Row, Publishers, 1956.

Gibran   Gibran, Kahlil. *The Prophet.* New York: Alfred A. Knopf, 1923.

Gilder, George. "In Defense of Monogamy." *Commentary,* November 1974, pp. 31–36.

Glatzer, Nahum N. "The Jewish Family and Humanistic Values." *Journal of Jewish Communal Service,* Summer, 1960, pp. 269–273.

Glazer, Nathan. "The Rediscovery of the Family." *Commentary,* March, 1978, pp 49–56.

Glenn, Jacob B. "Sex and Marriage in Judaism." *The Jewish Forum,* February, 1961, pp. 21–22.

Goldstein, Sidney E. *The Meaning of Marriage and the Foundations of the Family.* New York: Bloch Publishing Company, 1942.

Goodman   Goodman, Philip and Hanna. *The Jewish Marriage Anthology.* Philadelphia: Jewish Publication Society of America, 1965.

Gordis, Robert. *Love and Sex.* New York: Women's League for Conservative Judaism, 1978.

Gordis, Robert. "The Jewish Concept of Marriage." *Judaism,* July, 1953, pp. 225–238.

Halberstam, Yitta. "Today's Shadchan: Popular and Expensive." *The Jewish Digest,* February, 1978, pp. 23–27.

Handelman, Sheina Sarah. "The Paradoxes of Privacy." *Sh'ma,* November 10, 1978, pp. 2–5.

L. in SH   Harris, Monford. "The Concept of Love in Sepher Hassidim." *Jewish Quarterly Review,* July, 1959, pp. 13–44.

————. "Marriage As Metaphysics: A Study of the 'Iggereth Hakodesh.' " *Hebrew Union College Annual,* vol. 33, 1962, pp. 197–220.

PMSE   ————. "Pre-Marital Sexual Experience: A Convenantal Critique." *Judaism,* vol. 19, no. 2, Spring, 1970, pp. 134–144.

————. "Reflections on the Sexual Revolution." *Conservative Judaism,* vol. 20, no. 3, Spring, 1966), pp. 1–17.

WMM   ————. "The Way of a Man with a Maid—Romantic or Real Love." *Conservative Judaism,* vol. 14, no. 2, Winter, 1960, pp. 29–39.

Hastings, James, ed. *Encyclopaedia of Religion and Ethics.* vol. 8, pp. 460–463, 741–743.

Hertz   Hertz, Joseph, ed. *The Pentateuch and Haftorahs.* London: Soncino Press, 1960.

Heschel   Heschel, Abraham Joshua. *The Sabbath.* New York: Farrar, Straus; & Cudahy, 1951. Reprint; New York: Harper Torchbooks, 1966.

Heult, Heoze and Hudson. *Courtship and Marriage.* Boston: Little, Brown & Company, 1976.

HRB   Hirsch, Samson Raphael. *Horeb; A Philosophy of Jewish Laws and Observances.* Translated by Dayan Dr. I. Grunfeld. 2 vols. London: The Soncino Press, 1962.

Hoenig, Sidney B. *Jewish Family Life: The Duty of the Woman.* New York: Spero Foundation, 1961.

Jacobs, Louis. *What Does Judaism Say About . . . ?* New York: Quadrangle/The New York Times Book Company, 1973.

Jakobovits, Immanuel. *Jewish Law Faces Modern Problems.* New York: Yeshiva University Press, 1965.

_____. *Order of the Jewish Marriage Service.* New York: Bloch Publishing Company, 1959.

_____. *Jewish Medical Ethics.* New York: Bloch Publishing Company, 1959, 1975.

JE   *The Jewish Encyclopedia.* Edited by Isidore Singer. New York: Funk and Wagnalls Company, 1902–1907.

Jew. Mar.   Jewish Marriage Educational Council, *The Jewish Marriage.* London: Soncino Press, n.d.

Josephus, Flavius. *The Life and Works of Flavius Josephus.* Translated by William Whiston. New York: Holt, Rinehart and Winston, n.d.

Jung   Jung, Leo, ed. *The Jewish Library.* Vol. 3: *Woman.* London: Soncino Press, 1970.

Jung, Moses. *Modern Marriage.* New York: Appleton-Century-Crofts, Inc., 1940.

MJL   Kahana, Kalman. *The Theory of Marriage in Jewish Law.* Leiden: E. J. Brill, 1966.

Kehimker, H. S. *The History of the Bene Israel of India.* pp. 128–150. Tel Aviv: Dayag Press, 1937.

Keyserling, Count Hermann. *The Book of Marriage.* New York: Harcourt, Brace & Co., 1942.

Klein, Isaac. *Responsa and Halakhic Studies.* pp. 13–21. New York: KTAV Publishing House, 1975.

Kominsky, Neil. "Rabbinic Ethics and Mixed Marriage: An Exercise in 'Catch 22.'" *CCAR Journal,* Autumn, 1976, pp. 64–66.

Lamm, Maurice. *I Shall Glorify Him.* New York: Bloch Publishing, 1961.

WDM   _____. *The Jewish Way in Death and Mourning.* pp. 184–187. New York: The Jonathan David Publishers, 1969.

HR   Lamm, Norman. *A Hedge of Roses.* New York: Philipp Feldheim, Inc. Fourth Edition, revised 1972.

EJ'74   _____. "Judaism and the Modern Attitude to Homosexuality." *Encyclopaedia Judaica Yearbook,* 1974, pp. 18–28. Jerusalem: Keter Publishing House, Ltd., 1974.

Landau, Sol. "The Jewish Interpretation of Love." *The National Jewish Monthly,* December 1961, pp. 6–7.

Lauterbach, Jacob Z. "The Ceremony of Breaking a Glass at Weddings." *Hebrew Union College Annual,* vol. 2, 1925.

Lewis   Lewis, C. S. *The Allegory of Love.* London: Oxford University Press, 1938.

Lewisohn   Lewishohn, Ludwig. *What Is This Jewish Heritage?* New York: B'nai B'rith Hillel Foundations, 1954.

Lifschutz, Ezekiel. "Merrymakers and Jesters Among Jews." *YIVO Annual of Jewish Social Science,* vol. 7, 1952, pp. 43–53, 60–61, 68–83.

Linzer, Norman. *The Jewish Family: A Compendium.* New York: Commission on Synagogue Relations, Federation of Jewish Philanthropies of New York, 1975.

Livneh   Livneh, Eliezer. "Love and Eros." *Israel Magazine,* May, 1973, pp. 81–84. (See also: *Bet Mikra* [1977].)

HM   Mace, David R. *Hebrew Marriage.* New York: Philosophical Library, 1953.

MEW   Mace, David and Vera. *Marriage: East and West.* Garden City, New York: Doubleday & Company, Inc., 1960.

Maller, Allen S. "Jewish-Gentile Marriage: Another Look at the Problem." *CCAR Journal,* Winter, 1976, pp. 65–74.

Massarik   Massarik, Fred. "Rethinking the Intermarriage Crisis." *Moment Magazine,* vol. 3, no. 7, June, 1978, pp. 29–33.

Matt   Matt, Hershel J. "Sin, Crime, 'Sickness or Alternative Life Style?': A Jewish Approach to Homosexuality." *Judaism.* vol. 27, no. 1, Winter, 1978, pp. 13–24.

Maybaum, Ignaz. *The Jewish Home.* London: James Clarke & Company, Ltd., 1946.

Mehler.   Mehler, Barry Alan. "Gay Jews." *Moment Magazine,* February/March, 1977, pp. 22–24ff.

Meiselman. Meiselman, Moshe. *Jewish Woman in Jewish Law.* New York: KTAV Publishing House, Inc./Yeshiva University Press, 1978.

Meislin, Bernard J. *Jewish Law in American Tribunals.* New York: KTAV Publishing House, Inc., 1976.

Morgan, Douglas N. "Love in the Hebrew Bible." *Judaism,* Winter, 1956, pp. 31–45.

Neuman, Abraham A. *The Jews in Spain: Their Social, Political and Cultural Life During the Middle Ages.* vol. 2, pp. 42–46. 2 vols. Philadelphia: Jewish Publication Society of America, 1942.

EB   *The New Encyclopaedia Britannica.* Chicago: Encyclopaedia Britannica, Inc., 1976.

Niebuhr   Niebuhr, Reinhold. "Christian Attitudes Toward Sex and Family." *Christianity and Crisis,* April 27, 1964, pp. 73–75.

Novak, Michael. "The Family Out of Favor." *Harper's,* April, 1976, pp. 37–46.

Parnes, Hannah. "Abortion—A Time to Respect Halacha." *Sh'ma,* November 15, 1974, pp. 164–165.

Pelcovitz, Ralph. "The Intermarriage Issue: Crisis and Challenge." *Jewish Life,* October, 1973), pp. 38–47.

Pickett, Robert S. "Monogamy on Trial." *Alternative Lifestyles,* vol. 1, no. 3. August, 1978, pp. 281–301.

Posner, Zalman. "Modernity Must Make Room for Modesty." *Sh'ma,* November 10, 1978, pp. 1–2.

Rabbinical Council of America. *Procedure in Obtaining a Religious Jewish Divorce.* New York.

Rabinowicz, Harry. "The Shadchan." *The Jewish Spectator,* October, 1961, pp. 14–16.

Rabinowitz, Stanley. *A Jewish View of Love and Marriage.* Washington, D.C.: B'nai B'rith Youth Organization, 1961.

Rackman   Rackman, Emanuel. *One Man's Judaism.* pp. 225–237. New York: Philosophical Library, 1970.

Rilke   Rilke, Rainer Maria. *Rilke on Love and Other Difficulties.* Edited by John J. L. Mood, pp. 25–37. New York: W. W. Norton, 1975.

Rosenthal   Rosenthal, Gilbert S. *Generations in Crisis,* pp. 9–41. New York: Bloch Publishing Co., 1969.

Rosner, Fred. *Modern Medicine and Jewish Law.* New York: Bloch Publishing Co. for Yeshiva University Press, 1972.

Rougemont, Denis de. *Love in the Western World.* New York: Pantheon, 1956.

Ruppin   Ruppin, Arthur. *Jews in the Modern World.* New York: Macmillan & Company, Ltd., 1934.

Santayana, George. *Character and Opinion in the United States.* Reprint, Garden City, New York: Doubleday and Anchor Books.

Schlesinger, Benjamin. *The Jewish Family: A Survey and Annotated Bibliography.* Toronto: University of Toronto Press, 1971.

Schulweis, Harold M. "Jewish Theology and the Sexual Revolution." *Davka,* Fall, 1974, pp. 31–35.

Schwartz, Barry Dov. "Homosexuality—A Jewish Perspective." *United Synagogue Review,* Summer, 1977, pp. 4–5ff.

Schwartz, Tony, *et al.* "Living Together." *Newsweek,* August 1, 1977, pp. 47–50.

Shapiro, David. "Be Fruitful and Multiply." *Tradition,* Spring/Summer, 1973, pp. 42–67.

Shapiro, Miriam and Pearl, Chaim H. "The Woman's Role: A Continuing Discussion." *Conservative Judaism,* Fall, 1978, pp. 63–70.

Sheed   Sheed, F. J. *Society and Sanity.* pp. 107–166. New York: Sheed and Ward, 1953.

Sheehy   Sheehy, Gail. *Passages.* New York: E. P. Dutton, 1974.

Silver   Silver, David. "Halakhic Status of Intermarried Jews." Mimeographed. New York: Rabbinical Council of America, n.d.

Smith, CR   Smith, Charles Ryder. *The Bible Doctrine of Womanhood.* London: The Epworth Press, 1923.

Smith, WR   Smith, William Robertson. *Kinship and Marriage in Early Arabia.* Cambridge: 1885.

JBS: AE   Soloveitchik, Joseph Dov. *Adam and Eve.* Edited by Abraham R. Besdin. Mimeographed. New York: Yeshiva University, 1971.

JBS: TRT   Soloveitchik, Joseph Dov. "A Tribute to the Rebbitzen of Talne." *Tradition,* Spring, 1978, pp. 73–83.

Steiman, Sidney, *Custom and Survival; A Study of the Life and Work of Rabbi Jacob Molin (Moelln).* New York: Bloch Publishing Company, 1963.

Steinberg, Avraham. "Abortion in Traditional Jewish Law." *Jewish Digest,* November, 1976), pp. 9–12.

Steinsaltz, Adin. *The Essential Talmud.* New York: Basic Books, 1976.

PR   Tendler, Moses. *Pardes Rimonim: A Marriage Manual for the Jewish Family.* New York: The Judaica Press, Inc., 1977.

———. "Population Control—The Jewish View." *Tradition,* vol. 8, no. 3, Fall, 1966, pp. 5–14.

Thielicke   Thielicke, Helmut. *The Ethics of Sex.* New York: Harper and Row, 1964.

Tsuriel, Yeruham. "The Kedusha of Monogamy: A Personal Perspective." *Response,* vol. x, no. 32, no. 4, Winter, 1976–77, pp. 65–70.

Tucker, Ray M. S. "Open Abortion Laws Allow Mature Decision." *Sh'ma,* November 14, 1974, pp. 162–163.

Umansky, Ellen M. "The Liberal Jew and Sex." *Response,* vol. 10, no. 32; no. 4; Winter, 1976–77, pp. 71–74.

Von Rad   Von Rad, Gerhard. *Genesis: A Commentary.* Philadelphia: Westminster Press, 1961.

Weinberger, Bernard. "The Growing Rate of Divorce in Orthodox Jewish Life." *Jewish Life,* Spring, 1976, pp. 9–14.

Zeitlin, Solomon. "The Offspring of Intermarriage." *Jewish Quarterly Review,* October, 1960, pp. 135–140.

Zelizer, Viviana A. "The Unmarried Jew: Problems and Prospects." *Conservative Judaism,* Fall, 1978, pp. 16–21.

"Zero Population Growth and the Jewish Community: A Symposium." *Analysis,* no. 60; November/December, 1976, pp. 1–12.

Zimmels, H. J. *Ashkenazim and Sephardim,* pp. 164–187; 333–340. New York and London: Oxford University Press, 1958.

Glossary

agunah: Literally, "an imprisoned woman." A woman whose marriage is terminated in fact, but not by the law. Such a woman has no legal proof of her husband's death, or no legal divorce. She is not able to remarry.

ahavah: Love, such as love of God, of good or evil, or one's neighbor, etc. It is distinguished from *yichud* love.

ailonit: Pseudo-hermaphrodite. A female with only primary, but no secondary sexual characteristics.

akarah: A barren woman.

am ha-aretz: One who cannot be trusted on ritual matters. Folk usage: an ignoramus.

androgyne: Hermaphrodite.

armalta: Aramaic for "widow" in marriage contract.

arusah (arusot): Betrothed woman, betrothed women.

ashkenazim: Specifically denotes German Jewry and their descendants in other countries. More broadly, the entire Ashkenazi religious and cultural complex in contradistinction to Sephardi, originating in Spain.

asmakhta: A contract which is not legally binding because of the lack of complete *da'at.*

asufi: A foundling, abandoned in a public place, both of whose parents are unknown; a "doubtful *mamzer*".

basar echad: one flesh.

bedeken: The veiling of the bride by the groom before the wedding ceremony.

be'rit: Covenant.

be'rit nissuin: Marriage covenant.

bet din: A Jewish court.

be'tulah: A virgin; betulta (Aramaic).

bi'ah: A coming; sexual intercourse.

birkhat erusin: Blessings of betrothal.

birkhat mitzvah: Blessing recited before the performance of a *mitzvah.*

chalal, chalalah: A person whose religious defect derives solely from a specific *kohen* violation. The *chalal* is unfit for the priesthood; the *chalalah* may not marry a priest.

chalippin: A form of acquisition effected by transfer of an object of significance as a symbolic substitute.

chalitzah: Ceremony of release from the Levirate bond.

chalutzah: A Levirate widow after her release.

chatan: Groom.

chaver: Companion; a scholar's title.

chazakah: Acquisition of real estate by an act which improves the property; presumptive continuance of an actual condition until evidence of change is produced; legal status.

cherem: See *herem*.

cheresh: Literally, a deaf mute; refers to one who is retarded.

chibbur: A joining; the Kabbalistic term for sexual intercourse implying a spiritual union.

chillul ha-shem: Defamation of God's name; disgracing the Jewish religion.

*chiyyuv:*See *hiyyuv*.

chok: A law or decree without an obvious rational basis.

chuppah: The bridal canopy; as a legal term, the ceremony that completes the marriage.

da'at: Willing consent.

davka: Exactly. Commonly used as a term of obstinacy.

derekh eretz: The way of the land. Commonly, good manners; sometimes a euphemism for sexual connection.

edim: Witnesses.

erusin: Betrothal, the first part of the marriage ceremony; not an engagement, technically. (In modern Hebrew "*erusin* is "engagement.")

eshet ish: A married woman.

etrog: The citron used as part of the Sukkot service.

ezer: Helpmeet; companion.

family purity: The laws of sexual abstinence and immersion in a *mikvah* that follow the menstrual period.

gematria: The use of letters for their numerical value; homiletic interpretation based on the numerical value of Hebrew letters.

gemillut chasadim: Acts of kindness.

ger: Convert to Judaism.

ger arayot: A "lion proselyte"; one who converts to Judaism for ulterior motives.

ger tzedek: One who converts to Judaism out of religious motives.

gerusha: Divorcee.

get: A Jewish religious divorce.

gilui arayot: "The uncovering of the nakedness"; a biblical euphemism for prohibited sexual acts.

giyoret: Female convert to Judaism.

hakhnasat kallah: The tradition of accompanying the bride during the wedding; funds for poor brides.

Halakhah: The body of Jewish law as written in the Talmud.

Hanukkah: the Festival of Lights celebrating the Maccabean victory.

hashchatat zera: "Wasting of seed," masturbation or onanism.

haskamah: Consent, even if given unwillingly.

havchanah: A ninety-day waiting period following divorce or *chalitzah,* or death of husband, that serves to determine pregnancy.

havdalah: Separation; blessing recited at the conclusion of Sabbaths and holidays.

hefker: Ownerless property; act of abandonment; unbridled lust; an unprotected woman.

hekdesh: Property of the temple.

herem: A rabbinic excommunication.

hiyyuv: A positive obligation.

ikkar ketubah: The essential condition of the marriage contract; namely, the *mohar,* a promise of a cash gift of the groom to the bride in the event of divorce or husband's death.

ish: Man.

ishah: Woman.

ishut: Laws of matrimony; marital state.

issur asei: A prohibition that arises as a corollary of a positive commandment.

issur lav: A prohibition that arises as a corollary of a negative commandment.

Kabbalists: Those who studied and taught esoteric teachings of Judaism and Jewish mysticism.

kallah: Bride.

karet: Excision from the Jewish people; punishment decreed by Heaven, usually a shortened life or sudden death.

kasher: Permitted, correct.

katan: A minor boy before Bar Mitzvah.

kavanah: Intent.

ke'desha: Prostitute; "set aside" from society.

ke'dushah: Sanctity; "set above" society.

ke'lal yisrael: Rabbinic term used for the Jewish community as a whole, in regard to its common responsibility and relationship with God.

ke'negdo: Opposite.

kesef: Money; the only form of *kichah* practiced in modern wedding ceremonies.

ketubah: Marriage contract.

ketubah de'irkhesa: Replacement marriage contract.

kichah: Taking; acquisition.

kiddush: The blessing recited before the Sabbath meal.

kiddush ha-shem: The sanctification of God's name, extended to include active avoidance of actions likely to bring disgrace on Judaism.

kiddushin: Sanctity; the betrothal stage of marriage that precedes *nissuin;* also used as a synonym for marriage.

kinyan: A formal act that effects a change in status, either financial, social or ritual.

kitel: A white garment worn by some on high holidays; also worn on festive occasions by many and by grooms at their weddings; also the dress for the deceased.

Kohelet: Ecclesiastes.

kohen: A hereditary priest of the Jewish people (singular); kohanim (plural).

Lag Ba-Omer: Thirty-third day of Omer counting, which is celebrated as a semi-holiday; traditional mourning observances kept during Omer are suspended, and marriages permitted.

levi: Descendants of the tribe Levi; assisted kohen at temple service. Retained special status as distinct from kohen and Israelite.

levir: Latin for yavam; the brother of a married man who died childless and left a widow, whom the brother is biblically obligated either to marry or to give chalitzah, release.

lulav: A palm branch taken as part of Sukkot service.

mamzer: Offspring of incestuous or adulterous union (singular); mamzerim (plural); mamzeret (feminine); mamzerut (the state of being a mamzer).

mattan: Additional gift made by the husband and included as a standard condition of the marriage contract.

me'kudeshet: Dedicated (to); sanctified; betrothed.

metarakhta: Aramaic term for divorcee used in the marriage contract.

met mitzvah: A corpse that is unattended or has insufficient attendants for proper burial.

mi-de'oraita: Of biblical derivation.

mi-de'rabbanan: Of rabbinic derivation.

Midrash: A genre of rabbinic literature extending from talmudic times to the tenth century, which constitutes an anthology of homilies and forms a running Aggadic commentary to specific books of the Bible.

mikvah: A ritual pool used for purposes of ritual purification.

minchah: The daily afternoon religious service.

minyan: A group of not less than ten adult Jewish males, which serves as the basic unit of community for purposes of Jewish prayer.

mishkav zakhur: Pederasty.

Mishnah: Legal codification of Jewish law, redacted by Rabbi Judah ha-Nasi in the third century, on which the Talmud is based.

mitat bet din: Death decreed by a Jewish court.

mitzvah: Commandment; commonly used as "good deed."

mohar: A cash gift promised in the marriage contract by the groom to the bride. It is so important that it is called "the essence of the ketubah," ikkar ketubah.

mored: One who refuses obedience, especially a husband or wife who refuses marital duties; moredet (feminine).

mumar: Apostate; convert to another religion; especially one who is an open opponent of Jewish law.

naddan: Dowry.

navi: Prophet; visionary.

ne'dunya: Aramaic term for dowry as used in marriage contract.

niddah: A menstruating woman.

nikhsei melog: The bride's private property, only the "fruit" of which belongs to the husband during marriage.

nissuin: Nuptials.

onah: The obligation of the husband to maintain regular marital relations with his wife.

onanism: Coitus interruptus.

oneg: Pleasure, enjoyment, delight, as in *oneg shabbat,* Sabbath delight.

ones: Duress or an act done unwillingly.

panim chadashot: "New faces" required for the recitation of the seven marriage blessings during the first week of marriage.

pe'ritzut: Licentiousness, impudence.

pe'ru ure'vu: "Be fruitful and multiply."

pe'rutah: An inexpensive coin.

pesikta: One of the oldest homiletic *midrashim;* technically, *Pesikta de-Rav Kahana,* a Palestinian text, probably of the fifth century.

pe'sul: Defect.

pileggesh: Concubine.

Purim: Holiday celebrating the victory of the Jews over the Persian enemies in the time of Esther and Mordecai.

Rabbis: When capitalized, refers to the Rabbis of the Talmud.

rachmanut: Compassion.

re'a: Friend.

re'ach get: A "scent" of a divorce.

Responsa literature: A genre of Jewish literature consisting of replies by halakhic authorities to questioners, which covers every aspect of Jewish belief and practice.

Rosh Hashanah: The Jewish new year.

Sages: When capitalized, refers to the Rabbis of the Talmud.

Seder: Order; especially the order of the ritual meal of the first two Passover nights.

Sefer Torah: The scroll of the Torah.

Sephardim: Jewish religious and cultural complex of Jews whose ancestors lived in Spain or Portugal before 1492.

se'udat mitzvah: Meal taken in connection with the celebration of a *mitzvah.*

shadkhan: Matchmaker.

shalom: Peace.

shaveh kesef: Commodities other than cash.

Shavuot: Holiday of Pentecost, the Feast of Weeks, celebrated seven weeks after Passover.

Shekhinah: The indwelling of God's presence.

shelom bayit: Domestic peace.

sheloshim: Thirty days of mourning after the burial of one of seven relatives.

she'mad: Conversion of a Jew to another religion.

Shemini Atzeret: The eighth day of assembly, following Sukkot.

she'niyot: Secondary incest, rabbinically instituted.

she'tar: Contract.

she'tuki: Hush-child; a child of an unknown father.

Sheva Berakhot: Seven marriage benedictions recited first under the marriage canopy and then in the grace following every meal during the seven days that follow (only if a *minyan* is present).

shidukh: Marriage match.

shidukhin: Conditions established upon an agreement to marry.

Shiva: Seven days of mourning following the burial of one of seven relatives.

shofar: The ram's horn blown on the New Year and at the close of the Day of Atonement.

shoteh: One who is deranged.

sifra: A Tannaitic halakhic Midrash to Leviticus, probably compiled in Eretz Israel in the late fourth century. Also known as *Sifra de-Vei Rav* or *Torat Kohanim.*

simchah: Joy; rejoicing or party.

Sukkot: Feast of Tabernacles or Booths.

ta'avah: Sensual desire.

taba'at: Ring.

taharah: Ritual purification.

taharat ha'mishpachah: See family purity.

tallit: Prayer shawl.

talmid chakham: A rabbinical scholar; traditionally, the ideal toward which every individual was expected to strive.

Talmud: The body of teaching that comprises the commentary and discussions of the *Amoraim* on the Mishnah of Rabbi Judah ha-Nasi. Its editing was completed c. 500 C.E.

tannaim: Rabbinical scholars whose works comprise the *Mishnah.*

tefillin: Phylacteries; black leather boxes bound to the arm and head during prayer.

te'naim: A formal engagement contract.

tevilah: Immersion in a *mikvah.*

to'avah: Abomination; evil.

tosefet ketubah: The *mattan,* an additional gift included in the marriage contract promised by the groom to the bride in case of death or divorce.

tum'ah: Religious impurity.

tumtum: One who has underdeveloped or ambiguous genitalia; according to the law, a doubtful male or female.

tze'niut: Modesty, privacy.

yada: Knowing; refers to physical rather than spiritual (e.g., carnal knowledge).

yavam: See *levir.*

ye'diah: Knowledge; (as in *yada*).

yibbum: Levirate marriage.

yichud: Together; a couple alone in a room or enclosure; privacy; the term used to describe the Jewish concept of marital love; the ceremony that effects the second and final stage of the marriage ceremony.

yichus: Pedigree; genealogy.

Yom Kippur: Day of Atonement.

yosher: Righteousness; fairness.

ze'nut: Prostitution; harlotry.

zikah: The tie that exists between the widow and the Levir, before *chalitzah* releases her from the Levirate marriage.

zimmun: The presence of three adult Jews at the meals, who then have the duty to recite grace after meals as a unit.

Zohar: The basic work of Jewish mysticism.

zonah: A woman who is halakhically unfit to marry a *kohen;* a degenerate, a harlot.

zuz: Silver coin, one fourth of a shekel.

Index